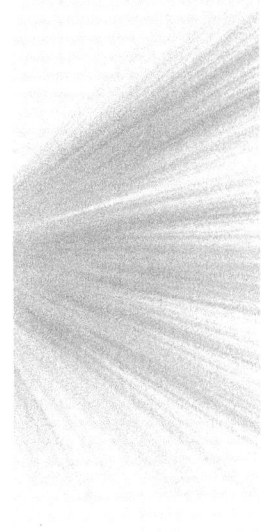

Leadership and Growth

Commission on Growth and Development

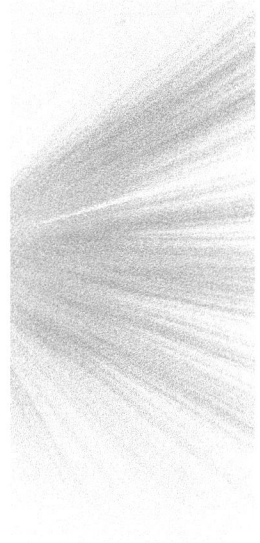

Leadership and Growth

Edited by David Brady and Michael Spence

Contributions by
David Brady
Michael Spence
Daron Acemoglu
Sadiq Ahmed
Fernando Henrique Cardoso
Alvin Eng
Eduardo Graeff
Milton A. Iyoha
Sandeep Mahajan
Wahiduddin Mahmud
Benjamin William Mkapa
Edward Robinson
James Robinson
Thomas Rusuhuzwa Kigabo
Tan Yin Ying

COMMISSION ON GROWTH AND DEVELOPMENT

On behalf of the Commission on Growth and Development
1818 H Street NW
Washington, DC 20433
Telephone: 202-473-1000
Internet: www.worldbank.org
        www.growthcommission.org
E-mail: info@worldbank.org
        contactinfo@growthcommission.org

This volume is a product of the Commission on Growth and Development,
which is sponsored by the following organizations:

Australian Agency for International Development (AusAID)
Dutch Ministry of Foreign Affairs
Swedish International Development Cooperation Agency (SIDA)
U.K. Department for International Development (DFID)
The William and Flora Hewlett Foundation
The World Bank Group

The findings, interpretations, and conclusions expressed herein do not
necessarily reflect the views of the sponsoring organizations or the governments they represent.
    The sponsoring organizations do not guarantee the accuracy of the data
included in this work. The boundaries, colors, denominations, and other
information shown on any map in this work do not imply any judgment on
the part of the sponsoring organizations concerning the legal status of any
territory or the endorsement or acceptance of such boundaries.
    All queries on rights and licenses, including subsidiary rights, should be
addressed to the Office of the Publisher, The World Bank, 1818 H Street
NW, Washington, DC 20433, USA; fax: 202-522-2422; e-mail: pubrights@
worldbank.org.

ISBN: 978-0-8213-8100-7
eISBN: 978-0-8213-8101-4
DOI: 10.1596/978-0-8213-8100-7

Library of Congress Cataloging-in-Publication Data
Leadership and growth / edited by David Brady and Michael Spence.
    p. cm.
 Includes bibliographical references and index.
  ISBN 978-0-8213-8100-7 —ISBN 978-0-8213-8101-4 (electronic)
  1. Leadership—Developing countries. 2. Developing countries—
Economic policy. 3. Economic development--Developing countries.
I. Brady, David W., 1940 II. Spence, Michael.
  HD57.7.L43143 2009
  303.3'4091724--dc22
                                                        2009030393

Cover design: Naylor Design

Contents

Boxes

Figures

Tables

Preface

In this book, former policy makers and practitioners reflect on the role of leadership in economic growth. Citing many examples of leaders making decisions that contributed materially to accelerating and sustaining long-term growth, they do not doubt that leadership matters. The role of Deng Xiaoping in China is one concrete example in which a choice to allow farmers to grow crops in excess of quotas yielded economic growth. The decision in the early 1960s by President Park of the Republic of Korea to industrialize the country is another example of leaders playing an important catalyzing role in economic growth. Although practitioners emphasize the role of leaders in economic growth, the social sciences have been slow to measure and include leadership in their economic growth models, largely because of the endogeneity problem. That is, although one can claim that Deng and Park made decisions that led to economic growth in China and Korea, respectively, it is possible that whoever was in power in China and Korea would have made the same decision or a decision sufficiently similar to yield much the same result. In China, Deng's agricultural reform followed the failure of the Cultural Revolution. In Korea, the rural economy was slumping, protestors were in the streets, and martial law had been in place since the end of World War II. Both countries were facing serious economic and political problems, and change was both necessary and probable. If any other leader had made similar choices, how could we model or measure leadership? Since history does not repeat itself—we cannot substitute Zhou En-lai for Deng and rerun the time period—we are left with examples and the endogeneity problem.

The basic question of which wields more influence over events, the leader or the times, is an ancient one. The emphasis on one or the other waxes and wanes over the years. Thomas Carlyle's history (1841) emphasizing great men was dominant a century ago. Such theories have since waned, and those emphasizing exogenous factors have waxed. Jared Diamond's analysis of successful economies (1997) emphasizes external factors at the expense of decisions made by leaders. Recent work in economics, however, has shown that leaders can make a difference in countries' growth rates. Particularly important is Jones and Olken's (2005) careful study, which controls for endogeneity by examining the consequences of leaders dying in office, from either accidents or natural causes.

In this book, which is part of the work of the Commission on Growth and Development, we do not purport to solve this long-standing problem. We do not have a single study in which we measure and model leadership in some way so as to avoid the endogeneity problem. Rather, our approach has been to commission a series of chapters that cover countries, institutions, and policy decisions in an attempt to show how leaders' decisions affect economic growth and development.

Sometimes the leaders' actions are quite specific, set in a given country and dealing with a specific problem. In others, the leaders' roles evolve over time. Some chapters explore the general characteristics of policy choices across countries. In addition, we include chapters about the importance of leaders choosing the right institutional arrangements as well as the right policies. In short, we take an eclectic view toward the role of leaders in generating economic growth and development, the better to gain purchase on a difficult topic.

The book begins with an overview essay by the editors. The chapter by Brady and Spence draws on the Commission's findings, papers, and testimony to distill what is known about the role of leadership in economic growth. The principal claim is that political leaders' decisions matter and that at various stages in the process they appear to matter more. The choice of a growth model is especially important. It is crucial to adopt an approach that leverages the global economy, exploiting large international markets and the stock of foreign knowledge. The leader must also build a consensus in favor of the model, because any strategy needs sufficient time to succeed. Visible evidence of success builds over time and is far from instantaneous. If leaders succeed in generating rapid growth, they are also likely to encounter the concomitant challenges associated with such growth: middle-class demands, inequality, shifting emphasis from cheap to skilled labor, and so on. Successful leadership requires adaptation to the new problems. This can take the form of wise investments in education, the creation of new institutions, and, often, second-best political/economic compromises, which keep the politics stable and the growth rate positive.

The volume then features seven chapters dealing with a broad range of issues and countries. Given this breadth, one of the editors' roles is to focus the reader's attention on what we take to be common issues across these chapters. In our view these common problems are fourfold: (1) promoting national unity, (2) building good, solid institutions, (3) choosing innovative and localized policies, and (4) creating political consensus for long-run policy implementation. All of the chapters focus on one or more of these themes in one or more countries. They also cover more than these four factors and should be read for the full set of their insights. Our hope is that these studies will stimulate further advances in the theory of the political economy of economic growth and development and of the role of leaders and political leadership at various stages in the process.

Making the right strategic choice (or better choices) for economic growth and development often entails overcoming local or sectional differences to bring about unity. In developing nations that were new to independence, nationhood, and sovereignty, leaders had to unite disparate interests to create a nation capable of economic growth. Tribal, ethnic, and racial differences often persist because the countries' borders were drawn by parties not interested in creating a unified country. Under this myriad of possible disunities, one of the leader's key responsibilities is to unite "the nation" so as to move toward common goals. In a sense, the challenge is to create a shared sense of identity as a foundation for making the intertemporal choices that are required for growth. Factionalism tends to focus the politics on the division of the pie rather than on increasing its size.

Three of this book's leadership chapters deal with the notion of national unification. Mkapa, in his chapter on Tanzania, argues that the success or failure of independence depended on the founding president. The first leader establishes the role(s) that the successors will play and forms an early set of institutions that the nation will be able to live with and amend over time. The leader should be seen as strong and decisive, competent and honest. Charismatic leadership, such as Gandhi in India or Mandela in South Africa, helps create unity because the people identify the country with the leader. Mandela's commitment to fairness without retribution after the years of apartheid yielded a government focused on shared progress, rather than one preoccupied with revenge, as many had predicted.

In Tanzania, Mkapa argues that President Nyerere's immediate move to create a sense of nationhood among the 126 tribes present in the new country was crucial to the unification of the country. The significance of a single-party system for nation building is discussed and analyzed, as is the danger of having a single-party system in place for too long. Mkapa makes the case that a one-party system was important for unifying the country under Nyerere. Across Africa, it was single parties such as Nyerere's, Nkrumah's in Ghana, and Kenyatta's in Kenya that were instrumental in ending colonial rule. These single-party systems under the leadership of the liberator carried over into the first national elections in Malawi, Mali, Senegal, and Tunisia, among other countries. Success in the first election carried over for about 20 years in Tanzania. Mkapa argues that as long as the single party is democratic within itself and ultimately leads to a multiparty system, the effect on unity and development is positive. In short, the one-party system was sufficiently unifying, democratic, participatory, and inclusive to be a positive force in development.

It should be noted that this use of a single-party system bears some similarity to the one-party systems in Asia. Most important, it aligns incentives such that the governments' policies have time to work. A major difference is that in African countries the leaders had to create a country out of tribal differences, whereas in China and Japan, for example, the national culture had been created over a much longer period, allowing leaders to concentrate on economic development.

Rusuhuzwa Kigabo's piece on Rwanda emphasizes the lessons learned from the civil war and the 1994 genocide. Rwanda is a country with almost no natural resources and, thus, almost entirely dependent on human capital. The genocide in 1994 destroyed human capital and the economy, leaving Rwanda a divided and impoverished nation. Thomas argues that the will and clear vision of the post-1994 leadership were crucial for the subsequent good performance of the economy. The leaders united the country around the idea that "the key of development is within the Rwandans' hands." They also stressed that internal peace and economic and social development are inherently linked: without peace there is no development, and vice versa. The aftermath of the genocide had to be dealt with, and here the leadership urged reconciliation and established policies and institutions crucial to healing the divide. The national decentralization process is an example of a policy with working institutions that can lead to lasting solutions. The policy-making process included all relevant stakeholders, and the decentralization policy became the instrument for empowerment, reconciliation, integration, and economic growth. The specific institutions needed to solve Rwanda's problems were the National Commission for Reconciliation and the village assemblies, *gacaca,* that brought rural villagers' preferences to the attention of the government.

In their analysis of Singapore's economic development, Tan, Eng, and Robinson make the general argument that the absence of natural resources can be overcome by, among other things, effective leadership. Specifically, strong institutions and capable leaders can arrive at the right set of pro-growth policies and adapt such policies to changing circumstances. Sometimes this process involves making less than ideal choices and then correcting them. All of these steps are contingent on building a social consensus, which spans the various ethnic and economic interests, in favor of the pro-growth policy. The authors maintain the view that national unity encouraged people to put aside individual desires and work for the greater good. The state institutionalized this by providing scholarships to bright students who would then work for the government and by paying civil servants well, thus reducing the probability of bribery. Moreover, they argue that building national unity in an inclusive way lessens the likelihood of social unrest, which enhances the prospects for economic growth. The chapter emphasizes that the consensus is twofold: between different social groups and between the society and government. Because long-term growth generates short-term pain, people must have confidence and trust in their leaders' honesty and integrity. Otherwise, the pain of change causes social unrest, and growth is lost.

The necessary consensus for economic growth is difficult to achieve because incentives have to be aligned over a broad range of interests, some of which will feel acutely the sacrifices of economic change. These essays show that there is no single road that leaders must follow; rather, they show that leaders decide and implement policies within specific historical, cultural, and economic contexts. Good leaders are, in a sense, home grown because they have to understand and balance all these factors. It is also clear that choosing the wrong economic policy affects unity in adverse ways. Pain for no discernible gain is not helpful. Creating unity across interests is a necessary but not sufficient condition for economic growth and development.

Economists have long argued that growth depends, to a large degree, on the institutions that a country creates. Indeed, the Commission itself states that "mature markets rely on deep institutional underpinnings, institutions that define property rights, enforce contracts, convey prices, and bridge informational gaps between buyers and sellers," among other things. The problem is that developing countries often lack these institutions. Growth can occur without them: these institutions co-evolve with the progress of the economy. However, we do not know in detail how these institutions are created and sustained. Therefore, the effect of policy shifts and reforms is harder to predict in developing economies. Given the importance of creating institutions compatible with economic growth, we are fortunate to have three essays that shed light on this problem.

Acemoglu and Robinson argue that the main differences in prosperity across countries reflect differences in economic institutions. The ability of leaders to change these economic institutions will determine the level of economic development achieved. The authors argue that such reforms are hard because the institutions are, in the final analysis, the end product of the political forces at play in a country. The distribution of political power in a country is often in a rough equilibrium, the settled result of a country's political culture and political institutions. Leaders trying to change the relevant economic institutions thus face the problem of changing the distribution of political power, which confounds the problem of institutional reform.

Acemoglu and Robinson provide several examples of the pitfalls of institutional reforms. They spell out that economic solutions are grounded in politics. Knowing the nature of the problem helps to specify the nature of the trade-offs necessary to move nations onto an appropriate reform path. Understanding these trade-offs is a sine qua non for leadership, as is the skill of determining the moment and condition under which change may be achieved.

Iyoha's chapter argues that in the Nigerian case, inconsistent leadership based on military coups has led to constant changes in institutions. This institutional upheaval has been associated with a poor record of long-term economic growth. From 1960 to 2000, per capita income grew less than 0.5 percent per year. This poor economic performance is attributed to the dominance of military governance, as well as regional and ethno-religious conflict. Leaders, both military and civil, were motivated by factors leading to "adverse redistributions." They failed to reform the macroeconomy, strengthen governance institutions, or make necessary structural changes in the economy.

Iyoha argues that the leadership changes begun in 2001 and culminating in 2003 resulted in strong economic growth. The 2003 measures focused on macroeconomic reform, structural reform, governance and institutional reform, and public sector reform. These reforms, in combination with increased aid revenue, a new monetary policy, and better debt management, resulted in a growth rate of 7.1 percent per year from 2003 to 2006. These changes were the result of good elected leaders making good choices implemented in a rational fashion.

The broad-ranging chapter by Tan, Eng, and Robinson claims that a country's institutional base determines whether natural endowments enrich or impoverish a nation. Using measures of institutional quality such as prudence in spending and judicial independence, the authors show that sustained growth is tied to quality institutions, and that good governance ensures maintained quality.

These three papers clearly show that the creation of economic institutions capable of generating and sustaining economic growth is best seen as a political economy problem. That is, creating economic institutions that enhance efficiency and generate economic growth often entails changing the distribution of political power within a country or a region. Leaders must balance the economics and the politics to sustain both growth and political order. Countries that have generated sustained growth over 25 years have succeeded in this juggling act, at least for long stretches.

Economic development in the United States and Western Europe did not occur all at once across the whole country or entire continent; rather, it first occurred in certain regions and states. The pattern of localized industrial centers is not random. In the United States, states differed in their interests and cultures, and their economics differed accordingly. It is almost as though the states were laboratories for different economic experiments. In China, Europe, Japan, and Korea, various regions, prefectures, and states developed at different rates over time. Surely much of the differential rates of industrialization are attributable to the natural advantages that a region or state had, such as a river or harbor, or to an entrepreneur such as Gutenberg, who invented the printing press in a specific spot and thus began an industry in a specific place. Given the comparative advantage of certain areas over others for initial economic growth, it is possible for leaders to make bad choices about which regions should be industrialized. Decisions by nineteenth-century socialists in the United States to place agricultural collectives in New England rather than the more fertile Midwest is one such example. In short, to promote growth and development, policies must be selected based on their fit with the local environment.

A canny political leadership should appreciate that different areas will respond differently to its policies. Deng's innovative agricultural policies were not met with the same response in all regions, and, as Jean Oi (1999) has shown, the response of local party leaders to national policies in China had an important effect on growth rates. In choosing policies and implementing them, leaders must pay due respect to local conditions or at least allow local advantages to come to the fore and flourish. This principle is illustrated in the work of Rusuhuzwa Kigabo on Rwanda, Cardoso and Graeff on Brazil, and Tan, Eng, and Robinson on Singapore.

Rwanda adopted a national decentralization policy to achieve three main goals: good governance, pro-poor service delivery, and sustainable economic development. The decentralization helped solve ethnic/tribal problems, bad governance, and extreme poverty. In addition, the decentralization was viewed as an instrument for political empowerment of the people, reconciliation, and creating the basis for local social integration. One example of this localized policy was *ubedehe,* whereby local citizens participate in assessing needs and growth and work together with government support to address the identified issues.

Again, the general purpose chapter by Tan, Eng, and Robinson argues that growth comes from policies applied at the local level with an understanding of local context. The Singapore case shows the importance of implementing policies at the right time and reviewing those policies on a regular basis so that they can be adapted as required.

Further thoughts on this problem are offered by Cardoso and Graeff, two important participants in Brazil's progress toward consolidating democracy and generating sustained economic growth. The chapter begins from the dual premise that there is no "recipe" for development that opens the doors of globalization to all if only they do their homework, but that Latin Americans are not condemned forever to underdevelopment. In 1990 Brazil was characterized by economic stagnation, a foreign debt moratorium, hyperinflation, and a democracy slipping away because of a lack of governability. The chapter describes how the Real Plan (to deal with the inflation problem) was formed by an experienced and creative new team at the Finance Ministry, which submitted a short-term plan (a first step) to dissolve the relationship between inflation and the public purse. The broad approval for the plan convinced firms and citizens that such a policy had a chance to succeed. The next steps were to dismantle the wage and price indexation and end the debt moratorium.

The success of the program was illustrated when inflation dropped from 47 percent per month to less than 3 percent per month (in 30 days). It went on to decline further and has since remained in single digits per year. To capture these advantages and begin to sustain growth, it was necessary, according to the authors, to choose a role for the state somewhere between the state-run and the neoliberal minimalist models: "the necessary state." The new leaders proposed a series of amendments to the constitutional policies on state monopolies, social security and pensions, and public service, among others. The passage of these reforms had long-lasting effects that occurred on several fronts. The authors show how political institutions can slow down, block, and shift economic policy solutions. Their analysis shows how a crisis or a series of crises can be useful in shifting policy through good choices to foster economic growth. The analysis of plebiscitary versus consensual democracy admirably lays out alternatives and the economic tradeoffs implicit in both, as the comparisons with Argentina and Chile make clear. The section "Opportunity, Passion, and Perspective" offers a unique overview and interpretation of the forces driving Brazil's recent economic success.

To succeed, a leader must both choose the right policies and create the political conditions necessary for them to work. In the wake of the genocide, the Rwandan leadership astutely combined peace and economic progress with a decentralization policy, allowing more local input and control. The Brazilian case is a classic example of the interaction between politics and economics within a specific cultural and institutional framework. Progress in political economy will need more case studies detailing the nature of these tradeoffs within specific locations.

Change from the status quo almost always entails some pain in the short run, whereas the benefits often take time before they are readily observed or felt by ordinary citizens. Precisely because the time horizon for gain is either unknown or of some lengthy duration, leaders must create stability for the economic reforms to take place. The leader may be trusted by the people to have their best interests at heart, thus earning time, or leaders may create a consensus around the plan sufficient for it to have the time to succeed. Whether the stability is created by trust, consensus, or institutions such as single-party dominance, it seems that stability is a necessary but not sufficient condition for economic growth.

This point is mentioned in many of the chapters in this book. Brady and Spence argue that good economic policies need time to have impact, and creating stability in the political system gives the policy a chance to succeed. In Asia a single dominant party system has, at times, aligned the incentives of the major economic and political actors in the initial phases of the plan. Over time, as the economic gains are realized and new interests created, either the dominant party adapts to the new economic reality, as in China, or a multiparty system develops where parties alternate in power.

The Cardoso and Graeff chapter emphasizes the president's role in creating a broad consensus across multiple political parties in support of specific policies, thus creating stability and time for the policies to take effect. The authors also emphasize the necessity of the leader being able to explain complicated economic choices to the general public. Without said explanations, neither support nor stability is present.

The chapter by Mahmud, Ahmed, and Mahajan on Bangladesh examines the pre- and post-1990 performance of the economy. The country emerged from the war of independence poor, overpopulated, and physically damaged. The development strategy in Bangladesh has undergone successive shifts often associated with regime change in government. The early years were dominated by state control and a socialist ideology. In 1975 General Ziaur Rahman took control and moved toward privatization, followed by a second period of divestment under General Ershad. The 1980s witnessed a period of market-oriented development strategy under the guidelines of the World Bank and the International Monetary Fund.

The transition to parliamentary democracy in the early 1990s was associated with the movement toward a more comprehensive program of economic reform featuring currency convertibility, reduced import duties, and removed controls on foreign private capital. The authors argue that the economic growth since the 1990s has been led by strong export growth, which provided a growth stimulus to other parts of the Bangladesh economy. The authors show how economic growth has greatly improved Bangladesh's record on human development indicators such as child mortality and female school enrollment. They also assess the country's record on governance and poverty reduction.

These four problems are not the only difficulties that leaders face in trying to generate economic growth, and our authors cover a variety of other problems. These chapters, we believe, represent an excellent first step toward understanding the role of leadership in generating economic growth, and we hope that they generate ideas and lead to new research on the problem of leadership in economic growth.

References

Carlyle, Thomas. 1841. *On Heroes, Hero-Worship, and the Heroic in History.* Whitefish, MT: Kessinger Press.

Diamond, Jared. 1997. *Guns, Germs, and Steel.* New York: W. W. Norton.

Jones, Benjamin, and Benjamin Olken. 2005. "Do Leaders Matter? National Leadership and Growth since World War II." *Quarterly Journal of Economics* 120 (3): 835–64.

Oi, Jean. 1999. *Rural China Takes Off: Institutional Foundations of Economic Reform.* Berkeley: University of California Press.

Workshop Participants

Acemoglu, Daron, Massachusetts Institute of Technology
Ahluwalia, Isher, Indian Council for Research on International Economic Relations
Ahluwalia, Montek, Commissioner and Deputy Chairman, Planning Commission of India
Backeus, Karl, Ministry of Foreign Affairs of Sweden
Boediono, Dr., Commissioner and Governor, Bank of Indonesia
Brady, David, Stanford University
Cardoso, Fernando Henrique, former President of Brazil
Derviş, Kemal, Commissioner and Director, United Nations Development Programme
Ffrench-Davis, Ricardo, University of Chile
Fuhr, Harald, University of Potsdam
Gelb, Alan, World Bank
Goh, Chok Tong, Commissioner and Senior Minister, and Chairman of the Monetary Authority of Singapore
Graeff, Eduardo, São Paulo State Government Representation Office in Brasilia
Hesse, Heiko, Economist, World Bank
Hübner, Danuta, Commissioner and European Commissioner for Regional Policy
Jämtin, Carin, Commissioner and former Minister for International Development of Sweden

Kharas, Homi, Visiting Fellow, Wolfensohn Center for Development, Brookings Institution

Kingsmill, William, Department for International Development

Kuczynski, Pedro Pablo, Commissioner and former Prime Minister of Peru

Lee, Chung Min, National University of Singapore

Leipziger, Danny, Growth Commission Vice Chair and Vice President, World Bank

Lim, Edwin, China Economic Research and Advisory Programme

Mkapa, Benjamin William, former President of Tanzania

Nankani, Gobind, Global Development Network

Nowak, Dorota, World Bank

Okonjo-Iweala, Ngozi N., Commissioner and Managing Director, World Bank

Perry, Guillermo, former Chief Economist, World Bank

Pinto, Brian, Economic Adviser, World Bank

Ramos, Maria, Transnet, Ltd

Robinson, James, Harvard University

Romer, Paul, Stanford University and Hoover Institution

Solow, Robert, Commissioner and Professor Emeritus, Massachusetts Institute of Technology

Spence, Michael, Growth Commission Chair and Professor Emeritus, Stanford University

Toruan, Henry, Coordinating Ministry for Economic Affairs of Indonesia

Venner, Sir K. Dwight, Commissioner and Governor of the Eastern Caribbean Central Bank

Wolfowitz, Paul, President, World Bank

Zagha, Roberto, World Bank

Zedillo, Ernesto, Commissioner and Director, Yale Center Study of Globalization

Professional affiliations identified are as of the time of the workshop.

About the Editors and Contributors

Daron Acemoglu is the Charles P. Kindleberger Professor of Applied Economics at the Massachusetts Institute of Technology. His research interests include political economy, economic development, economic growth, economic theory, technology, income and wage inequality, human capital and training labor economics, and network economics. He is the recipient of numerous awards and honors, including the John Bates Clark Medal from the American Economic Association (2005), Distinguished Science Award from the Turkish Sciences Association (2006), and Honorary Doctorate from the University of Utrecht, the Netherlands (2008).

Sadiq Ahmed is former Senior Manager, South Asia region, at the World Bank. He joined the Bank in 1981 and held various positions throughout his career at the World Bank, including Economist for the Arab Republic of Egypt, Indonesia, Papua New Guinea, Pakistan, and Sri Lanka (1981–95); Chief of the Bank's Resident Mission in Pakistan and later the Country Director for Afghanistan and Pakistan (1995–99); Chief Economist for South Asia Region (1999–2001); Sector Director for Poverty Reduction and Economic Management (PREM) and then Senior Manager for Regional Programs in the South Asia Region (2007–09). Since August 2009, he has been the Vice Chairman of the Policy Research Institute of Bangladesh. Mr. Ahmed was educated at the London School of Economics and Boston University. He has written and published extensively in the areas of public finance, monetary economics, development economics, and poverty analysis.

David Brady is the Bowen H. and Janice Arthur McCoy Professor of Political Science and Leadership Values, Professor of Political Science,

School of Humanities and Sciences, Stanford University; Deputy Director and Davies Family Senior Fellow, Hoover Institution; Senior Fellow, Stanford Institute for Economic Policy Research, and Morris M. Doyle Centennial Chair in Public Policy, Stanford University. Professor Brady's research focuses on the American Congress, the party system, and public policy. He also has written on Internet voting, the women's movement, regulation of the nuclear industry, apportionment, the Supreme Court's handling of abortion, and Korean and Japanese politics. He presently heads a joint project between the Brookings Institution and the Hoover Institution on Polarization in American Politics.

Professor Brady began his teaching career at Kansas State University in 1970; from there he moved to Houston, Texas, where he taught at both the University of Houston and Rice University, where in 1981 he was named Autry Distinguished Professor of Social Science. In 1986 he moved to Stanford University with a joint appointment in the Graduate School of Business (GSB) and Department of Political Science. While at Stanford he has served as Associate Dean for Academic Affairs in the GSB and as Vice Provost for Distance Learning. He has twice been a Fellow at the Center for Advanced Study in the Behavioral Sciences and was elected to the American Academy of Arts and Sciences in 1987. Professor Brady's teaching focuses on nonmarket strategy for corporations and ethical applications in building quality companies. In addition to his GSB teaching he teaches an undergraduate course in public policy. He has been awarded several teaching awards, including the prestigious Dinkelspiel and Phi Beta Kappa distinguished teacher prizes.

Fernando Henrique Cardoso is the former President of Brazil (1995–2002) and is currently President of the Instituto Fernando Henrique Cardoso (São Paulo, Brazil) and honorary President of the Brazilian Social Democracy Party (PSDB). He is a member of the Board of Directors of the Club of Madrid (Madrid, Spain), and in the United States, he is a member of the Clinton Global Initiative (New York) and a member of the Board of Directors of the Inter-American Dialogue, the World Resources Institute, and the Thomas J. Watson Jr. Institute for International Studies at Brown University (Providence, RI). He is author of *The Accidental President of Brazil: A Memoir,* published by Public Affairs Books (2006).

Alvin Eng is a Senior Economist at the Macroeconomic Surveillance Department, Monetary Authority of Singapore.

Eduardo Graeff is a Head of the State of São Paulo liaison office in Brasilia. He was Chief Congressional Liaison Officer and General Secretary to the President of Brazil in Fernando Henrique Cardoso's administration (1995–2002).

Milton A. Iyoha is a Visiting Research Scholar in the Research Department, Central Bank of Nigeria, Abuja. He is on leave of absence from Igbinedion University, Okada, Nigeria, where he holds concurrent Professorships in the Department of Business Administration and Department of Economics and Development Studies. He graduated (summa cum laude) from Oberlin College, Ohio, United States in 1966, and from Yale University in 1970 with a Ph.D. in economics. A former Research Fellow at the Brookings Institution in Washington, DC, Dr. Iyoha has taught at the State University of New York at Buffalo, United States and the University of Benin, Benin City, Nigeria. He has also been a Visiting Research Scholar at the International Monetary Fund in Washington, DC, and a Visiting Professor of Economics at the University of Lagos and the University of Botswana. Professor Iyoha's research focuses on macroeconomic policy, growth, trade, and international development.

Sandeep Mahajan is Lead Economist in the Africa Region of the World Bank. At the time of the writing of the chapter he was the World Bank's Senior Country Economist for Bangladesh and lead author of the report *Bangladesh: Strategy for Sustained Growth*. Dr. Mahajan's research interests cover macroeconomics, economic growth, volatility and inequality, and financial sector development. Born in New Delhi, India, Dr. Mahajan received his B. Com (Hons) from Delhi University in 1990 and his Ph.D. in economics from Georgetown University in 1996.

Wahiduddin Mahmud is Professor of Economics at the University of Dhaka. He has held teaching and research appointments at Cambridge University, the Institute of Development Studies at Sussex, the International Food Policy Research Institute, and the World Bank, among others. He has carried out numerous assignments for several international organizations and has led many committees of the Bangladesh government, such as those pertaining to bank reform, national income estimation, and poverty monitoring. He is a founder and chairman of the Palli Karma Shahayak Foundation (PKSF), Bangladesh's apex institution for funding the microcredit programs of nongovernmental organizations. He was Minister of Finance and Planning in the caretaker government of Bangladesh in 1996. His recent and forthcoming books include an edited volume of the International Economic Association titled *Adjustment and Beyond: The Reform Experience of South Asia* (Palgrave-Macmillan) and another edited volume, *Handbook of South Asian Economies* (Edward Elgar).

Benjamin William Mkapa is a seasoned diplomat, journalist, and politician. He was President of Tanzania (1995–2005); Tanzania's Ambassador to Nigeria (1976), Canada (1982–83), and the United States (1983–84); Managing Editor of prominent newspapers; and Press Secretary to the founding President of Tanzania, Mwalimu Julius K. Nyerere. His ministerial portfolios included foreign affairs; information and communication; and higher education, science and technology. He always worked to strengthen Tanzanian democracy, entrench civil rights, and fight poverty, while increasing the country's exposure to international trade and investment. He was Co-Chair of the World Commission on the Social Dimension of Globalization (2002–04) and was a member of the Commission for Africa (2004–05).

He is Chairman of the South Centre, Co-Chair of the Investment Climate Facility for Africa, and Co-Chair of the Africa Emerging Markets Forum

(AEMF). He is on the board of trustees of the Africa Wildlife Foundation (AWF) and served on the United Nations' Commission on the Legal Empowerment of the Poor (2006–08), as well as the United Nations' review panels on UNCTAD and UN System-wide Coherence. President Mkapa is a member of the Club of Madrid, InterAction Council, and the Africa Forum. He is patron of the UN committee of the 2008 International Year of Planet Earth. He is active in conflict resolution and political reconciliation in the Great Lakes Region of Africa, including in Kenya in early 2008, and currently in Eastern Congo (Democratic Republic of Congo). Educated at Makerere University in Uganda, and Columbia University in New York, he also has seven honorary doctorate degrees from universities in Africa, Japan, the United Kingdom, and the United States.

Edward Robinson is Executive Director of the Economic Policy Department, Monetary Authority of Singapore.

James Robinson is Professor of Government at Harvard University and a Faculty Associate at the Weatherhead Center for International Affairs. Professor Robinson studied economics at the London School of Economics, the University of Warwick, and Yale University. He previously taught in the Department of Economics at the University of Melbourne and the University of Southern California; before moving to Harvard he was a Professor in the Departments of Economics and Political Science at the University of California at Berkeley. His main research interest is why countries are different: particularly why some are more prosperous than others, and why some are more democratic than others. Professor Robinson is a member of the Canadian Institute for Advanced Research's program on Institutions, Organizations and Growth.

Thomas Rusuhuzwa Kigabo is Chief Economist, National Bank of Rwanda, and Professor, Department of Economics, National University of Rwanda.

Michael Spence is Senior Fellow, the Hoover Institution, and Philip H. Knight Professor Emeritus of Management, Graduate School of Business, Stanford University. He was awarded the Nobel Memorial Prize in Economic Sciences in 2001. Mr. Spence was Philip H. Knight Professor and Dean of the Stanford Business School from 1990 to 1999. Since 1999 he has been a partner at Oak Hill Capital Partners. From 1975 to 1990, he served as Professor of Economics and Business Administration at Harvard University. Mr. Spence was awarded the John Kenneth Galbraith Prize for excellence in teaching in 1978 and the John Bates Clark Medal in 1981 for a "significant contribution to economic thought and knowledge." He was appointed Chairman of the Economics Department at Harvard in 1983 and served as the Dean of the Faculty of Arts and Sciences from 1984 to 1990. At various times he has served as a member of the editorial boards of *American Economics Review, Bell Journal of Economics, Journal of Economic Theory,* and *Public Policy*. Professor Spence is the Chair of the Commission on Growth and Development.

Tan Yin Ying is a Senior Economist at the Economic Policy Department, Monetary Authority of Singapore.

Acknowledgments

The editors are most grateful for the strong support provided by the sponsors of the Commission on Growth and Development: the governments of Australia, the Netherlands, Sweden, and the United Kingdom; the William and Flora Hewlett Foundation; and the World Bank. Danny Leipziger, former Vice President of the Poverty Reduction and Economic Management Network at the World Bank, was generous in providing resources for this effort. We are much obliged to the participants in the workshop on leadership and growth sponsored by the Commission, especially the chapter authors, for their numerous and diverse insights and the time they dedicated to engaging in discussions of the issues. Roberto Zagha, Secretary of the Commission, was a constant source of good ideas, encouragement, and stimulation. Roberto brings out the best in others, while keeping a sharp focus on the driving issues at hand. The level of discussion and the quality of the chapters that follow reflect his enthusiasm and wisdom.

A team of colleagues in the Growth Commission secretariat—Muriel Darlington, Diana Manevskaya, and Dorota Nowak—were dedicated to making every aspect of the Commission's work successful. They gave us what felt like undivided attention in organizing the workshops and producing this book—one of many of the Commission's activities with pressing deadlines and low tolerance for error. The whole process was only possible due to their marvelous organization and steady hard work. Aziz Gökdemir was pragmatic, accommodating, and diligent in preparing the manuscript for publication. He kept the book on track when we occasionally needed to shift our deadlines. Stephen McGroarty oversaw the publication process with great skill and Nora Ridolfi managed the printing of the book to ensure the highest quality. We owe a special debt of thanks to Romy Saloner, who read the papers and helped us think through our approach to editing the volume, and to Mandy MacCalla for her excellent copyediting of our initial attempts.

David Brady
Michael Spence

Abbreviations

AIDS	acquired immune deficiency syndrome
APRM	Africa Peer Review Mechanism
AU	African Union
BNP	Bangladesh Nationalist Party
BPI	Bribe Payers Index
CAGR	compounded annual growth rate
CBN	Central Bank of Nigeria
CCP	Chinese Communist Party
CFS	Computers for Schools
CIA	Central Intelligence Agency
CPF	Central Provident Fund
CPI	Corruption Perception Index
CPP	Cambodian People's Party
DAC	Development Assistance Committee
DJP	Democratic Justice Party
EAC	East African Community
EDB	Economic Development Board
EU	European Union
FDI	foreign direct investment
G-8	Group of 8
GDP	gross domestic product
HIC	high-income countries
HIPC	highly indebted poor country
HIV	human immunodeficiency virus

ICF	Investment Climate Facility
ICT	information and communication technology
ICTR	International Criminal Tribunal for Rwanda
IFI	international financial institution
ILD	Institute for Liberty and Democracy
ILO	International Labour Organization
LDP	Liberal Democratic Party
LIC	low-income countries
MMD	Movement for Multiparty Democracy
MNC	multinational corporation
MNR	Movimiento Nacionalista Revolucionario
NAPEP	National Poverty Eradication Program
NBR	National Bank of Rwanda
NEEDS	National Economic Empowerment and Development Strategy
NEPAD	New Partnership for Africa's Development
NWC	National Wages Council
ODA	official development assistance
PAN	Partido Acción Nacional
PDC	Partido Demócrata Cristiano
PFL	Partido da Frente Liberal
PJ	Partido Justicialista
PMDB	Partido do Movimento Democrático Brasileiro
PPB	Partido Progressita Brasileiro
PPP	purchasing power parity
PRD	Partido de la Revolución Democrática
PRI	Partido Revolucionario Institucional
PS	Partido Socialista
PSDB	Partido da Social Democracia Brasileira
PT	Partido dos Trabalhadores
PTB	Partido Trabalhista Brasileiro
PWT	Penn World Table
REC	regional economic grouping
RPF	Rwanda Patriotic Front
SAP	Structural Adjustment Program
SEC	Securities and Exchange Commission
SNTV	single nontransferable vote
SOE	state-owned enterprise
SSA	sub-Saharan Africa
TI	Transparency International
UCR	Unión Cívica Radical
UNDP	United Nations Development Programme
VAT	value-added tax
WTO	World Trade Organization
YOY	year on year

All dollars are U.S. dollars.

CHAPTER 1
Leadership and Politics:
A Perspective from the Commission
on Growth and Development

David Brady and Michael Spence

The Role of Leadership in Growth and Development

In May 2008, the Commission on Growth and Development (the Growth Commission) issued its report entitled *The Growth Report*. In it the Commission attempted to distill what had been learned in the past two decades, from experience and academic and policy research, about strategies and policies that produced sustained high growth in developing countries. It became clear in the course of the work that politics, leadership, and political economy (the interaction of economic and political forces and choices) were centrally important ingredients in the story. Dealing with the politics and the interaction of political and economic forces is a work in progress in research—an important one.

This article was originally published in 2009 in *Oxford Review of Economic Policy* 25(2): 1–14 [doi: 10.1093/oxrep/grp017]. ©2009 David Brady and Michael Spence. Published by Oxford University Press. For permissions, please e-mail: journals.permissions@oxfordjournals.org.

In this chapter we do not try to present any general theory. Rather we have tried to illustrate with cases that there is a potentially important political analogue to the sort of economic policy formation and adaptation that supports sustained growth and development. These cases are far from representative. They come from Asian countries that have achieved sustained high growth over an extended period of time. Our hope is that by understanding the details in these cases, the process of developing a more general theory that integrates economic and political inputs to growth and development will be advanced. One can think of the cases as suggesting hypotheses that can be embodied in a more general theory and ultimately tested.

An analysis of the components of successful sustained economic growth and development strategies and dynamics appears to require inclusion of three components: (1) an economic component dealing with the issue of which models of growth and development work best and what kinds of policies tend to support sustained growth models, (2) an institutional component dealing with the question of which institutions enhance and facilitate economic growth and development and how those institutions come into existence and become stronger, and, finally, (3) a component that deals with the politics of growth featuring the ways in which countries deal with the issues created by growth, such as inequality. Each of these three components has complexities and problems associated with it, ranging from measurement and causation to particularism. Our knowledge in all three areas is considerable and improving all the time based on experience and careful scholarly work, but it is still incomplete. It seems clear that all three are necessary for there to be a reasonably complete description of growth and development.

Based on the experience of growth in a range of countries (with varying degrees of success in achieving and sustaining high growth) and on research on growth and development, a rough description of the right mix of economics, institutions, and politics supporting growth and development is something like the following:

1. An open-economy growth strategy that leverages both global demand and knowledge. Competition is allowed to work and produces the structural change that forms the microeconomic dynamic underpinning of high growth. While there is much more to it, including high levels of public and private sector investment and savings, these seem to be at the heart of sustained high-growth cases.[1]

2. Institutions characterized by openness, rule of law or some considerable degree of predictability, competent bureaucracy, and incentive structures that keep politicians focused on citizens' long-term well-being.

---

[1] The Growth Report identifies 13 countries that grew at an average rate of 7 percent or more for a period of 25 years or more. This is very hard to do. These cases have many idiosyncratic features, but all exhibit the open-economy approach (leveraging global knowledge and demand), and all have mobile resources and change the structural composition of the economy rapidly, using dynamic market forces of competition. The subtler policy judgments have to do with opening the economy up in such a way as to maintain balance between new job creation and job destruction and to avoid excessive volatility.

3. A set of political interactions and structures where there is sufficient stability early on for the right model to work in terms of sustained investment and, later on, where rotation in power and adaptation to the endogenous rise of important interest groups (a growing middle class, for example) is possible and peaceful.

At any specific point in time, a given country may be at any point in the three-dimensional space defined roughly by the degree of development in these three dimensions. Progress and likely future growth would be defined as being on a track toward the relevant zone where a supportive economic policy environment and adaptive political system are achieved. Maintaining such a trajectory and support for it can be thought of as one of the primary functions of political leadership.

Beyond the essential features, there is considerable allowable variance around the choice of an economic model and the institutions and politics that embrace growth and development.

There is not, therefore, and should not be a recommendation for a single path in any of these three dimensions. Indeed, the Growth Commission's work and the 13 high-growth cases show us that there is no single path or formula for sustained growth.

The 13 sustained high-growth cases in the postwar period are shown in Table 1.1. In addition, the Growth Commission believed that the structural

Table 1.1. 13 Success Stories of Sustained, High Growth

Economy	Period of High Growth[b]	Per Capita Income[c]	
		At the Start of the High-Growth Period	2005
Botswana	1960–2005	210	3,800
Brazil	1950–80	960	4,000
China	1961–2005	105	1,400
Hong Kong, China[a]	1960–97	3,100	29,900
Indonesia	1966–97	200	900
Japan[a]	1950–83	3,500	39,600
Korea, Republic of[a]	1960–2001	1,100	13,200
Malaysia	1967–97	790	4,400
Malta[a]	1963–94	1,100	9,600
Oman	1960–99	950	9,000
Singapore[a]	1967–2002	2,200	25,400
Taiwan, China[a]	1965–2002	1,500	16,400
Thailand	1960–97	330	2,400

Source: Commission on Growth and Development 2008; based on data from World Bank, World Development Indicators and Penn World Table (http://pwt.econ.upenn.edu).
a. Economies that have reached industrialized countries' per capita income levels.
b. Period in which GDP growth was 7 percent per year or more.
c. In constant U.S. dollars of 2000.

conditions were in place for India and Vietnam to be on track to achieve this kind of performance with a little more time, given a later and/or slower start.

In some very general sense, making the right choices over this set of components is what leaders in the high-growth economies have done. *The Growth Report* identifies 13 economies that have achieved sustained, high growth, specified as 7 percent or higher for 25 years or more, during the postwar period. Over time, the leaders in these 13 countries (and those in others, such as India and Vietnam, which appear to be on sustained, high-growth paths but at an earlier stage) chose some variant of a successful growth strategy or approach, put together coalitions of business, agriculture, labor, and other political segments that were sufficiently stable to allow the economic choices a chance to attain sustainable growth. Moreover, over time leadership in these countries managed the transition from rural to urban, from relatively closed to more open institutions and, in several cases, the change from autocratic to more democratic government. Thus, it seems clear that leadership plays a role in generating sustained growth. It has the primary task of making basic choices and building consensus without which the economic dynamics cannot get off the ground.

There is no one style of leadership that covers all the high-growth economies. Nor is leadership the only input. At best one can venture that effective leadership involves seizing opportunities created by the political-economy dynamics to institute change in strategy, structure, and direction. Opportunity can be created by a crisis, or the unanticipated discovery of natural-resource wealth, for example, but there needs to be a catalyst that turns change, adversity, and opportunity into a new direction with some degree of coherence and shared understanding of the direction.

Although leadership seems an obvious component of growth to some, the academic literature has not, until recently, been able to demonstrate the importance of the role of leaders in growth economies. Recent work on leadership has begun to demonstrate what seems obvious to the business, government, and interest groups who have witnessed the economic growth of the 13 countries. The problem for social scientists is that there is more than a little endogeneity with respect to leaders and economic growth. Thus, how does one know if the leader really makes a difference in causing growth, or to put it slightly baldly, that growth just looks good when it happens?

In a careful empirical study, Jones and Olken (2005) look across all post–Second World War economies and find 57 cases in which the country's leader suddenly dies or resigns, for example, thus allowing them to use the natural experiment change in leadership for exogenous reasons to solve the endogeneity problem. That is, the unexpected death of a leader gives us a chance to measure the leader's effect on growth. Of course, the change can be positive or negative. They found that the change of national leaders is related to economic growth. The effects were strongest (both positive and negative) in autocratic settings where one or a few leaders have centralized authority. In democratic settings, there were no significant findings. This may be a result of the fact that consensus building is a lengthier and more complex process in some democratic settings. The long time lags make it difficult to pick up the effects in cross-sectional regressions. For example, the reforms that began in India in the late 1980s and that accelerated in response to a crisis in the early 1990s are only now showing up in terms of a pattern of high growth.

In addition, they found that "individual leaders can play crucial roles in shaping the growth of nations" (Jones and Olken 2005: 835). Moreover, they found that a leader's effect on policy outcomes is most significant in monetary policy. This last result is interesting not only because of the use of natural experiments but also because they find that when there are more or stronger institutions (probably financial and governmental) present, the effect of individuals is lessened or harder to measure. This is not surprising. One of the functions of well-built institutions is to pool expertise and to apply brakes to poor policy choices, including those of the leadership group. It is, of course, harder to study the effect of leaders within institutions and the institutions' subsequent effect on economic growth. The endogeneity problem, combined with the measurement problems, makes the task exceedingly difficult.

That does not, of course, mean that leadership (defined to be the making of fundamental choices about strategy, consensus building, and adapting the political institutions to support economic and social objectives) does not make a difference, only that for a variety of reasons we cannot yet accurately measure the effect of such leadership. In this chapter, we assume that practitioners and observers and a wide range of scholars are right in believing that, at least at times, leadership makes a difference in terms of altering the trajectory of a developing economy, while acknowledging that the support for this view is not airtight or universal.

Given these constraints, our approach has been to separate the development process into different periods and to analyze leaders' roles at the various stages. The obvious first stage is where the leadership chooses an economic model or strategy, a general overall approach to development and growth, and then builds coalitions, institutions, or both, capable of sustaining a politics that allows the plan time to bring dividends in terms of growth. The second stage is in some sense not delimited in time because it concerns how leaders adjust strategies and choices to changing circumstances—economic and political. These adjustments can be responses to shocks or unanticipated external events, but they also occur in response to the endogenous evolution of characteristics of the economy in the course of growth. These latter challenges can and do range from rising income inequality, a rising middle class, competitive pressures from the global economy, rising incomes and wages causing shifting comparative advantage, and institutions not adapted to the evolving characteristics and state of development economy.

In all these cases, there is the element of problem solving within a specific institutional context that itself may or may not be changing. Thus, in none of the adjustment phases of economic growth will we be able to specify exactly what choices leaders should make over growth strategies, coalitions, and institutions. That tends to be very context specific. It would be nice to imagine a general theory or framework for doing this, but given our current knowledge, that is out of reach. Rather, we attempt with examples to draw what generalizations we can in regard to leadership and economic growth.

Founding or Shifting to Sustained High Growth

The general dimensions of leadership in growing and developing economies are characterized over time, first, by a founding or creating process where an economic model is chosen and implemented, and then by adjustments that either ensure growth or prevent other interests from subverting growth. The founding can be thought of as a period in which a leader or leaders choose the correct model—normally export-driven growth models—while simultaneously building a political consensus to support the model. Note that a leader or leadership group can choose a model that will not work (economically), or they can have, as Mao Tse-tung and Nehru did, other goals besides economic growth. Since we are trying to identify leadership's role in creating and sustaining development, our focus is on cases where leaders made the right decision and built a consensus for their choice.

We normally think of consensus as a negotiation. But it can and usually does include trust. History does to some extent tell citizens and interest groups something about the objectives of leaders. If the behavior gives evidence of concern for the present and future well-being of the citizens, then that can count for a lot. It is a form of intangible capital that makes the consensus-building process easier. In general, inclusiveness, by intent and historical experience, is a powerful underpinning of consensus building. It gives the leadership and the government time to implement the strategy and to wait for results to emerge.

Choosing the right model has generally meant relying on global demand, inbound knowledge and technology transfer, and high levels of investment and savings. For a fuller description of the critical policy ingredients and choices associated with sustained high growth, interested readers should see *The Growth Report*.

The choice of a correct model and subsequent adjustments have led 13 countries to sustained economic growth, with India and Vietnam set to follow. There are, therefore, many other countries that have not achieved this pattern of sustained high growth. The obvious question is, Why is the pattern of sustained high growth so limited? We believe that at least some of the explanation of the lower growth patterns lies with leaders who have chosen economic models that have not led to sustained growth.[2]

---

2   There are, of course, other problems. One is the political economy of self-interest and theft and the related corruption of the democratic process. A second is a failure on the economic side to get public-sector investment up to the level that will support private-sector investment and sustain high growth.

Part of the answer may have to do with opportunity. In many of the 13 high-growth cases plus India and Vietnam with which we are familiar, the choice of a correct model and the political machinations necessary to convince those who share power with the chooser to follow the model are associated with a crisis. The Japanese after the Second World War, the Koreans in 1961, the Chinese after the Cultural Revolution, the Taiwanese-Chinese in 1949, and Singapore after separating from Malaysia were all facing dire economic and political conditions. The crises gave leaders from Deng Xiaoping to President Park an opportunity to change course with a reduced level of resistance. In some cases, the crises are fiscal, and in some they are political, ranging from losing the Second World War to protests on the streets, as in Seoul in the mid-1980s.

Crises in India in 1991 and Turkey in 2001 were financial crises and are more recent examples of leaders having more room to choose new economic plans and policies. In both India and Turkey, the leadership responded by making major structural changes in the economy, which resulted in future economic growth. Kemal Derviş used the crises as an opportunity to get legislation through the Turkish parliament, which probably could not have been passed under normal circumstances. The 19 major reforms that were passed during and immediately after the crisis have helped Turkey grow its economy. Since the average per capita income of the 13 countries at the start of their growth was less than $1,000, widespread poverty itself may have been the basis for an enhanced willingness to contemplate major change. Telecommunications technology, which increasingly makes "the alternative" much more visible than it was in the past, may help create a political environment more conducive to change. This appears to be particularly true when proximity is added and citizens can see that other countries are doing better, as in the case of East and West Germany. It is widely believed within and outside India that China's growth, size, and proximity enhanced the incentives for reform and change of strategy in India. Deng Xiaoping's understanding of alternative strategies and possibilities was strongly influenced by visits to Singapore and New York in the 1970s before the adoption of a market-oriented system. More broadly, demonstration effects seem very real and more powerful as a result of information and communications technology and the increasing availability of information, through television, the Internet, travel, and other channels.

The crisis conditions, whether financial, political, poverty, or, as is most often the case, a combination of the three, have occurred more frequently and over many countries where wrong choices were made. The evidence does not support the conclusion that those crises drive right choices. Rather, the more modest hypothesis is that crises create conditions where leaders have fewer constraints on their choice over both economic policy and structural and institutional reform. Occasionally the relaxing of political constraints results in a new dynamic. The Japanese after the Second World War faced a major crisis, as did President Park in the Republic of Korea in 1961. The

Cultural Revolution in China was a disaster for the economy, of course, and, in each case, the leadership chose economic models that met most of the conditions specified above.

However, it does seem likely that there is a positive kind of contagion. The Japanese success after the Second World War induced other Asian countries to choose export-driven growth plans, including, in some cases, creating similar institutions. Examples and cases appear to have powerful effects.

The notion that crises create conditions for economic and political change is not limited to the founding period but also applies to crises generated by the very success of the economic plan. Ten to 20 years of economic growth generates winners, relative losers, and increased income and wealth inequalities. That creates new problems to resolve. It may be the case that, after per capita income has risen sufficiently, there are more limits (explicit and implicit) in general on decision makers because the society is more complicated. However, even then crises give leaders an opportunity to change structures and institutions.

Choosing the right economic model is only one part of the first phase of sustaining economic growth. Building support for these economic choices requires, as a sine qua non, enough political stability for the economic plan to work. In theory, a purely autocratic, one-person, absolute rule in some sense provides the greatest political stability—only one person to consult, convince, decide. No country has such a system, but there is evidence from Jones and Olken (2005) that economic growth is associated with autocracy in a subset of autocratic systems. However, there are fully functional democracies among the high-growth cases. Perhaps more important, there are many catastrophically poorly performing autocracies, and there are a number of failing democratic structures as well.[3] Jones and Olken (2005) further show that the effects of leaders (positive and negative) are very strong in autocratic settings, but much less so in the presence of democratic institutions. Their study was not confined to the 13 growth economies, but it is plausible that political stability and the absence of effective dissent allow the time necessary for economic choices to bear fruit. The idea is that in an autocratic country, a leader or a small group of leaders have greater latitude with respect to economic policy choices in the early stages when there is no track record to rely on. They can choose an export strategy, an import substitution policy, an isolationist policy (as in the Democratic People's Republic of Korea or Myanmar), and so on. Given that this authority does not guarantee the right choice, it surely says they will have more effect on growth independent of their decision. That is, a bad choice leads to slow or no growth, while a good choice leads to growth. An unexpected change in leadership is more likely to change growth.

---

3   Recent research in political economy and development is shedding new light on the endogenous economic and political forces that give rise to both superior and inferior economic performance. Acemoglu and Robinson (2006) is particularly good.

Examples from Growth Commission Countries

There are various ways to build political stability, from military takeover, to building one-party states, to consent over economic policies between the leading political parties. Many of the growth economies on our list formed or tried to form one-party or dominant-party structures—China; Hong Kong, China (where the British served as a single party and as the rule maker); Japan; Korea; Singapore; and Taiwan, China. The idea of a one-party state in Japan (the first high-growth economy along with Brazil) meant combining the Liberal and Democratic Parties in 1955 when the Socialist or Left Parties threatened to win majority status in parliament. The combination of these parties provided stability for the Japanese economic model to work. Combining the two conservative parties into a single power that continuously won reelection entailed specific electoral rules, malapportionment, accepting new faction leaders and new factions, and forming and reforming new interest groups. The Kwomingdong in Taiwan, China, maintained a similar feature in their electoral system, as did the Koreans (Groffman et al. 1999, especially pp. 383–85).

The key ingredients in the dominant party systems were multimember districts with a single, nontransferable vote. That had the effect of enhancing the seats in parliament of national parties. The Singaporean electoral system also facilitated single-party rule. Suffice it to say that, in our view, aligning stable political majorities enhances the time available to governments to allow their plan to work and makes it harder for short-term political movements to shift policy. We explain later the link between the voting structures and the staying power of the dominant party.

Any economic plan will have short-term winners and losers. If politicians have an incentive to appeal to those interests in order to win power, they will do so. In the single-party system, the arrangements make it harder for politicians to organize short-term losers into majorities. Over time, as the growth economies' wealth is increased and widely shared, the majority party will be able to sustain majorities more easily. The most important time for political stability is in the early years of a model's implementation. If after three to five years the plan is not working, the political stability may persist, as in India under the Congress Party, but ultimately the lack of economic growth and development will cause strategy and policy shifts and sometimes regime change.

Ultimately, a dominant single-party system changes the incentives, in that ambitious politicians tend to concentrate in the dominant party, since seats tied to power are more valuable than seats in the minority party. In successful cases, since the dominant party favors a growth-oriented strategy, more ambitious politicians see their ultimate success tied to whether or not the economy grows; thus, they support "the plan." In multiparty systems, as in Latin America, many more ambitious politicians do not have an incentive to support "the plan," since their fate is not tied to it. In the short run, generating growth dramatically shifts the status quo. In many cases, a majority or near majority are asked to make sacrifices (with the benefits more distant in time), and they are, relatively speaking, worse off. Politicians appeal to the majority or near majority by criticizing "the plan." This scenario differs by country. In the Taiwanese case, the legislative Yuan majority was relatively permanent. In Japan, by contrast, the Liberal Democratic Party was close to losing its majority status to the Progressive parties. Nevertheless, building a single dominant party gets the incentives for politicians more in line with the economic plan (choice model) than is the case for multiparty systems.

There are various ways to design an electoral system in which, with roughly one-third to 40 percent electoral support, a party can control the legislative body and the government. The most obvious way is to create districts unequal in size and to over-represent dominant party voters. During the transition from an agricultural to an industrial economy, rural interests are usually subsidized and overrepresented at the expense of urban districts. The highly subsidized farmers in Japan, Korea, and Taiwan, China, are proof of the merits of the strategy, at least from the dominant-party perspective. These differences are often quite extreme, with some rural districts having 10 times or more the voting strength of urban residents. These rural-urban differences persist even at present after electoral reforms in Japan, Korea, and Taiwan, China. In the present Korean National Assembly, the five largest Korean cities have about 50 percent of the population, but only about 35 percent of the seats. The nine provinces with 50 percent of the population get 65 percent of the seats. In Japan, during the early period of growth, the degree of malapportionment was 2 to 1, rural to urban, and in the later period of development the ratio was still 1.6 to 1 (Hata 1990).

Another way to maintain single-party dominance is to structure the electoral system to the advantage of the dominant party. The most common of these mechanisms in Asia has been to combine the single nontransferable vote (SNTV) with multimember districts (seat magnitude). In this system the voter has one and only one vote in a district that elects from two to five members to the government, which creates coordination problems for political parties competing nationwide. In a series of articles Cox and Niou (1994) and Cox (1996) showed that in both Japan and Taiwan, China, the system benefits the governing party in "that two governing parties (the LDP of Japan, the Kuomintang of Taiwan, China) have been significantly more efficient at securing as many seats as possible out of a given number of winnable seats than have their respective oppositions." The reason is that dominant parties can more easily overcome their collective-action problems by allocating government resources to reward supporters and decrease opposition strength. The Korean electoral system prior to the late 1980s reforms had both SNTV and multimember districts, which resulted in advantages to the dominant party (Brady and Mo 1992).

One might have assumed in the cases of Japan, Korea, and Taiwan, China, that when the one-party rule ended, the growth would slow. In Japan, the major changes to the electoral system (district magnitude) occurred post-growth; however, in both Korea and Taiwan, China, the major electoral reforms occurred well before the end of the high-growth period and did not affect the growth rate. Thus, it seems that economic success can lead to change in the democratic structures without necessarily affecting economic growth, because Korea, Singapore, and to a certain extent Taiwan, China, have democratized without losing 7 percent a year growth. Some caution is needed here. Advanced economies cannot grow at rates like 7 percent. Therefore the high-growth economies will eventually slow down as the per capita income levels rise. Depending on how that inevitable slowdown compares with the evolution of the political structures, it may be hard to disentangle the two effects.

Another example of growth led by a different kind of single party is China. In 1950, the per capita income in China was $439, not at the bottom of the list but much lower than that of many developing countries. China was, in short, a very poor country. In the 1960s, Mao Zedong's strategy of "four modernizations" essentially involved the introduction of high-accumulation, low-consumption policies; giving priority to the development of heavy industry; adopting capital-intensive guidelines; and setting highly protective import substitution policies. In Justin Lin's terms, China adopted a comparative-advantage-defying strategy and (as elsewhere) it largely failed.[4] The Cultural Revolution did further damage to the economy and to the accumulation of important intangible assets such as human capital.

Deng Xiaoping (having been banished during the Cultural Revolution) returned to the dominant party hierarchy. Inherited from the pre-reform period were important tangible and intangible assets: widespread basic education, land reform of a certain type, the abolition of officially sanctioned caste and class distinctions, and some important rural infrastructure. Building on that, Deng and his fellow reformers introduced a new and successful three-step development plan:

1. The Chinese leadership adopted the market system of incentives and resource allocation by introducing, with regional variation, market mechanisms in the agricultural sector where 82 percent of the population resided. Many of the early gains in productivity and income in the five to seven years after 1978 were due to these reforms.
2. The country made use of its comparative advantage in labor resources and pursued an opening-up policy.
3. China used the world economy to stimulate export growth and realized liberalization of trade and investment, and, perhaps most important, started a process of importing knowledge and technology from the global economy. Over time, the reforms developed to include various forms of private ownership, led by Wan Li from Anhui Province. Reforms in education, science, and technology increased the human capital in China. The new Wenzhou model (local economy formed mainly by private businesses) lived side by side with state-owned enterprises or, in the words of Deng Xiaoping, "one country, two systems."

---

4   Justin Lin, the Marshall Lectures, University of Cambridge, October 31 to November 1, 2007.

In many ways China illustrates both the upside and the downside of autocratic systems. In the period from 1949 to 1978, economic policy led to poor economic performance (in large part because the leadership got some but not all—and not enough—of the pieces of the strategy right), and there were few if any constraints on the policy choices that led to these results. Over time, the success of the Chinese economy was achieved under a one-party system where political stability provided a backdrop against which the new export-driven market forces could drive growth in China. The role of Deng Xiaoping as a leader in China's economic growth took place within the confines of the Chinese Communist Party (CCP). In the prevailing ideology, there was deep distrust of market systems and capitalism. Even today, political legitimacy and support depend on sustained inclusive economic growth. The eleventh Five-Year Economic Plan shows that the current one-party leaders understand that their future depends on both increasing growth and redistributing wealth and services.

In sum, each of the 13 growth states eventually chose an economic growth model (frequently after prior failed experiments) but established a stable political environment, which allowed persistence in the policies and time for their economic choices to allow the economy to grow. Thus, leadership entailed not only making correct choices over the economy but also building coalitions and creating a stable political environment where their choices had time to bear economic fruit.

Adjustments Induced and Required by Sustained Growth

A country that sustains growth of over 7 percent a year for a decade dramatically changes the structures of the economy, society, culture, and often the institutions of government. Growth in Botswana, China, Indonesia, Japan, Korea, Singapore, and other countries over several decades generated new patterns of ownership, new interest groups, a sizeable middle class, and a class of the very wealthy. These changes led invariably to new challenges. Among the most familiar are large increases in inequality, middle-class demands for a political democracy comparable to the freedoms established by the marketplace, and the pressure to accommodate new forces and individuals within the existing system. In addition to these problems, leaders face the problem of economic change. Economies that grow cannot always be based on abundant cheap labor. The rising price of labor causes comparative advantage to shift. Successful formulas for growth need to be abandoned. Thus leaders need to shift priorities, policies, and investments in a variety of ways to support the structural evolution of the economy and its changing role in the global economy. It is natural for both governments and citizens to resist this kind of change because it is hard to abandon a successful formula even after it has outlived its usefulness. The policy shifts tend to be toward horizontal policies to encourage information technology, education, and a human-capital-intensive economic structure. These economic adjustments are often accompanied by or tied to demands for political change. For example, the success of the economies of Japan, Korea, and Taiwan, China, generated intense pressure for democratic reforms ranging from redistricting, to more open, fair elections and a decline in the effects of money on politics. An example from the Japanese or Korean cases might demonstrate the complexity of the problems.

In Japan, the economic growth generated the rise of efficient large-store retail outlets at the expense of small mom and pop retailers. Pressured by competition from the new large retailers, mom and pop storeowners formed local organizations and were, by the late 1960s, voting for the Japanese Socialist Party. The dominant growth party, the Liberal Democratic Party (LDP), had been losing seats in the Diet and was faced with the prospect of a loss of control to a combination of Progressive parties that were anti–free trade, against Japan's special relationship with the United States, and for empowering unions and redistributing wealth (Hancock 1993; Baron 2005: 649–51). The successful post–Second World War leadership of the LDP was therefore faced with accommodating the new interests and winning elections. The party chose for the 1972 elections to be led by Mr. Tanaka, who was not part of the elite, Todai-educated, LDP post–Second World War leadership group. Indeed, Tanaka had not gone to college at all and had formed his new faction of the LDP against opposition. Nevertheless, the party made Tanaka the prime minister, thus accommodating some of the new interests generated by economic growth. Tanaka, as prime minister, made a deal with small retailer organizations and passed the Large Store Retail Act, which allowed local mom and pop organizations to delay, obstruct, and, in some cases, deny large retailers the store space necessary to capture economies of scale. The mom and pops voted LDP again, and the party dominated for another decade. A similar deal was struck between the LDP and farm organizations, which kept foreign agriculture products out of the country (Bouissou 2001). The Japanese, as a result, had, relative to the other developed economies, disproportionally high numbers of both farmers and small businesses. It is an example of how political leaders have to trade off accommodating new groups, setting growth policies, and ensuring that antigrowth coalitions do not stop economic development. The concessions to agriculture and small business interests were not economically efficient, however. The choices made were second best from a narrowly economic point of view. While sacrificing efficiency and productivity, they protected the long-range growth for at least a decade on the assumption that the success of the Japanese Socialist Party would have hurt economic growth.

The success of the Korean economy generated an increasing middle class and allowed a large number of Korean youth to attend college. By the mid-1980s, increasing numbers of college students, the middle class, and union members were protesting in the streets over the autocratic nature of the political system and elements of corruption that went with it. The Korean system had relied in part on an electoral college that guaranteed a victory for the candidate of the dominant Democratic Justice Party (DJP). That institution became the focal point of protest for those seeking political freedoms consistent with the economic freedoms. The presidential-designee of the DJP was the former General Roh Tae Woo. The problem he faced was how to get the protest out of the street and into the electoral system, which meant he had to agree to eliminate the electoral college and change the method of election to the National Assembly (Brady and Mo 1992).

Roh agreed to a "real" presidential election, betting that his two primary challengers, Kim Young Sam and Kim Dae-jung, could not agree on which one of them should run. The electoral result in the three-man race was a narrow victory for Roh Tae Woo and the preservation of Korea's export-driven, education-rich economic plan. The reforms of the National Assembly included changing the system from a single nontransferable vote in multimember districts to a U.S.-style single-member, first-past-the-post system with 75 proportional representative seats tacked on. The effect was to reduce the ability of the dominant party to leverage a minority voter support position into a larger parliamentary majority (Brady and Mo 1992).

The first election under the new system resulted in the loss of majority status for the DJP. In short, the reforms resulted first in divided government and ultimately in a multiparty, competitive party system where parties of the left often have control. Again, we have an example of economic growth generating change, which leaders have to deal with. In this case, the institutional changes took protest off the street, institutionalizing it in the electoral system, creating a genuine multiparty democracy where powers and interest rotate in government, which accommodates pressure for change from newly created interests.

These two examples are certainly not exhaustive, nor perhaps even representative, given the diversity of the 13 growth cases. But they do illustrate an important dimension of the political economy of growth. The success of an economy in terms of sustained growth over decades generates impressive and important changes in the society, the culture, the politics and the behavior and preferences of citizens. Leaders, particularly political leaders, need to respond to these changes such that economic growth is not thwarted and the new problems are dealt with successfully. Leaders who achieve this end have, among other things, learned to listen to the business and financial leaders who must compete under changing conditions in world markets.

Successful choices often do not fit the simple economic model of "stabilize, privatize, and liberalize." Leaders often have to make second-best decisions, as in the case of subsidizing farmers and small businesses in Japan, and China's operation of state-owned factories, or Mexico's continued ownership of Pemex. The small steps taken by actual leaders across high-growth economies clearly indicate the truth of Sir Arthur Lewis's well-known observation that "governments may fail because they do too little, or because they do too much."

The start-up period where sustained growth begins may be a less constraining environment and may be conducive for leaders to make good choices. The decision in China to allow farmers to raise crops above the quota and to sell the surplus on the market increased productivity, enriched farmers, and gave Chinese consumers more choices; in sum, for the most part win–win. There was some protest from the urban sector that had to pay somewhat higher prices for food than previously, but food was more plentiful. As growth increases wealth, it makes society more complex in terms of interest groups with significant potential power. Economic policy involves increasingly complex trade-offs between competing interests. When the average income is below $500 per year and 90 percent of a people are in agriculture, the diversity of interests is lower and the economic institutions are less complicated than when per capita income is $8,000 and only 30 percent are in agriculture. This does not mean that leaders cannot make bad decisions in the early stages. Robert Bates (1981), for example, has shown how a coalition of labor and urbanites in East Africa can sustain a political equilibrium, which hurts economic growth. Our claim is that as economies grow, decisions about how to maintain growth become ever more complex because they entail changing, or establishing, political institutions that can meet the challenges generated by growth, and that these political and policy choices are an important part of the growth and development dynamic.

The changes wrought by economic growth lead naturally to another question: after the strong leader, what kind of institutions give a country and its leaders the best chance to grow and develop an economy? The founding or choosing period, associated as they often are with crises, in many cases opens up opportunities for leaders to choose a better model and enhances prospects for convincing others to go along with a new direction. Over time, it appears that leaders have learned that strategies based on leveraging the global economy's knowledge work better than the alternatives. Once the plan is chosen, stability is crucial for it to have a chance to work, and many leaders seek stability by building a dominant party. In China and Taiwan, China, a stable party system already existed and did not need to be built.

The Political Economy of Growth and Development

The challenges for leaders, policy makers, and analysts are formidable. Along the lines of the discussion above, sustained growth appears to require a choice of a viable open growth model. It also requires time to work, persistence, and coherence, and hence a reasonable amount of stability in the policy-making process. How that is achieved (or not) in a variety of kinds of political structure is an important element in the growing body of research in political economy and development. But stability and persistence are not enough. The endogenous dynamics produce the need for continuous economic and structural change in the economy and for similar change in the supporting policies and investments. The argument here is that this need for continuous adaptation appears in case studies to extend to the political system and the evolution of political interests and power. Accomplishing these adaptations without disrupting the growth dynamics is a huge challenge. It falls mainly to political leaders using a combination of insight, experience, and political skill in finding compromises and second-best choices that are least damaging to the growth process.

Reasons for opening up the political and policy-setting processes are many. The old elite might open up institutions and politics to prevent violence (Acemoglu, Johnson, and Robinson 2005: 564–66) to ensure that decision making is not on the streets but within the institutions and political arrangements. Or business input is required in policy setting so that the business sector can compete effectively in the global economy and in the world marketplace. The most striking protests that occur are either violent or near violent and are associated with the downsizing of farm populations and the movement of people to urban areas. Likewise, rising middle classes sometimes take to the streets in favor of opening up the political system, as was the case as Korea and Taiwan, China, moved to two-party systems.

Opening up, in this view, includes transparency, rule of law, and either allowing new elites into dominant party systems or alternating political parties because, in each case, it signals that the regime is changing to accommodate diverse interests generated by the increasing complexity of the growing economy. The mix of factors that determine the countries' growth will also influence the interests that need to be accommodated. That is, a country with initially higher foreign direct investment (FDI) will develop differently than Korea, which relied far less on FDI than other countries.

Various forms of democracy are often held to be preferable because, in general, they accommodate more interests and let different combinations guide economic development at various points. In a democracy, one party or a coalition prefers (because of citizen preferences) less globalization and more protections, while the other party or coalition of parties prefers globalization, and, as they alternate power, policy shifts slightly, and politics is ballots not bullets or the street. However, it is not at all clear that Western-style democracies will be the right institution-politics mix for all countries or all stages of growth. There appears a fine line between opening and accommodating evolving economic and political interests, and the maintenance of some degree of stability, coherence, and persistence in policy space.

There would seem to be some basic institutional shifts that are de minimis. Among these would be the opening of the dominant party to the new interests (think of the CCP and the number of technocrats in the elite over time), or a shift from a single dominant party to a two- party system (Korea and Taiwan, China). Another necessary shift would seem to be the creation of a bureaucracy educated to understand global economic competition and competent enough to carry out regulatory and coordinating activities and the creation of a political process (wherever centered) that factors in diffuse interests, both domestic and international, into its decision process.

Leadership, in this view, has the crucial role of deciding where the fine line referred to above is. That means balancing the accommodation of emerging interests while maintaining the essential elements of a growth strategy. Relative to pure economic policy choices, these are most often second-best choices. In a sense, the challenge is to accommodate the distributional issues because they emerge in the political process of building and maintaining a governing coalition of interests, without undercutting the economic dynamics of the growth process.

References

Acemoglu, D., S. Johnson, and J. Robinson. 2005. "The Rise of Europe: Atlantic Trade, Institutional Change, and Economic Growth." *American Economic Review* 95 (3): 546–79.

Acemoglu, D., and J. Robinson. 2006. *Economic Origins of Dictatorship and Democracy*. Cambridge: Cambridge University Press.

Baron, D. 2005. *Business and Its Environment*. Englewood Cliffs, NJ: Prentice Hall.

Bates, R. 1981. *Markets and States in Tropical Africa: The Political Basis of Agricultural Policies*. Berkeley: University of California Press.

Bouissou, J.-M. 2001. "Party Factions and the Politics of Coalition: Japanese Politics under the System of 1955." *Electoral Studies* 20: 581–602.

Brady, D., and J. Mo. 1992. "Electoral Systems and Institutional Choice: A Case Study of the 1958 Korean Elections." *Comparative Political Studies* 24: 405–29.

Commission on Growth and Development. 2008. *The Growth Report: Strategies for Sustained Growth and Inclusive Development*. Washington, DC: International Bank for Reconstruction and Development and the World Bank.

Cox, G. 1996. "Is the Single Nontransferable Vote Superproportional? Evidence from Japan and Taiwan." *American Journal of Political Science* 40: 740–55.

Cox, G., and E. Niou. 1994. "Seat Bonuses under the Single Nontransferable Vote System: Evidence from Japan and Taiwan." *Comparative Politics* 26: 221–36.

Groffman, B., S. C. Lee, E. A. Winckler, and B. Woodall. 1999. *Elections in Japan, Korea, and Taiwan under the Single Nontransferable Vote*. Ann Arbor: University of Michigan Press.

Hancock, R. 1993. "Grocers against the State: The Politics of Retail Food Distribution in the United States and Japan." Ph.D. dissertation, Stanford University.

Hata, H. 1990. "Malapportionment of Representation in the National Diet." *Law and Contemporary Problems* 53: 157–70.

Jones, B. F., and B. A. Olken. 2005. "Do Leaders Matter? National Leadership and Growth since World War II." *Quarterly Journal of Economics* 120: 835–64.

CHAPTER 2
Leadership for Growth, Development, and Poverty Reduction:
An African Viewpoint and Experience

Benjamin William Mkapa

By 1967, six years after Tanzania's independence, the first president, Mwalimu Julius Kambarage Nyerere, knew enough about the challenges of development facing a poor, postcolonial African country like his. In that year, he published his treatise—the Arusha Declaration—on those challenges and called on the leadership to address them. Among other things, he distilled four core prerequisites for Tanzania's development:

- *Land,* and hence the focus on agriculture and rural development. He believed that Africa could best develop by making maximum use of what it had, in this case land, for food security and economic growth through processed agricultural commodity exports. He believed that because Tanzania did not have money, it could not depend on money for development unless it was willing to sacrifice its hard-won independence.
- *People,* especially with regard to human development, human resource capacity and skills development, and sheer hard work.
- *Good policies,* which aimed at self-reliance and which for him were essentially egalitarian, comprising three main components: (1) a Villagization Program (Ujamaa villages) as a cornerstone of rural

transformation and development through collective production and distribution (from each according to his ability, to each according to his needs), as well as the facilitation of social service delivery and development infrastructure; (2) the public ownership and centralization of main economic activities; and (3) a basic industry strategy to add value to agricultural commodity exports and for import substitution.

- *Good leadership,* which for him included training for capacity building and stringent standards of integrity and ethical behavior.

Clearly, he was a socialist idealist and visionary, but his focus on leadership was not misplaced, and it has now entered the mainstream of development.

Today the discourse on African development is increasingly focusing on capacity for leadership and governance, as well as on its role in engendering economic growth, promoting development, and ensuring poverty reduction. Examples include the Report of the Commission for Africa and work on governance by the World Bank Institute, the International Monetary Fund, and the African Development Bank. Moreover, there is ongoing work on governance by the Economic Commission for Africa and the New Partnership for Africa's Development (NEPAD) and its Africa Peer Review Mechanism (APRM), as well as the establishment of several African leadership training initiatives and institutions.

The connection between leadership and governance, on the one hand, and outcomes in terms of economic growth, development, and poverty reduction, on the other hand, is not too difficult to discern. What are not so easy to determine are the circumstances that can produce the kind of leadership qualities, in an African context (historical, cultural, and sociological), that are able to make a positive impact on the continent's development. This makes comparison difficult. Even more difficult is the effort to develop a theoretical framework for this imperative and synthesize the various experiences into one theory of leadership suitable for wider application on the continent. There is no theory of leadership in postcolonial Africa, except one of "muddling through," learning as we move forward; it is theory: not as articulated, but as lived.

However, the end of the Cold War has made African introspection possible. Africa has now learnt to come to terms with its postcolonial history. NEPAD and especially the APRM would not have been possible under the cloud of the Cold War. By focusing internally, it has now become possible for African leaders, under the auspices of the African Union (AU), to agree on a set of core principles, guidelines, and values that can guide African governments toward improved leadership and governance for development, without the resentment that such a framework would have elicited if it were prescribed for Africa by developed countries. African ownership of the governance agenda is paramount.

Africa cannot forever hold its history of slavery and colonialism responsible for its current poverty levels and economic woes. A discussion of leadership and governance in Africa will be seriously deficient, however, if it fails to put previous and current leadership, and the developmental challenges they faced, in their proper historical, cultural, and sociological context.

In terms of the historical development of independent nations, African nations are in their infancy, still heavily influenced by their colonial heritage. European colonial powers ruled most of Africa from 1885 to 1960, a period of 75 years. In 2007, Ghana, the first sub-Saharan African country to become independent, celebrated its 50th anniversary, a very short time in the lives of nations. That Antoine Gizenga, who in 1960 was deputy prime minister to the first prime minister of the Democratic Republic of Congo, Patrice Lumumba, is still active and competent to assume the role of prime minister (from December 30, 2006, to October 10, 2008) in the current administration illustrates how truly young African nations are.

African leaders in the period before the end of the Cold War can be put into six categories:

- The visionary idealists, such as Lumumba, Nkrumah, Nyerere, and Senghor
- The pragmatists, such as Khama and Kenyatta
- The incompetents, such as Idi Amin
- The military juntas, of which there are too many to list
- The tyrants and thieves, such as Bokassa and Mobutu
- A combination of two or more of the foregoing.

Whatever category of leaders one looks at, it is important for the sake of objective analysis to look beyond what they did, and beyond the dreary economic statistics used as evidence of lost decades in terms of development, to understand how these leaders came to power, why they behaved in the way that they did, and the environment in which they operated.

An objective analytical framework for African leadership should go beyond the usual criticism of governance and policies and address the following three key factors:

- Ability and skills, which imply the need for some form of preparation for leadership
- The wherewithal to act, in terms of tools and resources (financial and human), and the state of institutions
- The domestic and external environment (regional and global) that could have been supportive, ambivalent, or obstructive to what those leaders set out to do.

This chapter is not intended to absolve any leader or government of any lapses of governance. Before, however, we pass judgment on the performance of the earlier generations of African leadership, and before we look at the economic statistics from those years, we have to answer these questions: What preparation for leadership did the first generation of leaders have that would have given them the capacity, the ability, and the skills to produce better results? What tools and resources—financial, human, and institutional—did they have at their disposal to design and implement policies? How was the internal and external policy and operational environment? Was it supportive or obstructive?

It has become common to compare Asia and Africa in a way that projects the image of better leadership for development in Asia and poor leadership for development in Africa. Using the same three-point analytical framework, it should be possible to see if such a comparison and such criticism of African leadership is justified, and if so, to what extent. Such a comparison is not within the scope of this chapter, but enough has been published to show fundamental differences between Asia and Africa in all three areas.

Perhaps the greatest challenge facing African leaders today is the pressure—domestic and external—to deliver simultaneously on the three issues of sustainable economic growth (in terms of GDP), sustainable development (in its transformational nature), and poverty reduction (in its distributional sense). This entails addressing the challenge of setting priorities among priorities in the context of resource constraints, as well as the proper sequencing of policies and interventions in the context of fledgling institutions and low human resource capacity, while retaining the wide political support necessary for democratic legitimacy under current multiparty political dispensations.

My own leadership experience, as well as that of my country, convinces me that the following 10 issues are critical for leadership in Africa if the continent is to make greater headway in growth, development, and poverty reduction:

- The leadership capacity and ability to create and/or sustain *politically stable and peaceful states*.
- The leadership capacity and ability to create and/or sustain *stable and viable economies,* in terms of their internal capacity for survival, as well as their external capacity for significance and relevance. This includes capacity for regional integration and significance in a global economy.
- The political will to create and sustain *democratic, responsive, and accountable governments*—both national and local—that bestow legitimacy upon any government.
- The imperative to focus on *agriculture, food security, and rural development* as a cornerstone of poverty reduction efforts.
- *Human development*, including education and health (especially with regard to diseases such as HIV/AIDS, malaria, and tuberculosis).
- Constituting *strong governments with effective, efficient, and capable institutions,* including regulatory ones.
- Leadership to develop and facilitate *skills for contemporary Africa, business environment, local entrepreneurship,* and guarantees for the *property rights of the poor*.
- Investment in *integrative market and economic infrastructure*.
- Economic and financial *market facilitation and intermediation*. This includes the advocacy and institutional promotion of a savings and investment culture.

- Leadership that ensures *participation and sharing, not only of political power, but of economic prosperity* as well.

These are the core African leadership challenges of the future.

Partly because I knew him quite well and partly because even his detractors recognize him as one of the greatest postcolonial African leaders, I will use Mwalimu Julius K. Nyerere as a reference point in discussing a number of leadership issues. Granted, some will not want to remember him for his economic achievements, but he will always be remembered for the leadership in creating a united and politically viable, stable, peaceful, cohesive, and sustainable nation, where at independence there was none. For postcolonial African countries, this has to be the priority among priorities: *building a strong political foundation on which an economy can subsequently be built.* In reality, most if not all of those countries referred to as "failed states" were never states to begin with. They did not fail; they were never built. As history has proved many times, in the long run it does not pay to build an economic mansion on a foundation of political sand. Côte d'Ivoire is an example of what can happen to an economy that is not built on a firm political foundation and a shared sense of nationhood. Its real GDP per capita declined from $924 in 1980 to $574 in 2004 (World Bank 2006: 35).

I am credited with having presided over deep and very far-reaching economic reforms in Tanzania between 1995 and 2005. I could do that only because of the strong political culture and foundation that Nyerere, the founding president, laid between 1961 and 1985.

The new environment in Africa today, with initiatives such NEPAD and APRM, taken together with declining incidences, levels, and intensity of conflicts on the continent, makes it possible for African leaders to focus on the 10 core leadership issues that I have identified.

Outcome, in terms of growth, development, and poverty reduction, will require much more than good leadership at the national level. It will also require a conducive regional context, in terms of peace, security, and stability. It will also depend on the responses of the bilateral and multilateral development partners to the recommendations of the Report of the Commission for Africa and various G-8 Summit declarations beginning with the 2002 Kananaskis Summit. Likewise, it will depend on the outcome of the Doha round of global trade negotiations, as well as negotiations between the European Union (EU) and the African, Caribbean, and Pacific group of nations for Economic Partnership Agreements. The Doha round of trade negotiations was meant to be a "development round." It is not one yet. With political will it still can be.

This chapter seeks to emphasize the importance and role of leadership for African growth, development, and poverty reduction. It also attempts to project a more objective assessment of leadership issues during the first three to four decades of African independence. Agreeing on shared responsibilities for Africa's failures in its early years will enable all who want to take part in the continent's renewal to focus on the partnership that is now needed to close a sad chapter in Africa's history and open a new one. The core elements of such a partnership have evolved in the last decade, and this chapter argues passionately for the political will, in Africa and outside, for their realization.

The Colonial Legacy

Considerable debate has taken place about the extent to which the European colonial legacy has affected postcolonial Africa and what influence, if any, this legacy continues to have on the African continent. More to the point, how helpful and constructive, or unhelpful and destructive, was the colonial legacy in terms of the development of postcolonial Africa? How responsible was this legacy for the quality and character of postcolonial African leadership?

The Colonial Legacy Is Enduring

As mentioned earlier, for the majority of African countries, the period that they spent under colonial rule is still far longer than the subsequent period during which they have enjoyed independence and self-rule.

It is not surprising, therefore, that until recently the effect of colonial rule on African politics, economics, and social life has remained strong, and not just because Africans were taught and pressed to think and speak in the languages of their colonizers. It is also because at independence Africans inherited, with a few variations, the political and economic systems of their colonizers. An objective evaluation of political systems, processes, and governance in contemporary Africa has to go back to its colonial past and ask: What did Africa learn and adopt from the colonial rulers, and how has it shaped and directed postcolonial leadership, political systems, and governance on the continent?

In all of those years of colonialism, the relationship between the rulers and the ruled was basically one of master and servant. Every white man, woman, or child was made out to be superior in all respects, including color and culture, and the black man, woman, or child was made to feel inferior. African confidence and dignity were deliberately undermined. Humiliation was pervasive. This is a historical fact. Slavery, which in itself was an enforced inferiority on the black people, was superseded by colonial administration that made little if any effort to disabuse the black people of such imposed inferiority. In other words, Africans were protected from slavery abroad, but were condemned to be an underclass at home.

The white people's democratic values that were maturing in Europe in the nineteenth century were not spread to Africa, and any efforts by Africans to demand democratic rule and civil rights were ruthlessly suppressed. Traditional political and administrative systems in Africa were also rendered inferior to the colonial administrative systems, which were developed specifically for the colonies. These too were presented as superior, except where local chiefs could, through carrots and sticks, be enlisted to be part of different forms of indirect rule. It is also a historical fact that indirect rule, coupled with "divide and rule" tactics, characterized most colonial administrations in Africa and planted the seeds of postcolonial ethnic conflict, the most tragic manifestation of which occurred in Rwanda and Burundi.

How Prepared Were the First Leaders?

Leadership is both a science and an art. One can also be born with what is called natural leadership traits. Yet the fact remains that even divinely bestowed qualities of leadership need preparation to make them relevant to the challenges of the day.

Among the first generation of independent African leaders were very gifted, charismatic, and visionary leaders. How else could they have mobilized and earned the following of their compatriots in the face of sometimes very brutal repression by the colonial authorities? The question is, was there any effort by the colonial administrators to train and prepare these potential leaders before independence?

Even before we look for evidence, this clearly is an unlikely scenario. The colonial authorities would naturally consider those agitating for independence enemies of the realm to be stopped, incarcerated, or even killed. They would not see them as potential leaders of independent Africa to be properly trained for the job. It would also have been tempting for the departing colonial powers to leave a country in the hands of incompetent leaders who would mess up so much that the nationals would long for the more "efficient" or "orderly" colonial administration. Champions of African independence would then be seen as having been irresponsible in pushing for premature independence and handing over countries to weak and incompetent leaders. Weak and incompetent leaders would also create a perfect environment for the political influence and economic advantage of the colonial powers to persist.

Could Traditional African Leadership Be Helpful?

Attempts have been made, especially in the African Diaspora, to see if precolonial African systems of leadership and administration could have provided a better alternative to postcolonial governance. It is true that precolonial Africa is replete with examples of traditional leadership and governance that evolved over time, developing institutions and styles of leadership suited to the realities of the time. The debate continues also about whether in precolonial Africa there existed social and cultural norms, political structures, and processes, as well as philosophical underpinnings of governance, that could find relevance and applicability in modern Africa. If they existed, were they fundamentally transformed by colonial experience and insertion into the rest of the world, or were they stopped in their historical development, frozen in time, such that they could be unlocked, brushed up, and used to create an essentially African system of democratic governance? This debate is relevant and should be encouraged as long as it is appreciated that the circumstances and times under which such traditional governance and leadership models developed are completely different from today's national and global realities.

For instance, precolonial Africa comprised largely nonmonetary, tribe-based economies. The kind of preparation needed to rule in such precolonial African economies had to be different from the realities of leadership skills needed for the African economies of the second half of the twentieth century. Political entities in precolonial Africa were mostly ethnically homogenous. The new leaders of Africa inherited, for the most part, an amalgam of diverse, sometimes antagonistic tribes that were forced into one geographic entity whose boundaries were decided by colonial powers in Berlin in 1884–85. As I will explain later, addressing this challenge required a completely new set of leadership skills and governance systems for the newly independent nations.

The global system of which Africa is part today—whether political, economic, social, or cultural—is heavily influenced by factors that have nothing to do with traditional Africa. The current system was designed and spread by Africa's erstwhile colonial masters, through whom Africa was inserted into a global political and economic system initially as a mere appendage of the European powers.

Nevertheless, it is important to recognize certain important features and characteristics of precolonial African governance, administration, and democracy that could be used to enrich present-day African governance systems, institutions, and processes. What is needed is practical adaptation, not idle romanticism.

There must be something worth adapting. Not all traditional African leadership was without any restriction or responsibility to be responsive and accountable to the citizens. The 2003 literature review that Al-Yasha Ilhaam Williams conducted shows clearly that democracy and accountability were not anathema in traditional African governance. In fact, they were the cornerstone of legitimacy. Williams reveals that

> The political structure and stability of pre-colonial African kingdoms, some relatively large such as Ghana, Songhai, Benin, Bornu, and Sokoto, and others relatively small such as Nso', Bafut, Kom reveals a combination of leadership strategies, including the important role of democratic processes in traditional governance. . . . Specific formal practices (which may vary between cultures) positioned the citizenry to authorize, critique and sanction the ascension of their ruler, his/her continued reign and the selection and ascension of his/her successor." (Williams 2003: 61)

Williams adds that from the evidence "traditional leadership was not just the authority of 'kings and queens' . . . but was rather composed of queen-mothers and councils, secret societies and mystics, rituals and ceremonies, rules and doctrines, and subject-citizens. . . . On this account, perhaps African redemption is to be found not in the 'return to royalty' but to the democracy which makes a respected leadership possible" (Williams 2003: 64). I will return to this theme in due course.

Was Colonial Education Helpful?

Leadership of newly independent African countries that were no longer traditional African entities but appendages of colonial powers, inserted into a global political and economic order unfamiliar to most Africans except the educated few, required adequate preparation and capacity building. The first preparation for leadership should have been a good formal education for more Africans. Educating the "natives" beyond basic literacy was not, however, a priority for colonial governments, which for the most part left it to Christian missionaries to produce the clerks and the messengers needed to staff the lower echelons of colonial administration.

A few differences existed, however, between the approaches to education by the two main colonial powers in Africa, the British and the French.

The French, with their background of the 1789 French Revolution that emphasized notions of equality and egalitarianism, adopted an assimilation policy toward their colonies. It was as if they were saying: "Africans are of equal worth to us as long as they are as cultured as we are." Such a philosophical outlook would make education an important part of the French strategy to create an African elite imbued with metropolitan cultural and political values, such that they could even sit in the French parliament. By its nature, however, such an education was inherently elitist, geared toward denying one's Africanness and embracing a new culture irrelevant to the real challenges of leadership and development in Africa at independence.

Jules Ferry was twice prime minister of France between 1880 and 1885. In a speech to the French Chamber of Deputies on March 28, 1884, just before the Berlin Conference of 1884–85 at which Africa was officially parceled out into colonies of European powers—Belgium, Britain, France, Germany, Portugal, and Spain—he justified and defended the current French colonial policy: "The policy of colonial expansion is a political and economic system . . . that can be connected to three sets of ideas: economic ideas; the most far-reaching ideas of civilization; and ideas of a political and patriotic sort" (Ferry 1897). In further justifying the civilization aspect he added, "Gentlemen, we must speak more loudly and more honestly! We must say openly that indeed the higher races have a right over the lower races. . . . I repeat that the superior races have a right because they have a duty. They have the duty to civilize the inferior races."

The British for their part had no pretenses of the equal worth of people, nor any intention to turn Africans into black Englishmen. Using various sources, the British historian David Cannadine (2001: 5) described the British philosophy as follows: "Like all post-Enlightenment imperial powers, only more so, Britons saw themselves as the lords of the entire world and thus of humankind. They placed themselves at the top of the scale of civilization and achievement, they ranked all other races in descending order beneath them."

One can only imagine the place of Africans in that descending order. To make matters worse, an African was made to understand that he or she can be considered civilized only on embracing the language, religion, ways, and mannerism of citizens of the colonial power. Cannadine (2001) adds,

> By the end of the nineteenth century those notions of racial hierarchy, supremacy and stereotyping had become more fully developed, and stridently hardened, as exemplified in Cecil Rhodes's remark that "the British are the finest race in the world, and the more of the world they inhabit, the better it will be for mankind," or in Lord Cromer's belief that the world was divided between those who were British and those who were merely "subject races."

The British, unlike the French, preferred to rule indirectly through existing traditional systems and (with few exceptions) educated to the appropriate level only those few Africans needed for clerical or technical duties to make the wheels of colonial administration turn. In reality, however, the British colonial education also ended up, to a large extent, detaching educated Africans from the real challenges of development at the local level. These educated Africans were to form the core of the administration of newly independent African countries.

Some of the Africans who received this education realized its effect on them—that it was not preparing them for leadership that addressed the development challenges facing newly independent African countries, but rather was putting them in an ivory tower, much removed from the realities and challenges that their people faced. A review of postcolonial African literature by Omoregie (1999) found it replete with concerns shared by African and Caribbean writers as to the effect of colonial education on them. He quotes, for instance, Walter Rodney (1981: 263), who said:

> Education is crucial in any type of society for the preservation of the lives of its members and the maintenance of the social structure. . . . The most crucial aspect of pre-colonial African education was its relevance to Africans in sharp contrast with that which was later introduced (that is, under colonialism). . . . [T]he main purpose of colonial school system was to train Africans to participate in the domination and exploitation of the continent as a whole. . . . Colonial education was education for subordination, exploitation, the creation of mental confusion and the development of underdevelopment.

Omoregie also mentions other African writers such as Amilcar Cabral, Ngugi wa Thiongo, Ferdinand Oyono, Chinua Achebe, Mongo Beti, Charles Mungoshi, Okot P'Bitek, Leon Dumas, S. Ousmane, Pepetela, Frantz Fanon, and Tchicaya U'Tamsi, all of whom lament that colonial education made those few Africans who received it privileged political and economic functionaries in a colonial system that militated against the interests of their own people. He concludes, "Colonial education, therefore, creates a black elite to succeed it and perpetuate its political and economic interests in the post-independence period" (Omoregie 1999). In other words, not only did colonial education not prepare those who received it for leadership, but it was also not directed to the solution of economic and social problems of newly independent countries.

It is true that most of these writers wrote in the 1960s and 1970s, a time of particular revolutionary fervor in Africa. But there is no gainsaying

Box 2.1. Issues on Education Raised by Nyerere at the UN in 1956

- In Tanganyika education is racial. There are separate schools for the children of different racial groups. All European children and all Asian children receive primary education. Only 40 percent of the African children go to school.

- When I sat for the Makerere College entrance examination some fourteen years ago there were only three schools in the country which could send students to that college for higher education. That number remains the same today with the addition of one school for the girls.

- In 1949 and 1950 five African students, including myself, received government scholarships to study in universities in the United Kingdom. We were the first and the last.

- For a country like Tanganyika, the importance of higher education cannot be overemphasized. Our leadership and progress towards self-government depends on higher education.

Source: Nyerere 1966: 41–42.

the depth of feeling they had that colonial education was not the best preparation for the leaders of postcolonial Africa.

Tanzania's founding president, Mwalimu Julius K. Nyerere, was one of the few educated Africans at the independence of what was then called Tanganyika (mainland Tanzania today). He was equally unhappy about colonial education. A few days before his country became independent, he wrote an article in *East Africa and Rhodesia,* a journal that was published in London at that time, in which he said the following (Nyerere 1966: 133): "Our whole existence has been controlled by people with an alien attitude to life, people with different customs and beliefs. They have determined the forms of government, the type of economic activity—if any—and the schooling that our children have had. They have shaped the present generation of Tanganyikans, more than any other influence."

In addition to the inappropriateness of colonial education in terms of preparing Africans for self-rule, the fact was also that too few Africans received any education at all, let alone higher education and specialized skills. When he was still fighting for the independence of Tanganyika, President Nyerere raised the need to educate Africans in his statement to the United Nations Fourth Committee on December 25, 1956, only five years before independence (box 2.1).

Nyerere was pleading with the United Nations that people from his country should be educated in preparation for independence. The human resource capacity for development needed to be built. As I will show later, however, his pleas and those of other African leaders largely fell on deaf ears. As a result, at Tanganyika's independence in 1961:

- Only 15 percent of adults were literate
- Only 23 percent of Tanganyika men and 7.5 percent of Tanganyika women over 15 years of age had attended any formal school at all
- There were only 3,100 primary schools with 486,000 students in a population of 9 million

- There were only about 20 secondary schools with 11,832 students
- The first Tanzanian to get a university degree graduated outside the country in 1952, only nine years before independence
- The few professionals the country had at independence included only one agricultural engineer, one surveyor, 16 medical doctors, 12 accountants, 158 professional nurses, 50 agricultural scientists, and 427 government administrators. And that is about all. (Nyerere 1973: 296–97)

That was Tanzania's starting point—hardly the right preparation and capacity building for leadership of a newly independent country.

The case of what was then called the Belgian Congo is also instructive. As Larry Devlin, the first U.S. Central Intelligence Agency (CIA) Chief of Station in the Democratic Republic of Congo at independence, has noted in his recent memoirs (Devlin 2007: 7):

> The Congolese were well-educated and trained but only to a limited level. At independence, the country had one of the most literate and healthy indigenous populations in Africa. But out of fourteen million people, there were fewer than twenty university graduates. There was no Congolese cadre of doctors, dentists, engineers, architects, lawyers, university professors, business executives, or accountants. The *Force Publique*, the country's army soon to be re-named *Armée Nationale Congolaise* (ANC), was officered exclusively by Belgians. . . . What seemed clear was that Brussels planned to allow the Congolese their political freedom while keeping the military, economic, and commercial levers of power in their own hands.

A similar situation prevailed in practically the whole of colonial Africa. With the late exception of Namibia and South Africa (where the United Nations deliberately helped to train postcolonial and postapartheid leaders), there was not a concerted effort by the colonial powers to train and prepare Africans for democratic self-rule and development. Even when, through the United Nations, countries did offer scholarships to African students in preparation for independence, the colonial powers prevented many of them from traveling abroad for studies.

A review of United Nations General Assembly Resolutions in 1960 and 1961 reveals great international concern that although the poor preparations for independence should not be used as an excuse to further delay self-rule, it was imperative and urgent to train Africans, to build institutions, and to support the new governments with human and financial resources. The following are a few examples.

Resolution 1534 (XV) of December 15, 1960, on "Preparation and Training of Indigenous Civil and Technical Cadres in Non-Self-Governing Territories," among other things, resolved:

> *Considering* that the existence of adequate personnel of this kind is indispensable for the effective implementation of plans and programs of development in the educational, social and economic fields,
> *Bearing in mind* that suitably trained indigenous civil and technical cadres are essential to the efficient functioning of the administration of the Territories,
> *Believing* that the absence of such cadres has, in the past, resulted in serious administrative dislocation in certain Territories upon their attainment of independence . . .

1. Urges the Administering Members to take immediate measures aimed at the rapid development of indigenous civil and technical cadres and at the replacement of expatriate personnel by indigenous officers.

Resolution 1643 (XVI) of November 6, 1961, among other things:

1. *Notes with regret* that full use is not being made of all offers of study and training facilities for inhabitants of Trust Territories; . . .
3. *Urges* the Administering Authorities to provide all the necessary facilities to enable students to avail themselves of offers by Member States of study and training facilities.

Resolution 1696 (XVI) of December 19, 1961, reiterated these concerns regarding colonial authorities deliberately obstructing the use of scholarships by inhabitants of their colonies. The resolution, among other things:

Recognizing the importance of rendering assistance to colonial countries and peoples in the field of general and specialized education . . . ,

Noting with satisfaction the further response to its resolution 845 (IX) inviting Member States to extend their offers of study and training facilities to the inhabitants of Non-Self-Governing Territories,

Expressing regret that, despite the increased interest among inhabitants of the Non-Self-Governing Territories in such offers, a large number of the scholarships offered by Member States remain unutilized,

Further expressing regret that in several instances students who have been granted scholarships have not been accorded facilities to leave the Non-Self-Governing Territories in order to take advantage of such scholarships . . . ,

Invites once again the Administering Members concerned to take all necessary measures to ensure that all scholarships and training facilities offered by Member States are utilized by the inhabitants of the Non-Self-Governing Territories and to render effective assistance to those persons who have applied for, or have been granted, scholarships or fellowships, particularly with regard to facilitating their travel formalities.

Resolution 1697 (XVI) of December 19, 1961, says:

Reiterating that the existence of adequate indigenous civil servants and technical personnel in the Non-Self-Governing Territories is necessary for the effective implementation of satisfactory plans and programs of development in the educational, social and economic fields . . . ,

Believing that the rapid preparations and training of indigenous civil and technical cadres in Non-Self-Governing Territories will help towards the achievements of the purposes of resolution 1514 (XV),

1. *Considers* that the situation prevailing in various dependent territories in respect of the strength, composition and state of training indigenous civil servants and technical personnel is unsatisfactory;
2. *Regrets* that due attention has not been paid to that problem;
3. *Urges* the Administering Members to take immediately all necessary measures to increase the strength of indigenous civil service and technical cadres and to accelerate their training in public administration and other essential technical skills.

Did the Rest of the World Care?

Another problem was the general lack of interest in Africa among Western countries, other than the colonial ones. At most it was missionaries from those countries rather than governments that had significant contact with Africa. Addressing the Empire Club of Toronto on March 22, 1962, the Director of Operations of Crossroads Africa, Inc., Dr. James H. Robinson, referred to this lack of interest in Africa as follows:

> At the end of World War II, almost no great nation in the world had any significant plans for relating to what was shortly to be the cataclysmic events of emerging African nations. Most European nations, with the possible exception of Great Britain, still evolved their policies of relationship to the areas of Africa they controlled, in terms of what they thought would be an indefinite extension of colonial relationships. The United States, at the time, did not even have a desk of any consequence in the Department of State to advise on Africa and obviously had no well defined African policy. Our policies, if any, were related to Africa through our colonial allies. (Robinson 1962: 226–27)

This was quite a disappointment for the African intellectuals of the post–World War II era who, having studiously absorbed the American War of Independence, had expected the United States to be at the forefront not only of championing and actively supporting decolonization efforts in Africa, but also in helping to prepare the new corps of leaders of independent Africa. Dr. Robinson pointed out that in the late 1930s there were fewer than 500 African students studying in European and American universities (Robinson 1962: 239–40).

In his address to the Toronto Empire Club, Robinson also referred to an encounter that he had with students in Accra, Ghana, in 1954. In discussing the Mau Mau unrest in Kenya, he referred to the freedom fighters as terrorists, at which one student promptly chastised him by saying, "Dr. Robinson, they are not terrorists, they are like your patriots in 1776 fighting for their land, their freedom, and for independence" (Robinson 1962: 233).

The natural instinct of the independence leaders in most of Africa was to turn to the West for support in building their newly independent countries. Even those who turned to the East did so as a last resort, having been rebuffed by the West. It was only after being ignored by the United States that Lumumba turned to the Soviet Union. Nkrumah, like Nyerere, maintained good relations with Britain at independence and kept British advisors, and administrators, for quite a while. The French left Guinea in a pique, even ripping out telephones. Yet Sékou Touré, the first president, turned to the United States for help, and after he was turned down he went to the Soviet Union. Sékou Touré wanted genuine independence, but he did not want to distance himself from France. It was France that did not want to have anything to do with him. Only the Lusophone countries became independent as communist-leaning countries. The rest had more open minds.

In other words, despite the colonial history, most independence leaders in Africa reached out to Western countries for assistance, whether in education and capacity building or in economic development. The Western countries had the first option to develop mutually beneficial relations with newly independent Africa. They did not always do so, but instead drove some of the African leaders eastward and then undermined them in a communism containment policy.

The Argument

I believe that Africa's trajectory of development would have been very different and much more positive had the departing colonial powers behaved differently, including treating Africans with greater respect, helping them to train and build capacity for independence leaders and administrators, helping them to build strong institutions to deal with the challenges that the new countries faced rather than trying to perpetuate institutions intended to promote, sustain, and defend Western economic and political interests, and giving the new governments space and the wherewithal to realize the vision and dreams they had for their newly independent countries.

Regrettably, it was the colonial legacy that prevailed, and the resulting friction as African governments sought to reassert their rights as independent nations derailed development efforts to a significant extent by shifting the focus and priorities away from helpful trends.

Moreover, the colonial economic legacy meant that African countries would become independent with very little wherewithal with which to promote development and meet the phenomenal expectations of the people for a better life. It is common knowledge that colonial economic policy and strategy was never meant to develop the colony in question and reduce poverty. Rather it was an imperialistic economic policy and strategy to secure sources of raw materials for Europe's industrialization through a settler economy, whether plantations or mining operations, as well as to create the infrastructure to make this happen.

Quite a few modern metropolises were built across Africa during colonialism to cater to the needs, convenience, and comfort of the colonial and settler community. They were largely islands of prosperity in a sea of poverty. Leopoldville (now Kinshasa) was one. To this day, however, the countryside has little to show for Belgian colonial economic policy except the lasting effect of cruel resource exploitation. As Devlin (2007: 6) describes it, "The Belgians . . . exploited the huge natural riches of the country. For Leopold, the lure had first been ivory then rubber; for his successors, it was copper, cobalt, and diamonds. Belgians, not Congolese, controlled all economic and commercial enterprises."

The following list presents the context in which most African countries became independent:

- Very low levels of education, and hardly any preparation for leadership, whether political or economic.
- Very low governance resources, financial and human, and weak, if any, institutions of independent governance and economic development.
- A hostile external environment, partly because of the Cold War and partly because of lingering colonial power political interests. The domestic environment, especially with regard to the settler and colonial commercial interests, was equally obstructive, if not outright hostile.

These are the realities that have to be factored into any objective analysis of Africa's leadership of development and poverty reduction during the early years of independence. Africa's colonial legacy is not the only reason for Africa's poor economic performance, but it is a significant one, and it should never be forgotten or trivialized.

Postcolonial Cold War Years

The term "good governance" has always eluded a comprehensive definition. The World Bank (1994) tried to make a distinction between good and bad governance in the following terms:

> Good governance is epitomized by predictable, open and enlightened policy-making, a bureaucracy imbued with professional ethos acting in furtherance of the public good, the rule of law, transparent processes, and a strong civil society participating in public affairs. Poor governance (on the other hand) is characterized by arbitrary policy making, unaccountable bureaucracies, unenforced or unjust legal systems, the abuse of executive power, a civil society unengaged in public life, and widespread corruption.

If we take this as our working definition, then, with few exceptions, it is obvious the leaders of the newly independent African countries were not prepared for good governance, and colonial rule was not a good example for them, because it was indeed the epitome of bad governance (except perhaps for widespread corruption).

Leadership Capacity and the Wherewithal for Development

Before we pass judgment on the first African postcolonial leaders, we have to understand to what extent they had the capacity and the wherewithal to do what we think they should have done. Here I am referring largely to the African leaders who were visionary and pragmatic, not the tyrants and looters, or the inept ones.

In 1971, Tanzania's founding president, Mwalimu Julius K. Nyerere, reminisced on those early days of independence as follows (1973: 263):

> And in December 1961, Tanganyika did not attain economic power—and certainly not economic independence. We gained the political power to decide what to do; we lacked the economic and administrative power, which would have given us freedom in those decisions. For it is no use deciding to import more goods than you have foreign currency to pay for, or deciding to provide free books for all children if you have neither the teachers, the buildings nor the money to make a reality of that decision. A nation's real freedom depends on its capacity to do things, not on the legal rights conferred by its internationally recognized sovereignty.

Recalling the number of African civil servants at his disposal at independence, Nyerere said that "as late as April 1960, only 346 of the posts classified as "senior" were filled by Africans. By independence the position had improved somewhat; 1,170 out of 3,282 senior posts were held by citizens" (1973: 264).

So, largely unprepared for leadership, with very few educated citizens at their disposal, with economies that were basically economic outposts of the metropolitan powers (dominated by a settler community), with an infrastructure geared to consign Africa to a supplier of raw materials for metropolitan economies, and with no recent democratic tradition to look to or institutions to count on, the new African leaders had to contend with the following immediate challenges.

First, they had to move quickly to ensure national unity. Independence had removed colonialism from the scene, the one thing that united African people of diverse ethnic and religious affiliations. Once the shared hatred for colonialism had been assuaged, it was important for the new leaders to find something else to keep the people united. As John Reader (1999: 632–33) puts it:

> In Africa, the injustices of colonial rule inspired nationalist movements that united the most diverse of ethnic groups in the drive for independence. Once independence had been achieved, however, the nationalist movements are too often fractured into political groupings of purely ethnic dimensions, whose struggles for power and wealth not only left national issues inadequately addressed and injustices largely unremedied, but also polarized economic and social discontent along ethnic lines—with some dreadful consequences.

Second, they had to move quickly to prove to their people and the outside world that they were leaders of truly independent countries, at a time when some former colonial powers were waiting for them to fail, or actually plotting to make sure they failed. Two particularly striking examples were the Belgian Congo and French Guinea.

Colonial powers did not prepare Africans for democratic self-rule. The forms and systems of government that they introduced were not democratic by any measure, they were not concerned about human rights, and those who demanded their rights, including democratic rights, often were incarcerated. Should we have been surprised when postcolonial leaders also incarcerated their opponents? They learned from colonialism that this was the way to deal with dissent and opponents.

The education that colonial powers gave Africans was not meant to prepare them for leadership but to help perpetuate their rule. That is why educated Africans were dismissed from their jobs once they ventured into politics.

The concept of "African Big Men" is used in vilification of African leaders, or as an illustration of what others may want to portray as African proclivity toward tyranny and dictatorship. But, as Cannadine (2001: 32) reminds us: "The (British) governor was 'the fountain of honour and the distributor of patronage and rank,' by (among other things) determining who should (and should not) be invited to Government (nowadays State) House."

Patrice Lumumba, the first prime minister of the Democratic Republic of Congo after independence, was brutally killed with the knowledge and connivance, or at least the acquiescence, of some Western countries simply because he refused to be part of a framework of independence in which, in the words of Gen. Emille Janssens, head of the army, "Before Independence = After Independence."

De Witte (2002: 184) presents damning evidence of Western involvement in his death. In a letter to his wife, Patricia, before he was assassinated, Lumumba said:

> Throughout my struggle for the independence of my country, I have never doubted for a single instant that the sacred cause to which my comrades and I have dedicated our entire lives would triumph in the end. But what we wanted for our country—its right to an honorable life, to perfect dignity, to independence with no restrictions—was never wanted by Belgian colonialism and its Western allies, who found direct and indirect, intentional and unintentional support among certain senior officials of the United Nations, that body in which we placed all our trust when we called on it for help. They have corrupted some of our countrymen; they have bought others; they have done their part to distort the truth and defile our independence.

Lumumba's vision and views on the independent nation, and his willingness to die for them, should be contrasted with those of the man the Western powers helped to put in charge of the Democratic Republic of Congo—Mobutu Sese Seko. With the benefit of hindsight, Mobutu was a good student of King Leopold II. The colonial methods of rule, exploitation, human rights abuse, and personal wealth accumulation had an impact on some of the postcolonial African leaders, prominent among who was Mobutu.

Mobutu, like Leopold II, treated the country as his personal possession, plundering and looting its wealth at will. Like Leopold II he used the armed forces to enforce his will. During the Cold War, such leaders could literally get away with murder as long as they were on the right side of the war.

In 2002 the Belgian government apologized to the Congolese people for its role in Lumumba's death, but not for the looting of the country during the colonial era, and not for the clear efforts to ensure that political independence did not harm the commercial interests of the Belgians. The Democratic Republic of Congo crisis may be an extreme case of what is generally believed to have been the hope of departing colonialists across Africa—that their commercial interests, and their exploitative nature, would be safeguarded by a compliant corps of African leaders. At the country's independence celebrations, not only did King Baudouin of Belgium outrageously imply in his public address that Congolese independence was a kind of gift, a natural consequence of an undertaking by the "genius of King Leopold II," but also he must have thought the new leadership so inept that he counseled them to keep Belgian structures and institutions intact, including the army and security services.

Third, the new independence leaders had to address the immediate expectations of the people, many of whom wanted rapid improvements in their welfare. The leaders realized that unfulfilled expectations carried with them the seed of instability. As President Nyerere said immediately after the independence of his country in 1961: "Our policy is to make haste slowly, but it may be hard to sell this to the people. Freedom to many means immediate betterment, as if by magic. We are not magicians. But unless I can meet at least some of these aspirations, my support will wane and my head will roll just as surely as the tickbird follows the rhino" (*Time* 1961).

At independence, hardly any African country had an economy—an indigenous economy—to speak of. Basil Davidson, the acknowledged writer on African history, puts the situation in the following terms: "To these political difficulties on the road to stability, all of which were built into the situation on the day of independence, others of an economic and social nature were added. For what the new governments were obliged to take over . . . was not a prosperous colonial business, but, in many ways, a profound colonial crisis" (Davidson 1994: 209).

Writing only a week after Tanganyika's independence, *Time* magazine described the economic situation of the newly independent country in the following terms: "[The] biggest immediate problem facing Nyerere is Tanganyika's economic malnutrition. Average per capita income for the country's 9,240,000 people (all but 139,600 of whom are black) is only $55 a year. Periodic famine is a fact of life; only one-third of the country is arable. Industrial development is difficult because the huge deposits of iron ore, coal and columbite in southwest Tanganyika are far from transport" (*Time* 1961).

In view of the colonial legacy discussed above it is naive to imagine that the euphoria of political independence could, simply by virtue of having a national flag, a national anthem, and other paraphernalia of statehood, herald a new era of good democratic governance and economic management and prosperity.

This legacy meant that independent African states were destined from the beginning to remain small, fragile, unstable, and beholden to the departing colonial powers. When Guinea, for instance, refused autonomy and demanded full independence, France responded by immediately and precipitately withdrawing all economic aid, all civil servants, all skilled people, and even uprooting infrastructure and utilities, knowing well that it had never trained the Guineans to take over. Add to this the haste with which some of the colonial powers left (in 1960 alone, France granted independence to 14 African countries), and one can only have a recipe for instability.

The British historian Thomas Pakenham (1991: 671) summarizes this phase as follows: "The scramble out of Africa in the eleven years from 1957 to 1968 was pursued at the same undignified pace . . . as the scramble into Africa more than half a century earlier. . . . For one thing, these countries perceived that the race was to get out through the door before they were kicked through it." He adds that "Britain, France and Belgium ruled the mandates as arbitrarily as they ruled their other colonies. There was no supervision by the League, no progress towards self-government, very little education above primary level, abject poverty. The mandates, like the colonies, were . . . *prisoners of the world economy*" (673, emphasis added).

At independence, most African countries were making—for the first time—the transition from systems of governance that were blatantly undemocratic, oppressive, exploitative, and racist. It is unrealistic to expect that after half a century under such systems of governance—which exploited ethnicity to divide and rule and thrived on domination and abuse of human rights—the newly independent African country would, simply on account of a hastily drawn constitution, be a perfect democracy and a thriving economy. The colonial powers, when in power, never taught Africans democracy, human rights, or economic management. What Africans experienced and learned from decades of colonialism was domination, divide and rule, patronage, exploitation, and the abuse of human rights.

It was the ultimate insult that at the independence celebrations for what was then called the Belgian Congo (now the Democratic Republic of Congo), in what was then called Leopoldville (now Kinshasa), King Baudouin of Belgium had the temerity, bearing in mind the reality, to say, "It is now up to you, gentlemen, to show us that you are worthy of our confidence," immediately provoking an understandable and justified angry diatribe from Lumumba (Hochschild 2000: 301).

The Challenges of Nation Building

All changes, reforms, and transitions carry with them the seed of instability—and the same could be expected with the independence of the African countries. The most vulnerable spot was the gray zone between the old (colonial rule) and the new (self-rule). The old had not completely died, and the new had not yet taken form and root.

The successes or failures of the first few years of independence depended enormously on the founding president. To be able to hold the new nation together, such a president needed to be charismatic, strong, capable, and honest. Both Nkrumah and Nyerere had these qualities, but *Mwalimu* (Teacher) Nyerere was also credited with greater humility than the *Osagyefo* (Redeemer) Nkrumah. Both were didactic. Nelson Mandela's similar qualities enabled him to hold together a nation that for decades had been built on separateness (apartheid).

Going back to the 1960s, however, the first leaders, at least those with vision and committed to creating nations out of the many ethnic groups they inherited, had to contend with some formidable challenges.

The first challenge was how to build nation-states where before there was none. Oswaldo de Rivero (2001: 4) puts this challenge in its historical context:

> In the majority of the industrialised states, national identity preceded the forma-tion of the state authority. The nation, reflected above all in the joint emergence of a middle class and a market of national dimensions, formed the base of the modern state. In contrast, in most of the so-called developing countries, this sequence was reversed. The political authority—the state—emerged from the independence process before the nation, that is, before the development of a true bourgeoisie and unifying national capitalist economy.

What the first generation of African leaders inherited at independence were not nations. They were only an amalgamation of diverse and often-antagonistic tribes bundled together within ridiculous borders drawn by colonial powers in Berlin in 1884–85. The challenges of nation building at independence and their impact on development should never be underestimated, considering that colonial rulers taught one tribe or religion to distrust another, and that the colonial policy of divide and rule fed on and accentuated ethnic and religious differences and antagonism. It is not surprising that in some countries the departure of the colonial administration triggered coups d'état, civil war, conflict, and instability and accentuated tribalism.

Pakenham (1991: 678–79) explains what happened when the Belgians scrambled out of the Democratic Republic of Congo in 1960: "Unprepared for party politics, the country [Congo] split along ethnic and regional fault lines. When the Belgians scuttled out of the Congo in July 1960, they had left the country well prepared for civil war and anarchy. The prospect of their departure from Ruanda-Urundi, though delayed for two years, had the same disastrous effect." One can only imagine the challenge, after decades of indirect rule and divide and rule, of uniting the 250 ethno-linguistic groups of Nigeria into one nation-state. To appreciate the magnitude of the challenge, it is instructive to consider the views of two prominent independence-era Nigerian leaders.

Abubakar Tafawa Balewa from the North, who became the first federal prime minister of independent Nigeria, is quoted by Martin Meredith (2005: 8) to have said: "Since 1914 the British Government has been trying to make Nigeria into one country, but the Nigerian people themselves are historically different in their backgrounds, in their religious beliefs and customs and do not show themselves any sign of willingness to unite.... Nigerian unity is only a British invention." Meredith also quotes Obafemi Awolowo, a prominent Yoruba leader: "Nigeria is not a nation. It is a mere geographical expression." Both of these comments were made in the late 1940s, but the feelings endured long after Nigeria's independence.

Tanzania was one of a few exceptions among African nations that managed to build a sense of nationhood among its 126 different tribes. Other countries were not so lucky to have the visionary leadership that made nation building a priority. In this enterprise, however, Nyerere was helped by the fact that no tribe was big enough to be dominant. He also abolished chiefdoms early on and promoted Kiswahili as a lingua franca. His policies of one-party democratic state and of socialism also helped his nation-building efforts.

So, generally, under these circumstances, it is not surprising that many African countries focused more on the pursuit of the so-called fruits of independence, engaging in redistribution before production had grown sufficiently to create the surplus necessary for such redistribution. Throughout the 1960s and 1970s, Tanzania invested heavily in health and education infrastructure before it had an internal economy with the capacity to maintain, supply, and sustain such an extensive network of social services. Was it wrong, considering where the colonial government had left the country?

The challenge of nation building also required strong leadership and other unifying forces. The first leaders had to symbolize the new nations and had to be strong. It is easy today to accuse them of having been autocratic, or in other ways deficient in their democratic credentials. This criticism has to be weighed, however, against the imperative to hold the new "nations" together.

As Meredith (2005: 162) notes, "As founding fathers, the first generation of nationalist leaders—Nkrumah, Nasser, Senghor, Houphouët-Boigny, Sékou Touré, Keita, Olympio, Kenyatta, Nyerere, Kaunda, Banda—all enjoyed great prestige and high honour. They were seen to personify the states they led and swiftly took advantage to consolidate their control." Today it is easy to discredit the words of Houphouët-Boigny when he said, "Democracy is a system of government for virtuous people. In young countries such as our own, we need a chief who is all-powerful for a specific period of time" (2005).

The one-party political system was also considered an important unifying factor for newly independent African countries. The fact that shared opposition to colonial rule united Africans helped the emergence of dominant single parties during the first elections, such as in Côte d'Ivoire, Malawi, Mali, Senegal, Tanzania, and Tunisia.

The experience has been that a single-party system, as long as the party was democratic within itself, was a useful tool for nation building and focusing national attention and priorities. Tanzania is a good example of a country that used a democratic single-party system for about 20 years and then transited to a multiparty system when it was confident that the foundation of the postcolonial state had been built and strengthened sufficiently to withstand the potentially divisive politics of a multiparty political dispensation.

In his terms of reference to the Presidential Commission for the Establishment of a One-Party Political System, President Nyerere instructed the commissioners to ensure that key elements of good governance were adhered to. These included the rule of law, equity and inclusiveness, transparency, accountability, responsiveness, and participation (box 2.2).

In other words, Tanzania's single-party political system was to embrace all ingredients of a good democratic system except for the absence of opposition political parties. It should be remembered that Tanzania was in any case a de facto one-party state before the decision in 1963 to make it a de jure one-party state. Clearly Nyerere opted for a one-party system not because he had dictatorial proclivities, but because he wanted to concentrate the national mind on the core challenges of nation building and unity during those early years. He also did not think that a multiparty system was necessarily the best option:

> The British and American tradition of a two-party system is a reflection of the
> society from which it evolved. The existence of distinct classes and the struggle

Box 2.2. Terms of Reference to the Presidential Commission for the Establishment of a One-Party Political System

a) Tanganyika shall remain a Republic with an executive Head of State;

b) The Rule of Law and the independence of the Judiciary shall be preserved;

c) There shall be complete equality for all Tanganyikan citizens;

d) There shall be the maximum political freedom for all citizens within the context of a single national movement;

e) There shall be the maximum possible participation by the people in their own Government and ultimate control by them over all organs of State on a basis of universal suffrage;

f) There shall be complete freedom for the people to choose their own representatives on all Representative and Legislative bodies, within the context of the law.

In addition, Nyerere promulgated an eight-point national ethic to be embraced by the Commission, one point of which was as follows:

3. Every individual citizen has the right to freedom of expression, of movement, of religious belief, of association within the context of the law, subject in all cases only to the maintenance of equal freedom for all other citizens.

Source: Nyerere 1966: 261–62.

between them resulted in the growth of this system. In Africa, the Nationalist movements were fighting a battle for freedom from foreign domination, not from domination by any ruling class of our own. Once the foreign power— "the other Party"—has been expelled, there is no ready-made division among the people. The Nationalist movements must inevitably form the first Government of the new states. Once a free Government is formed, its supreme task lies ahead—the building up of the country's economy. This, no less than the struggle against colonialism, calls for the maximum united effort by the whole country if it is to succeed. There can be no room for difference or division. (Meredith 2005: 167)

Cranford Pratt (1999) nicely summarized the safeguards that Nyerere instituted to ensure that the one-party system was sufficiently democratic, participatory, inclusive, and a unifying factor. He termed the system "a hybrid constitutional order, democratic one-party state," adding that:

A few of its [the one-party system in Tanzania] most original features can be mentioned to indicate that it was neither a subterfuge for oligarchic rule nor for an ideological vanguard party on the Leninist model. Membership in TANU (the party) was open to all and any member could be nominated to run for the National Assembly or the representative organs of the party. In each constituency a large and representative body, the annual district conference of TANU, ranked the candidates for election to the National Assembly in order of preference. The National Executive Committee of the party then decided which two candidates would appear on the ballot, an arrangement which had the potential to become an instrument of oligarchic control but whose actual use, Nyerere ensured, was infrequent and unthreatening. The elections, which then followed operated within a set of rules that were designed to ensure as fair a contest as possible. No candidate could spend any money on his own campaign. All election meetings in every constituency were organized by the party and were to be addressed by both candidates. No tribal language could be used at these meetings and no appeal for votes could be made on grounds of race, tribe or religion. No politician or other prominent Tanzanian could campaign on behalf of any candidate. The system was thus designed to avoid the emergence of national factions, be they ideological, regional or tribal, while also securing the election in each constituency of a member in whom the citizens had confidence. Nyerere and his government had thus found a way for popular discontent to replace MNAs (Members of the National Assembly) who had become unpopular, while avoiding the highly divisive impact, which competitive party elections can have in countries whose national unity is fragile.

Matthew Lockwood, reviewing the literature, found that indeed single-party political systems tended to strengthen national unity and stability. He says (2005: 116): "It is also true that regimes that did *not* introduce a centralized one-party system soon after independence in Africa tended to be more unstable, often leading to military coups and sometimes state collapse (Allen 1995). In some cases (but certainly not all), political stability has been created out of chaos by authoritarian rule, Rawlings and Museveni being two examples."

But Mwalimu Nyerere also knew that if the one-party system is sustained for too long it has its own risks.

A few months before he passed away, he was interviewed by Ikaweba Bunting (1999) for the *Internationalist Magazine*. He was asked whether, since in 1990 he supported the creation of a multiparty political system in Tanzania, he thought it had been a mistake for so many African nations to opt for a one-party state. He answered:

> I never advocated this (one-party system) for everyone. But I did it for Tanzania because of our circumstances then. In 1990 the Chama Cha Mapinduzi (CCM) abandoned the one-party state for a multi-party system. But we do not have an opposition. The point I was making when I made the statement was that any party that stays in power for too long becomes corrupt. The Communist Party in the Soviet Union, the CCM of Tanzania and the Conservative Party of Britain all stayed in power too long and became corrupt. This is especially so if the opposition is too weak or non-existent.

African Leadership and Socialism

It is generally believed that the pursuit of African socialism, in its various hues and shades, was somehow partly responsible for Africa's poor economic record compared with Asia. Evidence does not support this view. Some Asian countries that started with socialist leanings are more developed than African countries that started with capitalist leanings. Likewise, African countries that began with capitalist leanings are not necessarily much better off than those who aspired to be socialist.

Second, the value of African socialism should not be seen only in economic terms. One also has to understand and appreciate the political, cultural, and historical basis of African socialism.

Hallen (2002: 72–89) has attempted to identify the philosophical underpinnings of the attractions that the early leaders of independent Africa found in various forms of socialism (rarely Marxism). Only the Portuguese colonies emerged from colonialism with Marxist or communist leanings. The majority of African countries called themselves socialists, of various kinds. Even capitalist-leaning Kenya called itself socialist. Clearly African socialism was much more than an economic system.

It is true that independent Africa was born into the Cold War, and the temptation to side with the noncolonial East against the colonial West must have been great. However, as Hallen and others have shown, and as I know from first-hand experience, very few if any newly independent African countries were spiteful toward the West. Not only had most of their leaders studied in the West, acquiring in the process great admiration for some of its historical figures, events, and institutions, but they were also not ready to throw away one form of domination for another. *Time* magazine (1961) intimated admiration for "Nyerere's moderation and his strongly pro-Western attitude."

The adoption by a number of leaders of some form of pragmatic African socialism (rather than scientific socialism or Marxism) was partly an effort to pursue an independent, authentic, and hence nonaligned political, social, and economic framework for development. They looked back to precolonial Africa to find guideposts and inspiration toward an authentic African philosophy, if not ideology, for social organization and economic development.

Capitalism as a form of economic organization and management had a clear disadvantage in postcolonial Africa, being firmly associated with colonial powers. Not that private property was anathema in precolonial Africa: rather, the paramountcy of community over private welfare tended to smooth the rough edges of the African version of capitalism.

In reviewing the two most notable exponents of African socialism, Nkrumah and Nyerere, Hallen (2002: 73) points out that (contrary to those who thought Africa was becoming communist per se) the vision of these early leaders was that "socialism in the African context was to be a formalized, (economically and politically) institutionalized expression of indigenous humanitarian social moral values."

Criticism in the literature has been brought to the effect that people such as Nkrumah, Nyerere, and others tended to romanticize precolonial systems of social organization. In any case, there was no uniformity of culture or social organization in precolonial Africa. There is no doubt, however, that the vast majority of precolonial African politics shared some or all of the following thoughts advocated by Nkrumah and Nyerere:

- Individual self-interest, when pursued at the expense of community interest, carried with it seeds for the erosion of moral values
- The notion of one, and shared, humanity
- The equal and intrinsic value of the human being and of humanity.

These early efforts by African leaders to chart an independent, authentic, African adaptation of precolonial and postcolonial Africa were misconstrued as necessarily taking sides in the Cold War, or becoming communists, and hence a fair target in the Cold War. The West could not countenance the emergence of a successful socialist experiment in Africa under those circumstances. Many independent African political systems and economic policies were deliberately obstructed from maturing for fear that they would be communist. As Devlin (2007: 66) admits with regard to the Democratic Republic of Congo, "In those days, when everything was measured in Cold War terms, we were convinced that we were observing the beginning of a major Soviet effort to gain control of a key country . . . as a spring board to control much of the continent. With the full backing of Headquarters, the station began work on a plan to remove Lumumba from power." This was despite the fact that, as he admits in another part of his memoirs (2007: 25), "Most of us at the Embassy regarded him as a disaster in the making. There was (however) no reason to believe that he was a Soviet agent or even a communist, but he was all too close to the Soviet Union for comfort."

The articulation of African socialism rang a positive chord among many African people. That is why even those African countries that had capitalist leanings had also some socialist pretenses in word, if not in deed. African socialism added legitimacy to postcolonial governance, while one-party states were an important strategy in ensuring national unity during the early years of independence.

One of the greatest tragedies of postcolonial Africa was the use of power and ethnicity for personal economic gain. The other was the emergence of the category leaders I referred to earlier as tyrants and looters. This harmed efforts at nation building and ultimately led to political instability and economic collapse.

Nyerere, from the beginning, was a vehement opponent of the use of public office for private gain. It seemed as if he had a disdain for personal wealth, which made the people trust him enormously. He believed that the pursuit of personal wealth would exacerbate the issues that could undermine unity, such as ethnicity and abuse of power. In outlining his objectives for a socialist Tanzania he said (Nyerere 1968: 340): "This is the objective of socialism in Tanzania. To build a society in which all members have equal rights and equal opportunities; in which all can live at peace with their neighbors without suffering or imposing injustice, being exploited, or exploiting; and in which all have a gradually increasing basic level of material welfare before any individual lives in luxury."

It is this spirit of justice and equality that helped to cement the links that strengthened the sense of nationhood in Tanzania for so long.

The Cold War and Military Coups

One terrible effect of the Cold War on governance in Africa was the possibility it gave some African leaders to play one power bloc against the other, get away with lots of misdemeanors, and misplace their national priorities. Oswaldo de Rivero (2001: 5) describes this phenomenon as follows:

> During the Cold War, many of the unfinished national projects, euphemistically called "developing countries," acquired strategic value. . . . This provided them with room for manoeuvre, enabling them to obtain economic aid and political support from one of the two power blocs, and to finance their economic non-viability in this manner. This strategic subsidy allowed many countries to survive despite profligate economic policies and excessive state interventions and it allowed them to indulge in extravagant dreams.

Another sad chapter in early postcolonial Africa was the phase of military coups d'état. Some were externally instigated or influenced as part of the Cold War. Some were internal as leaders failed to keep independent African countries united. Some were a result of the crisis of unfulfilled expectations for the "fruits of independence." Some were preemptive as people in the military feared for their lives or wealth. Some were manifestations of, or responses to, ethnicity in politics and commerce. And some were a combination of one or more of the foregoing. With the benefit of hindsight the question should be asked: Were those military coups a consequence of bad leadership, or were they in fact the main cause of bad governance across Africa?

The outcome, as Reader points out (1999: 667), was that between the first sub-Saharan military coup d'état that led to the assassination of the Togolese president, Sylvanus Olympio, in 1963 to the overthrow of Mobutu in 1997, more than 70 coups had taken place in 32 countries over a period of 34 years, an average of two military coups each year.

It did not take long for the military in Africa to realize their power. Colonel Gamel Abdul Nasser had grabbed power away from King Farouk in Egypt in 1952. In 1963 the military took power in Togo. In Algeria, Ahmed ben Bella's socialist schemes did not work well and created discontent, and in 1965 he was overthrown by Houari Boumedienne. In November 1965 in the Democratic Republic of Congo, the army, led by Mobutu, overthrew the president, Joseph Kasavubu, which started Mobutu on more than 30 years of corrupt rule. In January 1966, the military in the Central African Republic overthrew civilian rule. Three days later in what was then called Upper Volta (today Burkina Faso) the military took power. That same month the military took power in Nigeria, and the following month the military in Ghana overthrew Nkrumah. In 1967 the military came to power in Sierra Leone. In 1969 Colonel Muammar Gaddafi overthrew the monarchy in Libya, and that year army officers took power in Somalia.

Nzongola-Ntalaja (2002: 2) describes the Congolese experience in the following terms:

> The negation of democracy and the popular will through Mobutu's usurpation of power in 1960, 1965 and 1972, and through Kabila's self-proclamation in 1997, were made possible by the external backing and/or endorsement that these actions obtained in the international community. For these external forces with a vested interest in the Congo's enormous size, geographical location and bountiful

resource endowment, it is preferable to deal with rulers who they can hope to influence and manipulate, rather than democratically elected leaders who are accountable to their national constituencies.

He adds that "Since then (1885) the enormous wealth of the country has served not to meet the basic needs of the people but to enrich the country's rulers and their external political allies and business partners" (2002).

In his study of military coups and coup attempts in Africa, Naison Ngoma (2004) came to the conclusion that although democratic governance is a good deterrence for military coups, this has not always been the case in Africa. Many democratically elected governments, beginning with that of Lumumba in Congo, were removed unconstitutionally regardless of their democratic credentials and origins. He says:

> The democratic governance-stability connection should not be accepted uncritically. The continuation of (coups) in an environment that seeks both political and economic pluralism clearly shows that the mere transition to democratic governance is no guarantee that military coups will not occur . . . sheer greed and the crises of expectations play a significant role as "push factors". . . . Military coups are prevalent in Africa because of the generally low levels of literacy. Such uninformedness leads the majority of the citizens to respond—or indeed react— to political economic reforms in a manner that is premised on naivety, ignorance or gullibility. The role of some foreign governments and foreign business is another issue that has been articulated.

There is no doubt that military coups are to blame for a significant part of Africa's economic problems and poor record in terms of poverty reduction. Military coups disrupt economic activity at home and certainly discourage foreign direct investment (FDI). The evidence also shows, however, that the military coups were not always caused by bad governance and poor leadership—certainly not during the Cold War when most of the coups took place. At that time a government's democratic record was subordinated to where it stood in the East-West divide of the Cold War. This too has to be factored in if we want an objective analysis of Africa's poor economic performance in its first 50 years of independence.

Wars of Liberation and Other Conflicts

It was not only the Cold War that affected negatively leadership for development. An equally significant distraction from development was the liberation struggle in some parts of Africa, principally Southern Africa and to an extent West Africa.

At Ghana's independence, Kwame Nkrumah said the freedom of his country was meaningless if the rest of the continent remained under colonial occupation or supremacist minority rule. This was a sentiment shared by most newly independent African countries.

Colonies were the creation of Western countries, and white minority regimes on the continent were a legacy of Western imperialism. The West could have ensured a peaceful and quick end to colonialism, apartheid, and white minority rule. Western countries did not, which pushed Africa closer to Eastern countries that were willing to support African liberation efforts. Whether this was only another dimension of the Cold War is not the issue. The issue is that Western attitudes toward decolonization in Africa made it necessary for African liberation movements and supportive governments to look to the East for support. However, this did not, ipso facto, make every liberation movement and any supportive government communist.

Ongoing conflicts in Africa still unnecessarily hamper economic and social development, but the conflicts around the liberation struggle in the 1960s, 1970s, and 1980s were necessary, and the disruption of economic and social development was equally a necessary price to pay for African freedom, human rights, democracy, and dignity. The disengagement from South Africa that countries of the Frontline States in the liberation war in Southern Africa had to undertake bore far-reaching economic and social implications for the region. Lives were lost, resources were directed away from development, infrastructure was destroyed, and agricultural production suppressed, but the struggle was a top priority for the leaders of the independent countries in the region. Statistics on economic performance during those years do not tell this side of the story. There was no way, however, that countries in Southern Africa could focus on growth before the conclusion of the freedom agenda.

Development in the southern part of Tanzania was almost frozen in the 1960s and 1970s as the liberation war against Portuguese colonialism in neighboring Mozambique, which Tanzania fully supported, raged on.

In 1970, Guinea, which like Tanzania actively supported the liberation struggle in what was then Portuguese Guinea (today's Guinea-Bissau), was invaded by opponents of the then president, Sékou Touré, supported by the Portuguese. Guinea prevailed in what was henceforth referred to as Portugal's Vietnam in Africa, but the effect on the economy was unavoidable.

Many other African conflicts have also caused much suffering and economic and social disruption, and not all of them were instigated by, or a consequence of, Western action. However, many were made possible by the Cold War, and others, such as those in Burundi, the Democratic Republic of Congo, and Rwanda, were a direct legacy of Belgian colonialism.

Among the conflicts that the West supported, instigated, or otherwise acquiesced to, the most tragic is Uganda. The West, led by Britain, thought that Uganda under Milton Obote and his "Common Man's Charter" was becoming too socialist. With the benefit of hindsight, to think that one would consider Idi Amin a better alternative to Obote, whatever Obote's problems, would be laughable if it were not so tragic. One must look at the implications of this tragic mistake for the development, not only of Uganda, but of the whole of East Africa.

The East African Community, which by the early 1970s was far ahead of the European Economic Community in terms of the level of integration, was dealt a fatal blow with the emergence of Idi Amin as president of Uganda. Invading Tanzania in 1978, Idi Amin forced the country into a war that eventually removed him from power, but proved exceedingly costly for Tanzania at a time when commodity prices were tumbling and the oil shocks were being felt. Not only did the war with Idi Amin disrupt economic activity in those years, but it took Tanzania more than 15 years to weather its long-term effects. To think, therefore, that Tanzania's poor economic performance in the 1980s was simply a leadership or governance issue would be incorrect. Much more was involved than governance.

Economic Crises and Failed Experiments

In looking at Africa's postcolonial economic history one often comes across statistics that show that Africa was performing better in the early 1960s than, say, in the "lost decade" of the 1980s. These statistics are not always put in their proper historical context, however. Africa's main exports then (as now for non-oil-exporting countries) were agricultural commodities. Prices of such commodities were historically high during the late 1950s and early 1960s. The 1980s, on the other hand, were a time of great volatility and depressed commodity prices.

Second, the plantation economy of the colonial era and the early postcolonial era accounted for a substantial share of the commodity exports. Twenty years later some of the settler community that owned and managed the plantations had left, either because of uncertainties that they felt or because of nationalization, as happened in Tanzania under socialism.

Socialism in Tanzania was a major factor in engendering a sense of mutual respect, dignity, unity, and national identity. On the other hand, it is also true that economic performance under that framework was not too impressive.

In his interview with Ikaweba Bunting, Nyerere was asked where he stood with regard to the Arusha Declaration and the socialist policies he had so passionately and energetically promoted. His reply is instructive for its candor and enlightenment. He emphasized the role of the declaration and socialism in nation building and insisted on its virtues, but he was equally critical of some of its outcomes. When asked if the Arusha Declaration would still stand up at that time, he replied (Bunting 1999):

> Tanzania had been independent for a short time before we began to see a growing gap between the haves and the have-nots in our country. A privileged group was emerging from the political leaders and bureaucrats who had been poor under colonial rule but were now beginning to use their positions in the Party and the Government to enrich themselves. This kind of development would alienate the leadership from the people. So we articulated a new national objective: we stressed that development is about all our people and not just a small and privileged minority.
>
> The Arusha Declaration was what made Tanzania distinctly Tanzania. We stated what we stood for, we laid down a code of conduct for our leaders, and we made an effort to achieve our goals. This was obvious to all, even if we made mistakes—anywhere one tries anything new and uncharted there are bound to be mistakes.

The Arusha Declaration and our democratic single-party system, together with our national language, Kiswahili, and a highly politicized and disciplined national army, transformed more than 126 different tribes into a cohesive and stable nation. . . .

The floundering of socialism has been global. This is what needs an explanation, not just the Tanzanian part of it. George Bernard Shaw, who was an atheist, said, "You cannot say Christianity has failed because it has never been tried." It is the same with socialism: you cannot say it has failed because it has never been tried.

When asked what he thought his main mistakes as a Tanzanian leader were, or what he would, given the chance, do differently, Nyerere said (Bunting 1999):

There are things that I would have done more firmly or not at all. For example, I would not nationalize the sisal plantations. This was a mistake. I did not realize how difficult it would be for the state to manage agriculture. Agriculture is difficult to socialize. . . . The land issue and family holdings were very sensitive. I saw this intellectually but it was hard to translate it into policy implementation.

This chapter does not seek to underestimate the effect of policy choices, economic management, and leadership on economic performance in Tanzania in the first three decades of independence. We do now realize, and I personally advocated this during my presidency, that macroeconomic fundamentals when properly tailored to what we want to accomplish nationally are critical for success. However, in those years, the prescriptions of the international financial institutions, especially the structural adjustment programs, were unacceptably arrogant and unrelated to the reality in the field and their impact on people. The Washington Consensus prescription was in fact not a consensus at all because the patients were not consulted.

It is now admitted that the Structural Adjustment Programs of those years made the patients worse off, especially in terms of human development. In Tanzania it became difficult to maintain the wide network of social delivery services, especially education, health, water, and the maintenance of infrastructure. School attendance and literacy, which had climbed steadily after independence, plunged, and health care deteriorated to the point where public clinics often faced acute shortages of drugs.

In addition, in the case of Tanzania, events completely outside the control of the government in the 1970s resulted in a really difficult time in the 1980s. These events included the following:

- The drought of 1973–74
- The breakup of the East African Community in 1977
- The war with Idi Amin's Uganda in 1978–79
- The oil crises of 1973 and 1979
- The commodity price crashes of the 1970s and 1980s.

This list shows, at least in the case of Tanzania, that although issues of governance and leadership may have had some impact in terms of our poor economic performance, external factors were also responsible to a significant extent.

There were also cases of economic crises and failed experiments in other African countries. A typical case is where ambitious industrialization programs, all with good intent and with external concurrence and support, either did not produce the desired results or, like in Nkrumah's Ghana, diverted attention from agriculture before industrialization could take up the slack in exports and GDP contribution. Again it was not simply a question of governance and leadership.

Land

One thing that Nkrumah and Nyerere had in common was their approach to land ownership and usage. This is one of the precolonial aspects of Africa that they wanted to adapt to modern-day Africa. In most of Africa, it is land usage that was personal, not land ownership. Land was communal, but the people of that community had user rights over the land.

The logic behind this "communal ownership, private use" dichotomy is that for Africans land is much more than a factor of production, to be acquired, used, and disposed of like other factors of production. An elemental spiritual attachment to land is felt that escapes outsiders who argue for wholesale free-hold rather than lease-hold forms of land ownership.

Failure to understand this logic has led to too much trouble in Africa so far and carries with it seeds for even greater trouble in the future. Whatever others may think, to the vast majority of Africans the land redistribution process in Zimbabwe was both necessary and long overdue. One may question how it was done, but not why. The impatience with the speed of land redistribution that is done differently in South Africa and Namibia is something to watch. Over the last few months we have read of violent conflicts over land in several African countries.

Some of Africa's active or latent land conflicts are a colonial legacy, such as in Zimbabwe, where at independence 75 percent of prime farmland was owned by 4,500 white farmers out of a population of 8 million. Others are ethnic. Yet others are a result of commercialization of land, and the competition between different land uses. Whatever the cause, competition for arable land and pastures is increasing, and open conflicts over land are increasing.

The North-West province in Cameroon has witnessed open land conflicts on almost a yearly basis. In 2006 angry villagers beat their chief to death and burnt his corpse, and they stoned to death the policeman sent to arrest the suspects, because they suspected that their chief had sold farmland to wealthy cattle breeders. A year later, in 2007, in the same province, villagers burnt down 300 homes, forcing thousands of people to flee over a dispute about farming land.

Between December 2006 and early February 2007, about 60 people were killed and tens of thousands fled from their homes because of escalating clashes over fertile land in the Mount Elgon region of Kenya. A local member of parliament, John Serut, was quoted in a story by Jeremy Clarke (2007) for Reuters saying that a group calling itself the Sabaot Land Defense Force was responsible, claiming to represent people forced off their ancestral land by successive governments. According to the member of parliament, the problems in the fertile area dated back to the 1960s.

Although the land policies and laws of countries such as Tanzania have sometimes been criticized as an obstacle for development, they have actually spared Tanzanians from some of the worst land conflicts on the continent by guaranteeing access to land for everyone.

The spiritual attachment that Africans have to land, especially ancestral land, and the fact that the majority of them depend on arable land and pastures for their very sustenance, make land potentially one of the most destabilizing factors in Africa. It is, therefore, a critical area for leadership, and it is encouraging that a number of bilateral development partners, as well as the World Bank in its report "Land Policies for Growth and Poverty Reduction," have recognized the importance of land issues.

Additionally, it should be recognized that secure property rights over land and other immovable assets are now taking center stage in poverty reduction efforts.

The Post–Cold War Years

Especially with regard to governance, I have always maintained that next to independence the best thing to have happened to Africa was the end of the Cold War, which had turned Africa into the battleground of East and West. The end of the Cold War also helped to accelerate the dismantling of the apartheid regime in South Africa and make Africa truly free in the political sense.

Independent African countries were literally born into the Cold War. Decolonization itself became part of the Cold War, which forced countries to look externally rather than internally at an important defining moment of their history and formation as nation-states.

With the end of the Cold War, and denied the opportunity to play one side against the other, African leaders were forced to look inward, and they were also increasingly held to higher standards of governance by development partners and international financial institutions.

In terms of political governance, economic governance, regional integration and cooperation, and results in terms of stability and economic performance, Africa has much to show following the end of the Cold War. Although the 1980s were literally a lost decade for Africa, the continent changed in very profound ways—politically, economically, and socially—albeit from very low levels. The facts speak for themselves:

- The number of conflicts in Africa dropped to just five in 2005, from a peak of 16 in 2002.
- There was a time when more than half of African governments were military juntas. There are none as of this writing (early 2007), and the

AU has served notice that it will neither recognize nor accept in its councils any leader who comes to power through unconstitutional means.

- Since 1990 many African countries have undergone political transformation. Political competition and participatory processes improved more in Africa during the 1990s than in any other region, even if from a low base. In 1982 only one-tenth of African countries had competitively elected executives. Today the majority of leaders are competitively elected.

- Civil society is much more engaged and vibrant, and a thriving private media is generally free to criticize most governments. Human rights are being taken much more seriously, and women are participating more in representative and decision-making bodies. Judiciaries and legislatures are being strengthened and are more free and independent than before.

- The African Peer Review Mechanism to which about half of the African countries have submitted themselves is a welcome innovation for mutual support along this path. Its mandate is to ensure that the policies and practices of participating states conform to the agreed political, economic, and corporate governance values, codes, and standards that are contained in the AU Declaration on Democracy, Political, Economic and Corporate Governance.

- On average, between 2002 and 2005 over two-thirds of African countries had single-digit inflation. More than ever before countries are attaining macroeconomic fundamentals.

- Net private flows into Africa rose from an average of $6.8 billion in 1998–2002 to $17 billion in 2005. Africa is more open and attractive to investment, both domestic and foreign.

- Between 1995 and 2005, 17 sub-Saharan African countries grew at average rates exceeding 5 percent annually, up from only five countries during the previous decade. By 2005, nine countries were near or above the 7 percent growth rate threshold needed for sustained poverty reduction. The growth momentum was sustained, with overall real GDP growth rate of 5.7 percent recorded in 2006 compared to 5.3 percent and 5.2 percent in 2005 and 2004, respectively. For the second consecutive year, Africa's average growth rate remains higher than that of Latin America (4.8 percent). Twenty-eight countries in Africa recorded improvements in growth in 2006 relative to 2005, and 25 recorded improvements in 2005 relative to 2004 (ECA 2006: 3–5).

- Corruption remains a problem, but many countries have begun in earnest to deal with it through institutional reform, legislation, and more robust investigation and prosecution.

This optimism has dominated the debate on Africa in recent years and is captured in the Report of the Commission for Africa, of which I was a member. The real challenge now is where we go from here, for it remains a fact that, despite positive trends, sustainability is not yet ensured, and whether Africa will meet the Millennium Development Goals remains doubtful for a good number of countries.

The Way Forward

As more African countries stabilize politically, socially, and economically, the time has come for the leadership to think in a more structured and strategic way, focusing on long-term and sustainable growth strategies. For all their worth, the Millennium Development Goals are only minimal development goals, hardly ambitious in terms of the people's right to development. They are also short-term and not directly focused on growth. Yet there can be no poverty reduction without growth—long-term and sustainable growth. *Africa must think beyond survival.* That is a challenge of leadership. Africa has to move from social and economic crisis management to strategic positioning and planning.

Strategic thinking is about making choices, however, and at Africa's level of development the choices are very difficult. Yet they have to be made.

Africa had quite a few political strategist and visionary leaders at independence, such as Nkrumah, Nyerere, Leopold Senghor, Sékou Touré, and finally Nelson Mandela. Nyerere, whom I know much better than the others, made very difficult but visionary and strategic political choices at independence. Those choices helped to forge a united nation where before there was none. With others, Nyerere championed the liberation struggle in Southern Africa, constituting and chairing what was called the Frontline States (against colonial and minority rule in Southern Africa).

Today, one does not see the same sense of mission, vision, and willingness to make difficult strategic choices—this time not political, but economic. Where are the new Frontline States against poverty and for growth? It is one thing for African economies to be on the growth path; it is another to actually move along that path. It is one thing to be on the runway; it is another to take off. It is the take-off that needs the greatest power.

The strategic and visionary economic thinking needed has to have a domestic, regional, and global dimension. Globalization is a reality, and the challenge of leadership is how to position ourselves in such a way as to maximize its benefits and minimize its side effects. In the World Commission on the Social Dimension of Globalization, which I cochaired with the president of Finland, H. E. Tarja Halonen, we exhorted Africa and other affected developing countries to *begin at home* (ILO 2004: 54–74).

Beginning at home brings into focus three critical issues. The first is developing national capabilities and policies, especially in relation to governance (both political and economic), economic liberalization and the role of the state, addressing the special needs of agriculture and the informal sector, enabling and empowering people through education and skills, work and employment, as well as through sustainable development and resource productivity.

Second, it is about empowering people and institutions at the local level, including strengthening participatory local government, strengthening the local economic base, and using and protecting local values and cultural heritages that are helpful in strengthening accountable government and participation.

Third, it is about regional integration and cooperation as a stepping stone for profitable engagement at the global level.

Beginning at home requires strategic economic leadership that not only better positions a country nationally and regionally, but also engages the outside world in a strategic compact for growth and development. On the one hand, this involves a nationally determined strategic engagement with bilateral and multilateral development partners. On the other hand, it involves determining parameters of a mutually rewarding engagement with international private capital.

Regardless of positive trends, Africa will not get far without the correct and significant engagement of these two players—the development partners and private capital. As the Commission for Africa report showed, we need a surge of official development assistance over a period of at least another 20 years to address the fundamental and paralyzing weaknesses of African economies, not only in terms of governance and policies, but also in terms of human resource capacities, institutional and other structural reforms, and the creation of the infrastructure that will get African markets to actually work within and across its borders.

This calls for a big push in terms of external support to what Africa is doing. For no matter how much the new generation of African leaders focuses on the priority issues, and no matter how clear their strategic choices are, they do not on their own have at their disposal the wherewithal to see them through.

If, on the other hand, through NEPAD and APRM, the OECD countries were to agree to a surge of aid resources to ensure that any of the weaknesses that APRM identified is actually dealt with, and that the strategic economic choices are fully funded, we could have indeed a new group of Frontline States against poverty and for growth. Also, *Africa needs an APRM compliance dividend* as an incentive for others to join. Only about half of the African countries have acceded to the APRM. Those countries that have not yet acceded would like to see if it is worth their while to open up to so much external scrutiny, which I am sure no rich developed country would agree to. If those who have already acceded have nothing to show for it, why should they join?

In a way, it is like HIV/AIDS. Once you assure people that if found HIV positive everyone will receive care and treatment, more people will come forward to test. There is no incentive to know one's status if there is no treatment. Likewise, there is no need to join the APRM if no one will help African countries address the weaknesses in governance that the process will identify.

Foreign Direct Investment

The debate on whether Africa needs FDI for its development has long ended among serious people. African leaders must now accept that attracting and retaining FDI must be an integral part of efforts and policies to engender economic growth, social development, and poverty reduction. The attraction of FDI must, however, go hand in hand with deliberate efforts to build domestic productive capacities and an indigenous middle class. At the current level of African development, especially its low capacity for manufactured exports, it is equally important for African leaders to create the policy framework and guidelines that will ensure that FDI is better integrated into the local economy, not only in terms of technology transfer, skills development, and managerial know-how, but equally important in terms of forward and backward linkages to the domestic economy. If this is not achieved, efforts to attract FDI, especially in the natural resources sector, will not be politically sustainable in the long term on a democratic and democratizing continent.

Here too you need African leaders who can earn the trust and confidence of the people, and who can provide strong leadership. For them to succeed, however, they will need, perhaps more than ever, the support and cooperation of foreign investors and developed countries.

The truth is that with its present geography and structure of investment and trade, Africa cannot as yet develop through trade. The truth is that many sub-Saharan African countries are still locked into an exploitative and asymmetrical relationship with their major trading partners, supplying raw materials to North America, Europe, and recently Asia, and importing consumer goods, capital goods, and manufactures.

The outside world now has to decide if it wants to work for Africa's interests in changing this state of affairs or to continue to consign Africa to its current status as a supplier of raw materials. Properly managed and supported, FDI from the economic North, as well as from the economic South in the context of South-South cooperation, is the most viable way to wean Africa from the current exploitative relationship with the outside world.

It is of little benefit for rich countries to offer Africa duty-free access for products that it cannot competitively produce.

FDI and the Domestic Economy

Africa simply does not have the capital and technology necessary to produce sustainable growth, and hence to make a decisive impact on poverty. Any discussion of African economic growth and poverty reduction must, therefore, include a discussion of the important role of private investment capital, mostly FDI.

Properly targeted and facilitated FDI will not only bring into Africa needed capital and technology, but it will also improve government revenues for social service delivery, create skilled and semiskilled jobs for a restive growing number of African young people, and bring with it a new culture of management and an opening to the global marketplace.

The question is thus not whether, but how best, to do it. Here the challenge for leadership again is vision, courage, and focus. Difficult choices have to be made. It is certainly not enough to have an open economy with an attractive investment climate. That alone will only lead African countries into the so-called race to the bottom because each wants to portray itself as the fairest of them all. It will also not be politically sustainable in a democratic dispensation when the benefits of opening up the economy are seen to be too narrowly distributed, or when the outcome is not indigenization of foreign capital, but externalization of the domestic economy.

As shown earlier, recently a significant increase of FDI has been directed toward Africa, driven by a combination of an improving investment and business climate and rising global demand for minerals, oil, and gas. It remains uncertain how long this interest will last. It is for this reason that Africans have to capitalize on the present trend to send out a more positive image of the continent, while at the same time trying hard to anchor FDI more firmly in the domestic economy.

Each African country has to do much self-diagnosis in the context of strategic thinking on how best to attract FDI and link it with the domestic economy so as to build linkages that will help to maximize returns at the local level. Here too leadership is about vision and determination. If the focus is on urgent export promotion to take advantage of preferential trade market access (such as through the African Growth and Opportunity Act, Everything but Arms program, and others), then one might focus on things such as textiles. If, however, the interest is on a technologically driven economy, special efforts might be needed to attract FDI in the technological field.

Africa should not necessarily extend a blanket invitation and facilitation for FDI. It may wish first to develop a strategic direction for growth and poverty reduction within specific timeframes, then determine the kind of FDI necessary for that strategic direction to take shape. Once such a determination has been made, the relevant African government should do what is necessary to attract that kind of FDI, even if it means actually head-hunting and providing special incentives, not only to come in, but also to be embedded into the domestic economy.

Legal and Economic Empowerment of the Poor

Linking FDI with the local economy is one aspect of empowering the poor. The other is linking the small, formal, legal domestic economy with the large, informal, and extralegal economy.[1] Looking forward, and as African economies are increasingly becoming market economies, we need the hardware of the market (such as physical infrastructure) and the software

---

1   For the ILD, "extralegal" refers to economic activity that takes place outside the law or is limited or handicapped by the law. It is not synonymous with "illegal" or "lawless."

of the market (macroeconomic fundamentals, business environment, entrepreneurship, saving culture, a legal system, and so forth) to make the market system work and produce growth and development. If the goal is poverty reduction, then we have to find ways to bring the majority poor into the market, *not to be exploited but to participate and benefit,* and to make the legal system an accessible asset working for them, rather than an obstacle to their economic emancipation.

To me, of equal if not greater importance to giving African people the right to democratic participation is the importance of giving them the right to economic participation.

One of my greatest fears for the future of Africa, politically and economically, is that we are giving the people more room for political participation without a corresponding increase in economic participation. For me economic inclusion is not ideology, it is political common sense. We are giving people political power over an economic system in which they have no personal stake. They are politically included, but economically excluded. Consequently, income inequalities are increasing across Africa. That is political dynamite, and it has to be addressed as a matter of urgency.

African governments and their development partners have to find ways to connect the island of the formal legal sector of African economies with the vast ocean of informal extralegal economic activity that characterizes and defines the life of the rapidly increasing semi-urbanized population. To a large extent this population constitutes a separate economy that does not always appear in the national accounts.

Sub-Saharan African countries have the highest rates of rural-urban migration in the world. We note in the Commission for Africa Report that, at about 5 percent, urban growth in Africa is twice as fast as in Latin America and Asia. Close to 40 percent of Africans now live in cities, and that figure will rise to more than 50 percent over the next 20 years. But sub-Saharan African cities are not ready for such a huge influx of people. The size of its cities bears no resemblance to their economic wealth and capacities. That is why over 166 million people live in slums.

The vast majority of these people end up operating on the margins, if not completely outside the formal market, with its laws and regulations. Regardless of government efforts to improve the business environment, these people will not be in a position to make use of an expanded market until they are able to operate within its formality and legality. They also cannot come to the market empty-handed, but what they have is not recognized by formal market players.

This situation makes the work of Hernando de Soto critical for political stability and economic participation and inclusion. African governments cannot give the poor the capital with which to take part in a market economy, but they can help them unlock their own dead capital. As de Soto (2000: 7) said: "The poor inhabitants of these nations—the overwhelming majority—do have things, but they lack the process to represent their

Figure 2.1. Legal Status of Businesses and Property in Tanzania

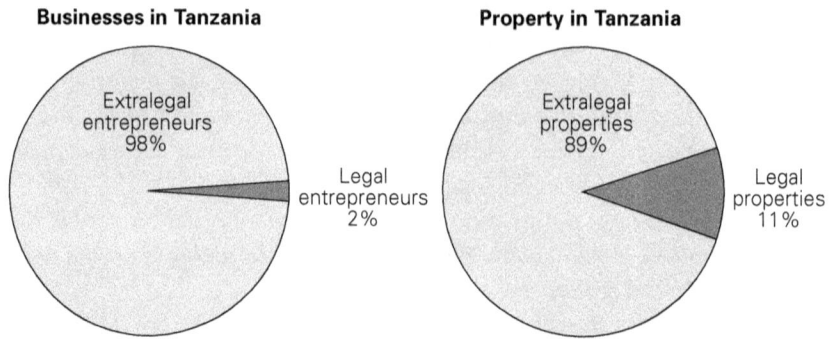

Businesses in Tanzania

Extralegal
entrepreneurs
98%

Legal
entrepreneurs
2%

Property in Tanzania

Extralegal
properties
89%

Legal
properties
11%

Source: ILD 2005.

property and create capital. They have houses but not titles; crops but not deeds; business but not statutes of incorporation."

Working with de Soto's Institute for Liberty and Democracy (ILD), we conducted a diagnostic study of the informal, extralegal sector in Tanzania and found that a staggering 98 percent of all businesses operate extralegally (a total of 1,482,000), and 89 percent of all properties are held extralegally (1,447,000 urban properties and 60,200,000 rural hectares, of which only 10 percent is under clan control) (see figure 2.1). Whatever margin of error one may provide for; there is no gainsaying the magnitude of the problem.

Second, we tried to put a value to this wealth that is held outside the law. We found these assets to be worth about $29.3 billion, or almost 10 times all FDI accumulated since independence, and four times the net financial flows from multilateral institutions in the same period (see figure 2.2). Again, whatever criticism one may have for the methodology we used, and providing for any margins of error, there is no gainsaying the huge value of assets that the poor hold outside the formal, legal economy.

Third, we realized that having failed to make the transition from informality to formality these people have developed their own archetypes of organization and processes to transact business among themselves. In other words, they have learned to operate outside the mainstream of government.

Tanzania has a legal and administrative system largely inherited from colonial days that makes it difficult if not impossible for the poor to identify with it or access its services. For them, the law is distant, inaccessible, incomprehensible, costly, and in reality an obstacle rather than a facilitator and protector.

We found that it is difficult for 90 percent of Tanzanians to enter the legal economy. The obstacles they would have to overcome to access the legal system and obtain organizational structures, credit, capital, markets beyond their immediate families, and legal property rights are formidable.

If a poor entrepreneur obeys the law throughout a 50-year business life, it will require him or her to make cash payments of $91,000 to the state

Figure 2.2. Tanzanian Relevant Indicators in 2005 (US$ billions)

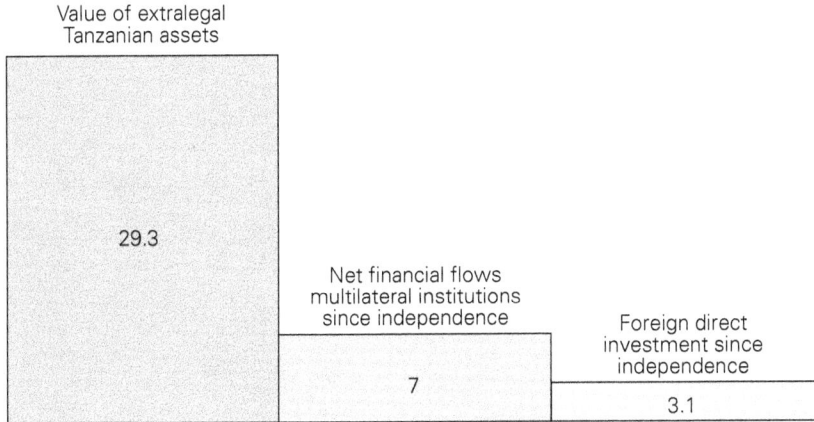

Value of extralegal
Tanzanian assets

29.3

Net financial flows
multilateral institutions
since independence

7

Foreign direct
investment since
independence

3.1

Sources: ILD, World Development Indicators 2005. Adjusted by U.S. consumer price index.

for the requisite licenses, permits, and approvals, and spend 1,118 days in government offices petitioning for them (during which the entrepreneur could have earned $9,350). The same entrepreneur would have to wait another 32,216 days for administrators to resolve all his or her requests, and during that time lose another $79,600 in potential income. The grand total of these costs is almost $180,000—enough money to create 31 additional small enterprises (ILD 2005).

Again, whatever criticism one may have for the methodology we used, and providing for any margins of error, there is no gainsaying the huge obstacles that the poor would have to contend with before making the transition from informality to formality—from exclusion from the rule of law to inclusion in the rule of law with the protection it provides.

I believe that this is a fundamental aspect of governance that has to be addressed if the war on poverty is to be won in the context of market economies. At the international level, the Commission on the Legal Empowerment of the Poor, cochaired by Madeleine K. Albright and Hernando de Soto and hosted by the UNDP, aims to make legal protection and economic opportunity not the privilege of the few but the right of all. As its Web site (http://legalempowerment.undp.org) explains, we want to address the challenges of those locked out of prosperity by the legal system (box 2.3).

If African countries and their development partners agree to give the legal and economic empowerment of the poor as much attention as they give to political rights, democracy, and corruption, then we will have a balanced and more comprehensive onslaught on poverty.

Microfinance is without doubt a key instrument of economic empowerment, but without the rule of law that includes everyone, it will always be difficult for the poor to take advantage of the expanding and expanded market.

Box 2.3. Locked Out of Prosperity

The majority of the world's 3 billion poor—many of them women and children—live outside the rule of law, without the basic legal protection that recognizes their homes, assets, and hard work.

Without property rights, they live in fear of forced eviction.

Without access to a justice system, they are victims of corruption and violence.

Without enforceable labor laws, they suffer unsafe and abusive work conditions.

If they own an informal business, they cannot access the legal business protections that entrepreneurs in the developed world take for granted—they are locked out of economic opportunity in their own countries and in the global marketplace. Many are unregistered from birth and have no access to basic public services. Outside the law, the ability of the poor to create wealth is frustrated; without legal empowerment, their dignity is violated.

Although most of the world's poor possess assets of some kind, they lack a formal way to document these possessions through legally recognized tools such as deeds, contracts, and permits. These people live and work in the "informal economy," outside a set of widely recognized and enforceable rules. For many people, a confusing patchwork of overlapping and conflicting regulations makes access to the formal system impossible. Laws and legal procedures that would guarantee rights are often not enforced and are not designed to work for the poor.

Source: http://legalempowerment.undp.org/challenge.

Investment Climate Facility for Africa

The Commission for Africa Report zeroed in on the link between growth and poverty reduction—not just growth in aggregate terms, but growth in which many more poor people, including women and youth, participate. The goal mentioned in the report—of 7 percent growth by the end of the current decade sustained over the long term—is achievable, judging from what is already happening in some African countries. Evidence of the political will in Africa to work for such levels of growth is abundant, and NEPAD as well as various declarations of the AU are examples of that. What is not in evidence is the external support in terms of actually facilitating FDI to Africa, doubling support for infrastructure projects in Africa, and supporting African efforts in improving the investment and business climate, including entrepreneurship and skills training for all levels of business activity.

Moreover, the bad news from Africa is still eclipsing the good news from the continent, and this has a negative impact on the possible role of international capital in Africa's economic growth. Too much of inward FDI to Africa is still invested in extractive industries that are not sufficiently linked to the domestic economy. This does not portend well for sustainability, both economic and political.

A similar two-pronged approach is necessary for the success of the Investment Climate Facility for Africa (ICF) (see box 2.4). African leaders must continue to improve economic governance and create a conducive environment for private sector participation in the economy. Specific and targeted policy instruments might be needed to focus private investment so that it forms part of a collective strategy for sustainable economic growth.

Box 2.4. The Investment Climate Facility

The ICF is a new vehicle for improving investment conditions in Africa. It has been endorsed by key African institutions, including NEPAD, major donor agencies, and key private sector interests. It provides the private sector, G-8 countries, and donor agencies with a practical opportunity for reducing barriers to investment in Africa. The ICF will be managed according to business principles and will support appropriately targeted practical interventions. It will systematically focus on areas where practical steps can be taken to remove identified constraints and problems.

The extent to which a given country provides an enabling business environment strongly influences the decisions of domestic and international investors. Business environments are created by government policies, laws, and regulations, and the way in which these are implemented. African policy makers are increasingly recognizing that obstacles to both domestic and international investment are seriously impeding Africa's development.

- *Intra-African trade*—improving Africa's import and export environment and improving and simplifying administration to facilitate cross-border trade.
- *Facilitation of business development and expansion*—focusing on ICT and infrastructure development, business registration, and licensing and property rights.
- *Facilitation of financial and investment environment*—developing capital markets, increasing access to finance for enterprises, improving the regulatory environment for second- and third-tier institutions, and facilitating improved digital infrastructure.

The initial phase of ICF operations will be driven by three strategic themes:
The ICF will also work toward improving Africa's image as an attractive investment destination, publicizing, among other things, improvements made to the investment climate.

The objectives of the ICF are to:
- Build the environment for investment climate reform
- Encourage, develop, and work with coalitions for investment climate reform, and support business-government dialogue
- Get the investment climate right
- Support governments in creating a legal, regulatory, and administrative environment that encourages businesses at all levels to invest, grow, and create jobs
- Encourage business to respond
- Improve Africa's image as an investment destination through a coordinated effort to publicize improvements in the investment climate.

Source: http://www.investmentclimatefacility.org.

On the other hand, special efforts are needed to present a more objective and balanced image of Africa to the outside world.

The ICF is, therefore, an initiative to bring together all previous initiatives to enhance investments in Africa into one big, coherent push. These important previous initiatives and commitments include the G-8 Africa Action Plan that came out of the 2002 G-8 Summit in Kananaskis, reinforced at the 2004 G-8 Summit in Sea Island, and fully embraced at the 2005 G-8 Summit in Gleneagles. The 2005 report of the World Bank "A Better Investment Climate for All" was very helpful in designing the ICF.

The ICF provides an innovative, and in a sense a unique, opportunity for African governments, developed countries, the private business sector, and international and regional financial institutions to work jointly, in partnership, to tackle barriers to domestic and foreign investment, to create a more attractive investment climate, and to spread a more positive image of Africa where warranted. This is a partnership underwritten by a shared commitment to respond to the needs of African governments, depending on their own self-determined priorities, and following a clear commitment to reform. The ICF does not get involved where such a commitment is in doubt.

The ICF's efforts also have to be supported externally to reduce the element of political and business environment risk. As mentioned earlier, the ICF engages in only those countries with a proven political will for reform, and by implication, those with the lowest political risk. Especially during the transition, foreign and domestic investors would need the comfort of insurance against such risks, until those countries' track records begin to speak for themselves.

Of equal importance is the role that the ICF can play in providing a good governance dividend for the truly reforming African countries.

Harnessing Technology

A defining characteristic of globalization is the rapid development and use of technology, not only to speed up and reduce the cost of production and services, but also to speed up and reduce the cost of business and trade.

Africa cannot expect to benefit from globalization unless it develops a clear strategy—nationally, regionally, and continentally—to identify, internalize, and use available technology to enhance productivity and facilitate cost-effective business and trading regimes. It is hoped that Africa can design and develop its own technology.

This is a question of leadership. At present it is as if technology is imposed on Africa from outside, rather than that Africa is identifying and attracting the kind of technology best suited to its needs and its level of development. I fear that sometimes Africa opts for unnecessarily expensive and complicated technology without much value addition in terms of the core objective of increasing production and improving productivity, as well as facilitating cost-effective commerce.

Globalization is also about instant communication, and the cellular phone has, perhaps more than any other device, helped to produce a phenomenal surge in the capacity for instant communication among Africans. First, the number of cellphone service subscribers increased tremendously in a relatively short period, and evidence suggests that this has helped to facilitate and speed up commerce. Second, cellphones have shown that Africans can indeed hook into the kind of technology needed to participate in the broader market that globalization provides. Third, cellphone usage has shown that even those Africans in rural or poor urban areas, and those in the informal sector, can fairly quickly understand and apply new technology.

This also helps to emphasize my other point that Africa has to choose, rather than simply take, available technologies for its use. To most Africans, what they need is a basic handset that enables voice and text message communication. There is nothing wrong for people who can afford it to have handsets that are more for status than for their utility. Moving across Africa, one can see people with handsets loaded with costly features that they do not need, they never use, and perhaps not even understand. It is a challenge for leadership, through fiscal or other policy measures, to make sure that anyone who needs a cellphone can have access to one. A combination of booming numbers of subscribers and fiscal measures targeting basic handsets should enable such handsets to be very cheaply available to more subscribers.

What I have said about cellphones is equally true for computers. The youth of Africa will be highly constrained in participating in the broader labor and economic market without a certain level of computer access and literacy. Africa needs computers not as status symbols, but as essential basic tools for education and capacity building in an interactive global economy.

Canada, a G-8 member country, has an impressive program called Computers for Schools (CFS), through which government, crown corporations, and private companies and institutions donate used computers to the program. The computers are fully refurbished and distributed to schools, libraries, and other not-for-profit learning centers across Canada. The program Web site (http://cfs.ic.gc.ca) states that since its inception in 1993, CFS has distributed 775,000 computers to schools and public libraries, with a current annual capacity of distributing 113,000 additional computers from over 50 refurbishment centers the program oversees across Canada. The centers are staffed by volunteers, including current and retired telecommunications professionals and students, who acquire technical skills in the process.

As far as I know Kenya is the only African country, as I write in early 2007, that has learned from the Canadian program and created a similar one that is up and running (http://ctsk.org). Canada is ready to share this experience. Yet Africa, with the lowest worldwide access rate to computers, has not fully embraced this shortcut to rectifying the problem. The other option, of course, is the $100 laptop computer program. This is a problem essentially of leadership.

Some African leaders even discourage the importation of used computers to Africa, invoking among other things the challenge of e-waste management and disposal and its environmental implications, as well as the thought that the technology is obsolete. This is misguided, for the following reasons:

- If Canada, a wealthy country, cannot afford new computers for its children, there is no way Africa can.
- The e-waste disposal challenge is not confined to refurbished computers; even new ones will in due course have to be disposed of if they cannot be refurbished.

- Rather than creating an e-waste problem, computer refurbishment centers actually deal with the problem by making it possible to postpone the disposal issue through recycling.
- The CFS program in Canada has shown that even much older computers versions can still be used. One refurbished Pentium III or IV computer can act as a server for a whole classroom of refurbished Pentium I computers.

With progress being made on Education for All, soon all African villages will have schools, which in turn could become village e-centers (or tele-centers) not only for training children, but also for enabling parents to leverage technology in their income-generating activities as well as creating possibilities for e-government.

Coming to the actual application of technology for development, a recent good example is the Ghanaian software firm that has developed and launched an innovative and interesting agricultural market information service called *tradenetINTL*. This service is based on a simple and straightforward model of providing an online clearing house for offers and price alerts for products that Africans produce and wish to trade in. The service, according to its Web site (www.tradenet.biz), enables producers and traders across Africa to exchange product prices, contacts, and offers using their cellular phones.

One of the pressing challenges of leadership in Africa is how to increase intra-Africa trade. Yet, as I write (in early February 2007), only 11 African countries (Benin, Burkina Faso, Côte d'Ivoire, Ghana, Guinea, Mali, Niger, Nigeria, Senegal, Togo, and Uganda) have signed up for the tradenetINTL service. Even as Africa has to focus on addressing the infrastructural and fiscal obstacles to intra-African trade, the momentum can be built now by linking buyers and sellers using available technology.

This service also provides a good opportunity for private-public partnership, with governments providing facilitative and capacity-building services. There is also no reason, with the technology available, not to launch similar services at the national or regional level, such as the East African Community, Southern African Development Community, Common Market for Eastern and Southern Africa, or Economic Community of West African States.

There is also the case for leadership in ensuring wider application of technology on the production side. The vast majority of Africans subsist on agriculture and can develop only by improving the yields and quality of their agricultural produce. Also, there is the need to reduce postharvest losses that currently beset African producers.

Possibilities for enhanced agricultural production using modern technology go beyond modern agricultural practices, e-commerce in agricultural goods, agroprocessing, soil analysis, or better weather forecasting. Information and communication technology (ICT) in particular offers a digital solution to the chronic problem of the property rights of the poor. A pilot program in Tanzania has made it possible to embark on e-registration of land ownership, providing accurate and reliable data on land, housing, and farming activities. Such registration has made it possible for banks to offer farmers loans with which to improve agriculture. Ultimately the application of ICT can help to increase transparency and reduce transaction costs for trade and service delivery, as well as increase the scope for good governance.

Trade and Development

One of the greatest challenges, indeed, imperatives, facing leaders of the first category of countries is not just the attainment of Millennium Development Goals, important as they are, but, equally important, how to wean their countries off dependence on external aid. This should now be a priority for them.

This implies not only a conducive investment regime but also equally improved capacity for domestic revenue generation. Clear targets have to be set by which year-after-year domestic revenue yields would enable these countries to meet most of their budgetary needs from their own economies.

To succeed, this requires a very high level of political commitment and clarity of vision. Increasing domestic revenues requires expanding the tax base, and not everyone would be glad to be caught in the tax initiatives net. The outside world has a role as well. In the medium term, most sub-Saharan African governments would depend on tariffs to enhance their revenues. If the rich industrialized countries want Africans to reduce their dependence on aid, and hence develop with dignity, they should not impose on Africa conditions, the effect of which is to undercut Africa's revenue base. It is true there are long-term benefits in trade liberalization and open markets. But Africa needs gradual, managed trade liberalization, and it needs leaders who can articulate and defend this position, in addition to arguing for "fair" rather than simply "free" trade.

A recent study commissioned by the United Nations Economic Commission for Africa looked at the economic and welfare impacts of the EU-Africa Economic Partnership Agreements and, although mindful of their imperative and importance, strongly discouraged the adoption of full reciprocity in trade liberalization between the two groups of countries. The report says that "full reciprocity will be very costly for Africa irrespective of how the issue is looked at, in terms of revenue losses, adjustment costs associated with de-industrialization and its undermining effect on regional integration" (ECA 2006).

If the EU is truly eager to help Africa develop through production and trade, it should not impose on Africa policies that in effect undermine Africa's capacity to produce competitively and trade. It would be scandalous for the World Trade Organization (WTO) to demand compliance with reciprocity requirements, especially for least developed countries.

Recommendations from the ECA report should guide African leaders in their negotiations with the EU, or even in the broader framework of the WTO. The following points are particularly pertinent:

1. The focus in the next 10–12 years should be on deepening intra-African trade, through stronger and effective regional economic groupings (RECs).
2. The RECs should be given practical support and sufficient lead time to allow member countries to build diversified supply capacities and the competitiveness with which eventually to engage the rest of the world.
3. The EU and other development partners should facilitate intra-African trade through, among other things, supporting the development of infrastructure to facilitate and reduce the transaction costs of intra-Africa trade. In addition, the donor community should provide compensation for those countries in Africa that will suffer verifiable revenue losses from dismantling barriers to intra-Africa trade.
4. Unrestricted and tariff-free access to the EU market for African exports must continue for at least 15 years before introducing reciprocity.

Aid Effectiveness

Central to Africa's development efforts always has been the subject of resources, especially from external sources. Admittedly, the continent has benefited from external financing in the form of official development assistance (ODA), including debt relief and FDI with significant cross-country variations in the receipt of such finance. In particular, FDI has favored countries rich in oil and other natural resources.

By 2004 aid levels to Africa had recovered from their 1990s dip. Much of the recovery, however, came in the form of debt relief and emergency assistance that, although helpful, did not expand the fiscal space for governments. One source estimates that direct aid to African governments declined from $24 billion (in 1993) to $20 billion (in 2004) in real terms. Over the same period, emergency and debt relief grew from 15 to 32 percent of total ODA. More important than the total aid amount is its sectoral composition. Between 1994–95 and 2003–04, the share of aid going to social sectors grew from 27 to 43 percent and that to productive sectors declined from 16 to 14 percent, as did budget and program support, from 20 to 11 percent.

The literature on aid contains much criticism revolving around the issue of aid effectiveness, and rightly so. The record of aid effectiveness in most African countries, especially in the 1970s and 1980s, is far from impressive. The progress achieved in recent years, however, and the new aid modalities emerging from best practices, should ensure that this will no longer be an obstacle to increasing aid volumes. Both sides must be ready to learn from past mistakes.

As pointed out elsewhere, aid and concessionary loans will be needed even more in the days ahead if the external world is to give the new leaders of Africa the tools with which to realize the goals and objectives encapsulated in the NEPAD document and subsequent African Union decisions and declarations. No amount of good leadership and democratic governance can produce the growth and development results that one would wish to see in Africa in the medium term without this new push in external support.

For that to happen, the genuine and widely shared concerns for improving aid effectiveness must be adhered to, and there is no better place to start than to review what went wrong in the 1970s and 1980s.

The review must objectively balance responsibility for poor aid effectiveness. It is true that some African leaders bear large responsibility for this state of affairs. The outside world, however, both bilateral and multilateral partners, must bear its fair share of the blame.

It is true, for instance, that some of that early aid was not properly targeted, prioritized, and sequenced. This was not, however, simply a result of leadership problems among African governments. That era saw much less domestic ownership of the development agenda than we are trying to create now. Aid allocation was as much a factor of domestic politics as it was a factor of politics in donor countries and institutions.

It is true that some of the aid and loans were misused or misappropriated. This was especially true during the Cold War, when aid and loans became part of the Cold War arsenal, as both sides sought to contain each other's influence in Africa while promoting their own. Much of the thieving during the Cold War was with the full knowledge, connivance, or acquiescence of some of the donor countries.

It is true that some of the aid and loans never reached the project level, but this problem was not the monopoly of African leaders. Projects have been undertaken in Africa in which over 80 percent of aid resources ended up meeting the administrative overheads of the aid bureaucracy, including salaries, allowances, medical care, and traveling expenses of expatriates and consultants—including ensuring their comfort in Africa through the construction of special, air-conditioned houses furnished from Europe or the United States. All those expenses were counted as part of the aid to Africa. Add to this "tied aid," where aid programs could very well be considered part of the export strategy of donor countries.

I could go on and on, and I do not accept people's talk of problems of aid effectiveness as if it was inherently a problem of African leadership. The blame must be shared equally.

Today there is a better understanding of what it takes to make aid more effective—an understanding that spreads fairly the burden of ensuring that this indeed is the case. The efforts of the Organisation for Economic Co-operation and Development's Development Assistance Committee (DAC) in this direction are highly welcome. The Rome Declaration on Aid Harmonization and the Paris Declaration on Aid Effectiveness are landmarks in a long journey to make aid more effective. The decision of some DAC members to evaluate themselves against agreed benchmarks in these areas is welcome and encouraged for others. The initiative of the Center for Global Development (http://cgdev.org) to rank donors against a *commitment to development index* is a good innovation that helps everyone to focus on the core objective of development and poverty reduction. At the national level, a system of Joint Assistance Strategy as we have in Tanzania and in a few other countries, as well as the Independent Monitoring Group, provides a much better environment to make aid more effective on the ground.

The outcome of these welcome initiatives is to put more ownership, responsibility, and trust in African leaders and provides the instruments needed for transparency and accountability to ensure that we do not relapse into the aid mismanagement and inefficiencies of the 1970s and 1980s. Some people are still hesitant in making the transition from project to program aid, and from project support to budgetary support. The challenge for the few African governments that are pioneers in this transformation in aid relationships and channels is to prove that it is workable and make it possible to spread the mechanism to other countries. The bottom line is good governance, transparency, and accountability.

The commitment of the donor community, both bilateral and multilateral, to this transformation must be clear and unequivocal. Everyone has to focus less on politics and more on the growth, development, and poverty reduction priorities of the African countries.

Corruption

There is now no doubt whatsoever that corruption, in its broad sense, is bad for economic growth, development, and poverty reduction. Although it does not always get reflected in the international media, it has also been established without a doubt that the vice of corruption and bribery is not the monopoly of Africa and other developing countries. The motivation and methods for corrupt behavior may be different. How governments react to corruption may differ. Capacities to prevent, investigate, and prosecute corruption and bribery cases may differ. But there are no saints.

First, I fear that there is some exaggeration as to how much corruption, especially in the post–Cold War era, is responsible for the continued underdevelopment of Africa. It has become common, especially in the international media, to simply write off Africa's misery as the outcome of bad governance and corruption. This is naive and an oversimplification of very complex phenomena, which may have the effect of removing the incentive to look for other equally important causes of poverty. We need a better balance between an appreciation of the harmful effects of corruption and bad governance, and the extent to which we can hold bad governance and corruption responsible for the development problems of different countries around the world.

Second, what type of corruption and bribery is worst for development? Is it the petty type of corruption, of hungry Africans bribing hungry

Africans, or is it the grand corruption in which rich companies from rich developed countries bribe poor Africans? For a country at Tanzania's level of development, the big contracts and licenses that would attract grand corruption would normally involve aid-funded projects and companies from rich industrialized countries.

Third, we must not forget intellectual corruption. We have journalists who would mold public opinion for or against someone, or some cause, for a price. We have academics and researchers for hire. With their low wages, they will produce research findings or evaluation reports to the tune picked by the payer. Sometimes government decisions, in either donor or aid-receiving countries, are based on such research findings or evaluation reports. The debate about corruption in Africa should take a broader perspective, shifting away from the narrow confines of bureaucratic corruption, to political corruption, legislative corruption, intellectual corruption, and the whole spectrum of issues that mold societal thinking and provide the information base for decision making.

Finally, what examples do the rich industrial countries give Africa?

I appreciate the World Bank's efforts in fighting corruption. I especially appreciate the concrete action in terms of blacklisting those companies found to have won World Bank–financed contracts through corruption and bribery. Most of the over 400 blacklisted companies are not African companies, and I have not heard evidence that action against these companies has been taken in their home jurisdictions. What I hear, on the contrary, is that some countries want the World Bank to take it easy on the corruption agenda.

In 1999 Transparency International (TI) developed the Bribe Payers Index (BPI), but it is far less known than the Corruption Perception Index (CPI). Although the CPI comes out yearly, the BPI has come out only three times in eight years. Comments by TI officials (box 2.5) on releasing the latest BPI expose a weak link in the war on corruption and bribery because

---

Box 2.5. Bribe Payers Index

"Bribing companies are actively undermining the best efforts of governments in developing nations to improve governance, and thereby driving the vicious cycle of poverty," said Transparency International Chair Huguette Labelle.

"It is hypocritical that OECD-based companies continue to bribe across the globe, while their governments pay lip-service to enforcing the law. TI's Bribe Payers Index indicates that they are not doing enough to clamp down on overseas bribery," said David Nussbaum, Chief Executive of Transparency International. "The enforcement record on international anti-bribery laws makes for short and disheartening reading."

"The rules and tools for governments and companies do exist," said Nussbaum. "Domestic legislation has been introduced in many countries following the adoption of the UN and OECD anti-corruption conventions, but there are still major problems of implementation and enforcement."

Source: http://www.transparency.org/news_room/in_focus/bpi_2006#pr.

Box 2.6. Tax Havens Cause Poverty

"Taxes are what we pay for civilized society"

The world's leading development agencies have taken a lead in the current debate about corruption and development, but have ignored civil society concerns about how tax havens encourage and enable capital flight and tax evasion. In a world of globalized capital markets, tax havens create an offshore interface between the illicit and licit economies. This interface corrupts national tax regimes and onshore regulation, and distorts markets by rewarding economic free-riders and misdirecting investment.

Tax havens are a major cause of inequality and poverty. They function as a result of collusion between banks and other financial intermediaries and the governments of states and microstates that host their activities. The major culprits include the United States, Britain, Switzerland, and other European countries that promote tax havens and prevent efforts to clamp down on their activities.

Source: http://www.taxjustice.net/cms/front_content.php?idcat=2.

the perception is that although all rich developed countries have signed and ratified the OECD Convention on Bribery of Foreign Public Officials in International Business Transactions, many have yet to ratify the United Nations Convention against Corruption, and in both cases little has been achieved in terms of actually prosecuting the culprits in those countries. Another aspect is the one raised by Eva Joly and carried in the journal *Development Today* (2007). Joly supports supporting the Tax Justice Network's point (box 2.6) that tax havens are part of the corruption network and should be brought into the war on the vice. That this idea has been received coolly by TI, and coldly by rich industrialized countries, will keep open this escape route for big companies as we seek to prosecute corrupt bureaucrats and politicians in poor countries.

Theory of Leadership

Just as we could not discern a single theory of leadership for development in the first three to five decades of Africa's independence, we cannot prescribe a single theory of leadership for development in the years ahead. As in the past, however, so will it be necessary in the future to keep in mind the centrality of the following:

- A strong sense of nationhood and shared destiny
- Good democratic governance, preferably with constitutional term limits
- Good economic governance, especially in terms of macroeconomic fundamentals, as well as strong, capable, and facilitative regulatory institutions, a strong financial sector, and promotion of entrepreneurship
- Greater investment in infrastructure
- Human resource capacity building, including health, education, and skills for contemporary Africa

- The advocacy and institutional promotion of a savings and investment culture.

Although no two African countries are the same, recent trends enable us to put African countries in three categories in terms of trying to venture a broad range of leadership challenges in the years ahead.

The first category is those African countries that are ahead of the pack in terms of nationhood, peace and security, good democratic governance, stable macroeconomic fundamentals, and openness to business. These would include countries such as Kenya, Mali, Mozambique, Senegal, South Africa, Tanzania, and Uganda. These countries must now resolutely shift from a short-term crisis management mode to a longer-term strategic leadership mode. Nationally, this requires a new set of leadership qualities that can balance the enhanced risk element that a bold strategic vision may entail, as well as the need to safeguard achievements to date in terms of political stability and growth prospects.

Externally, this will require a new and heightened engagement by the development partners, both bilateral and multilateral. The concept of local ownership of the development agenda will have to be deepened more than ever before, while being supported even more than before. If these sub-Saharan African countries that are ahead of the pack keep to their current commitment to peace and security, good democratic governance, and sound economic management, and with a new surge of external support, they can cross the threshold toward a new era of sustainable growth, development, and poverty reduction.

The second category includes most African countries that are in transition toward stable and democratic political and economic dispensations, but that still need more careful nurturing to avoid back-sliding. These are the countries on the verge of getting debt relief, or that have had their first democratic elections, or that have recently ended an era of conflict, for example, Burundi, the Democratic Republic of Congo, and Liberia.

These countries need leadership skills that emphasize nation building and unifying leaders who can earn the respect and trust of previously antagonistic groups. They also, however, need to produce quick results in terms of peace dividends. In this respect, for instance, following the Second International Conference on the Great Lakes in Nairobi in December 2006, external support for regional growth and development has to be forthcoming soon, either bilaterally or through a dedicated African Development Bank window.

The third category of countries consists of what has come to be known as "failed states" or "dysfunctional states," in the sense that operationally their statehood is little more than nominal and territorial. These are the countries such as Somalia, but the category includes countries that are currently in conflict situations, such as Côte d'Ivoire.

For these countries, the top priority should be peace and security, the smooth transition to functioning democratic political dispensations, and the fundamentals of economic management. Such countries need statesmen or stateswomen in the true definition of the term. They must be leaders willing and able to rise above personal or parochial interests. They must be willing to sacrifice short-term gain for long-term stability and the common good. Attempting to build an economy on shaky political foundations will only produce an economic house of cards.

Last, Africa needs strong, capable, and effective states. We cannot on the one hand lament "failed" or "dysfunctional" states while on the other hand we impose or pursue policies whose ultimate result is the weakening of what are already very weak states. So I cannot understand when people say that true democracy is when political competition is such that no party is too strong. At Africa's level of development I ask: too strong for what? If a party is strong for development, that is good. If it is not strong for development, the other parties will coalesce into a stronger opposition that can win subsequent elections. But democracy that presupposes weak governments, or that believes a victory by the ruling party implies no true democracy, is not developmental democracy in Africa.

It is naive to see African democracy through the lens of Western democracy. Italy can afford to change governments almost on a yearly basis, and that does not undermine the state. In Africa a similar scenario would be the recipe for "failed" or "dysfunctional" states. To be an effective state in Africa is to be a strong but democratic and accountable state. To think that democracy in South Africa and Tanzania is deficient just because the ruling parties have an overwhelming majority is to miss the point. The real issue is that at Africa's level of development, the agenda for development is pretty clear-cut, and the policies and strategies would not really differ very much from one serious party to another. Any significant difference would be on how and who, rather than on what needs to be done.

Conclusion: Development Democracy for Africa

It is generally accepted now that good democratic governance is important for economic growth, development, and poverty reduction. What remains unresolved is to what extent good governance is required, and therefore what other requirements are needed for growth, development, and poverty reduction. What I fear is the debate shifting from one extreme, like during the Cold War when not much attention was focused on governance, to another extreme, where governance is peddled as the panacea. As those in this business know, development, especially in Africa, is a very complex matter. There are no simple solutions, only a combination of necessary ingredients, of which good democratic governance is one.

Matthew Lockwood (2005: 115–16) argues strongly for "developmental states" in Africa, but based on several studies he also concludes the following: "The case for democracy is far from straightforward. Statistically the general relationship between democracy and poverty reduction is weak (e.g., Moore et al. 1999, pp. 8–9). In Africa, the advent of multi-party systems did not make a decisive difference to overall economic performance in the early 1990s (van de Walle 2001, pp. 247–54)."

The Commission for Africa Report (2005: 133–56) singles out governance as Africa's core problem. It says that without improvements in governance, that economic, social, cultural, and other reforms will have limited impact in the race to eradicate poverty in Africa. It points out that good governance is about much more than periodic multiparty elections, sound policies, and the challenge of putting policies into effect. It places strong emphasis on capacity building for governance and on getting systems of governance right. African leaders are urged to improve accountability, and to do so by broadening the participation of citizens in governance.

The report also made reference to the role of colonialism in establishing nonviable states. I have tried to explain in this chapter how this has affected social attitudes and shaped the moral and institutional foundations of politics in Africa today.

As I look back over our recent history, I am convinced that Africa needs a home-grown new democracy, focused on development. After almost half a century of independence, and bearing in mind our precolonial and colonial experience, we should now know enough about what works and what does not work in Africa to be able to develop a synthesis based on our history, our experience, and global realities.

Such a synthesis has to revolve around the following eight points.

Education

The first is education. There is no denying the fact that low levels of education were one of the major problems related to governance during the first years of our independence. Many people were given important positions of leadership without the education, skills, and experience needed to discharge their duties properly. In addition, they were deliberately denied the preparation that they needed to assume leadership. Thus poorly equipped, they had to courageously muddle through unknown terrain.

Today we are independent. Free, fair, and regular periodic elections in multiparty political systems are very important, but they are not enough for the new democracy for Africa that I envisage. We must also properly prepare our people for leadership, not simply by expanding enrollment in different levels of our education systems, but also by improving the quality and the relevance of that education to the needs and challenges of today and tomorrow. We also need to identify potential leaders early and develop and nurture them.

Education is also the means by which ordinary people can acquire the tools and the courage to make informed choices during elections, and to hold leaders to account after elections. Without this, free and fair elections will not amount to much. For us in Africa, education must be not just for social mobility, wealth creation, and poverty reduction, but also especially a means to encourage and facilitate good democratic governance.

Building Capable and Sustainable Institutions and Systems

The second point is building capable and sustainable institutions and systems for good democratic governance. Today one hears a lot of talk about the capacity of African institutions to deliver on good governance and development. In extreme cases, we are concerned about the so-called failed states.

It is obvious from history that colonial powers focused only on those institutions and systems that worked to ensure firm control over their colonies. They did not focus on developing institutions and systems to ensure democratic governance and development after independence. Neither was the development of such institutions and systems a priority during the Cold War in most African countries.

Today, in the era of multiparty politics, with the divisive tendencies they often spawn, and in the competitive environment of the market nationally, regionally, and internationally, the question of effective, efficient institutions and systems to guide, regulate, and monitor the political, economic, and social life of our peoples and countries becomes pertinent and urgent. Moreover, we must now create systems of political and economic management that are strong, that are resilient, and that are capable of outliving their founders and current leaders.

Tolerance and Inclusion

The third point concerns tolerance and inclusion. As I pointed out earlier, the colonial legacy in Africa is one of divide and rule, of playing one African group against another—one religion against another, one tribe against another, one clan against another. Today, from the experience of the last few decades, we can attribute most civil wars and cross-border conflicts to the legacies of the policies of bigotry, intolerance, and exclusion. The new African democracy that I advocate must have at its heart the politics of tolerance and inclusion, not as a product, but as a fundamental, deliberate goal and priority.

I am sure that if we look far back enough into our history, to the period before colonialism, we can find archetypes of politics of tolerance and inclusion that can today inform our efforts to design a new, more inclusive, form of democracy with African characteristics. Today there are people who ridicule the African extended family. It is true that some aspects of it are now anachronistic and unhelpful, but the extended African family is an expression of a sense of belonging, inclusion, and participation. Yet, when we embraced Western forms of democracy, we fell into the trap of making political parties, not as mechanisms for tolerance and inclusion, but of intolerance and exclusion. The concept of "winner takes all" has no African roots. Traditional Africa is corporate, if not communal. It is inclusive.

In the new African democracy, political parties will not be an excuse to exclude people, but a reason to bring them together. Political parties must never be based on divisive things such as religion, tribe, or race. Some religions are minorities, some tribes are a minority, and some races will always be a minority. No political system should institutionalize the disadvantages generated by such minority status. No one wants to be perpetually excluded, and if someone sees no light at the end of the tunnel, that person may take desperate measures to be taken note of, and to be included in governance.

Additionally, inclusion must also cover the social and economic spheres. Africa must avoid social and economic policies and practices that exclude some people from the benefits of national ownership of natural resources, national investment, and growth and development. As in politics, people who feel permanently excluded from the benefits of growth can be desperate and hence be a potential force for instability. Inclusion is necessary in politics, but it is equally necessary in development and prosperity. This is not ideological posturing; it makes political sense in Africa for leaders who want to entrench stability. The widening income inequalities in Africa are a recipe for instability and must be addressed as a matter of policy.

Participation

The fourth aspect is participation, which I deliberately want to treat separately from inclusion. Inclusion is one thing. Actual participation is another. Here too we can find in traditional African societies archetypes of participation in the social, economic, and political systems on our continent. We have to think out of the box and refuse to be constrained by what we have been conditioned to accept as the gospel of democratic participation.

An African proverb made famous by U.S. Senator Hillary Clinton says, "It takes a whole village to raise a child." This is the kind of participation that I should like to see emerging in the new African democracy. The relationship between governments and people should not be about us and them, only about us—one team, one destiny. It is common now to hear of the imperative of ownership in socioeconomic development, but ownership is pointless without actual participation, including the full participation of women.

Decentralization of government—of resources and of responsibilities—is one way to address the needs of inclusion and participation. But it has to go far, embodying and illustrating more trust and more confidence in the people. Former colonial rulers underestimated the capacities of Africans. Today governments in independent Africa must not repeat the same prejudices and mistakes. They must never underestimate our people's capacity to plan, to prioritize, and to do things for themselves, with government support. In traditional African societies people used to sit under a tree or around a fire and discuss issues thoroughly until solutions with buy-in from everyone were found. This may be considered inefficient in today's fast-paced societies, but we can always find ways of incorporating some of these positive elements in a new democratic paradigm for today's Africa.

Transparency

The fifth aspect is transparency. The attitudes of political leaders and public officials about the necessity to be more open and transparent in the operations of governments need to change. It is not about being open on all government matters, at all stages of formulation and implementation, but about acknowledging the people's right to know what the government is doing in their name. Inclusion and participation will not be possible if people are not well informed. Effective participation requires effective government communication.

In the new African democracy that I envisage, it is the government's duty to communicate. I use the broader concept of "communicate," not the narrow one of "inform." For, important as the duty to inform is, it is much more important to communicate, to create space for dialogue, and to facilitate a free flow of thoughts and ideas.

Communication, rather than information, builds stronger institutions and processes for good governance. It is about improving interaction between governments and the governed, in whose name decisions are made and government revenue spent. Elections every five years are important for democracy, but they are not sufficient to ensure that the people have a greater say in the way they are governed. Between elections, the people must continue to feel relevant, to feel that they are listened to. That is the heart and culture of the new democratic good governance for Africa that I am advocating. The multiparty constitutional order prevailing in most African states requires openness and accessibility as pillars of legitimacy, and as determinants of government popular support.

A democratic government thrives on popular support, but such support cannot be in the abstract. It must be based on what the people know. They cannot feel part of the general polity if they do not hear, and are not heard.

Accountability

The sixth point is accountability, which flows logically from the previous point of transparency. Being open is exposing oneself to public scrutiny and hence being accountable. When people are open and accountable, little room exists for the scourge of corruption. In the new African democracy that I envisage, all stakeholders have to be open and accountable. Those who want to hold the government accountable, such as the media, political parties, and civil society, must indeed themselves be examples of integrity, transparency, and accountability before they can demand the right to hold the government accountable.

Additionally, African media and civil society will have to develop an African agenda. It is my perception, rightly or wrongly, that not only are most civil societies in Africa externally funded, and hence beholden to those who pay the piper, but also they have no agenda of their own, preferring to echo and respond to an agenda set by others. It is likewise with our media. In Tanzania I always ask the media not to be like the proverbial knife, which, thinking it is only destroying an old sheath, is actually destroying its own home. An Ashanti proverb says, "Do not call the forest that shelters you a jungle." African media need to pay heed to this adage as they relate to their own countries and continent. It is bad enough that the international media hardly sees anything good worth reporting on Africa. The real tragedy is when they are fed the negative, stereotyped stories by Africa's own media. The media should not shy away from revealing the truth, but they should also strive for objectivity, balance, and professionalism.

Effective and efficient government communication critically depends on the quality of the mass media. For the media are the bridge between the government and the governed; they are the mechanism for interaction between these two entities, and a forum for the exchange of ideas. Once the credibility of the mass media is eroded, they cease to be effective partners to the government in the promotion of open and accountable governance. Very importantly, members of the media should not assume a role that could be construed as supplanting representative democracy. They should instead play better their role of societal watchdogs, whistle blowers, signalers, and initiators of action to promote good governance.

One problem that I discern is the trend to turn the concept of a free press upside down. Some think that the plethora of media is a reflection of a free press. Does the production in my commercial capital of Dar es Salaam of five English language and eight Swahili language *daily* newspapers truly empower our people to participate in democratic governance more effectively? The quintessential question of quality versus quantity needs attention.

Above all, a free African media should uphold African decency, respect for authority, and the right of maligned people to respond and to legal redress. A free press is not a license to lie, to misrepresent, and to insult. I yearn for a free press, with African characteristics: one that seeks to build, not to destroy; to heal, not to kill.

Constitutionalism and the Rule of Law

A seventh point is constitutionalism, and the rule of law. Governments and especially leaders must respect their oaths of office, which invariably include a commitment to respect the constitution and the rule of law. One of my great concerns, however, is that too many people in Africa have to operate outside the law because they cannot access the law. We have expensive legal systems in Africa that serve only a tiny minority of the people who can afford it and who can understand its intricacies. Justice only for the few is not only discriminatory, it is inherently unjust. All citizens deserve the protection of the law in practice, not only in theory. Certainly, the latent entrepreneurial spirit of Africans cannot be fully harnessed for development until the property rights of the majority poor are recognized and protected within the law.

Corruption

The eighth and last point is corruption. This needs no further elaboration. Corruption imposes a high cost on development, and indeed it undermines in a very serious way the development agenda. But corruption has to be fought on all fronts, including on the supply side.

With such a framework, I believe that Africa will have the kind of leadership that will translate recent gains into a new momentum for growth, shared development, and poverty reduction.

References

Allen, Chris. 1995. "Understanding African Politics." *Review of African Political Economy* 22 (65): 301–20.

Bunting, Ikaweba. 1999. "The Heart of Africa. Interview with Julius Nyerere on Anti-Colonialism." *New Internationalist Magazine* 309 (January–February). http://www.hartford-hwp.com/archives/30/049.html.

Cannadine, David. 2001. *Ornamentalism: How the British Saw Their Empire.* London: Allen Lane Penguin Press.

Clarke, Jeremy. 2007. "Dozens Killed as Kenyan Land Battles Resume." Nairobi, February 7. http://www.int.iol.co.za/index.php?art_id=qw1170795422449B254.

Commission for Africa. 2005. *Our Common Interest: Report of the Commission for Africa.* London: Department for International Development.

Davidson, Basil. 1994. *Modern Africa: A Social and Political History.* 3rd ed. London and New York: Longman.

De Rivero, Oswaldo. 2001. *The Myth of Development: The Non-Viable Economies of the 21st Century.* London and New York: Zed Books.

De Soto, Hernando. 2000. *The Mystery of Capital: Why Capitalism Triumphs in the West and Fails Everywhere Else.* London: Black Swan.

Development Today. 2007. "Eva Joly: TI Index on Corruption Should Put Spotlight on Tax Havens." *Development Today* (Oslo) 17 (3). http://www.development-today.com. magazine/2007/DT_3.

Devlin, Larry. 2007. *Chief of Station, Congo: A Memoir of 1960–67.* New York: Public Affairs–Perseus Books Group.

De Witte, Ludo. 2002. *The Assassination of Lumumba.* London and New York: Verso.

Economic Commission for Africa (ECA). 2006. *Economic Report on Africa 2006: Capital Flows and Development Financing in Africa.* Addis Ababa: Economic Commission for Africa. http://www.uneca.org/eca_resources/publications/books/era2006/full.pdf.

Ferry, Jules François Camille. 1897. "Speech before the French Chamber of Deputies, March 28, 1884." In Paul Robiquet, ed., *Discours et Opinions de Jules Ferry,* trans. Ruth Kleinman and J. S. Arkenberg, pp. 199–201, 210–11, 215–18. Paris: Armand Colin & Cie. http://www.fordham.edu/halsall/mod/1884ferry.html.

Hallen, Barry. 2002. *A Short History of African Philosophy.* Bloomington: Indiana University Press.

Hochschild, Adam. 2000. *King Leopold's Ghost: A Story of Greed, Terror and Heroism in Colonial Africa.* London: Papermac.

Institute for Liberty and Democracy (ILD). 2005. *Program to Formalize the Assets of the Poor of Tanzania and Strengthen the Rule of Law: Diagnosis Progress Report Vol. I.* Lima: ILD. Summary available at http://www.tanzania.go.tz/mkurabita/PDF/Executive%20Summary.pdf.

International Labour Organization (ILO). 2004. *A Fair Globalization: Creating Opportunities for All*. Geneva: ILO.

Lockwood, Matthew. 2005. *The State They're In: An Agenda for International Action on Poverty in Africa*. Bourton-on-Dunsmore: ITDG Publishing.

Meredith, Martin. 2005. *The State of Africa: A History of Fifty Years of Independence*. London: Free Press.

Moore, Mick, Jennifer Leavy, Peter Houtzager, and Howard White. 1999. "Polity Qualities: How Governance Affects Poverty." Working Paper 99, Institute of Development Studies, University of Sussex, Brighton.

Ngoma Naison. 2004. "Coups and Coup Attempts in Africa: Is There a Missing Link?" *Africa Security Review* 13 (3). http://www.iss.co.za/pubs/ASR/13No3/ENgoma.htm.

Nyerere, Julius K. 1966. *Freedom and Unity*. Dar es Salaam: Oxford University Press.

———. 1968. *Freedom and Socialism*. Dar es Salaam: Oxford University Press.

———. 1973. *Freedom and Development*. Dar es Salaam: Oxford University Press.

Nzongola-Ntalaja, Georges. 2002. *The Congo from Leopold to Kabila: A People's History*. London: Zed Books.

Omoregie, Fani Kayode. 1999. "Rodney, Cabral and Ngugi as Guides to African Postcolonial Literature." In *African Postcolonial Literature in English*, University of Botswana. http://www.postcolonialweb.org/africa/omoregie11.html.

Pakenham, Thomas. 1991. *The Scramble for Africa*. London: Abacus History.

Pratt, Cranford. 1999. "Julius Nyerere: The Ethical Foundation of His Legacy." http://www.queensu.ca/snid/pratt.htm#_edn10.

Reader, John. 1999. *Africa: A Biography of the Continent*. New York: Vintage Books.

Robinson, Dr. James H. 1962. "International Aspects of American Race Relations." In *The Empire Club of Canada Speeches 1961–1962*, pp. 226–40. Toronto: Empire Club Foundation.

Rodney, Walter. 1981. *How Europe Underdeveloped Africa*. Harare: Zimbabwe Publishing House.

Time. 1961. "Island of Peace." December 15. http://www.time.com/time/magazine/article/0,9171,827061-1,00.html.

Van De Walle, Nicholas. 2001. *African Economies and the Politics of Permanent Crisis, 1979–1999*. Cambridge: Cambridge University Press.

Williams, Al-yasha Ilhaam. 2003. "On the Subject of Kings and Queens: 'Traditional' African Leadership and the Diasporal Imagination." *African Studies Quarterly* 6 (4). http://www.africa.ufl.edu/asq/v7/v7i1a4.htm.

World Bank. 1994. *Governance: The World Bank's Experience*. Washington, DC: World Bank. http://www.gdrc.org/u-gov/governance-understand.html.

———. 2006. *Africa Development Indicators 2006*. Washington, DC: World Bank. http://siteresources.worldbank.org/INTSTATINAFR/Resources/ADI_2006_text.pdf.

CHAPTER 3

Leadership, Policy Making, Quality of Economic Policies, and Their Inclusiveness: The Case of Rwanda

Thomas Rusuhuzwa Kigabo

Fifteen years ago, Rwanda was considered a dead country, one whose future was simply unclear following the 1994 genocide against Tutsi. The entire system—from the economy to the security situation, to the justice framework, to the infrastructure—had been destroyed. However, important socioeconomic achievements have been realized in Rwanda since the genocide. Although economic development challenges remain, owing essentially to structural problems, the country has attained very good results and built a solid foundation for its development in the long term. These impressive achievements of the past 15 years are attributable to good leadership committed to finding durable solutions for Rwandan's people despite important challenges.

Rwanda is landlocked and far from ocean ports, a factor that raises transportation costs for both exports and imports. These natural barriers to trade hinder industrial and other forms of development.

Rwanda faces challenges in building its institutional capacity. Governance, including the management of public resources, remains insufficient because

The views expressed in the chapter are those of the author and should not be ascribed to the institutions of his affiliation.

of the lack of sound institutions and competent personnel. Although great progress has been made on this front, the severe shortage of professional personnel constitutes an obstacle to the development of all sectors. Lack of adequately trained people in agriculture and animal husbandry hampers modernization of this sector, while a shortage of technicians and competent managers constrains the expansion of the secondary and tertiary sectors.

The 1994 genocide against Tutsi devastated the Rwandan economy as well as its population. Gross domestic product (GDP) was halved in a single year, 80 percent of the population was plunged into poverty, and vast tracts of land and livestock were destroyed. The genocide exacerbated numerous constraints on development that existed before 1994. The poorly developed productive infrastructure was completely destroyed. The genocide devastated Rwanda's social, political, and economic fabric.

Since 2000 Rwanda has envisaged a set of policies with the goal of transforming the agrarian subsistence economy into a sophisticated knowledge-based society. These policies are defined in a framework called Vision 2020. The main socioeconomic objectives of Vision 2020 include transforming Rwanda into a middle-income country, with per capita income of about $900 (from $290 in 2000), and transforming the structure of the economy such that the industrial and services sectors will take over by 2020. It is expected that services will contribute 42 percent, industry 26 percent, and agriculture 33 percent of GDP. In 2007 the contribution of the three sectors was 42 percent, 14 percent, and 36 percent, respectively (based on 2007 statistics from the National Institute of Statistics of Rwanda). It is also expected that the population living under the poverty line will be reduced from 60 percent in 2000 to 25 percent by 2020, the population will grow, on average, 2.7 percent a year until 2020, the literacy rate will increase from 48 percent in 2000 to 90 percent in 2020, and average life expectancy will rise from 49 to 55 years (MINECOFIN 2000, *Rwanda Vision 2020*).

This chapter analyzes the role of political leadership, the process of policy making, and the process of policy learning in sustaining economic growth. It also examines the extent to which public policies in Rwanda are effective and inclusive.

The rest of the chapter is organized as follows. The first section highlights macroeconomic performance in Rwanda with regard to the dynamic of post-conflict economic growth. The second summarizes existing empirical findings on the sources of growth in Rwanda. The third analyzes the nature, goals, and objectives of the Rwandan leadership as well as the extent to which leadership in Rwanda is conducive to growth. The fourth section analyzes the economic reforms undertaken by the government of Rwanda with the expectations of sustaining growth.

Overview of Macroeconomic Performance in Rwanda: The Dynamics of Post-Conflict Growth

To understand the current macroeconomic performance in Rwanda, it is important to consider the Rwandan economy before and after the 1994 war and genocide against Tutsi. The post-conflict government inherited two sets of problems: the consequences of the 1994 genocide and the structural problems of Rwanda's economy. As a consequence of the genocide, the country lost not only 1 million people, including highly skilled people, but also economic infrastructure. The genocide also had strong social repercussions, including losses at different levels of society and increased poverty, leading, for example, to higher government transfers in the form of social security payments.

To deal with these problems, the government introduced macroeconomic and structural reforms. Among others, the government embarked on reforms in the following areas: the central bank was made independent in an effort to control inflation and achieve macroeconomic stabilization (National Bank of Rwanda, Annual Reports 2002–05); the tax system was reformed by creating an independent tax collection agency (Rwanda Revenue Authority) and introducing a value-added tax (VAT); state enterprises were privatized; the tariff structure and labor market were reformed; and trade was liberalized by removing price controls. Over the years, Rwanda has attained a reasonable level of macroeconomic stability and fiscal discipline. This has been achieved in spite of the ongoing heavy reliance on foreign savings to compensate for insufficient domestic savings. In 2005 Rwanda's economic reforms were advanced enough to qualify for the highly indebted poor countries (HIPC) debt cancellation. Under the enhanced HIPC, Rwanda gained an estimated $1.4 billion out of $1.5 billion as a result of the adoption of strict measures in public debt management. These reforms and different economic policies explain important economic achievements in Rwanda during the last five years. From 2004 to 2008, the economic growth in Rwanda was around 8 percent on average against –1.8 percent from 1990 to 1993. The real GDP per capita, which grew on average 0.1 percent from 1980 to 1989, rose by 5 percent per year from 1995 to 2003 (Ezemenari and Coulibaly 2008) and by 14.9 percent per year on average from 2003 to 2007 (2007 statistics from the National Institute of Statistics of Rwanda).

Economic reforms alone could not have brought about this degree of positive change in Rwanda. As Napoleon said in 1815, "Men are powerless to secure the future; institutions alone fix the destinies of nations" (World Bank 1997). Peace and stability must be established first and foremost. Democratic rule, supported by institutions of good governance and a strong political will, must exist concurrently. Involving people in governance and making them responsible for their own destiny are essential elements of legitimacy and consensus. Rwanda embarked on a program of decentralization of public administration to improve the delivery of services

Table 3.1. Real Economic Growth by Sectors from 2004 to 2008
(percent)

	2004	2005	2006	2007	2008
GDP growth	5.3	7.2	7.3	7.9	11.2
Agriculture	0.1	4.8	1.1	0.7	15.0
Food crops	−1.8	6.4	0.0	1.8	16.4
Export crops	58.2	−24.3	29.8	−33.1	20.3
Industry	12.8	7.5	10.9	10.2	10.7
Manufacturing	6.4	3.5	9.9	6.9	−4.1
Electricity, gas, and water	−16.1	17.4	28.0	3.7	16.9
Construction	20.1	9.1	13.2	11.6	25.9
Services	7.9	9.1	10.9	12.8	7.9
Wholesale and retail trade, restaurants and hotels	7.4	9.3	13.1	13.9	9.4
Transport, storage, and communication	11.7	10.6	16.4	18.4	11.4
Finance and insurance	17.2	10.5	20.3	22.7	12.0
Real estate and business services	3.0	8.3	4.5	10.5	14.2

Source: Ministry of Finance and Economic Planning 2008.

and empower people to participate in their own development programs. Important efforts were made to build peace, security, and reconciliation.

The following sections of this chapter analyze more deeply the dynamics of the Rwandan economy after the genocide, focusing on the role of the Rwandan leadership, because conflicts and development clearly should not be dealt with separately.

Summary of Empirical Studies on Sources of Growth in Rwanda

Two major studies have been conducted on sources of growth in Rwanda. One was conducted by Kene Ezemenari and Kalamogo Coulibaly at the World Bank (Ezemenari and Coulibaly 2006). Another study, titled "Convergence des économies de la CEPGL, cas du Rwanda et du Burundi," was conducted by the author of this chapter (Thomas 2006) and was commissioned by the African Economic Commission The results of these two studies are similar.

Rwanda's growth performance during the 1995–2004 period was significant, as compared to growth during 1980–89. Average annual real GDP per capita grew by over 6 percent during 1995–2004, whereas it averaged 0.1 percent during 1980–89. Rwanda's economic performance was far better than the combined growth rate of all sub-Saharan African[1]

---

1   Angola, Benin, Botswana, Burkina Faso, Burundi, Cameroon, Central African Republic, Chad, Comoros, Republic of Congo, Democratic Republic of Congo, Côte d'Ivoire, Ethiopia, The Gambia, Ghana, Guinea, Guinea-Bissau, Kenya, Lesotho, Liberia, Madagascar, Malawi, Mali, Mauritius, Mozambique, Namibia, Niger, Nigeria, Rwanda, São Tomé and Príncipe, Senegal, Sierra Leone, South Africa, Swaziland, Tanzania, Togo, Uganda, Zambia, and Zimbabwe.

countries, which on average was –1.6 percent during 1995–2003. The key question for Rwanda is how this performance has been realized and how this remarkable growth rate, which is required for sustained poverty reduction, can be sustained.

The economic growth in Rwanda was due mainly to factor accumulation before 1995. Since 1995, both factor accumulation and total factor productivity have contributed to growth. The determinants of growth analysis show that in addition to these factors, human capital, credit to the private sector/GDP, public investment/GDP, share of imports of capital goods/GDP, and official development assistance/GDP positively contributed to GDP growth This growth in GDP contrasts with the outcome of the appreciation of the real effective exchange rate in the late 1980s, as well as the aftermath of the 1994 genocide, which had a dampening effect on GDP growth.

In the two studies, annual real GDP growth was regressed on measures accounting for access to credit, human capital formation, exchange rate reforms, financial conditions, and investment.

The variable *human capital* exerts a large positive effect on economic growth because its estimated coefficient is both positive and significant (elasticity between 0.5 and 0.6). The variable *CREDIT* also has a positive effect on real GDP growth.[2] This suggests that financial reforms led to a financial deepening by making economic resources available throughout the economy. The real effective exchange rate had a negative and statistically significant impact on real GDP growth. The appreciation of the real effective exchange rate in the late 1980s made tradable goods from Rwanda less competitive than those from abroad. The coefficient of public investment over GDP is positive and significant, which suggests that public investment contributes to improving economic growth.

Additionally, capital has a positive significance, which illustrates that capital imports underscore the importance of new capital in incorporating new technology and, in many cases, enabling greater productive efficiency and therefore greater economic growth. In Ezemenari and Coulibaly (2006) the variable tax revenue collected on international trade exerted a positive and significant effect on the GDP growth rate. The positive connection between revenue and economic development suggests that collected revenues may have been directed to more productive projects that led to improvements in economic growth.

The variable official aid, as expected, was positive and significant. Since 1994 most aid that Rwanda has received from the international community has been used, for among other purposes, to build schools, pay teachers, provide school furniture, build hospitals, and purchase computers for workers and students. Such spending on education and health, along with increased training of civil servants, has contributed significantly to productivity growth and therefore greater economic development.

---

2   Broad money (M2) was also tested instead of private sector credit, but the results did not change significantly.

Finally, and predictably, the 1994 dummy variable, measuring the economic effects of the political events at that time, was both negative and significant, indicating a decrease in economic growth.

One of the specificities of the findings presented here is that the openness factor plays a nonnegligible role in the observed GDP growth.

Leadership and Economic Growth in Rwanda

Fourteen years ago, Rwanda was considered a shell of a country, racked by destruction, whose future was in doubt following the 1994 genocide. The entire system was destroyed, from the economy to security and justice systems to infrastructures. However, the condition of the country today has been called "the Rwandan miracle." Rwanda has achieved tremendous progress both politically and economically.

The fundamental causes of this decade of quick development are most likely the following: charismatic leadership, rich and positive ideology, strict political will, and lessons from the genocide and Rwandan history. A leadership is charismatic when it works to serve the general interest, rather than egoistic and selfish interests. Such leadership is always committed to finding durable solutions to community problems. Since its military victory over the forces who carried out the genocide forces, Rwanda Patriotic Front (RPF) leaders have worked to reestablish social harmony and promote sustainable economic development. For these purposes the RPF has created mechanisms, institutions, principles, and practices to serve the country efficiently. The results include the reestablishment of security, economic and social reconstruction, and promotion of the private sector and civil society.

The RPF's ideology is one of victory, an ideology of optimism, hard work, and community empowerment. The core of this ideology is summarized in nine points (Rwanda Patriotic Front 1997, revised 2003), one of which is strong social and economic development. It states that the key to the country's development is "within the Rwandans' hands," and nowhere else. This builds national self-confidence and the will for all Rwandans to own their own future.

This political will of Rwanda's leadership is manifested through the creation of structures, mechanisms, and practices that guarantee the participation of all citizens and transparency in management of public affairs. Reforms are enacted following mass consultative meetings to react efficiently to community problems. Another current mechanism for finding solutions to community problems in Rwanda is decentralization.

Leadership and Economic Growth in Rwanda

The links between peace and economic development are likely to be more evident in Africa than in any other part of the world. Many conflicts are ongoing in Africa at different levels of violence, and the most violent conflicts are correlated to a high level of poverty. Ibrahim A. Gambari (2004) argues that it is no accident that Africa is the most marginalized part of the world undergoing globalization. The continent's share of total world trade has declined from about 4 percent in the 1990s to less than 2 percent at present. Conflict is among the key variables determining such a position in world trade.

There is common understanding that conflicts in Africa are essentially crises of governance. They are violent responses to lack of democracy, freedom and to the politics of exclusion, mismanagement and tyranny by many African governments. Kofi Annan, in his 1998 report, "Causes of Conflict and Promotion of Durable Peace and Sustainable Development in Africa," recognizes that "conflicts and development should not be dealt with separately; rather, they need to be dealt with within a comprehensive framework of governance that addresses the root causes of conflict and sustainable development."

Considering this need for a comprehensive framework of governance, a postconflict country such as Rwanda cannot deal with economic growth separately from conflict resolution and building peace and security. Peace is a precondition for security, stability, and development. The leadership of Rwanda understands that it needs political stability to attract domestic and foreign investors, and it needs peace to implement development plans and growth. In 1997–98 the office of the president of the republic took the initiative to organize discussions about the future of Rwanda. On the basis of the ideas agreed upon at the discussions, the Vision 2020 project was born and further developed to become a high-level vision for the Rwanda's future. One of the key ingredients of this vision is building peace and security to facilitate productive initiatives. This will help realize the main goal of the vision: to transform Rwanda into a modern, strong, and united nation, proud of its fundamental values, politically stable, and without discrimination among its citizens.

In the aftermath of the 1994 genocide, Rwandans have been able to share the vision of peace and to work together without fear of civil crises. The environment of peace obviously has promoted the involvement of Rwandans in productive activities such as agriculture and business. This involvement in productive sectors is an important factor of growth.

After the genocide, national reconciliation has been and continues to be promoted as an official policy, understood as a prerequisite to economic development. Reforms in different areas of the Rwandan society have been realized and can be summarized as follows.

Political and Institutional Reforms

The postgenocide transition has been ended by the implementation of political institutions based on democracy and equity. Rwanda now is headed by an effective government that maintains law and order and demonstrates economic leadership. Mutual support and complementarity among different institutions have been shown to be essential for the attainment of stability and security in the country. The government also has much invested in good governance, and an important administrative reform based on decentralization has been completed. Today administrative services are decentralized to the low levels of sectors, so-called *umurenge*. This has greatly facilitated easy and quick access to public services for all Rwandans, especially those living in rural areas. Easy availability of public services has been shown to be less costly in terms of money and time.

Moreover, in the spirit of institutional development, different institutions have been created to contribute to the process of national reconciliation and socioeconomic growth, among them the following:

The *National Commission for Reconciliation* is a national organization that implements reconciliation mechanisms. This commission has trained Rwandans to participate in personal exchanges, business, and any other socioeconomic activity without discrimination. Its work has proved to be a good way to concentrate the national effort into activities of social and economic interest nationwide.

The *Rwanda Investment and Export Promotion Agency* has significantly contributed to economic growth by putting in place measures and incentives for investment and exports.

The *National Commission to Fight against HIV/AIDS* is a successful organization that tries to protect the Rwandan population through anti-HIV/AIDS programs. It is known that HIV-affected and -infected people are economically less productive or unproductive in the long term, especially in developing countries where methods of care for these people are inefficient. Therefore, fighting HIV/AIDS in Rwanda is, among other purposes, a way for providing and maintaining the workforce for the economy.

The *RWANDA Revenue Authority* has significantly contributed to allocating government revenues to finance public investment budgets.

Many other specialized programs and socioeconomic initiatives to support youth and women have been put in place and are significantly contributing to economic development. Important institutions with the objective of fighting corruption have been created. The Ombudsman deals with the national leader's property (personal wealth), the General Auditor's Office checks the management of public institutions, and the National Tender Board manages public procurement. In Africa, in postconflict situations, disarmament and demobilization programs have often left a power vacuum. There is a tendency to reduce the numbers of the police and the military without paying much attention to the challenges that lie ahead for the already weakened institutions to maintain order and security. The national commission for demobilization has developed a good program for reintegration of former soldiers and police into civil life by providing training and financial support in the implementation of small projects that generate income for the demobilized soldiers.

Judicial Reforms

After the 1994 genocide, the International Criminal Tribunal for Rwanda (ICTR) was created in Arusha, Tanzania, in November 1994 to try those accused of responsibility for the genocide. It targets those who masterminded the genocide and who bear the greatest responsibility for the crimes committed. As of December 2005, the ICTR had completed 26 trials, and cases involving 26 other accused were in progress. In March 2006, eight trials were being run concurrently, and 15 detainees remained in custody awaiting trial. There was optimism that all trials will be completed by the deadline in 2008 and appeals by 2010, but this has not been achieved.

However, individuals accused of "intermediate crimes" are tried in national jurisdictions. More than 100,000 accused persons face justice in Rwandan courts and traditional justice in village assemblies called *gacaca*. This process, whereby witnesses, suspects, and victims give testimony during neighborhood meetings, began in January 2005. Many international observers acknowledge that it is the best, if not the only, alternative. In fact, one of the main objectives of *gacaca* is to make reconciliation possible between victims of genocide and the perpetrators. By enabling Rwandans to live together, it provides incentives to work hand in hand and thus contribute to the socioeconomic development of the country.

The Process of Policy Making: A Way of Sustaining Economic Growth

The policy-making process is defined as the procedure by which policies are discussed, approved, and implemented. It is intended to be a dynamic and interactive process that involves all stakeholders. The process has an important impact on the quality of public policies, including the capacity of a given country to provide a stable policy environment, adapt policies when needed, implement and enforce policies effectively, and ensure that the policies that are adopted are in the public interest.

In Rwanda today the process of policy making is essentially characterized by the elements discussed in the following sections.

The Decentralization Policy as a Structure for the Mobilization of Economic Development Energies

The government of Rwanda adopted the national decentralization policy in May 2000 to achieve three main goals: good governance, pro-poor service delivery, and sustainable socioeconomic development. Through its willingness to succeed, Rwanda has successfully implemented the planned decentralization policies. This policy was developed from nationwide consultative processes aimed at determining the causes of genocide and outlining lasting solutions. Bad governance, extreme poverty, and exclusive political processes have been identified as some of the main underlying causes of the genocide (Ministry of Local Government and Social Affairs 2000). On the basis of these findings, and within the government's long-term Vision 2020 and poverty reduction strategy, the government of

Rwanda designed and adopted an implementation program to put the decentralization policy into practice.

Rwanda's decentralization policy has five specific objectives (Ministry of Local Government and Social Affairs 2000):

To enable and be reactive to local people's participation in initiating, making, implementing, and monitoring decisions and plans that concern them, taking into consideration their local needs, priorities, capacities, and resources by transferring power, authority, and resources from the central government to local government and lower levels.

To strengthen accountability and transparency by making local leaders directly accountable to the communities that they serve and by establishing a clear linkage between the taxes people pay and the services that are financed by these taxes.

To enhance the sensitivity and responsiveness of public administration to the local environment by placing the planning, financing, management, and control of service provision at the point at which services are provided and by enabling local leadership to develop organization structures and capacities that take into consideration the local environment and needs.

To develop sustainable economic planning and management capacity at local levels that will serve as the driving motor for planning, mobilization, and implementation of social, political, and economic development to alleviate poverty.

To enhance effectiveness and efficiency in the planning, monitoring, and delivery of services by reducing the burden on central government officials who are distanced from the point at which needs are felt and services delivered.

In this context, decentralization is taken as an instrument for people's political empowerment, reconciliation, social integration, and well-being. In particular, decentralization in Rwanda is understood as a platform for sustainable democratization and a structured arrangement for mobilization of economic development energies, initiatives, and resources. It is intended to give the power to the people and enable them to execute their will for self-development. In this regard, the following reforms, which can be considered as important ingredients of socioeconomic growth, have been established:

1. Community Development Committees have been created as planning organs answerable to the local population. Some of them have already had their planning capacities developed through training, and they have gone on to develop District Development Plans.
2. Fiscal responsibilities and financial resources have been transferred to decentralized units. The most important element of the fiscal and financial decentralization is the relative autonomy in budgeting and financial management at local levels, which facilitates prioritization of the expenditure needs in situations of inadequate financing.
3. Substantial improvements in the delivery of services have been registered, including local trade, small-scale industries, tourism and environmental protection through the practice of the *Umuganda* (Community Work), cooperatives and associations, local government roads, and others.

These results indicate that the decentralization policy is obviously pro-poor because it promotes small-scale economic activities, including small industries in the poorest areas (rural zones) of the country. Decentralization has also significantly reduced the cost of public services in terms of money, time, and energy. The savings probably are used in more productive activities. Decentralization in Rwanda is then worthy to be considered as an engine for economic growth.

Additionally, to make the decentralization policy more effective, local governments sign performance contracts with the president of the republic. These contracts include details on programs that are achievable within one year, and evaluation is performed every three months. For example, the evaluation done on April 2–3, 2007, indicated that the absorption capacity of districts has significantly increased. Therefore, the next budget revision is expected to allocate 10 percent of the national budget to the Common Development Fund.

Ubudehe: A Way of Improving People's Participation in Their Own Development

To promote and enforce participatory people-centered initiatives, *ubudehe* has been created. *Ubudehe* is the traditional Rwandan practice and cultural value of working together to solve problems (MINECOFIN, Concept Note, 2003).

The literal origins of the word describe the practice of digging up fields before the rains come and the planting season arrives. A group of households join together to dig their fields, acting collectively to share the burden of the work and make sure that everyone is ready for the planting season.

In the present context, the *ubudehe* process in Rwanda is a unique policy of promoting citizens' collective action in partnership with a government committed to decentralization. It is a policy designed to increase institutional problem-solving capacity at the local level by citizens and local governments, and it seeks to put into operation the principles of citizens' participation through local collective action. It also sets out to strengthen democratic processes and governance starting from the people's aspirations, ability, and traditions. As carried out under the Participatory Poverty Assessment, each *umurenge* (neighborhood) is expected to go through a process of collectively defining and analyzing the nature of poverty in its community. The first step is to look at local categories of poverty, the characteristics of each category, mobility between categories, causes and impacts of poverty, and the roles of security, risk and vulnerability, social cohesion, crime and conflict, and social exclusion. The *umurenge* then goes on to identify and analyze the characteristics of the problems that it faces. This list of analyzed problems is then ranked in terms of priority, using pairwise comparison, and the problem on which the community wants to spend the most time, effort, and resources is selected. From there, the people develop an action plan to address the problems that they have prioritized.

After this process, funds are made available to support the identified *ubudehe* collective action. The European Union until now has been the major donor supporting the *ubudehe* process. The flow of these funds can be summarized as follows: Once funds are deposited in the National Bank of Rwanda (NBR), they are released through the Strategic Planning and Poverty Monitoring Department in the Ministry of Finance and Economic Planning (MINECOFIN), which manages these funds and channels the money destined for the actual collective action from the NBR account to the district-level accounts. All cellules (an administrative unit) have set up an account in the Banque Populaire's nearest branch. The money, which is now at the district level, is then transferred to the cellule account.

This framework clearly shows the innovation and the usefulness of the *ubudehe* process as a tool to make Rwandan people at the grassroots level aware of their poverty-related problems and help them address these problems in a participatory way. *Ubudehe* has helped increase understanding of poverty in Rwanda and how it is felt by the people through the Participatory Poverty Assessment process.

Economic Reforms Conducive to Targeted Growth

Rwanda embarked on economic restructuring as a necessary step on a development path that would help rebuild an economy shattered by war and genocide. The instituted reforms emphasized the importance of efficient allocation of resources, transparency, putting an enabling environment in place to promote private investment, obtaining value for money, and accountability, among other themes. These reforms included the following activities.

Privatization of State Enterprises

Because of the effects of the war, many public enterprises were in a weakened state. The government resolved to carry out a privatization program to create a market-oriented economy; increase efficiency and production; provide employment; attract investment, technology, and innovation; reduce costs of production; and, as a result, increase competitiveness. The government decided to concentrate on policy matters while the private sector took over as a business operator. To empower the private sector to take up these challenges and to facilitate a market-oriented economy, legal reforms to deregulate the government from business operations were carried out. In the beginning of the process, there was not much demand for the state enterprises, and the private sector, mainly made up of the local business community, lacked both managerial and financial capacity.

The government revised investment laws to attract business from abroad and encouraged local business operators to team with foreign investors for mutual benefit. In the beginning, foreign investors were very slow to come to Rwanda because it was a postconflict country. However, different economic reforms and the creation of a good business environment have opened up the economy and attracted foreign direct investment in areas such as the construction industry, telecommunications, and the services sector. Consequently, skills have been acquired and employment increased. This in turn has resulted in increased demand for goods and services, stimulating more production and economic growth as a whole.

Reforming the Tax System

To improve government revenues, the tax system was reformed to increase efficiency and effectiveness. An independent tax collection agency was created and a VAT introduced, and the tax base was broadened to include more taxpayers. This reform has met its expectations, with tax revenues increasing each year since 2000. In nine years the revenue to GDP ratio almost doubled, from 7 percent in 1997 to 15.5 percent in 2005.

Despite this economic performance, Rwanda remains dependent on foreign aid, which currently provides resources to fund around 50 percent of the budget. Effective resource management and good governance are among the most important elements that ensure that foreign partners will continue funding the Rwandan government's programs.

An Appropriate Monetary Policy for Rural Sector Challenges

The 1994 genocide destroyed the banking system. Important measures were initiated for rebuilding the system, and the NBR was transformed into an independent institution. This enables the NBR to contribute significantly to controlling inflation and financing the economy. Direct control and orientation of credit was abolished, and the regulation of liquidity based on indirect instruments was established. An appropriate monetary policy reform has been adopted to address rural sector challenges. To provide funds for the agriculture sector in rural areas, Rural Investment Facilities have been put in place in the form of guarantee funds, managed by the NBR. Through this facility framework, the agriculture sector is being progressively financed and enormous socioeconomic effects are being observed. Table 3.2 shows the rural-sector funding through the three main facilities.

These facilities are conceived of as an important way of promoting growth, especially for a country whose economy is mostly based on agriculture. In particular, the facilities have had a positive impact on export production.

Table 3.2. Rural Investment Facilities
(amount in RF)

Facility	2002	2003	2004	2005	Total
Facility 1	—	—	109,370,912	637,430,762	746,801,674
Facility 2	—	—	758,200,000	548,412,000	1,306,612,000
Facility 3	481,546,339	782,329,378	1,265,794,041	1,252,121,409	3,781,791,167
Total	481,546,339	782,329,378	2,133,364,953	2,437,964,171	5,835,204,841

Source: National Bank of Rwanda, Capital and Money Market Department.

Rural Investment Facilities provide short-term credits for agriculture projects and long-term investment credits for rural economic agents. For a given project to be financed, the bank that funds the facility is responsible for economic, financial, and risk analysis. Next, the NBR makes its own analysis before providing the guarantee funds for the project. In collaboration with the commercial bank that deals directly with the rural economic agent in need of funds, a monitoring and evaluation framework is established and agreed on. Every three months, a credit reimbursement report is transmitted to the NBR. An account audit for the credit beneficiary is regularly made to ensure that the received credit has been used according to the credit contract. If it is found that the credit has been misused, the guarantee offered through the Rural Investment Facility is immediately canceled.

Regional Integration and Economic Growth

Rwanda has embraced the New Partnership for Africa's Development (NEPAD). The country is a member of its 15-member Implementation Committee and has also volunteered for the NEPAD African Peer Review Mechanism (APRM). In June 2005 Rwanda, along with Ghana, was one of the first states to submit an APRM report, which demonstrates its willingness to produce a self-critical and consultative evaluation about conditions in the country. Rwanda is also demonstrating economic leadership in Africa's regional institutions. Rwanda is a member of the Common Market for Eastern and Southern Africa, and it has already joined the East African Community (EAC). The regional integration is obviously creating a good environment for sustainable economic growth. Attempts at regional integration are reflecting the desire to deal with the perceived growth-inhibiting problems associated with the structure of Rwandan economy—its small size, its landlocked status, and the country's poor infrastructure. Regional integration is then envisaged as an important engine for high and sustainable economic growth in Rwanda. The integration in the EAC is an especially high interest for the country, because almost 70 percent of Rwandan imports come from East African countries. Trade liberalization is thus very important and should make transactions easy and cheap.

Given the lack of natural resources of Rwanda, the current leadership has adopted more investment in science and technology and in human development so that Rwanda can be competitive and benefit from regional integration, with a goal of transforming Rwanda into a knowledge-based economy. The eventual target that is under consideration is to produce 50 trained engineers and scientists per 10,000 population. This planning process is summarized in table 3.3.

Similar targets were defined in terms of qualified doctors and health professionals. The eventual target under consideration is for 10 trained doctors and 20 trained nursing professionals per 10,000 population. This will require additional investment in the development of courses and facilities to increase the training capacity in Rwanda.

Table 3.3. Development of Professionally Qualified Rwandan Scientists and Engineers

Institute	Average Number Studying Science and Technology[a]	Average Yearly Output Degrees and Diplomas	Total Degrees and Diplomas over 15 Years[a]	Enrollment Growth at 3%	Taking into Consideration KIST Rapid Expansion Plans
Kigali Institute of Science and Technology (KIST)	2,000	500	5,625	9,300	19,188
National University of Rwanda	1,300	325	4,875	6,044	6,044
Institut Supérieur d'Agriculture et d'Elevage	1,000	250	3,750	4,650	4,650
Kigali Institute of Education	1,000	250	3,750	4,650	4,650
Total	—	1,200	18,000	24,643	34,532
S-T trust fund	—	—	5,000	5,000	5,000
Revised total	—	—	23,000	29,644	39,532
Engineers and scientists per 10,000 in 2020	—	—	19	24	32

Sources: Murenzi and Hughes 2006, Rwandan Ministry in the President's Office in Charge of Science and Scientific Research, 2006
— Not available.
a. Estimated.

Conclusion

This chapter has analyzed the role of the Rwandan political leadership and the process of policy making in sustaining economic growth, indicating the extent to which public policies and several reforms have sustained economic growth.

The 1994 genocide has had deep consequences for Rwanda's social, political, and economic structures. In its willingness to promote socioeconomic development, the country's leadership is convinced that reconciliation, political stability, and security constitute a good environment for economic growth. In this regard, the main goal of the current leadership is the transformation of Rwanda into a modern, strong, and united nation, proud of its fundamental values and politically stable. Over the last 13 years, the government of Rwanda has invested enormous efforts into rebuilding the national peace and reconciliation process, which is considered a prerequisite to any economic development.

Rwanda's process of policy making has its own foundations and orientations that make it country specific. In effect, the process of policy making in Rwanda is a dynamic and interactive game that involves all stakeholders. The government of Rwanda adopted the national decentralization policy in May 2000 to achieve three main goals: good governance, pro-poor service delivery, and sustainable socioeconomic development. This policy was developed from a nationwide consultative processes aimed at determining the causes of genocide and outlining lasting solutions. In this context, decentralization is taken as an instrument for people's political empowerment, reconciliation, social integration, and well-being. In particular, decentralization in Rwanda is understood as a platform for sustainable democratization and a structure for mobilization of economic development energies, initiatives, and resources. Decentralization is currently giving the power to the people and enabling them to execute their will for self-development.

To reinforce decentralization and self-development, the *ubudehe* process was established in Rwanda. This is a unique policy of promoting citizens' collective action in partnership with a government committed to decentralization. It is a policy designed to increase the level of institutional problem-solving capacity at the local level by citizens and local governments. It has succeeded in putting into operation the principles of citizens' participation through local collective action.

To increase accountability and make the decentralization policy more effective, a strategy of local governments signing performance contracts with the president of the republic has been adopted. These contracts include details on the programs that are achievable within one year. Evaluations are performed every three months, which allows institutions to plan their activities and establish quantifiable indicators for evaluation.

The above public policies are enacting the willingness of the government to make Rwanda a middle-income country by 2020. Since 1994 Rwanda has attained impressive achievements following the turbulent war and genocide and since that time has been on a path of economic development and poverty reduction of its citizens. Recently attained economic performance and social and political achievements are strongly linked to a charismatic leadership that invests in the development of all Rwandans.

References

Adedeji, Adebayo. 2003. "Countries Emerging from Conflict: Lessons on Partnership in Post Conflict Reconstruction, Rehabilitation and Reintegration." Committee on Human Development and Civil Society, Addis Ababa.

Annan, Kofi. 1998. "Causes of Conflict and Promotion of Durable Peace and Sustainable Development in Africa." Report A/52/871-S/1998/318. United Nations, New York.

Ezemenari, Kene, and Kalamogo Coulibaly. 2006. "Sources of Growth in Rwanda: Four Different Complementary Approaches." Background paper to the Rwanda Country Economic Memorandum. World Bank, Washington, DC.

———. 2008. "Productivity Growth and Economic Reform: Evidence from Rwanda." World Bank policy working paper, No. 4552, World Bank, Washington, DC.

Gambari, Ibrahim A. 2004. "Conflict Prevention, Conflict Transformation and Economic Growth in Africa: Role and Contribution of Africa Diaspora." Peace Research Group and City College, New York.

MINECOFIN (Ministry of Finance and Economic Planning). 2000. *Rwanda Vision 2020*. Kigali: MINECOFIN.

———. 2003. "Ubudehe mu kurwanya ubukene." Concept Note. MINECOFIN, Kigali.

Ministry of Local Government and Social Affairs. 2000. National Decentralization Policy. May. Kigali.

Murenzi, Romain, and M. Hughes. 2006. "Building a Prosperous Global Knowledge Economy in Rwanda: Rwanda as a Case Study." *International Journal of Technology and Globalization* 2 (3–4): 254–69.

National Bank of Rwanda. Annual Reports 2002, 2003, 2004, 2005. Kigali.

Rusuhuzwa Kigabo, Thomas. 2006. "Convergence des économies CEPGL: cas du Rwanda et Burundi." Commission Economique pour l'Afrique.

Rwanda Patriotic Front (RPF). 1997, rev. 2003. Eight point political program of RPF. Originally published 1997. Kigali.

Rwandan Ministry in the President's Office in Charge of Science and Scientific Research. 2006. "Policy on Science, Technology and Innovation." Kigali.

Taylor, John B. 2003. "Economic Leadership in Brazil and United States." Under Secretary of Treasury for International Affairs. Remarks before the Brazil-U.S. Business Council, January 27, Washington, DC.

World Bank. 1997. *The State in a Changing World*. World Development Report. Washington, DC: World Bank.

CHAPTER 4

Perspectives on Growth:
A Political-Economy Framework—
Lessons from the Singapore Experience

Tan Yin Ying, Alvin Eng, and Edward Robinson

Until the 1970s, traditional neoclassical growth models emphasized differences in factor accumulation to explain differences in income per capita across countries. These models found factors such as saving rates (Solow 1956), preferences (Cass 1965; Koopmans 1965), or other exogenous parameters, such as total factor productivity growth, to be important. More recent strands of growth theory, following Romer (1986) and Lucas (1988), are similar in this approach but endogenize steady-state growth and technical progress.

Throughout the 1990s, it became increasingly evident that factor accumulation alone was insufficient for sustained growth. The growth experience of many countries in the 1990s and numerous extensive cross-country regressions provided evidence that good policies and sound institutions play an equally, if not more, important role in building and sustaining the momentum for growth. Although a consensus has yet to be reached on the impact that policies and institutions have on growth, a far greater amount of attention has been paid in an attempt to understand their roles in the growth story.

This chapter attempts to match a country's growth performance to a set of qualitative variables, with particular emphasis on political-economy variables covering institutions and geography. This discussion draws extensively on data from Penn World Table 6.2 (PWT6.2; Heston, Summers, and Aten 2006) to create a comparable database of growth performance for countries across the time period 1960 to 2003. Appendix 1 elaborates on the methodology used to sample PWT6.2.

The Global Growth Experience since 1960

An examination of the data dating back to 1960 brings forward interesting observations on the global growth experience. Notably, the median chain-weighted purchasing power parity (PPP)–adjusted per capita gross domestic product (GDP; henceforth real per capita GDP) of countries has increased steadily over the years, rising from $2,463 in 1960 to $6,025 in 2003 (figure 4.1a). The income gap between countries has also widened considerably, especially over the last decade or so. This can be seen from the increased income range, which was measured as the difference between the real per capita GDP of the wealthiest and poorest country (figure 4.1b). What this clearly shows is that the growth process over the last 43 years has benefited some countries more than others, and that this differential has persisted, contrary to theoretical predictions of (absolute) growth convergence models.

Following Durlauf, Johnson, and Temple (2005), this discussion next examines the global distribution of income at 10-year intervals from 1960 to

Figure 4.1a. Real per Capita GDP (1960–2000)

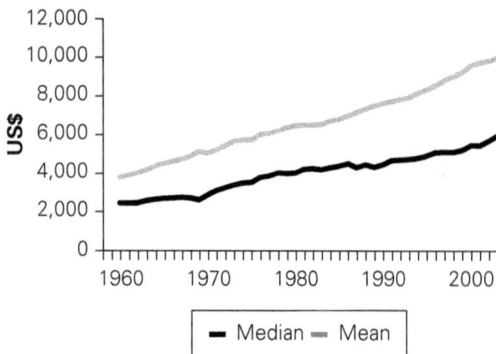

Figure 4.1b. Range of Real per Capita GDP (1960–2000)

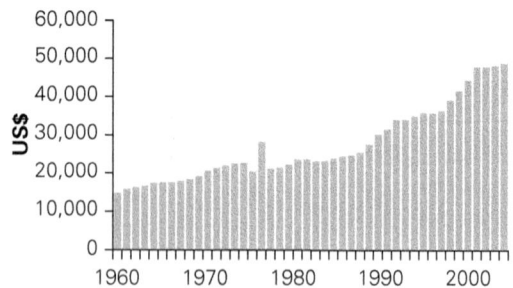

- Median - Mean

Sources: Heston, Summers, and Aten 2006; authors' calculations.
Note: Data are denominated in international PPP-dollars. This is equivalent to the purchasing power of a U.S. dollar in a given year.

2000 using kernel density plots. Figure 4.2 shows the estimated distribution functions for GDP per capita growth across countries, with the rightward shift reflecting the growth that has taken place since 1960. Noticeably, the distribution has become more "normal" (less peaked), suggesting a broadening of growth to more countries over the years. Nonetheless, the rightward shift of the "second peak" in the distribution across the time period corroborates our earlier observation that the income gap across countries has increased over time.

Figure 4.3 provides yet another perspective by showing the distribution of real per capita GDP relative to the benchmark, which here is taken to be the country with the highest real per capita GDP at each period. The rightward shift and normalizing of the distributions over the period 1970–90 suggests that growth had indeed broadened to many countries, even when compared against the benchmark that proxies for the economic "possibility frontier." However, perhaps because of the series of shocks in the late 1990s, the distribution in 2000 has reverted back to the distribution in 1960, albeit with a more pronounced "second peak." In other words, most countries have actually become worse off relative to the wealthiest country in 2000, with the emergence of a middle-income group of countries following the recent bout of shocks to the global economy.

The evolution of the distribution of global income reflects widely divergent growth performances over the years. To identify the countries that have done exceptionally well and those that have performed badly, the countries have been ranked by their compounded annual growth rates

Figure 4.2. Kernel Density Plot of Global Income Distribution (in international dollars)

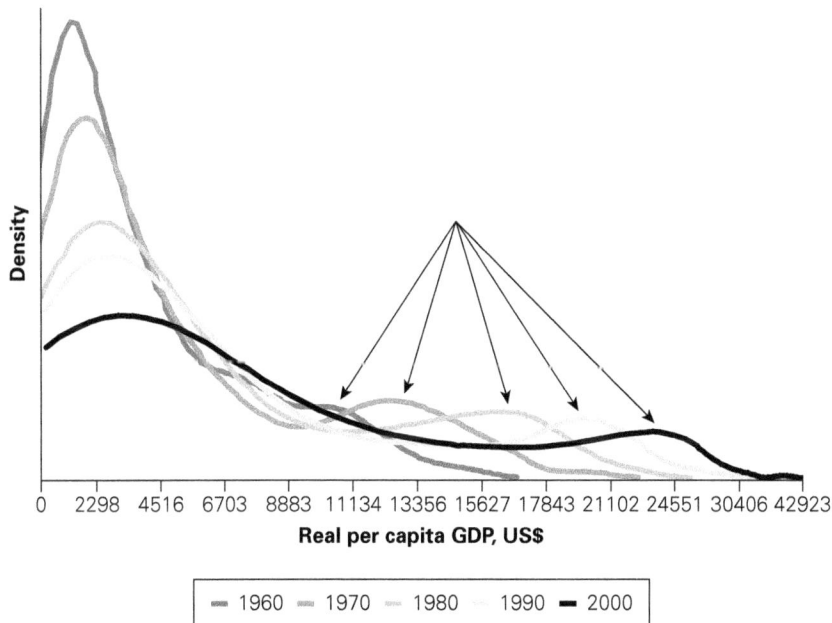

Source: Authors' estimates.

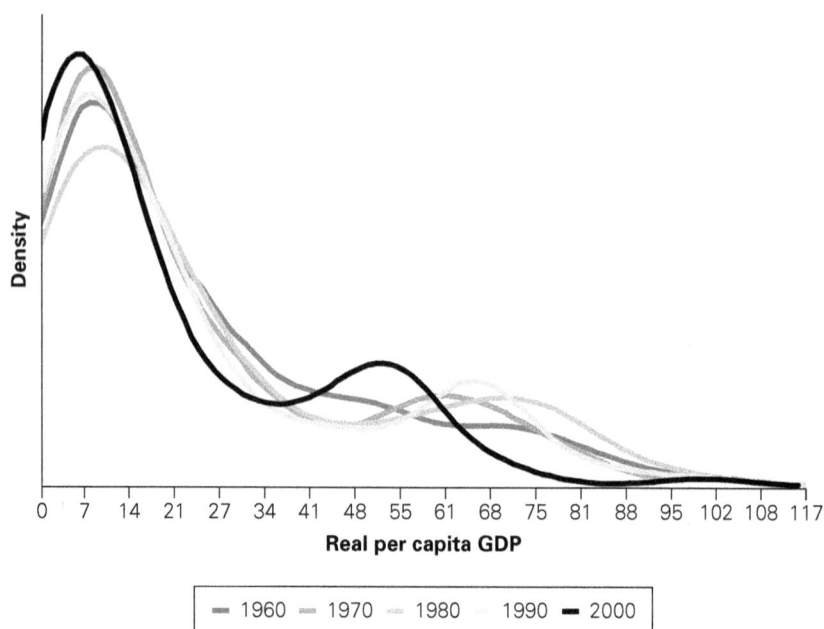

Figure 4.3. Kernel Density Plot of Global Income Distribution
(relative to benchmark country)

— 1960   — 1970   — 1980   1990   — 2000

Source: Authors' estimates.

(CAGR) of real per capita GDP over the period 1960–2003, and then the 10
best and 10 worst performers selected. For completeness, the average year-
on-year (YOY) changes and the coefficient of variation[1] over the period are
also shown (see tables 4.1 and 4.2).

1   The coefficient of variation is measured as the dispersion of YOY growth around the mean.

Table 4.1. Ten Growth Successes, 1960–2003
(real per capita GDP)

Growth Successes	CAGR %	Average YOY%	Coefficient of Variation
Taiwan, China	6.29	6.34	0.50
Botswana	6.03	6.20	0.99
Korea, Rep. of	6.02	6.05	0.69
Equatorial Guinea	5.96	8.18	3.07
China	5.75	5.92	0.97
Hong Kong, China	5.05	5.17	0.96
Thailand	4.58	4.65	0.81
Malaysia	4.54	4.60	0.78
Singapore	4.41	4.52	1.04
Cyprus	4.34	4.57	1.50
Average (growth successes)	**5.29**	**5.62**	**1.13**
World average	**1.65**	**2.08**	**3.14**

Source: Authors' estimates.
Note: Coefficient of variation is computed as the ratio of standard deviation of YOY percentage growth to average YOY percent
growth across economies from 1960 to 2003.

Table 4.2. Ten Growth Laggards, 1960–2003 (real per capita GDP)

Growth Laggards	CAGR %	Average YOY%	Coefficient of Variation
Congo, Dem. Rep. of	–3.47	–3.07	–2.98
Sierra Leone	–1.86	–1.72	–3.11
Madagascar	–1.19	–1.12	–3.24
Niger	–0.78	–0.57	–11.40
Central African Republic	–0.74	–0.55	–11.37
Nicaragua	–0.61	–0.46	–11.87
Chad	–0.59	–0.25	–33.53
Senegal	–0.54	–0.43	–11.33
Jordan	–0.24	–0.01	–491.07
Guinea	–0.14	–0.05	–80.23
Average (growth laggards)	**–1.02**	**–0.82**	**–66.01**
World average	**1.65**	**2.08**	**3.14**

Source: Authors' estimates.
Note: Coefficient of variation is computed as the ratio of standard deviation of YOY percentage growth to average YOY percentage growth across countries from 1960 to 2003.

Growth Successes and Laggards

Of the 10 growth success stories, seven have come from Asia (East and Southeast Asia), and sub-Saharan African economies dominate the list of growth laggards. The success stories' record is particularly impressive, with each one attaining growth rates nearly three times that of the world average. Landlocked Botswana, with a population of only slightly over 1.6 million, is one of two African countries in the list of top performers. Not only have the top performing countries grown at a significantly faster pace than the growth laggards, they have also done so with far greater consistency, as seen from their markedly lower coefficients of variation. Again, the Asian economies and Botswana stand out, with coefficients of variation lower than the average of that for growth successes. In contrast, growth is far more volatile in the growth laggard countries and in Equatorial Guinea. The latter, for example, has seen fast but volatile growth, its fortunes rising with the discovery of crude oil, which forms the bulk of its export earnings.[2]

If asked in 1980 which countries would do well in the next 20 years, an observer would almost certainly have, with the benefit of hindsight, fallen into the trap of identifying future winners by extrapolating past growth trends in 1960–80. Countries such as Ecuador or Paraguay, which enjoyed strong growth over 1960–80, might have been identified only to find them falling into a deep recession in the subsequent years. Table 4.3 lists the economies in

---

2 See United Nations (2005). Between 2002 and 2003, Equatorial Guinea exported $1.2 billion worth of crude petroleum, equivalent to 89.7 percent of total exports. Exports increased rapidly after the discovery of crude oil in the 1990s, rising to $1.3 billion between 2002 and 2003. In contrast, the economy's exports totaled $26.1 million between 1982 and 1983, when Equatorial Guinea exported no crude oil (data for 1982–83 from United Nations 1986).

Table 4.3. Average Growth (YOY %) over 1960–80 and 1981–2003

	G2 ≤ 0	0 < G2 ≤ 1.5	1.5 < G2 ≤ 3	G2 > 3
G1 ≤ 0	Central African Republic Congo, Dem. Rep. of Madagascar	Guinea Namibia Nigeria Senegal Togo	Chad Mali Uganda	Dominica São Tomé and Príncipe
0 < G1 ≤ 1.5	Bolivia Jordan Kenya Nicaragua Niger Sierra Leone	Benin Cameroon Gambia, The Jamaica	Algeria Bangladesh Burkina Faso Ethiopia Guinea-Bissau Nepal New Zealand Rwanda Tanzania	
1.5 < G1 ≤ 3	Burundi Comoros Côte d'Ivoire Guatemala Peru Venezuela, R. B. de Zambia Zimbabwe	Argentina Colombia Costa Rica El Salvador Honduras Iran, Islamic Rep. of Madagascar Mozambique Philippines South Africa Switzerland Uruguay	Australia Canada Chile Denmark Egypt, Arab Rep. of Germany Netherlands St. Lucia Sweden Turkey United Kingdom United States	Cape Verde China India Luxembourg Mauritius St. Kitts and Nevis St. Vincent
G1 > 3	Congo, Rep. of Ecuador Gabon Haiti Paraguay	Barbados Brazil Fiji Ghana Greece Mexico Morocco Papua New Guinea Romania Syrian Arab Rep.	Austria Belgium Dominican Republic Finland France Grenada Hungary Iceland Indonesia Israel Italy Japan Lesotho Norway Pakistan Panama Poland Portugal Spain Trinidad and Tobago Tunisia	Botswana Cyprus Equatorial Guinea Hong Kong, China Ireland Korea, Rep. of Malaysia Maldives Singapore Sri Lanka Taiwan, China Thailand

Source: Authors' estimates.
Note: Only economies with 10 or more observations in both periods are included.

Figure 4.4. Scatter Plot of Average Growth (YOY %), 1960–80 against 1981–2003

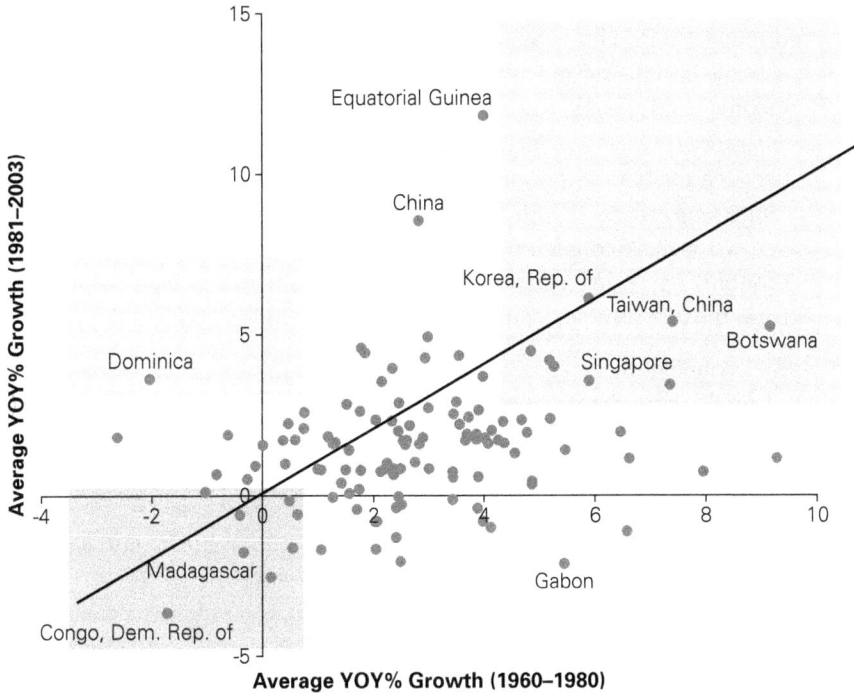

Average YOY% Growth (1960–1980)

Source: Authors' estimates.

Note: Economies in the upper-right (gray) area were the consistently high performers that achieved 80th percentile growth rate (or greater) in both periods. Economies in the lower-left (dark pink) area were the consistent underperformers that achieved 20th percentile growth rate (or lower) in both periods. Economies in the upper-left (light pink) area were the late achievers that registered 20th percentile growth rates in G1 but 80th percentile growth rates in G2.

various categories, classified by their average YOY growth rates of real per capita GDP in 1960–80 (G1) and in 1981–2003 (G2).

Clearly, past growth does not necessarily translate to future growth, although resources and institutions inherited from past growth do appear to feed into an economy's endowment in the next cycle. For example, it appears that economies that do not do well in G1 tend not to do as well in G2, with Dominica and São Tomé and Príncipe being the most notable exceptions. In comparison, economies that did well in G1 have by and large managed to maintain positive, albeit lower, growth in G2, as figure 4.4 illustrates.

Divergence in Growth Experiences

To attain finer granularity, it has been found to be useful to group the economies into three income bands: the top 50th percentile, the second quartile (the 25th to 50th percentile range), and those in the bottom quartile, according to their levels of real per capita GDP at five-year intervals over the period 1960–2003. Then the economies were classified into three broad categories based on their income trajectories:

1. *Advancers*—Economies that rose from one income band into a higher one for three consecutive observations or more, without slipping back to their original band. This would include an economy rising from the bottom quartile into the second, or one rising into the top 50th percentile from the income bands below.
2. *Average Performers*—Economies that remained in the income band between the bottom quartile and the 50th percentile.
3. *Underperformers*—Economies that fell from an income band into the ones below for three consecutive observations or more. This would include an economy regressing into the lowest quartile from the second, or one falling from the top 50th percentile into the income bands below.

By grouping these economies this way, those that have been ranked consistently above the 50th percentile ("developed" economies) have effectively been filtered out, as well as those that have persistently remained below the 25th percentile ("developing" economies). This leaves a set of 42 "developing" economies, categorized in the three groups according to table 4.4.

As is to be expected, a strong mapping of economies is seen from table 4.4 across to table 4.3, because the growth performance of economies over the years would directly impact their ranking within the band. The underperformers in table 4.4 are clustered around the top left-hand cells of table 4.3, whereas most advancers in table 4.4 are found in the bottom right-hand cells of table 4.3. Notably, most of the advancers have already moved into the top 50th percentile; the only exceptions are China (47th percentile), Sri Lanka (39th percentile), Indonesia (38th percentile), and India (32nd percentile). Given their growth momentum, it would not be surprising for China and India to rise into the top band within the next decade or so.

Table 4.4. Categorization of Economies Based on Income Trajectories

Advancers	Average Performers	Underperformers
Botswana	Bolivia	El Salvador
China	Cameroon	Fiji
Dominican Republic	Cape Verde	Guatemala
India	Comoros	Jamaica
Korea, Rep. of	Côte d'Ivoire	Jordan
Malaysia	Ecuador	Madagascar
Pakistan	Egypt, Arab Rep. of	Namibia
Romania	Grenada	Nicaragua
Sri Lanka	Guinea	Paraguay
St. Lucia	Haiti	Peru
St. Vincent	Honduras	Senegal
Taiwan, China	Indonesia	
Thailand	Morocco	
	Papua New Guinea	
	Philippines	
	Syrian Arab Rep.	
	Turkey	
	Zimbabwe	

Source: The economies are drawn from a sample of 118 from Heston, Summers, and Aten 2006.

Nearly all the growth advancers listed in table 4.4 also appear in our list of growth successes compiled in table 4.1. Hong Kong, China, and Singapore are two of the most glaring growth successes omitted from the advancers category. This is an artifact following the transition to PWT6.2 from PWT6.1. PWT6.2 omits data for 12 countries in 1960 as compared to PWT6.1. With seven out of 12 of these countries previously having higher incomes than Singapore, their omission under PWT6.2 boosts Singapore's relative ranking above the sample's 50th percentile. Hong Kong, China's classification reflects similar factors in the transition. Consequently, where both economies in 1960 were marginally below the 50th percentile under PWT6.1, they are now above the 50th percentile under PWT6.2. Having consistently remained above the 50th percentile throughout the sample period, they do not fit our definition of growth advancers and are thus not reflected in table 4.4.

A Conceptual Political-Economy Framework

The previous section documented the widely divergent trends in the global growth experience. In line with the evolution of growth and development economics, thinking about economic growth processes might be best done via an empirical, a posteriori framework induced from actual growth experiences. Singapore has seen strong economic performance over the last four decades since gaining independence as a sovereign state, and the conceptual framework that follows draws on insights from Senior Minister Goh Chok Tong, who served as prime minister of Singapore from 1990 to 2004. This framework of analysis will identify "necessary conditions of growth" under a few broad categories and will be applied in the analysis of the sample of countries in table 4.4. This will allow us to identify and highlight commonalities for each category of countries.

The three pillars in this conceptual framework (see figure 4.5) are as follows:

1. *Resources, which take the form of the following:*

   a) Natural endowment, or a country's geographical positioning, its land area, its natural resources, and its people. For example, Singapore's only natural resource was its superior geographical location and a natural deep sea harbor, which made it an ideal trading post for the British en route to China and India. The British experiment in growing agricultural crops floundered because Singapore's soil proved unsuitable. This contrasts with neighboring Malaysia, where rubber was successfully cultivated. Malaysia also had ample tin reserves and was once the world's largest producer of tin.

   b) Inheritance, or the institutions of bureaucracy and government, and the political and legal systems in a country. These are artifacts of history, handed down from previous generations, whether through monarchic rule or the outcome of revolutions and colonialism.

Figure 4.5. The Economic Growth Cycle

- Inheritance—institutions and systems
- Endowment—geography, natural resources, and people
- Accumulation—resources built up through sustained growth

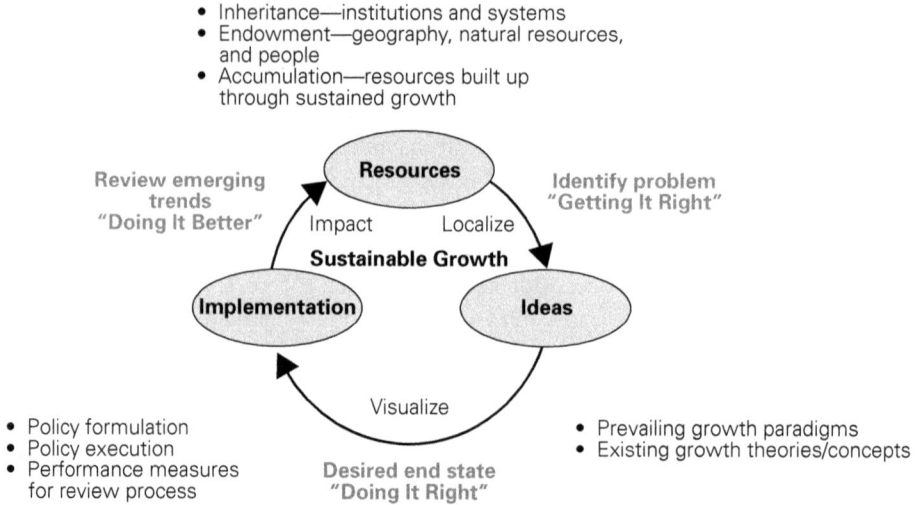

Review emerging trends "Doing It Better"

Resources

Identify problem "Getting It Right"

Impact   Localize

Sustainable Growth

Implementation   **Ideas**

Visualize

- Policy formulation
- Policy execution
- Performance measures for review process

Desired end state "Doing It Right"

- Prevailing growth paradigms
- Existing growth theories/concepts

Institutions	Leadership	People
• Effective administration • Independent judiciary • Responsible press • Vibrant private sector • Effective civil service • Responsible legislature • Good governance	• Selflessly devoted to national interests and not pursuit of party/individual interests • Visionary, competent, and diligent • Integrity, honesty, and incorruptibility • Able to mobilize people • Work through politics of convergence not divergence • Good leadership does not preempt a particular political system	• Common purpose and destiny • Supportive of leadership and government • Social cohesion among different groups • Entrenched stake in country

Source: Authors.

c) Accumulation, or the cyclical process that affects an economy's stock of resources. Economic growth, changes in government, or natural disasters all affect a country's stock of endowed or inherited resources. Resources accumulated from successful growth will feed into a country's inheritance in the next cycle, whereas shocks may deplete a country's endowment or destroy its inherited resources.

Resource availability will condition the growth paradigms that can be usefully applied to any economy. However, some caveats are necessary. First, the initial resource endowment of a country is not necessarily reflective of its future developmental potential. Although natural endowments may be less susceptible to change, inherited resources can change, and sometimes fairly quickly. Countries are thus, at times, able to make up for a shortfall in natural endowments by building on their inherited resources, such as reforming their institutions. When robust institutions are in place, they become valuable inherited resources that reduce the constraints on future growth. Similarly, countries with rich natural endowments could have very poor inherited resources, and losses on the latter may outweigh gains arising from the former. Second, being resource rich reduces the constraints to economic activity but does not create growth per se. The pragmatic assessment of growth paradigms, alongside an economy's resources and constraints, will enable the creation of good, tailored policies to boost growth, with more options available to economies that are richer in resources.

2. *Ideas, or the prevailing growth paradigms/concepts of the day.* Ideas cover a wide spectrum ranging from desired outcomes (such as growth as economic progress or a broader definition to include measures of well-being) and desired paths (such as Marxist dialectic or capital accumulation) to requisite preconditions (such as trade liberalization or quality of institutions). Ideas are fluid and varied, and there is thus no single yellow brick road to prosperity. A paradigm that is fashionable in one decade falls out of favor in the next, and may yet be resurrected in a third.

   Experience has also demonstrated that a wholesale application of ideas to an economy is no recipe for growth. The idea needs to be applied to its local context. A pragmatic assessment of the resources, constraints, and other structural peculiarities associated with the domestic economy is thus necessary for any growth practitioner seeking to understand how certain growth paradigms may actually work out in an economy.

3. *Implementation or formulating the right policies and effectively executing them.* The review channel then allows for feedback as to whether policies were correctly crafted and well implemented. Policy makers must constantly review the policy phase using appropriate performance indicators to determine (a) whether the idea has worked in the local context, (b) whether and how implementation and formulation could be improved, or more fundamentally, (c) whether one should rethink the original growth paradigm in light of possible changes in the operating environment.

Policy review is important, because sustained growth is often the result of persistent fine-tuning of policies. The discipline accorded by financial markets can sometimes be a useful yardstick for policy review, where international market response is positive. For example, this could manifest through foreign investors' willingness to invest or the successful export of a country's output; efforts can then be directed to refining policies along this track.

In a setup in which institutions are meant to enhance, not undermine, each other, and in which politics is convergent and not divergent, this review process, through honest self-reflection against clearly defined benchmarks, provides necessary checks and balances.

The successful implementation of policies depends, among other things, on the following:

1. *Robust institutions.* These include an effective administration and civil service, responsible legislature, independent judiciary, a vibrant private sector, and a responsible press. The underlying value entrenching these institutions is a commitment to good governance, which ensures that a

country's institutions remain effective and impartial, are devoted to the formulation and implementation of pragmatic and focused growth policies, and are not distracted by motives for self-enrichment or extraction of a country's resources and assets. These institutions are also responsible and serve to enhance, not undermine, each other's operations.

2. *Good leadership.* Such leaders are visionary and diligent, selflessly devoted to national, not party or individual, interests. For credibility, leaders must have integrity, be incorruptible (or have the incentives to remain so), and be honest. These leaders contribute to successful policy implementation by their ability to envision the road ahead, to mobilize the people, and to build consensus for their policies through a politics of convergence, not divergence.

3. *People consensus.* Sustained growth often requires trading short-term pain for long-term gain. The end point of growth and development— the well-being of a nation's people—will thus be meaningful only to a people united on the purpose and destiny of their country and who have an entrenched stake in the country. Policies that purport to bring about this end must have the consensus of the population; the people can then be supportive of the leadership and government, even when sacrifices are called for. Social cohesion is key: growth policies should not be divisive or benefit one group to the detriment of another, in line with the politics of convergence practiced by the government. In the absence of people consensus, social strife or political instability may render unfruitful even the most determined efforts to implement growth policies.

The three key elements of robust institutions, good leaders, and people consensus—the "horizontals"—interact with each other and have critical roles to play at each stage of the development path, from the inception of ideas, to efficient use of resources, to formulation of growth policies and their implementation and review.

Resources, ideas, and implementation form a self-reinforcing growth cycle. Policy makers who are able to accurately pin down the interactions between the three could thus generate sustained growth, which in turn boosts a country's resources, strengthens its institutions, and bolsters popular support for its leaders. Yet these same dynamics could be reinforced in a negative spiral, where the foundations for growth are repeatedly undermined. This makes poor growth outcomes more likely.

Singapore's experience may be rather unique, given its circumstances. The country's small size allows policy to be highly targeted and makes policy execution, coordination, and implementation somewhat easier. Yet, as the framework above illustrates, its development experience can have wider application for analyzing and promoting the growth of a small region, if not of a bigger country. Singapore has learned that resources and ideas are only necessary conditions, which are in and of themselves not sufficient to ensure sustained growth. Holistic implementation is key: there is no point in having first-class strategies and policies with third-class execution.

Singapore's Development Experience

The conceptual political-economy framework in the previous section was induced a posteriori from Singapore's own development experience. Singapore has grown 4.4 percent per year on a compounded annual basis over the last 40 years. Real per capita GDP has risen sharply, reaching $29,404 in 2003 from $4,219 in 1960. This is no coincidence: although Singapore lacked natural resources and had only its geography by way of natural endowment, it also inherited British-style institutions such as a civil service, which were built upon. Singapore's leaders adopted policies that entrenched Singaporeans' stake in the country and strove to bridge ethnic divisions with a shared vision of prosperity for all citizens.

The rest of this section applies the framework to interpret Singapore's history, examining five distinct phases in its development. Each phase starts with the laying out of the domestic and external economic contexts for that period before discussing the factors that underpin growth—resources, institutions, leadership, and social consensus—in turn.

First Phase: Import Substitution and Merger with Malaysia (1959–65) (Figure 4.6)

Newly independent, Singapore found itself saddled with a poorly educated population suffering from severe poverty and chronic unemployment. The country had little by way of resources, aside from its natural harbor and its reputation and role as a major entrepôt trade center for Asia. However, it had inherited the British legal system with entrenched rule of law, as well as a bureaucracy operating on the principles of meritocracy and incorruptibility. The country faced a challenging operating environment: Singapore's traditional economic activities—entrepôt trade and related supporting services and processing industries—were declining as direct trade routes between Southeast Asia and developed world markets opened up. A rising communist swell played on interracial tensions and

Figure 4.6. First Phase—Import Substitution and Merger with Malaysia (1959–65)

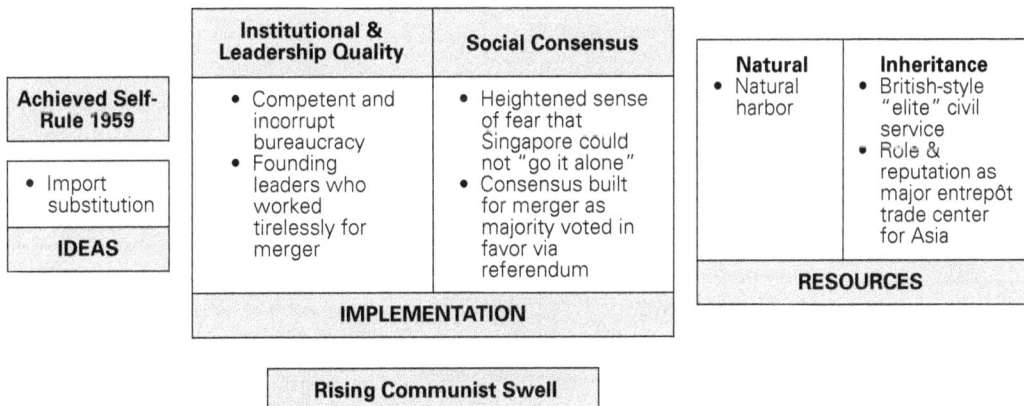

Achieved Self-Rule 1959	Institutional & Leadership Quality	Social Consensus	Natural	Inheritance
	• Competent and incorrupt bureaucracy • Founding leaders who worked tirelessly for merger	• Heightened sense of fear that Singapore could not "go it alone" • Consensus built for merger as majority voted in favor via referendum	• Natural harbor	• British-style "elite" civil service • Role & reputation as major entrepôt trade center for Asia
• Import substitution				
IDEAS			**RESOURCES**	
	IMPLEMENTATION			
	Rising Communist Swell			

threatened institutional stability. The business environment deteriorated as a consequence.

Neocolonial ideas of growth were percolating in the developing world, and chief among these was the import substitution paradigm. Similarly influenced, Singapore's social democratic government looked to create its own industrial base through import substitution. In adopting this paradigm, the country's leaders were aware that Singapore lacked natural resources, a sufficiently large domestic market, and a skilled workforce. They thus looked toward a common market with Malaysia that would be far larger than the country's small population of two million people. In addition, the government drew up a host of complementing policies such as tariffs on imports and a five-year education plan to boost math, science, and technical skills to support industrial development.

Implementing import substitution required building up existing institutions, as well as vigorous efforts by Singapore's leaders to drive the merger with Malaysia. The government created a scholarship system, which channeled its best and brightest into the civil service. The country's leaders led by Prime Minister Lee Kuan Yew were pragmatic and understood that industrialization would not happen simply because of a single policy decision, but would require a host of supporting measures. Social support for the merger was also strong, heightened by a sense of fear that Singapore could not "go it alone."

A majority of the people voted for a merger via popular referendum. Nonetheless, the economic opportunities that Singapore had expected from the merger with Malaysia failed to materialize, and indeed, the introduction of an additional layer of bureaucracy from Kuala Lumpur did not help the investment climate. Growth was erratic—after a recession in 1959, GDP growth rebounded but was highly volatile, ranging from 4 percent to 14 percent in alternate years.[3]

Second Phase: From Import Substitution to Export-Oriented Growth (1966–73) (Figure 4.7)

Singapore's brief union with Malaysia ended in 1965. With separation, the common market could not be realized, rendering import substitution unviable. The urgent need to create jobs in the economy was heightened with the impending closure of the British military base on the island, which would affect up to 70,000 jobs and bring a fifth of economic activity to a halt.

Industrialization could succeed only if Singapore tapped external markets that it had no privileged access to. Export orientation thus became the logical choice of growth paradigm, because firms could manufacture goods and create jobs for a market far larger than what domestic consumption alone could sustain. To this end, the government abolished tariffs, reduced import quotas, and passed a host of supporting policies, such as the 1967 Economic Expansion Incentives Act, which sharply reduced corporate tax

---

3 Based on GDP levels in pound sterling (Lee 1974).

Figure 4.7. Second Phase—From Import Substitution to Export-Oriented Growth (1966–73)

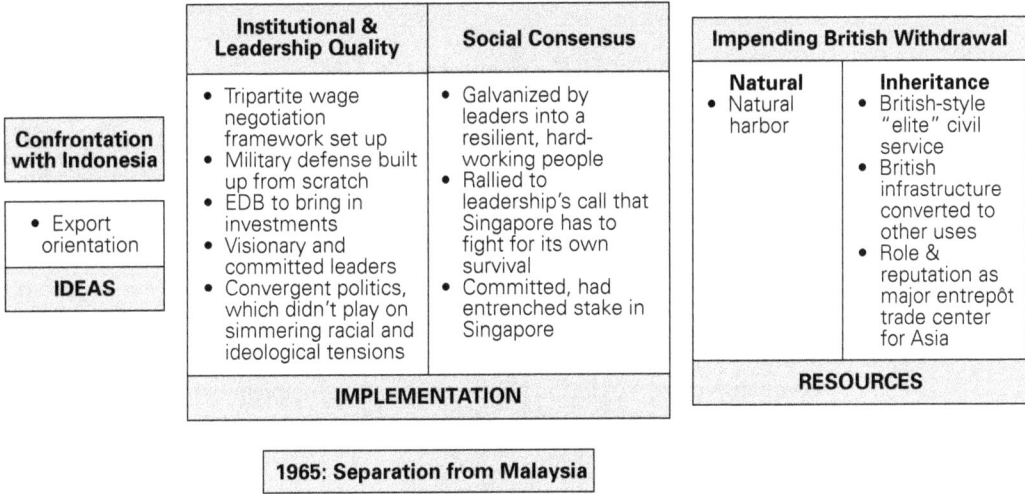

Institutional & Leadership Quality	Social Consensus	Impending British Withdrawal	
• Tripartite wage negotiation framework set up • Military defense built up from scratch • EDB to bring in investments • Visionary and committed leaders • Convergent politics, which didn't play on simmering racial and ideological tensions	• Galvanized by leaders into a resilient, hard-working people • Rallied to leadership's call that Singapore has to fight for its own survival • Committed, had entrenched stake in Singapore	**Natural** • Natural harbor	**Inheritance** • British-style "elite" civil service • British infrastructure converted to other uses • Role & reputation as major entrepôt trade center for Asia
IMPLEMENTATION		**RESOURCES**	

Confrontation with Indonesia

• Export orientation

IDEAS

1965: Separation from Malaysia

rates on exporting manufacturers. Singapore's efforts to bring in foreign investments were holistic in that they recognized the importance of ensuring harmonious industrial relations. The tripartite wage negotiation system was established to provide stability in the wage bargaining process and to deter labor militancy.

The institutional base for a fully sovereign state had already been laid, and the government continued to build up the capabilities of its bureaucracy. To implement its external-oriented growth policies, new statutory boards, such as the Economic Development Board (EDB), were created. Singapore's founding leaders eschewed potentially divergent politics that threatened to divide people along racial and ideological lines and dealt fairly with rising communal tensions. They also built up the country's defense capabilities to boost security and, in turn, Singaporeans' confidence in the country's future. Under the leadership's guidance, the population was galvanized into a resilient and hard-working people, determined to fight for their survival. They rallied to the leadership's reminder that "The world does not owe us a living. We cannot live by the begging bowl" (Lee 2000). Over time, the people thus developed a commitment to Singapore as an independent country in which they had a stake.[4] Policies such as the government housing programs helped to further entrench this commitment.[5]

Export orientation took off in this phase, and the economy was able to generate sustained growth. The EDB successfully attracted several multinational corporations (MNCs) to invest in the country, including National Semiconductor, Fairchild, Texas Instruments, and Hewlett-Packard. These firms helped to lay the foundations for the development

---

4   Chua (2006) details the process of nation building and the government policies that helped entrench Singaporeans' sense of belonging.

5   Home ownership became a major tenet in Singapore's nation-building program. In 1968 Singaporeans were allowed to use their savings with the Central Provident Fund (CPF) to purchase public housing. The CPF was a compulsory savings program first established in 1955.

of Singapore's electronics cluster. Policies were recalibrated and fine-tuned along the way.

Third Phase: Industrial Restructuring (1973–84)
(Figure 4.8)

By the 1970s and early 1980s, Singapore had established a substantial manufacturing base and capacity in terms of both infrastructure and skilled labor. It had a solid reputation as a stable environment where MNC operations could thrive. However, the economy also faced the impact from the oil shocks of 1973 and 1979, which drove up business costs and dampened economic activity. Excess demand in the domestic labor market began to put upward pressure on real wages, resulting in a loss of competitiveness in relation to other exporters. Incipient wage-price pressures had begun to emerge that, if not dealt with, would severely threaten Singapore's competitiveness.

Dealing with the issue of cost competitiveness required a two-pronged approach. First, it was necessary to stem the domestic cost and price pressures. The tripartite wage negotiation arrangements, which brought employers, employees, and the government to the bargaining table, were formalized in 1972 with the setting up of the National Wages Council (NWC). The NWC was also supported by a robust legal and legislative framework. This helped to ensure wage stability at a time when pressures to increase wages were substantial.

Second, Singapore's industrial sector had to shift to the manufacture of higher value-added products. As early as 1971, the government reviewed its industrialization program. Restructuring the industrial base toward more capital- and skill-intensive industries meant that the EDB became

Figure 4.8. Third Phase—Industrial Restructuring (1973–84)

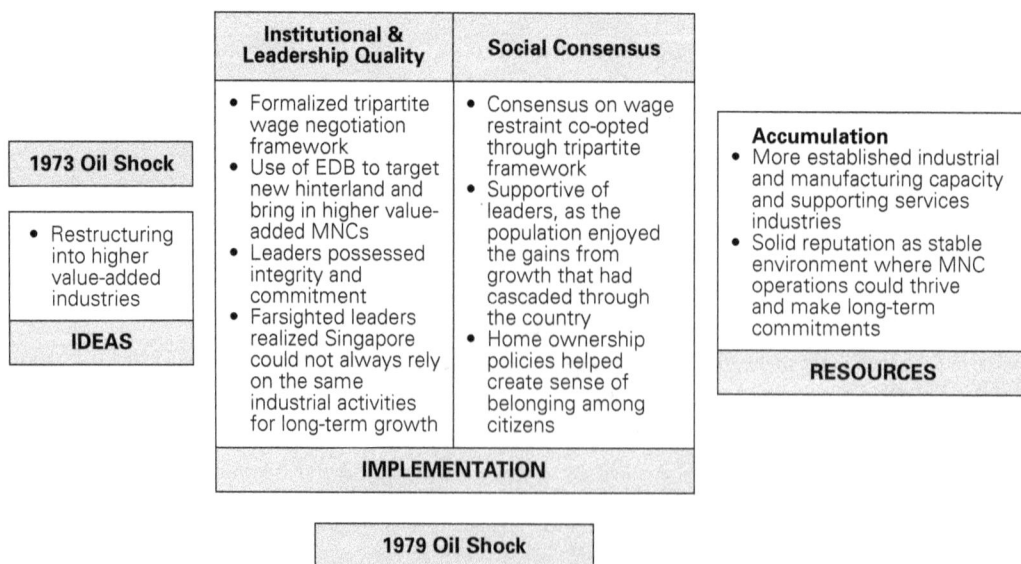

more selective in whom it wooed to Singapore. Firms requiring extensive protection (and that were likely to be low skilled or uncompetitive in the global market) were passed over or allowed to leave the country. The EDB also partnered with top European and Japanese MNCs to create training centers in Singapore, which helped to enhance the skills of their local workers and, later, to train a broader swath of Singaporeans. The government also introduced a levy on foreign workers to deter the hiring of low-skilled labor from abroad.

In this phase, the institutional capabilities and leadership of the EDB proved critical in the challenging task of fine-tuning Singapore's investment promotion strategies. For example, the Board decided to seek investments from U.S. MNCs over those from Taiwan, China, and Hong Kong, China, because the latter group at that time tended to produce lower value-added, labor-intensive products such as textiles. Singapore's leaders also appreciated the importance of maintaining investor confidence in the volatile environment. They were ready to uphold the country's business-friendly reputation, which was becoming a very important intangible asset.

The country's workers were supportive of the tripartite wage negotiation system. The implicit social compact between the government and the people—the promise that by exercising wage restraint to generate growth, the people would share in the benefits of growth—was upheld. The benefits of Singapore's sustained economic progress were shared with the people, in the form of government housing upgrades and a public medical savings/insurance program known as Medisave. Tripartism was successful, with no serious labor unrest over this period.

Consequently, Singapore enjoyed strong productivity growth and maintained its competitive edge. Unemployment remained steady at 4.5 percent even as economic growth slowed temporarily to 4 percent in 1975 from 13 percent in 1972, and inflation spiraled to 22 percent in 1974. Growth rebounded soon thereafter and remained robust from 1976–83, averaging 8.5 percent each year. Inflation was brought down to 3.9 percent over the same period. Singapore's industrial sector successfully moved up the value chain. For example, high-technology investment in capital-intensive industries such as component and precision engineering soon displaced investment in labor-intensive industries such as textiles and semiconductor assembly.

Fourth Phase: Industrial Diversification and Consolidation (1985–97) (Figure 4.9)

Having staved off the challenges of the 1970s, Singapore faced rising unit labor costs in the latter half of the 1980s, straining competitiveness and dampening demand for its traditional exports. New engines of growth were needed. The year 1985 marked the beginning of a new growth opportunity: post-Plaza Accord, a flood of investments rushed to Southeast Asia, as low- and mid-skilled manufacturing was outsourced from Japan.

Figure 4.9. Fourth Phase—Industrial Diversification and Consolidation (1985–97)

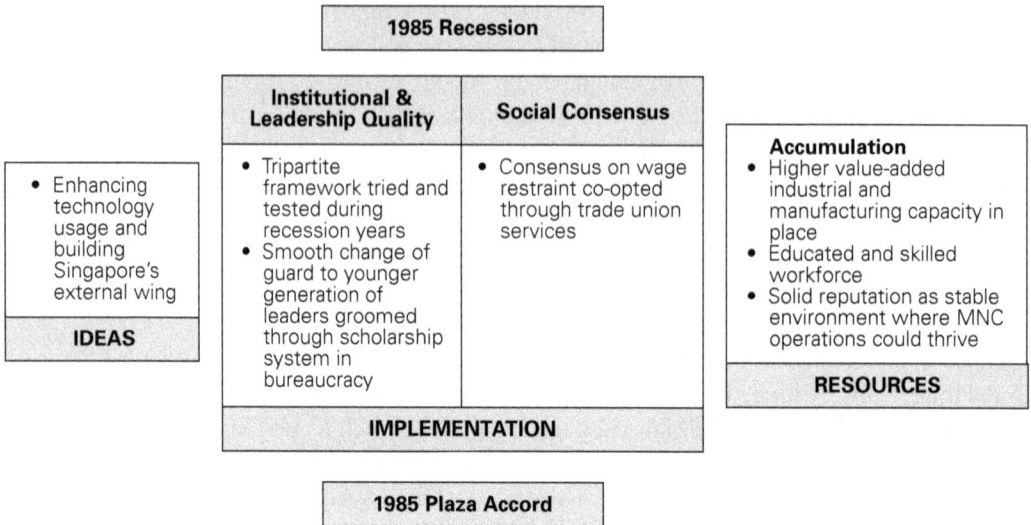

```
                              ┌──────────────────────┐
                              │    1985 Recession    │
                              └──────────────────────┘

                        ┌───────────────────┬───────────────────┐
                        │ Institutional &   │ Social Consensus  │
                        │ Leadership Quality│                   │
                        │                   │                   │      ┌──────────────────────────┐
┌──────────────────┐    │ • Tripartite      │ • Consensus on    │      │ Accumulation             │
│ • Enhancing      │    │   framework tried │   wage restraint  │      │ • Higher value-added     │
│   technology     │    │   and tested      │   co-opted        │      │   industrial and         │
│   usage and      │    │   during          │   through trade   │      │   manufacturing capacity │
│   building       │    │   recession years │   union services  │      │   in place               │
│   Singapore's    │    │ • Smooth change   │                   │      │ • Educated and skilled   │
│   external wing  │    │   of guard to     │                   │      │   workforce              │
│                  │    │   younger         │                   │      │ • Solid reputation as    │
├──────────────────┤    │   generation of   │                   │      │   stable environment     │
│     IDEAS        │    │   leaders groomed │                   │      │   where MNC operations   │
└──────────────────┘    │   through         │                   │      │   could thrive           │
                        │   scholarship     │                   │      ├──────────────────────────┤
                        │   system in       │                   │      │        RESOURCES         │
                        │   bureaucracy     │                   │      └──────────────────────────┘
                        ├───────────────────┴───────────────────┤
                        │           IMPLEMENTATION               │
                        └────────────────────────────────────────┘

                              ┌──────────────────────┐
                              │  1985 Plaza Accord   │
                              └──────────────────────┘
```

Singapore, however, could not compete with its immediate neighbors for low-end manufacturing outsourced from Japan. Industrial restructuring, in this context, involved the following steps:

1. *Developing the economy's external wing.* The island's labor-intensive industries were allowed to "hollow out" to lower-cost countries in the region, freeing the country to focus its limited resources on high value-added activities. This involved, in some instances, encouraging the creation of special economic zones. This policy also allowed Singapore to seek higher returns on domestic savings by tapping into the growth potential of the emerging economies in Asia.

2. *Attracting mid-end investments from Japan and the developed world.* Moving up the value chain in manufacturing and associated services required technology deepening. Within electronics, for example, Singapore shifted emphasis toward growing the computer peripherals segment, which was a higher-end activity than component testing. The government initiated the Local Industry Upgrading Program, which encouraged MNCs to "adopt" local subcontractors with the aim of developing specialized clusters of firms serving the MNCs' needs. Singapore also began promoting other industries that required skilled labor inputs, such as biotechnology, banking, and financial services.

3. *Maintaining some measure of cost competitiveness.* The government reduced employers' Central Provident Fund (CPF) contributions and made wages more flexible by introducing variable wage components. Under the auspices of the NWC, trade unions agreed to practice wage restraint and accepted CPF cuts during the recession years of 1985–86. Workers consented to wage restraints, as trade unions managed to deliver a range of social services to union members and the larger public, which helped to offset the pains of restructuring. These services included workers'

education, a cooperative movement, and social and cultural programs. Singapore's tripartite setup had passed a critical test.

Concurrently, the political landscape within Singapore was also changing. With the smooth change of the guard, policy making passed to a younger generation of Singaporean leaders who had been groomed through the scholarship system in the civil service, and who had now come of age. This helped to ensure the consistency and continuity that investors valued.

Together, the decisive measures helped the economy recover strongly after growth faltered in 1985–86. Growth averaged 9 percent from 1987 to 1997, even exceeding 10 percent in some years. Singapore's industrial sector successfully moved up the value chain and attracted middle-technology Japanese investments alongside the economies of Taiwan, China, the Republic of Korea, and Hong Kong, China. After the initial adaptation phase, the country was also able to grow its external wing. It made use of its experience in administration to develop economic zones in China and India. The relative success of this strategy demonstrated the transferability of good institutions and implementation practices.

Fifth Phase: Toward a Knowledge-Based Economy (1998 to present) (Figure 4.10)

Developing Asia's golden years came to an abrupt end with the Asian financial crisis in 1997. Singapore found itself in a far more challenging external environment in this phase. The region was struggling to recover

Figure 4.10. Fifth Phase—Toward a Knowledge-Based Economy (1998 to present)

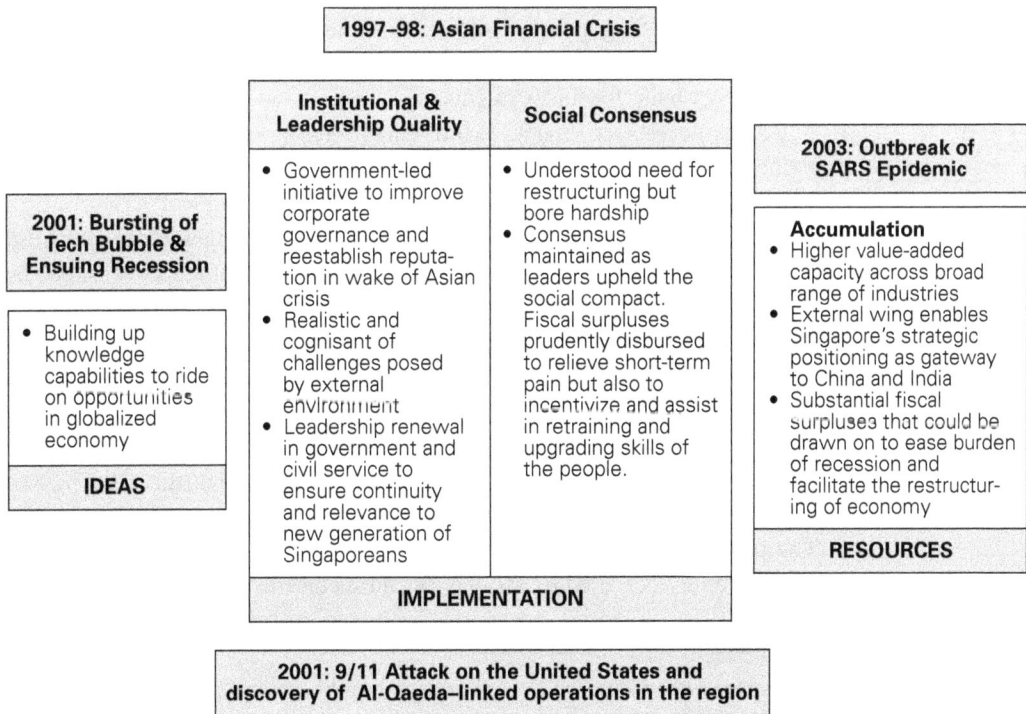

1997–98: Asian Financial Crisis		

2001: Bursting of Tech Bubble & Ensuing Recession	Institutional & Leadership Quality	Social Consensus	2003: Outbreak of SARS Epidemic
• Building up knowledge capabilities to ride on opportunities in globalized economy **IDEAS**	• Government-led initiative to improve corporate governance and reestablish reputation in wake of Asian crisis • Realistic and cognisant of challenges posed by external environment • Leadership renewal in government and civil service to ensure continuity and relevance to new generation of Singaporeans	• Understood need for restructuring but bore hardship • Consensus maintained as leaders upheld the social compact. Fiscal surpluses prudently disbursed to relieve short-term pain but also to incentivize and assist in retraining and upgrading skills of the people.	**Accumulation** • Higher value-added capacity across broad range of industries • External wing enables Singapore's strategic positioning as gateway to China and India • Substantial fiscal surpluses that could be drawn on to ease burden of recession and facilitate the restructuring of economy **RESOURCES**

IMPLEMENTATION		

2001: 9/11 Attack on the United States and discovery of Al-Qaeda–linked operations in the region		

from the debilitating effects of the crisis, and the rise of China posed a huge competitive challenge. The sense of external uncertainty was compounded by the attack on New York City's World Trade Center on September 11, 2001, and the discovery of terrorist groups in Asia linked to Al-Qaeda.

However, Singapore had a firm foundation on which it could build the capacity to face these challenges. The country had developed higher value-added activities across a broad range of industries. The relatively successful economic zones afforded the country the strategic opportunity to position itself as a gateway to Asia and to market itself as a hub for other regions in the world to establish inroads into the fast-growing economies of China and India.

Restructuring the economy to face the challenges in this phase meant equipping people and firms to operate in a globalized world, where production was more readily diffusible and where knowledge was a premium. Singaporeans and the country's firms had to be innovative, creative, and entrepreneurial to generate the technologies and efficiencies on which future productivity gains would come.

The government's role was thus to deregulate and liberalize economic activities to reduce business costs and preserve jobs during the crisis and its aftermath. Two packages, amounting to $12.5 billion, were introduced in 1998. These included policies to lower total wage bills by 15 percent; to reduce costs arising from industrial and commercial land rental, foreign worker levies, and other government charges for electricity, telecommunications, port, and airport services; as well as to provide rebates on property, income, and corporate tax. Yet another substantial package was introduced in 2001 amid a global recession. The government also liberalized Singapore's "software"—that is, policies relating to social, cultural, and human capital—to help make the city an attractive and vibrant place for globally footloose talents.

Economic restructuring was a bitter but necessary medicine, as Singapore's economic planners were realistic and cognizant of the need to respond quickly to a changing environment. A key aspect was renewal in the political leadership and the civil service. There was a need for new ideas and fresh perspectives and to engage the younger generation of Singaporeans. As the burden of economic restructuring would be borne by those suffering from structural unemployment, the government had to provide "social support to those adversely affected by the changes, to ensure that no one [was] left behind." The social consensus for remaking Singapore was maintained through the visible, prudent, and targeted use of fiscal surpluses, to ease adjustment pains in the short term. Yet it was critical that this support was implemented "without undermining the incentive to work" (Lee 2003). The people were thus incentivized to undertake retraining, and programs were carefully designed to avoid a "welfare culture."

Summary

Singapore's economic development story is not necessarily about its successful adoption of unique policies. Instead, it is about how the country managed to implement appropriate policies successfully. This has come about through robust institutions guided by visionary leaders, who have won the support of the general populace. The people have experienced the tangible benefits of growth and have thus backed the government's institutions and leaders. The successful implementation of growth policies has helped the country to earn credibility and develop a solid reputation, which has proven invaluable in Singapore's bid to attract foreign investment. The conceptual political-economy framework developed in the previous section has shown its usefulness in providing a broad interpretive filter through which the economic developmental experience can be better understood.

Natural Endowments, Institutions, Leadership, and People

This section will apply the conceptual political-economy framework to the growth performances of countries in table 4.4, to establish its broader applicability. In particular, an attempt is made to assess divergences in countries' growth by analyzing empirical measures identified as possible explanatory factors. Because many of the underpinnings of growth are not readily quantifiable, use has been made of existing surveys and research, and, in certain instances, appropriate proxies to indicators relevant to the conceptual framework on growth have been created. The framework covers four broad categories of indicators: resources, institutions, leadership, and people or social consensus (see appendix 2 for data sources and interpretations).[6] Together, these four criteria cover the pillars of growth as summarized in figure 4.5.

The most tangible resources available to a country are its natural endowments. A priori, having a rich natural endowment should benefit a country, because superior geography, abundant natural wealth, or a large population affords economies more choices. The advantages of superior geography, proxied by coastal access as a measure of the extent to which a country is landlocked, are telling. Of the 10 growth laggards listed in table 4.2, Niger, the Central African Republic, and Chad are completely landlocked, and another four have minimal sea access, in that their coastal boundaries account for less than a tenth of the country's total bounds.

---

6   The data used in the analysis cover the group of countries listed in table 4.4.

Table 4.5. Natural Endowments

	Advancers	Average Performers	Underperformers	Sample Average
Coastal access/ landlocked[a]	59.0	53.3	47.9	53.8
Resource richness[b]	41.8	57.0	46.7	49.7

Sources: Mineral Resources Data System 2005; PennWell Corporation 2006; CIA 2007; authors' estimates.
a. Score refers to the proportion of a country's coastal boundaries to its total boundaries (land + sea). A zero score refers to a landlocked country, and a full 100 score refers to countries with only coastal boundaries.
b. Higher score indicates greater wealth in natural resources.

Conversely, growth advancers enjoyed superior sea access as compared to average and underperforming economies, as seen in table 4.4.

Being rich in natural resources is no guarantee of prosperity. All other things being equal, growth advancers were resource poor compared to average growth economies or underperformers, although the former had the benefit of superior geographic location and sea access. By most counts, Africa and Central and South America are resource-rich continents; yet the natural wealth of ancient nations located in these continents, such as the Ashanti, Aztec, and Incan Empires, did not guarantee their peoples' prosperity in the subsequent centuries. Such reversals of fortune do occur, as Acemoglu, Johnson, and Robinson (2002) show.

Whether natural wealth enriches or impoverishes a country is heavily influenced by its institutional base. Strong institutions tend to implement policies that channel natural resources to the generation of sustained growth and the accumulation of national wealth; weaker ones could conversely lead to the implementation of exploitative policies that benefit select groups in the short term but that are detrimental to the economy and the broader populace over the longer term. Institutional structures and operations are path-dependent "carriers of history." Once created, they may persist for some time, unless impacted through the accumulation process or via shocks. The quality of institutions is also determined by the people staffing them.

The importance of the quality of institutions and leadership is clearly seen in tables 4.6 and 4.7. Unequivocally, the advancers ranked better on all measures of legislation, policy execution, and enforcement. They also had better scores on most measures of leadership as compared to the other

Table 4.6. Institutional Quality

	Advancers	Average Performers	Underperformers	Sample Average
Judicial independence	56.6	36.0	45.2	46.7
Prudence in government spending	50.4	38.9	42.9	44.3
Effectiveness of law-making bodies	52.1	40.1	37.3	43.9
Regulatory quality	56.6	36.1	48.5	45.6

Sources: Lopez-Claros, Porter, and Schwab 2005; Kaufmann, Kraay, and Mastruzzi 2006; authors' estimates.
Note: The higher the score, the more positive the average rating on the variable for each group.

Table 4.7. Leadership Quality

	Advancers	Average Performers	Underperformers	Sample Average
Corruptions perception index	39.1	26.3	35.6	32.5
Voice and accountability	52.6	39.1	51.2	46.3
Political stability	50.3	33.0	36.0	41.7
Government effectiveness	57.5	35.5	44.6	44.7

Sources: Kaufmann, Kraay, and Mastruzzi 2006; Transparency International 2006; authors' estimates.
Note: The higher the score, the better the average rating on the variable for each group. A high score on the corruptions perception index reflects lower corruption.

categories. The institutions were more efficient and effective, and the leaders were less corrupt and more accountable, which laid the ground for more stable political environments in the advancers.

Institutions and the values under which leaders and bureaucrats operate are important in helping us to understand why some countries persistently choose suboptimal policy mixes. This cannot be, over time, because of sheer ignorance of growth paradigms or poor knowledge of local constraints. Instead, it may be because institutions and leaders are hindered by local systems, structures, and values.

Notably, having quality institutions does not preempt a specific political system. As with economics, so the first principles in political science apply: checks and balances within a system are necessary, but they need not emanate from democratic systems alone. Table 4.8 shows that advancers are, on average, more democratic than underperformers, but high-performing economies can be identified that are more authoritarian than even the least democratic underperformer. Examples also exist of average or underperforming economies in which democracy is attained to a higher degree than in the highest-ranked advancer democracy. On broad averages across the different groups, however, our observations seem to confirm the Lipset hypothesis (Lipset 1959) that democracy requires higher levels of income to sustain it. At lower income levels, growth and democracy appear to be mutually inhibiting, and poorer countries with democratic systems tend to lapse into more authoritarian ones as incomes rise, only reverting to democratic systems at higher income levels. The findings above seem to support this hypothesis, because the advancers and underperformers display higher levels of democracy, whereas the average growth economies' score could represent the breakdown of fledgling democracy until higher income levels are generated and sustained. The measure of political rights is inconclusive as well. Indeed, countries classified as growth advancers afford both the highest and lowest levels of political rights across the sample and, on average, score more poorly in this measure relative to the other groups.

Institutions and leadership aside, the third major player in policy and reform is the people. Leaders share their vision with the people; institutions implement and enforce policies that affect society. If policies are tailored

Table 4.8. Democracy and Political Rights

	Advancers	Average Performers	Underperformers	Sample Average
Democracy[a]	−0.5	−2.6	−1.4	−1.5
Score range	−7.5 to 8.6	−12.8 to 10.0	−7.3 to 9.8	
Political rights[b]	3.3	4.4	3.5	3.9
Score range	1.2 to 6.7	2.1 to 6.5	1.8 to 5.1	

Sources: University of Maryland 2005; Freedom House 2006.
a. A higher score indicates greater democracy, averaged over 1960–2003. Score range: −10 = authoritarian, +10 = democracy. Scores < −10 indicate foreign occupation, collapse of government, or transitional or provisional government over most of the period. These readings are excluded from the computation of each group's average and the sample average.
b. A higher score indicates greater political rights, averaged over 1972–2005. Score range: 1 = least free, 7 = most free.

Table 4.9. Social Consensus

	Advancers	Average Performers	Underperformers	Sample Average
Consensus between society and state				
Brain drain[a]	53.0	38.1	40.7	44.5
Public trust of politicians[a]	39.6	27.5	30.0	33.0
Consensus across society				
Gini index[b]	39.9	46.1	49.4	45.0
Ethno-linguistic and religious fractionalization index[c]	0.52	0.49	0.57	0.52
Civil war (1960–2002)[d]	12.8	14.8	18.9	15.2

Sources: Annett 2001; Gleditsch 2004; Lopez-Claros, Porter, and Schwab 2005; World Bank Development Data Group 2006; CIA 2007; authors' estimates.
a. The higher the score, the less brain drain, and the higher the trust of politicians.
b. The higher the score, the more unequal is income distribution.
c. Score represents the probability that any two individuals picked at random will be from a different ethno-linguistic and/or religious backgrounds.
d. The higher the score, the more frequent were civil wars.

for growth, their final impact in terms of gains and distribution will matter to the population. Creating the right incentives for people to support and participate in the growth policies and reforms—creating social consensus—becomes relevant, especially if short-term pain is required for long-term gain. Table 4.9 summarizes the set of social consensus indicators.

The brain-drain variable can be interpreted as a measure of the trust that a (talented) person vests in the existing institutions and leadership to create sufficient opportunities and freedoms for the exercise of their talents. Unsurprisingly, a higher incidence of brain drain is found in average performers and underperformers as compared to advancers. The public's trust in its political leaders to make the right policies, improve standards of living, and enhance security is also considerably lower in average or underperforming economies than in advancers.

Social consensus can also be understood as the building of convergent interests across the different groups in society. Empirically, the Kuznets curve displays an inverted-"U" shape, meaning that economies with low levels of income, alongside economies with high levels of income, are likely to see lower income inequality and, thus, lower Gini coefficients. It is therefore unsurprising that growth advancers have lower relative income disparities as compared to average performers.

Ethnic fractionalization is a direct measure of intrasocietal divisions. Empirical studies on sub-Saharan Africa show that underperforming African economies that are more fractionalized along ethno-linguistic and/ or religious lines are also more prone to conflict, institutional capture, partial policy making, and divergent politics.

In 1960, 14 of the 15 most ethnically heterogeneous societies in the world were in Africa, and nearly all of these economies have remained in the bottom third of the global income spectrum. This is "Africa's growth tragedy" (Easterly and Levine 1997). More reasonably, the confluence of ethnic fractionalization with higher income inequality magnifies fault lines and weakens intrasocietal consensus. Biased policy making, obstructionist attitudes of the general public against pro-growth reforms, or even physical conflict between the different groups (civil war) could thus impede growth.

Fractionalization, however, thus tells only part of the growth story. After all, 11 of the 14 growth advancers also had above-average levels of fractionalization, and yet their success contrasts starkly with that of Africa, or even with that of average and underperforming economies. Growth advancers seem to have engaged in convergent politics and policy making and were able to create institutions to manage societal fault lines instead of diverting benefits to one group to the exclusion and/or at the expense of another. In average or underperforming economies, leaders and institutions were unable to build consensus across different factions. Notably, civil war occurred more frequently in growth underperformers, as institutions and leaders failed to forge unity and instead exploited differences for their own gain, possibly fighting for resource wealth.

Resources, institutions, leaders, and people all interact with each other, with institutional setups often the nexus of policy-making activity and consensus building between leaders and people. Countries may start with different natural endowments, but institution and leadership quality will determine their growth trajectory over the longer term. The people may be divided along several lines, but consensus can be built through robust institutions and competent, incorrupt, and trustworthy leaders. Advancers, by and large, are those that may not have had the fortune of geography but have enjoyed the fortunes of history. They have continued to build up institutions to meld existing fault lines in society, instead of allowing these divisions to wreck institutional and government operations.

Country data on each indicator are detailed in appendix 3. Country scores have been rescaled from 0 to 100, with a higher number indicating a more favorable score. This allows the derivation of a composite score for natural endowments, institutions, leadership, and social consensus. Natural endowments aside, growth advancers outscore average growth economies and underperformers on the composite measures in table 4.10. The divergence is especially stark when focusing on institutions and leadership.

Notably, Singapore scores better on overall indexes measuring institutional and leadership quality and social consensus, bettering the sample average and the growth advancers on aggregate (table 4.11).

Policy Lessons and Conclusion

By the late 1980s, growth practitioners and academics had come to a broad agreement on some of the macro- and micro-fundamentals that were deemed critical to sustained growth. Further case studies of other countries' growth experiences might shed light on how successful economies have been in mapping these fundamental economics first principles onto policy

Table 4.10. Composite Scores

Composite Score	Growth Advancers	Average Performers	Underperformers	Sample Average
Natural endowments	50.4	55.2	47.3	51.7
Institutional quality	56.2	36.3	43.7	44.4
Leadership quality	51.1	34.1	44.8	42.1
Social consensus	59.6	59.2	51.9	57.5

Source: Authors' estimates.
Note: Scores are derived from the individual components within each composite grouping. Scores on individual components are rebased from 0–100, with a higher score indicating a better outcome on that component.

Table 4.11. Composite Scores for Singapore on Framework Indicators

Composite Score	Singapore	Growth Advancers	Sample Average
Natural endowments	50.0	50.4	51.7
Institutional quality	84.0	56.2	44.4
Leadership quality	75.6	51.1	42.1
Social consensus	76.2	59.6	57.5

Source: Authors' estimates.
Note: Scores are derived from the individual components within each composite grouping. Scores on individual components are rebased from 0 to 100, with a higher score indicating a better outcome on that component.

outcomes. Summarized below are some of the broad perspectives gleaned from this study into the global growth experience:

Policy Formulation

1. Count the costs—know that sustained growth requires reforms that take place over a continuum of cost-benefit trade-offs. Growth, and the policies that jump-start and sustain it, incurs costs. For example, income inequality is typically low at low levels of income but may rise as growth takes place into the middle-income strata and decline as the country gets richer. The relevant lesson for developing economies at the lower end of the income scale is that there may be short-term pain to raise standards of living. For example, countries may have to live with less democracy or greater inequality in the short term to achieve sustainable growth in the long term.

2. Foundational economics first principles do not map onto well-defined, universal policy sets. Basic macroeconomic stability—a first principle—is essential if growth is to be sustained and permanent progress to be made in the war on poverty. Ideas as to how an economy can attain macroeconomic stability are fluid and varied, and there is thus no single yellow brick road to prosperity. A paradigm that is fashionable and relevant in one decade could fall out of favor and be irrelevant in the next, and may yet be resurrected in a third.

3. Policy formulation must have a localized context. Experience has shown that a wholesale application of ideas to an economy is no recipe for growth. The idea needs to be applied to its local context. A pragmatic assessment

of the resources, constraints, and other structural peculiarities associated with the domestic economy is necessary for any growth practitioner seeking to understand how certain growth paradigms may work out in an economy.

4. Leadership quality is important, because policy formulation is prone to capture. Although practitioners and academics alike have come to a consensus that there is no single policy that is universally applicable to all economies, it has been less acceptable to enunciate the view that there are economies that persistently choose poor policies. Good policy making requires high-caliber, impartial, selfless leaders in institutions that enhance, not undermine, each other. Singapore, for example, has a practice of ensuring that leaders in policy-making positions are well remunerated, thereby reducing the incentives for leaders to undertake corruption or rent-seeking activities. The government scholarship system has also allowed the civil service to harness talent for its use. Checks on and balances against individuals and institutions with vested interests are also required. Good leaders also contribute to successful policy implementation by their ability to convey their vision of the road ahead, mobilize people, and build consensus for their policies through a politics of convergence, not divergence.

Policy Implementation and Review

1. Robust institutions are key to policy implementation. Failure at the implementation stage drives a wedge between policy in theory and policy in effect. To reduce that wedge, institutions such as an effective administration and civil service, independent judiciary, a vibrant private sector, and a responsible press are needed. History has demonstrated the debilitating effects that institutions captured by vested interests have on growth; commitment to good governance ensures that a country's institutions remain effective and impartial and are devoted to the implementation of well-formulated growth policies.

2. People consensus matters as growth policy ultimately impacts the population directly. Two kinds of consensus are found at the social level—one, between society and the government, and two, within different social groups. Sustained growth often requires trading short-term pain for long-term gain, and even the best of policies can be undermined at the implementation stage if people do not believe in the capabilities of the leaders and government to plan or carry through policy well. This would also reduce public willingness to incur short-term pain given the uncertainty of future gains from growth. The people's confidence and trust in their leaders—the first kind of people consensus—is thus relevant for sustained growth. Furthermore, the end point of growth and development—the well-being of a nation's people—will thus be meaningful only to a people united on the purpose and destiny of their country and who have an entrenched stake in the country. In the absence of a unifying vision, social conflict becomes common, and directly undermines efforts to jump-start growth as well.

3. Start small and leverage on "demonstrable effects." Many gradual steps in the right direction may yield more benefits than wholesale "big bang" reforms. Small-scale reform can yield substantial gains (or "demonstrable effects") on the margin without necessarily incurring significant costs. This also buys policy makers critical time for building up consensus and participation. On a geographical basis, large countries that face substantial logistic and institutional difficulties in implementing growth policies on a broad base can instead adopt a targeted approach by jump-starting growth in a smaller region (for example, SEZs in China). Indeed, the promise of a big solution to a very big problem is an outlier in the practice of economics, where economists usually study how marginal changes to existing systems and policies can bring about general marginal improvements.

4. Avoid ideological lock-ins. A policy is only as successful as its impact. Policy makers must avoid pursuing a policy for its own sake and should instead assess whether a policy is still working and/or remains relevant. Also, policies can be captured by vested interest groups. Policy makers must thus constantly review, fine-tune, and calibrate policies. This allows them to assess whether (1) the ideas behind the policies have worked in the local context, (2) whether and how implementation could be improved, or more fundamentally, (3) whether one should rethink the original growth paradigms in light of possible changes in the operating environment. After all, policy makers rarely hit on the right policy mix from the beginning. Starting small and proceeding in a sequenced stepwise fashion will allow time for building up popular consensus and will prevent policy inflexibility that tends to come with the high sunk costs associated with "big bang" reform packages.

References

Acemoglu, D., S. Johnson, and J. A. Robinson. 2002. "Reversal of Fortune: Geography and Development in the Making of the Modern World Income Distribution." *Quarterly Journal of Economics* 117 (4): 1231–94.

Annett, A. 2001. "Social Fractionalization, Political Instability, and the Size of Government." *IMF Staff Papers* 48 (3): 573–77.

Cass, D. 1965. "Optimum Growth in an Aggregative Model of Capital Accumulation." *Review of Economic Studies* 32 (3): 233–40.

Central Intelligence Agency (CIA). 2007. *CIA World Factbook*. Washington, DC: Government Printing Office.

Chan, C. B. 2002. *Heart Work*. Singapore: Singapore Economic Development Board and EDB Society.

Chua, B. H. 2006. "Values and Development in Singapore." In *Developing Cultures: Case Studies,* ed. Lawrence E. Harrison and Peter Berger. New York: Routledge.

Durlauf, S. N., P. A. Johnson, and J. Temple. 2005. "Growth Econometrics." In *Handbook of Economic Growth,* ed. Philippe Aghion and Stephen N. Durlauf, vol. 1A, pp. 555–677. Amsterdam: North-Holland/Elsevier Science Publishers.

Easterly, W., and R. Levine. 1997. "Africa's Growth Tragedy: Policies and Ethnic Divisions," *Quarterly Journal of Economics* 112 (4): 1203–50.

Freedom House. 2006. *Freedom in the World 2006: The Annual Survey of Political Rights and Civil Liberties*. Westport, CT: Freedom House.

Gleditsch, K. S. 2004. "A Revised List of Wars between and within Independent States, 1816–2002," *International Interactions* 30 (3): 231–62.

Heston, A., R. Summers, and B. Aten. 2006. *Penn World Table Version 6.2*. Centre for International Comparisons of Production, Income and Prices at the University of Pennsylvania.

Kaufmann, D., A. Kraay, and M. Mastruzzi. 2006. "Governance Matters V: Governance Indicators for 1996–2005." Policy Research Paper, World Bank, Washington, DC.

Koopmans, T. C. 1965. "On the Concept of Optimal Economic Growth." *Pontificiae Academiae Scientiarum Scripta Varia* 28 (1).

Lee, H. L. 2003. "Remaking the Singapore Economy." Keynote speech in his capacity as deputy prime minister at the annual dinner of the Economics Society of Singapore.

Lee, K. Y. 2000. *From Third World to First: The Singapore Story: 1965–2000*. Singapore: Times Media Private Limited and The Straits Times Press.

Lee, S. 1974. *The Monetary & Banking Development of Malaysia & Singapore*. Singapore: Singapore University Press.

Lipset, S. M. 1959. "Some Social Requisites of Democracy: Economic Development and Political Legitimacy." *American Political Science Review* 53 (1): 69–105.

Lopez-Claros, A., M. E. Porter, and K. Schwab. 2005. *The Global Competitiveness Report 2005–2006: Policies Underpinning Rising Prosperity*. World Economic Forum. New York: Palgrave Macmillan.

Lucas, R. E., Jr. 1988. "On the Mechanics of Economic Development." *Journal of Monetary Economics* 22 (1): 3–42.

Mineral Resources Data System. 2005. *U.S. Geological Survey*. Reston, VA: U.S. Geological Survey. Available at http://tin.er.usgs.gov/mrds/.

PennWell Corporation. 2006. Special Report: Oil Production, Reserves, Increase Slightly in 2006. *Oil & Gas Journal* 104 (47, Dec.).

Romer, P. 1986. "Increasing Returns and Long-Run Growth." *Journal of Political Economy* 94 (5): 1002–37.

Solow, R. 1956. "A Contribution to the Theory of Economic Growth." *Quarterly Journal of Economics* 70 (1): 65-94.

Transparency International. 2006. *Global Corruption Report*. London: Pluto Press.

United Nations. 1986. *Handbook of International Trade and Development Statistics Supplement*. New York: United Nations.

———. 2005. *UNCTAD Handbook of Statistics*. New York: United Nations.

University of Maryland. 2005. *Polity IV Project: Political Regime Characteristics and Transitions*. College Park: University of Maryland.

World Bank Development Data Group. 2006. *World Development Indicators*. Washington, DC: World Bank.

Annex 1: Method for Sampling PWT6.2

The Penn World Table provides internationally comparable data on production, income, and prices on as many as 188 countries. In updating PWT6.1 to 6.2, several countries' data have been added or removed, as a result of political changes or improvements to the national accounts. This chapter was originally prepared using data from PWT6.1, but notable revisions were made with the release of PWT6.2 in September 2006. These revisions have the potential to skew the data dramatically, with the addition of data on, for example, oil-rich Middle Eastern countries in 1970 or poorer, former Soviet Union states after 1990.

Acknowledging that PWT6.2 has more updated information (extending to 2004 for a number of countries, and 2003 for most), the data are used for the rest of the analysis that follows in this chapter. Yet it is necessary to derive a consistent set of countries whose inclusion does not dramatically skew the analysis nor create artificial "structural breaks" in the database. As such, the following methodology was applied to derive a final count of 118 countries in the sample:

1. Choose countries that appear in *both* PWT6.1 and 6.2. This reduces the database to 145 countries from 188 in the full PWT6.2.
2. Data from the RGDPC variable, or PPP-adjusted GDP per capita (chain-weighted) for these 145 countries, are divided into five-year periods. The latest observation, 2003, is also included. Of the nine blocks of five-year periods (1960–2000) and the final set of observations from 2003, any countries with fewer than six observations in PWT6.1 are removed. These countries are similarly removed from PWT6.2.
3. PWT6.2 also lacks data on a number of countries where previously there were data under PWT6.1; these are similarly removed.

Annex 2: Data Sources and Interpretation

Variable	Year	Source	Interpretation of Score
Income and growth			
Real GDP per capita	1960–2003	Heston, Summers, and Aten (2006)	RGDPC variable, which refers to the chain-weighted, PPP-adjusted per capital GDP denominated in international dollars. Each international dollar has the PPP equivalent of $1 in a given year.
Table 5: Natural Endowments			
Coastal access/ landlocked	...	CIA (2007)	Score refers to a country's coastal boundaries as a share of its total land and sea boundaries. 0 = landlocked country, 100 = full sea access.
Natural resources	...	*Arable Land* Food and Agricultural Organisation of the United Nations	0 = poor in natural resources, 100 = rich in natural resources. This is a composite index derived from the highest score across four indexes:
			1. Arable land as percentage of total land area
		Oil Reserves and Gas Reserves PennWell Corporation (2006). Sourced from the Energy Information Administration.	2. Oil reserves (billions of barrels)
			3. Natural gas reserves (trillions of cubic feet)
			4. Number of mines with precious metals (gold, silver, platinum, and palladium) and gemstones
		Precious Metals and Gemstone Mines Mineral Resources Data System (2005)	Recognizing that some natural resources are mutually exclusive (for instance, a farm cannot be planted on top of an oil well), the highest score across the four categories, and not the average, is taken as indicative of a country's wealth in any natural resource.
			Authors' calculations
Table 6: Institutional Quality			
Judicial independence	2005–06	Lopez-Claros, Porter, and Schwab (2005)	1 = no, heavily influenced, 7 = yes, entirely independent. Final score rescaled such that maximum score = 100.
Prudence in government spending	2005–06	Lopez-Claros, Porter, and Schwab (2005)	Corresponds to "Wastefulness of government spending" variable. 1 = is wasteful, 7 = provides necessary goods and services not provided by the market.
			Final score rescaled such that maximum score = 100.
Effectiveness of law-making bodies	2005–06	Lopez-Claros, Porter, and Schwab (2005)	1 = very ineffective, 7 = very effective.
			Final score rescaled such that maximum score = 100.
Regulatory quality	2005	Kaufmann, Kraay, and Mastruzzi (2006)	−2.5 = poor governance outcomes, 2.5 = excellent governance outcomes.
			Final score rescaled such that maximum score = 100.
Table 7: Leadership Quality			
Corruptions perception index	2006	Transparency International (2006)	0 = highly corrupt, 10 = highly clean.
			Final score rescaled such that maximum score = 100
Voice and accountability	2005	Kaufmann, Kraay, and Mastruzzi (2006)	−2.5 = poor governance outcomes, 2.5 = excellent governance outcomes.
			Final score rescaled such that maximum score = 100.

Variable	Year	Source	Interpretation of Score
Political stability	2005	Kaufmann, Kraay, and Mastruzzi (2006)	−2.5 = poor governance outcomes, 2.5 = excellent governance outcomes.
			Final score rescaled such that maximum score = 100.
Government effectiveness	2005	Kaufmann, Kraay, and Mastruzzi (2006)	−2.5 = poor governance outcomes, 2.5 = excellent governance outcomes.
			Final score rescaled such that maximum score = 100.

Table 8: Democracy and Political Rights

Variable	Year	Source	Interpretation of Score
Democracy/ authoritarianism	1960–2003	University of Maryland (2005)	Country scores calculated as average over 1960–2003.
			Index units, −10 = strongly authoritarian, +10 = strongly democratic. Special cases: collapse of central authority (−77) and transition/provisional governments (−88). These special cases are dropped when calculating the average score for the group.
			Excluding the special cases, the final score has been rescaled such that maximum score = 100. Countries that average a score < −10 over the time period are scored 0.
Political rights	2005	Freedom House (2006)	Index units, 1 = most free, 7 = least free.
			Final score rescaled such that maximum score = 100.

Table 9: Social Consensus

Variable	Year	Source	Interpretation of Score
Brain drain	2004–05	Lopez-Claros, Porter, and Schwab (2005)	1= talented people leave country, 7 = talented people stay. Final score rescaled such that maximum score = 100.
Public trust of politicians	2004–05	Lopez-Claros, Porter, and Schwab (2005)	1 = very low, 7 = very high.
			Final score rescaled such that maximum score = 100.
Gini index	Various years	World Bank Development Data Group (2006)	Data adjusted such that a higher score is positively correlated with higher social consensus, that is, 0 = perfect income inequality, 100 = perfect income equality.
Ethnic fractionalization	1960s– 1980s	Annett (2001) Cameroon and Taiwan, China: authors' calculations based on population breakdown by ethno-linguistic group provided in *CIA World Factbook* (2007)	0 = homogeneous society, 100 = fractured society. Score refers to the percent probability that any two individuals selected at random in the country will be from different ethnic and/or linguistic backgrounds. Data adjusted such that a higher score is positively correlated with higher social consensus, that is, 0 = fractured society, 100 = homogeneous society.
Civil war	1960–2002	Extension of Correlates of War database (intrastate wars). Gleditsch (2004)	Binary, Yes = 1, No = 0 for any observation of civil war occurring in a country for any length of time in a given five-year period (for example, 1960–64). Score refers to proportion of five-year country observations with civil war.
			Data adjusted such that a higher score is positively correlated with higher social consensus, that is, 0 = civil war in every period, 100 = no civil war.

	Botswana	China	Dominican Republic	India	Korea, Rep. of	Malaysia	Pakistan	Romania	Sri Lanka	St. Lucia	St. Vincent	Taiwan, China	Thailand
Institutional quality	**69.57**	**50.05**	**32.21**	**56.15**	**57.76**	**71.45**	**41.27**	**41.23**	**41.88**	**72.72**	**72.72**	**63.23**	**60.48**
Judicial independence	85.86	48.57	34.29	75.71	60.00	77.14	37.14	37.14	42.86	...	...	61.43	62.86
Prudence in government spending	62.86	48.57	24.29	44.29	54.29	72.86	48.57	37.14	35.71	...	...	64.29	61.43
Effectiveness of law-making institutions	64.29	58.57	25.71	61.43	51.43	75.71	41.43	37.14	41.43	...	...	55.71	60.00
Regulatory quality	65.29	44.47	44.54	43.17	65.34	60.09	37.95	53.49	47.52	72.72	72.72	71.50	57.63
Leadership quality	**63.57**	**35.99**	**43.70**	**42.70**	**61.13**	**55.45**	**25.80**	**47.02**	**35.62**	**71.71**	**71.65**	**64.45**	**46.09**
Corruption perceptions index	56.00	33.00	28.00	33.00	51.00	50.00	22.00	31.00	31.00	...	...	59.00	36.00
Voice and accountability	63.65	16.83	54.02	57.06	64.78	41.89	25.34	57.13	44.71	70.70	70.70	65.88	51.39
Political stability	68.85	46.36	50.99	32.99	58.66	59.75	16.47	50.64	25.06	71.97	72.83	60.65	39.02
Government effectiveness	65.78	47.76	41.80	47.75	70.07	70.15	39.37	49.33	41.73	72.45	71.42	72.29	57.97
Social consensus	**60.94**	**59.86**	**50.52**	**42.90**	**74.54**	**63.87**	**45.36**	**57.21**	**44.21**	**67.80**	**73.50**	**74.21**	**59.35**
Public trust of politicians	57.14	47.14	18.57	30.00	42.86	67.14	27.14	27.14	22.86	...	...	52.86	42.86
Gini index	37.00	69.00	48.30	67.50	68.40	50.80	69.40	69.00	66.80	57.40	...	...	58.00
Ethnic fractionalization	52.00	40.00	54.00	10.00	100	30.00	39.00	71.00	29.00	46.00	47.00	72.56	37.00
Civil war	100	88.89	88.89	55.56	100	100	55.56	88.89	66.67	100	100	100	88.89
Brain drain	58.57	54.29	42.86	51.43	61.43	71.43	35.71	30.00	35.71	...	...	71.43	70.00
Geography	**22.86**	**69.80**	**50.32**	**45.16**	**79.80**	**70.18**	**21.26**	**23.86**	**57.14**	**53.23**	**58.97**	**67.14**	**35.63**
Coastal access	0	39.60	78.16	33.17	91.02	63.66	13.38	8.23	100	100	100	100	39.83
Resource richness	45.71	100	22.49	57.14	68.57	76.70	29.15	39.49	14.29	6.45	17.95	34.29	31.43
Politics													
Political rights index	27.27	95.24	32.90	32.03	44.59	54.11	68.40	72.29	41.99	16.48	24.73	54.55	47.62
Democracy/autocracy	87.76	12.31	24.44	92.96	40.74	76.06	22.69	24.17	81.57	...	...	32.41	27.59

Annex 3b: Indicator Scores for Average Performers

	Bolivia	Cameroon	Cape Verde	Comoros	Côte d'Ivoire	Ecuador	Egypt, Arab Rep. of	Grenada
Institutional quality	**32.71**	**34.44**	**45.76**	**17.31**	**31.06**	**24.78**	**48.26**	**57.19**
Judicial independence	31.43	31.43	...	...	...	17.14	...	...
Prudence in government spending	35.71	34.29	...	...	...	28.57	52.86	...
Effectiveness of law-making institutions	24.29	37.14	...	...	...	20.00	51.43	...
Regulatory quality	39.40	34.90	45.76	17.31	31.06	33.40	40.51	57.19
Leadership quality	**34.03**	**31.10**	**60.68**	**34.89**	**15.92**	**33.19**	**33.76**	**54.18**
Corruption perceptions index	27.00	23.00	...	...	21.00	23.00	33.00	35.00
Voice and accountability	48.16	26.18	66.59	44.47	20.00	46.71	27.08	66.75
Political stability	26.92	43.13	67.66	42.86	0.19	33.35	32.02	59.74
Government effectiveness	34.05	32.10	47.80	17.35	22.50	29.70	42.95	55.22
Social consensus	**44.35**	**46.44**	**76.00**	**85.89**	**56.13**	**50.06**	**63.52**	**73.00**
Public trust of politicians	20.00	27.14	...	...	...	17.14	...	...
Gini index	39.90	55.40	...	...	55.40	56.30	65.60	...
Ethnic fractionalization	29.00	18.25	52.00	94.00	13.00	34.00	75.00	46.00
Civil war	100	100	100	77.78	100	100	77.78	100
Brain drain	32.86	31.43	...	...	...	42.86	35.71	...
Geography	**48.57**	**16.88**	**55.71**	**67.94**	**31.39**	**73.48**	**56.81**	**52.94**
Coastal access	0	8.05	100	100	14.21	52.67	47.90	100
Resource richness	97.14	25.71	11.41	35.87	48.57	94.29	65.71	5.88
Politics								
Political rights index	41.13	88.74	48.57	69.05	84.42	45.02	77.92	30.88
Democracy/ autocracy	22.96	17.61	...	30.00	0	68.33	19.07	...

Guinea	Haiti	Honduras	Indonesia	Morocco	Papua New Guinea	Philippines	Syrian Arab Rep.	Turkey	Zimbabwe
31.54	**26.51**	**38.85**	**47.05**	**44.14**	**32.90**	**39.91**	**25.62**	**50.91**	**25.07**
...	...	34.29	45.71	44.29	...	38.57	...	51.43	30.00
...	...	37.14	51.43	45.71	...	34.29	...	40.00	28.57
...	...	42.86	50.00	44.29	...	37.14	...	58.57	35.71
31.54	26.51	41.12	41.07	42.26	32.90	49.65	25.62	53.65	5.99
25.66	**18.50**	**35.98**	**32.97**	**38.50**	**34.40**	**37.90**	**25.75**	**45.43**	**20.24**
19.00	18.00	25.00	24.00	32.00	24.00	25.00	29.00	38.00	24.00
26.41	21.83	47.24	45.73	34.70	49.03	50.13	16.68	49.19	16.92
27.76	11.88	34.49	21.65	41.39	33.73	27.81	31.85	39.14	18.45
29.48	22.28	37.21	40.50	45.91	30.84	48.67	25.47	55.37	21.59
60.90	**76.93**	**58.24**	**57.63**	**51.40**	**71.37**	**31.22**	**67.28**	**57.67**	**37.70**
...	...	27.14	41.43	34.29	...	20.00	...	37.14	22.86
59.70	40.80	46.20	65.70	60.50	49.10	53.90	...	56.40	49.90
23.00	90.00	75.00	21.00	53.00	65.00	16.00	79.00	81.00	47.00
100	100	100	100	77.78	100	33.33	55.56	66.67	44.44
...	...	42.86	60.00	31.43	...	32.86	...	47.14	24.29
30.02	**55.61**	**63.24**	**97.54**	**55.24**	**83.13**	**88.57**	**16.35**	**56.56**	**42.86**
8.60	83.11	35.04	95.08	47.63	86.27	100	7.89	73.11	0
51.43	28.11	91.43	100	62.86	80.00	77.14	24.80	40.00	85.71
93.07	87.88	49.35	71.43	65.37	30.48	47.62	92.21	44.16	75.76
16.09	0	42.22	28.70	14.06	100.00	53.24	0.00	73.24	30.00

Annex 3c: Indicator Scores for Growth Underperformers

	El Salvador	Fiji	Guatemala	Jamaica	Jordan	Madagascar	Namibia	Nicaragua	Peru	Senegal
Institutional quality	**45.24**	**42.99**	**34.75**	**50.85**	**57.95**	**43.65**	**54.14**	**29.50**	**34.05**	**43.92**
Judicial independence	44.29	...	35.71	58.57	67.14	41.43	68.57	17.14	28.57	...
Prudence in government spending	52.86	...	32.86	38.57	57.14	48.57	45.71	34.29	32.86	...
Effectiveness of law-making institutions	31.43	...	25.71	51.43	54.29	40.00	50.00	22.86	22.86	...
Regulatory quality	52.41	42.99	44.72	54.82	53.24	44.60	52.29	43.71	51.91	43.92
Leadership quality	**46.55**	**52.53**	**34.25**	**47.36**	**45.95**	**45.53**	**52.51**	**39.23**	**37.56**	**46.14**
Corruption perceptions index	40.00	...	26.00	37.00	53.00	31.00	41.00	26.00	33.00	33.00
Voice and accountability	55.14	53.53	42.66	61.40	35.29	49.89	57.28	49.75	50.85	55.97
Political stability	47.14	55.82	32.23	43.40	43.84	53.59	60.06	46.77	28.32	48.55
Government effectiveness	43.94	48.23	36.09	47.65	51.66	47.62	51.71	34.38	38.08	47.04
Social consensus	**54.49**	**72.00**	**42.83**	**58.56**	**57.33**	**45.96**	**46.40**	**43.63**	**38.42**	**59.23**
Public trust of politicians	32.86	...	21.43	28.57	51.43	28.57	38.57	18.57	20.00	...
Gini index	47.60	...	44.90	62.10	61.20	52.50	25.70	56.90	45.40	58.70
Ethnic fractionalization	85.00	44.00	48.00	65.00	48.00	13.00	22.00	50.00	34.00	19.00
Civil war	55.56	100	55.56	100	88.89	100	100	55.56	55.56	100
Brain drain	51.43	...	44.29	37.14	37.14	35.71	45.71	37.14	37.14	...
Geography	**48.02**	**55.47**	**51.83**	**57.92**	**5.07**	**77.14**	**32.84**	**62.68**	**62.22**	**19.80**
Coastal access	36.03	100	29.37	100	1.57	100	28.54	42.50	24.45	16.75
Resource richness	60.00	10.95	74.29	15.83	8.57	54.29	37.14	82.86	100	22.86
Politics										
Political rights index	40.69	48.92	52.38	26.41	72.29	56.71	38.57	59.31	53.68	55.41
Democracy/autocracy	13.70	67.94	42.04	98.78	17.31	37.50	80.00	21.76	37.04	29.09

CHAPTER 5

The Role of Institutions
in Growth and Development

Daron Acemoglu and James Robinson

Arguably the most important questions in social science concern the causes of cross-country differences in economic development and economic growth. Why are some countries much poorer than others? Why do some countries achieve economic growth while others stagnate? To the extent that we can develop some answers to these questions we can address the next ones: what can be done to induce economic growth and improve living standards in a society?

Economists long have recognized that output per capita in a society is intimately related to the amount of human capital, physical capital, and technology to which workers and firms in that country have access. Similarly, economic growth is related to the ability of a society to increase its human capital and physical capital and improve its technology. In this context, technology is construed broadly; technological differences refer not only to differences in techniques available to firms, but also to differences

This chapter was written as a background paper for the Commission on Growth and Development. We are grateful to Montek Ahluwalia, Gerard Padró i Miquel, Michael Spence, and Roberto Zagha for their comments and suggestions.

in the organization of production, which implies that some countries will be able to use their resources more efficiently. Nevertheless, differences in human capital, physical capital, and technology are only *proximate* causes in the sense that they pose the next question of why some countries have less human capital, physical capital, and technology and make worse use of their factors of production and opportunities. To develop more satisfactory answers to questions about why some countries are much richer than others and why some countries grow much faster than others, we need to look for potential *fundamental* causes that may be underlying these proximate differences across countries. Only by understanding these fundamental causes can we develop a framework for making policy recommendations that go beyond platitudes (such as "improve your technology") and minimize the risk of unintended negative consequences.

In this chapter we will argue that *institutions*, also very broadly construed, are the fundamental cause of economic growth and development differences across countries and that it is possible to develop a coherent framework for understanding why and how institutions differ across countries, as well as how they change. We will also argue that our state of knowledge does not yet enable us to make specific statements about how institutions can be improved (to promote further economic growth). Nevertheless, we can use this framework in several ways. One is to illustrate the potential *pitfalls of institutional reforms*. Although this in itself is not a solution to the problem of development, avoiding such pitfalls may be valuable enough to start with. We can also use the framework to structure our understanding of cases of economic success. Although such an ex post understanding is not a substitute for policy, it is the first step toward the goal of knowing how to reform institutions.

What Are Institutions?

Douglass North (1990: 3) offers the following definition: "Institutions are the rules of the game in a society or, more formally, are the humanly devised constraints that shape human interaction." Three important features of institutions are apparent in this definition: (1) that they are "humanly devised," which contrasts with other potential fundamental causes, such as geographic factors, that are outside human control; (2) that they are "the rules of the game" setting "constraints" on human behavior; and (3) that their major effect will be through incentives (see also North 1981).

The notion that incentives matter is second nature to economists, and institutions, if they are a key determinant of incentives, should have a major effect on economic outcomes, including economic development, growth, inequality, and poverty. But do they? Are institutions key determinants of economic outcomes, or are they secondary arrangements that respond to other, perhaps geographic or cultural, determinants of human and economic interactions?

Much empirical research attempts to answer this question. Before discussing some of this research, it is useful to emphasize an important point: ultimately, the aim of the research on institutions is to pinpoint *specific* institutional characteristics that are responsible for economic outcomes in specific situations (for example, the effect of legal institutions on the types of business contracts). However, the starting point is often the impact of a broader notion of institutions on a variety of economic outcomes. This broader notion, in line with North's conception, incorporates many aspects of economics and the political and social organization of society. Institutions can differ between societies because of their formal methods of collective decision making (democracy versus dictatorship) or because of their economic institutions (security of property rights, entry barriers, or the set of contracts available to businessmen). They may also differ because a given set of formal institutions are expected to and do function differently; for example, they may differ between two societies that are democratic because the distribution of political power lies with different groups or social classes, or because in one society, democracy is expected to collapse whereas in the other it is consolidated. This broad definition of institutions is both an advantage and a curse. It is an advantage because it enables us to get started with theoretical and empirical investigations of the role of institutions without getting bogged down by taxonomies. It is a curse because unless we can follow it up with a better understanding of the role of specific institutions, we have learned only little.

The Impact of Institutions

Tremendous cross-country differences exist in the way that economic and political life is organized. A voluminous literature documents large cross-country differences in economic institutions, as well as a strong correlation between these institutions and economic performance. Knack and Keefer (1995), for instance, looked at measures of property rights enforcement compiled by international business organizations, Mauro (1995) looked at measures of corruption, and Djankov and others (2002) compiled measures of entry barriers across countries. Many other studies look at variation in educational institutions and the corresponding differences in human capital. All of these authors find substantial differences in these measures of economic institutions, as well as significant correlation between these measures and various indicators of economic performance. For example, Djankov and others found that, although the total cost of opening a medium-sized business in the United States was less than 0.02 percent of GDP per capita in 1999, the same cost was 4.95 percent in the Dominican Republic, 0.91 percent in Ecuador, 1.16 percent in Kenya, and 2.7 percent of GDP per capita in Nigeria. These entry barriers are highly correlated with various economic outcomes, including the rate of economic growth and the level of development.

Nevertheless, this type of correlation does not establish that the countries with worse institutions are poor *because* of their institutions. After all, the United States differs from the Dominican Republic, Ecuador, Kenya, and Nigeria in its social, geographic, cultural, and economic fundamentals, so these may be the source of their poor economic performance. In fact, these differences may be the source of institutional differences themselves. Consequently, evidence based on correlation does not establish whether institutions are important determinants of economic outcomes.

To make further progress, one needs to isolate a source of exogenous differences in institutions, so that we approximate a situation in which a number of otherwise-identical societies end up with different sets of institutions. European colonization of the rest of the world provides a potential laboratory through which to investigate these issues. Beginning in the late fifteenth century, Europeans dominated and colonized much of the rest of the globe. Together with European dominance came the imposition of very different institutions and social power structures in different parts of the world.

Acemoglu, Johnson, and Robinson (2001) document that in a large number of colonies, especially those in Africa, Central America, the Caribbean, and South Asia, European powers set up "extractive institutions." These institutions (again broadly construed) did not introduce much protection for private property, nor did they provide checks and balances against the government. The explicit aim of the Europeans in these colonies was extraction of resources, in one form or another. This colonization strategy and the associated institutions contrast with the institutions Europeans set up in other colonies, especially in colonies where they settled in large numbers, for example, Australia, Canada, New Zealand, and the United States. In these colonies the emphasis was on the enforcement of property rights for a *broad cross section* of the society, especially smallholders, merchants, and entrepreneurs. The term "broad cross section" is emphasized here, because even in the societies with the worst institutions, the property rights of the elite are often secure, but the vast majority of the population enjoys no such rights and faced significant barriers preventing their participation in many economic activities. Although investments by the elite can generate economic growth for limited periods, property rights for a broad cross section seem to be crucial for sustained growth (Acemoglu 2008).

A crucial determinant of whether Europeans chose the path of extractive institutions was whether they settled in large numbers. In colonies where Europeans settled, the institutions were being developed for their own future benefits. In colonies where Europeans did not settle, their objective was to set up a highly centralized state apparatus, and other associated institutions, to oppress the native population and facilitate the extraction of resources in the short run. Based on this idea, Acemoglu, Johnson, and Robinson (2001) suggest that in places where the disease environments made it easy for Europeans to settle, the path of institutional development should have been different from areas where Europeans faced high mortality rates.

In practice, during the time of colonization, Europeans faced widely different mortality rates in colonies because of differences in the prevalence of malaria and yellow fever. These therefore provide a possible candidate for a source of exogenous variation in institutions. These mortality rates should not influence output today directly, but by affecting the settlement patterns of Europeans, they may have had a first-order effect on institutional development. Consequently, these potential settler mortality rates can be used as an *instrument* for broad institutional differences across countries in an instrumental-variables estimation strategy.

The key requirement for an instrument is that it should have no direct effect on the outcome of interest (other than its effect via the endogenous regressor). A number of channels can be identified through which potential settler mortality could influence current economic outcomes or may be correlated with other factors influencing these outcomes. Nevertheless, there are also good reasons for why, as a first approximation, these mortality rates should not have a direct effect. Malaria and yellow fever were fatal to Europeans who had no immunity, thus having a major effect on settlement patterns, but they had much more limited effects on indigenous peoples who, over centuries, had developed various types of immunities. The exclusion restriction is also supported by the death rates of native populations, which appear to be similar between areas with very different mortality rates for Europeans (see, for example, Curtin 1964).

The data also show major differences in the institutional development of the high- and low-mortality colonies. Moreover, consistent with the key idea in Acemoglu, Johnson, and Robinson (2001), various measures of broad institutions, for example, measures of protection against expropriation, are highly correlated with the death rates Europeans faced more than 100 years ago and with early European settlement patterns. They also show that these institutional differences induced by mortality rates and European settlement patterns have a major (and robust) effect on income per capita. For example, the estimates imply that improving Nigeria's institutions to the level of those in Chile could, in the long run, lead to as much as a sevenfold increase in Nigeria's income per capita, which accounts for the preponderance of the difference between the countries. This evidence suggests that once we focus on potentially exogenous sources of variation, the data point to a large effect of broad institutional differences on economic development.

Naturally, mortality rates faced by Europeans were not the only determinant of Europeans' colonization strategies. Acemoglu, Johnson, and Robinson (2002) focus on another important aspect: how densely different regions were populated before colonization. They document that in more densely settled areas, Europeans were more likely to introduce extractive institutions because it was more profitable for them to exploit the indigenous population, either by having them work in plantations and mines or by maintaining the existing system and collecting taxes and tributes. This suggests another source of variation in institutions that may have persisted to the present, and Acemoglu, Johnson, and Robinson (2002) show similar large effects from this source of variation.

Another example that illustrates the consequences of difference in institutions is the contrast between the Democratic People's Republic of Korea and the Republic of Korea. The geopolitical balance between the Soviet Union and the United States following World War II led to separation along the 38th parallel. The Democratic People's Republic of Korea, under the dictatorship of Kim Il Sung, adopted a very centralized command economy with little role for private property. In the meantime, the Republic of Korea relied on a capitalist organization of the economy, with private ownership of the means of production and legal protection for a range of producers, especially those under the umbrella of the *chaebols,* the large family conglomerates that dominated the Republic of Korea's economy. Although not democratic during its early phases, the Republic of Korea's state was generally supportive of rapid development and is often credited with facilitating, or even encouraging, investment and rapid growth.

Under these two highly contrasting regimes, the economies of the Democratic People's Republic of Korea and the Republic of Korea diverged. Although the Republic of Korea has grown rapidly under capitalist institutions and policies, the Democratic People's Republic of Korea has experienced minimal growth since 1950 under communist institutions and policies.

Overall, a variety of evidence paints a picture in which broad institutional differences across countries have had a major influence on their economic development. This evidence suggests that to understand why some countries are poor we should understand why their institutions are dysfunctional. This, however, is only part of a first step in the journey toward an answer. The next question is even harder: if institutions have such a large effect on economic riches, why do some societies choose, end up with, and maintain these dysfunctional institutions?

Modeling Institutional Differences

As a first step in modeling institutions, let us consider the relationship between three institutional characteristics: (1) economic institutions, (2) political power, and (3) political institutions.

As already mentioned above, economic institutions matter for economic growth because they shape the incentives of key economic actors in society. In particular, they influence investments in physical and human capital and technology and the organization of production. Economic institutions determine not only the aggregate economic growth potential of the economy, but also the distribution of resources in the society, and herein lies part of the problem: different institutions will be associated not only with different degrees of efficiency and potential for economic growth, but also with different distribution of the gains across different individuals and social groups.

How are economic institutions determined? Although various factors play a role here, including history and chance, at the end of the day, economic institutions are collective choices of the society. Because of their influence on the distribution of economic gains, not all individuals and groups typically prefer the same set of economic institutions. This leads to a *conflict of interest* among various groups and individuals over the choice of economic institutions, and the *political power* of the different groups will be the deciding factor.

The distribution of political power in society is also endogenous. To make more progress here, let us distinguish between two components of political power—*de jure* and *de facto* political power (see Acemoglu and Robinson 2006a). De jure political power refers to power that originates from the *political institutions* in society. Political institutions, similar to economic institutions, determine the constraints on and the incentives of the key actors, but this time in the political sphere. Examples of political institutions include the form of government, for example, democracy versus dictatorship or autocracy, and the extent of constraints on politicians and political elites.

A group of individuals, even if they are not allocated power by political institutions, may possess political power; for example, they can revolt, use arms, hire mercenaries, co-opt the military, or undertake protests to impose their wishes on society. This type of *de facto political power* originates from both the ability of the group in question to solve its collective action problem and the economic resources available to the group (which determines its capacity to use force against other groups).

This discussion highlights that we can think of political institutions and the distribution of economic resources in society as two *state variables,* affecting how political power will be distributed and how economic institutions will be chosen. An important notion is that of *persistence;* the distribution of resources and political institutions is relatively slow changing and persistent. Because, like economic institutions, political institutions are collective choices, the distribution of political power in society is the key determinant of their evolution. This creates a central mechanism of persistence: political institutions allocate de jure political power, and those who hold political power influence the evolution of political institutions, and they will generally opt to maintain the political institutions that give them political power. A second mechanism of persistence comes from the distribution of resources: when a particular group is rich relative to others, this will increase its de facto political power and enable it to push for economic and political institutions favorable to its interests, reproducing the initial disparity. We shall see later that these ideas are powerful in developing ideas about why reform is so difficult. Reform comes with pitfalls because either de facto or de jure power may persist even if other things change.

Figure 5.1. The Determinants of Institutions

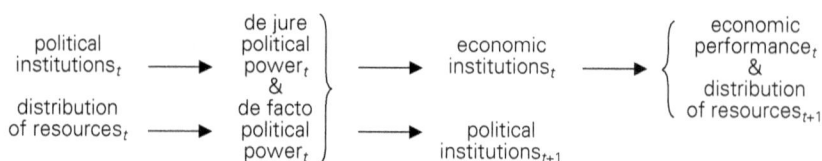

$$\left.\begin{array}{l}\text{political}\\\text{institutions}_t\\[1em]\text{distribution}\\\text{of resources}_t\end{array}\right\} \longrightarrow \left.\begin{array}{l}\text{de jure}\\\text{political}\\\text{power}_t\\\&\\\text{de facto}\\\text{political}\\\text{power}_t\end{array}\right\} \longrightarrow \begin{array}{l}\text{economic}\\\text{institutions}_t\\[2em]\text{political}\\\text{institutions}_{t+1}\end{array} \longrightarrow \left\{\begin{array}{l}\text{economic}\\\text{performance}_t\\\&\\\text{distribution}\\\text{of resources}_{t+1}\end{array}\right.$$

Source: Acemoglu, Johnson, and Robinson (2005b).

Despite these tendencies for persistence, the framework also emphasizes the potential for change. In particular, "shocks" to the balance of de facto political power, including changes in technologies and the international environment, have the potential to generate major changes in political institutions, and consequently in economic institutions and economic growth.

Acemoglu, Johnson, and Robinson (2005b) summarized this framework with the schematic representation shown in figure 5.1.

A Simple Historical Example

As a brief example, consider the development of property rights in Europe during the late Middle Ages and Early Modern period. Lack of property rights for landowners, merchants, and proto-industrialists was detrimental to economic growth during this epoch. Political institutions at the time placed political power in the hands of kings and various types of hereditary monarchies, so such rights were largely decided by these monarchs. The monarchs often used their powers to expropriate producers, impose arbitrary taxation, renege on their debts, and allocate the productive resources of society to their allies in return for economic benefits or political support. Consequently, economic institutions during the Middle Ages provided little incentive to invest in land, physical or human capital, or technology and failed to foster economic growth. These economic institutions also ensured that the monarchs controlled a large fraction of the economic resources in society, solidifying their political power, and ensuring the continuation of the political regime.

The seventeenth century, however, witnessed major changes in the economic and political institutions that paved the way for the development of property rights and limits on monarchs' power, especially in England after the Civil War of the 1640s and the Glorious Revolution of 1688, and in the Netherlands after the Dutch Revolt against the Hapsburgs between 1568 and 1648. How did these major institutional changes take place? In England until the sixteenth century the king also possessed a substantial amount of de facto political power, and leaving aside civil wars related to royal succession, no other social group could amass sufficient de facto political power to challenge the king. But changes in the English land market

(Tawney 1941) and the expansion of Atlantic trade in the sixteenth and seventeenth centuries (Acemoglu, Johnson, and Robinson 2005a) gradually increased the economic fortunes, and consequently the de facto power, of landowners and merchants opposed to the absolutist tendencies of the kings.

By the seventeenth century, the growing prosperity of the merchants and the gentry, based on both internal and overseas (especially Atlantic) trade, enabled them to field military forces capable of defeating the king. This de facto power overcame the Stuart monarchs in the Civil War and Glorious Revolution and led to a change in political institutions that stripped the king of much of his previous power over policy. These changes in the distribution of political power led to major changes in economic institutions, strengthening the property rights of both land and capital owners and spurring a process of financial and commercial expansion. The consequence was rapid economic growth, culminating in the Industrial Revolution and a very different distribution of economic resources from that in the late Middle Ages.

This discussion poses, and also gives clues about the answers to, two crucial questions. First, why do the groups with conflicting interests not agree on the set of economic institutions that maximize aggregate growth? Second, why do groups with political power want to change political institutions in their favor? In the context of the example above, why did the gentry and merchants use their de facto political power to change political institutions rather than simply implement the policies they wanted? The issue of *commitment* is at the root of the answers to both questions.

An agreement on the efficient set of institutions is often not forthcoming because of the complementarity between economic and political institutions and because groups with political power cannot commit to not using their power to change the distribution of resources in their favor. For example, economic institutions that increased the security of property rights for land and capital owners during the Middle Ages would not have been credible as long as the monarch monopolized political power. He could promise to respect property rights but then at some point renege on his promise, as exemplified by the numerous financial defaults by medieval kings. Credible secure property rights necessitated a reduction in the political power of the monarch. Although these more secure property rights would foster economic growth, they were not appealing to the monarchs, who would lose their rents from predation and expropriation as well as various other privileges associated with their monopoly of political power. This is why the institutional changes in England as a result of the Glorious Revolution were not easily conceded by the Stuart kings. James II had to be deposed for the changes to take place.

The reason that political power is often used to change political institutions is related. In a dynamic world, individuals care about economic outcomes not only today but also in the future. In the example above, the gentry and merchants were interested in their profits and therefore in the security of their property rights, not only in the present but also in the future. Therefore, they would have liked to use their (de facto) political power to secure benefits in the future as well as the present. However, commitment to future allocations (or economic institutions) is in general not possible because decisions in the future are made by those who hold political power at the time. If the gentry and merchants had been confident of their future de facto political power, this would not have been a problem. However, de facto political power is often *transient,* for example, because the collective action problems that are solved to amass this power are likely to resurface in the future, or other groups, especially those controlling de jure power, can become stronger in the future. Therefore, any change in policies and economic institutions that relies purely on de facto political power is likely to be reversed in the future. In addition, many revolutions are followed by conflict among the revolutionaries. Recognizing this, the English gentry and merchants strove not just to change economic institutions in their favor following their victories against the Stuart monarchy, but also to alter political institutions and the future allocation of de jure power. Using political power to change political institutions then emerges as a useful strategy to make gains more durable. Consequently, political institutions and changes in political institutions are important as ways of manipulating future political power, and thus indirectly shaping future, as well as present, economic institutions and outcomes.

Pitfalls of Reform

The framework we have sketched above is useful in delineating a range of dysfunctional political equilibria and consequent economic institutions. We have also emphasized how important it is to understand the political forces and institutions that keep these dysfunctional economic institutions in place and are often mutually self-reinforcing (complementary) with these economic institutions. Nevertheless, at present we do not have a satisfactory understanding of the circumstances under which dysfunctional political equilibria arise and sustain themselves. A natural idea would be to focus on specific political institutions such as democracy. Yet we know that democracy per se is not necessarily associated with better development outcomes, and we all know the famous examples of "developmental dictatorships" such as in the Republic of Korea or Taiwan, China. However, as yet, we do not understand why some dictatorships are developmental and others are not, or why, for instance, there has never been a developmental dictatorship in sub-Saharan Africa or Latin America.

Although we cannot yet say under what circumstances political equilibria that lead to economic growth will arise, we can illustrate the power of the ideas we have developed by examining the issue of institutional reform. If economic institutions do not create the right incentives in society, then a natural approach is to directly try to reform economic institutions. If security of property rights is the problem under kleptocracies, then why not introduce (or force dictators to introduce) more secure property rights? The potential problems facing such an approach highlight the first set of *pitfalls of institutional reform*. Our framework emphasizes that one should not try to understand or manipulate economic institutions without thinking about the political forces that created or sustain them. Although blatant disregard for property rights is a powerful distortionary force in kleptocratic societies, it is not the only instrument available to a dictator who wants to extract resources from the rest of the society.

The comparison of Ghana in the 1960s and 1970s to Zimbabwe today nicely illustrates these ideas. In Zimbabwe the mass expropriation and redistribution of agricultural land has led to a collapse in the economy (GDP per capita has apparently fallen by around 50 percent since the introduction of the fast-track land reform policy in 2000). In Ghana agricultural policies were also motivated by the desire to redistribute incomes (Bates 1981), but the property rights of rural producers were never challenged. Instead, a succession of governments used monopsony marketing boards to set very low prices for crops such as cocoa. The instruments were very different, but the motivation and economic effects were similar.

This reasoning suggests that direct institutional reform in itself is unlikely to be effective and that instead it might be more useful to focus on understanding and reforming the forces that keep bad institutions in place. It is therefore important to focus on political institutions and the distribution of political power as well as the nature of economic institutions in thinking about potential institutional reform or institution building. This raises the second potential pitfall of institutional reform; although we have recognized the importance of political institutions, we are still at the beginning of understanding the complex relationship between political institutions and the political equilibrium. Sometimes changing political institutions may be insufficient, or even counterproductive, in leading to better economic outcomes. Once again the use of a theoretical framework in thinking about these issues is useful both for academic research and in generating better policy advice.

The pitfalls of institutional reform are related to the fact that patterns of relative economic performance are very persistent. Indeed, our framework emphasized persistence. This is not to say that change does not occur: it does, and some countries manage to dramatically change their position in the world income distribution. However, it is a striking fact in the Americas, to take one example, that the rank order of countries in terms of income per capita has been basically unchanged at least since the middle of the nineteenth century. This suggests that it is difficult to change institutions and that there are powerful forces at work reinforcing the status quo. Examining the pitfalls of reform is one way of approaching this issue. We then move to examining successful change.

We begin our discussion by focusing at more length on whether reforming specific economic institutions is likely to be effective. We argue that such reforms may not work if they do not change the political equilibrium. We then examine if these pitfalls of reform can be solved by reforming political institutions (thus altering the distribution of de jure power in society). We argue that this may not work either, because de facto power may persist and may override the effects of reforms on political institutions. From this it might seem to follow that a successful reform necessitates changes in both de jure and de facto power. We show that simultaneously changing both may not achieve real reform either because the political equilibrium may be path dependent.

Persistence of Power and Incentives—The Seesaw Effect

Many dysfunctional economic institutions are supported by a system of specific laws and regulations that relate to these institutions. This is true of the labor-repressive agricultural societies of nineteenth-century Russia and Eastern Europe (Acemoglu and Robinson 2006b) or twentieth-century El Salvador and Guatemala, where the legal system kept workers in semi-servile status and blocked their mobility. It is also true of highly oligarchic societies with very concentrated industrial structures, such as modern-day Mexico, where specific barriers to entry block competition. An obvious idea might be to change the laws and regulations. For example, if Latin American countries grew slowly after the Second World War because they levied high tariffs on imports, then irrespective of what forces led these tariffs to be put in place, removing them ought to stimulate growth. This was the sort of reasoning that led to the famous Washington consensus.

The first pitfall of institutional reform is that directly reforming specific economic institutions (such as the trade regime) may not be sufficient, and may even backfire. The reason that reforms of specific economic institutions may be ineffective is that many different ways and a multitude of instruments may be used to achieve a specific goal. Taking away one instrument without altering the balance of power in society or the basic political equilibrium can simply lead to the replacement of one instrument by another. This phenomenon was dubbed the *see-saw effect* by Acemoglu and others (2003).

Case Study: Reform and the New Clientelism in Latin America

Prominent examples of reforms were those imposed on Latin American countries following the debt crisis of the 1980s. As part of packages to repay debt, Latin American countries abandoned many aspects of the economic institutions that had been prevalent since the 1930s and 1940s. Policy reforms that took place in the late 1980s and 1990s included deregulation of the trade regime and severe cuts in tariffs, privatization, and financial deregulation. Although this had been done earlier in Chile and attempted by the military regime in Argentina after 1976, this was now done wholesale in most Latin American countries. Even though there was an economic crisis, the acceptance of these policy reforms by such institutions as the Peronist party in Argentina appears to be quite strange. Enduring crises and many rounds of policy reform have not induced many African countries toward reform. One difference, of course, is that Latin American countries are more democratic than African ones, making it more difficult to maintain the status quo in the face of economic collapse. Another important difference is that Latin American politicians realized that the policies of neoliberalism could be manipulated to fulfill clientelistic ends. As Roberts (1995: 114) convincingly argues in his analysis of the reforms of Fujimori, "The Peruvian case demonstrates that it may be possible to craft populist formulas that complement neoliberalism." For example, privatization could be organized to redistribute rents by reducing competition and giving privatized assets as favors to political supporters (see Gibson 1997; Roberts and Arce 1998; Weyland 1998, 2002). There were, of course, differences: for example, in Argentina the Peronist party distanced itself from its traditional supporters in the labor movement. But such a strategy was feasible because the political power of the labor movement had been severely damaged by repression under the military. The Peronist party was able to reinvent itself (Levitsky 2003) and carry on with clientelism as usual.

The see-saw effect operates here in the following sense: to win power in Argentina, for example, the Peronist party traditionally engaged in redistribution of incomes and rents. The instruments it used to do this included rationing of foreign exchange or the distribution of rents via industrial licenses. The policy reforms of the 1990s meant that these old instruments could not be used. For example, the currency board took away the ability of ration access to foreign exchange. Other instruments were still available for use to achieve the same ends: for example, the labor movements were compensated for some deregulation by being able to benefit from privatization. Despite the crises in the 1980s, changes in the distribution of political power in Argentine society (the unions were weaker), and changes in the feasible instruments through which to pursue clientelism, the political incentive environment was remarkably stable over time, and as a consequence little improvement was seen in the economic incentive environment in Argentina.

Case Study: The Structural Adjustment of Politics in Africa

Another important example of the see-saw effect comes from the politics of structural adjustment in Africa. The attempt to induce African countries to implement institutional reforms such as reducing distortions was not a success (van de Walle 1993, 2000), mostly for the reason that international financial institutions did not take into account the political rationale for the inefficient policies that they were trying to reform. The most dramatic example of this is discussed by Herbst (1990) and Reno (1998). They argued that attempts by international financial institutions (IFIs) to induce downsizing of the public sector, for example, by closing down unprofitable parastatals, had played an important role in creating civil war in Liberia and Sierra Leone. Regimes in both countries had used public-sector employment as a method of redistributing rents to opponents or potential opponents of the regime and buying political support. Once these options had been taken away by structural adjustment, more opposition to the regimes emerged, and incumbents switched from using carrots to using sticks. In this story, policy reform induced a switch from one inefficient instrument, patronage through public-sector employment, to an even more inefficient one, repression. This is the see-saw effect in action.

General Lessons

Making or imposing specific institutional reforms may have little impact on the general structure of economic institutions or performance if they leave untouched the underlying political equilibrium. Of course, as the framework above emphasized, political power will to some extent reflect economic institutions, so it is possible that a change in economic institutions may induce a change in de facto power and ultimately in the broader political equilibrium. Nevertheless, as the above examples make clear, this is far from certain. A piecemeal approach may be dangerous. Often we see the symptoms, but they are precisely the symptoms of deeper causes. Dealing with the symptoms other than causes may backfire.

Despite all of the Washington consensus reforms that took place in Argentina, for example, little change occurred in the way politics worked. The political genius of Menem and the Peronist party after 1989 was to recognize that the policies of the Washington consensus could be bent to function as "politics as usual." In consequence there was little change in the underlying political equilibrium, although the instruments that the Peronists used after 1989 were different. This perspective is, of course, very different from that which claims that the Washington consensus reforms failed (Rodrik 2006). Our view is not that they failed, but that for them to have succeeded a change in the political equilibrium in Argentina would have been necessary. Although it is possible that such reforms could change the political equilibrium, it did not happen.

The points are related to those made by Stigler (1971, 1982) and Coate and Morris (2005) in their discussion of the political economy of income redistribution. Stigler pointed out that it was political incentives that led income redistribution to take a socially inefficient form. For instance, although it might be better to redistribute to farmers by giving them lump-sum transfers, subsidizing farm output might be more attractive politically because it was not perceived as income redistribution by other voters (see Coate and Morris 1995 for a formalization of this idea). This being the case, Coate and Morris (2005) noted that policy reform that aimed at banning the use of particular inefficient instruments might be counterproductive because rational politicians would already be using the least-cost way of redistributing, given the political constraints and incentives they faced.

Persistence of De Facto Power

The last section illustrated that reforming specific economic institutions without disturbing the underlying political equilibrium may not lead to improved economic institutions or performance. Moreover, we shall now argue that even reforming de jure power (for instance, enfranchising former slaves) or introducing democracy may not be sufficient to induce broader institutional change. The reason that changes in de jure power may not be sufficient to trigger a change in the political equilibrium is that the political and economic system is kept in place by a combination of de jure and de facto political power. An external or internal impetus to change de jure institutions may still leave the sources of de facto power intact, and groups that have lost their de jure power may use their de facto power to re-create a system similar to the one that has departed (Acemoglu and Robinson 2006c, 2008). The new system may be as inefficient as the old one.

This is not to argue that reform of de jure institutions is not possible or that it is irrelevant. For example, democratization in many European societies in the nineteenth century appears to have significantly changed economic institutions, for example, leading to sustained expansions of educational systems (Acemoglu and Robinson 2000; Lindert 2004). Nevertheless, this section emphasizes that such reforms come with pitfalls.

Case Study: The Persistence of the Southern Equilibrium

> De landlord is landlord, de politician is landlord, de judge is landlord, de shurf is landlord, ever'body is landlord, en we ain' got nothin.
> —Testimony of a Mississippi sharecropper to an official of the Agricultural Adjustment Administration in 1936 (Schulman 1994: 16)

An important example that illustrates our thesis is the continuation of the economic system based on labor repression, plantation, and low-wage uneducated labor in the U.S. South before and after the significant changes in political institutions brought about by the Civil War. Most obviously these changes in de jure power included the enfranchisement of the freed slaves.

Before the Civil War, the South was significantly poorer than the U.S. average income at about 70 percent of GDP per capita. The South lacked industry (Bateman and Weiss 1981; Wright 1986: 27, table 2.4), and in 1860 the total manufacturing output of the South was less than that of either Pennsylvania, New York, or Massachusetts (Cobb 1984: 6). The South had very low rates of urbanization (around 9 percent as opposed to 35 percent in the Northeast) and relatively little investment in infrastructure. For example, the density of railroads (miles of track divided by land area) was three times higher in the North than in Southern states. The situation with respect to canal mileage was similar (Wright 1986: 21, table 2.1). Perhaps more important, especially in the context of the potential for future economic growth and industrialization, the South was not even innovative for the sectors in which it specialized.

The relative backwardness of the South was because of the plantation economy and slavery. Wright (1986) argues that because slaves were a mobile asset, there was no incentive for planter interests to support investment in public goods such as infrastructure, and so manufacturing could not develop. Bateman and Weiss (1981) show that Southern planters did not invest in industry, even though the rate of return was superior to that in agriculture. A plausible explanation for the lack of innovation is that slavery limited the possibilities for productive investment. Slaves were forbidden to own property or to become educated in most Southern states, presumably because this made them easier to control. This pattern of labor repression, however, also condemned plantations to low-skilled labor forces and possibly removed the incentives of planters to innovate.

In the aftermath of the Civil War, the income per capita of the South fell to about 50 percent of the U.S. average. If the organization of the slave economy had been the reason that the South had been relatively backward in 1865, one might have imagined that the abolition of slavery in 1865 would have removed this blockage to Southern prosperity. The evidence and historical interpretations show that the abolition of slavery had a surprisingly small effect on the Southern economy. Although planters initially tried and failed to reintroduce the gang-labor system with the freed slaves, out of the ashes of the Civil War emerged a low-wage, labor-intensive economy based on labor repression. Cut off from the rest of the United States, income per capita remained at about half the national average until the 1940s, when it finally began slowly to converge. Just as before the Civil War, there was systematic underinvestment in education (Margo 1990). The main incentive for this seems to have been to impede migration (see Wright 1986: 79). In 1900 all but two of the non-Southern states had enacted compulsory schooling laws, whereas no states in the South had such laws except Kentucky (Woodward 1951: 399). Although industrial development did begin more systematically after 1865, Cobb (1984: 17) notes: "The industries that grew most rapidly in the post-Reconstruction decades were typical of an underdeveloped economy in that they utilized both cheap labor and abundant raw materials. . . . [S]uch industries hardly promised to elevate the region to economic parity with the rest of the nation."

Why did the economic system of the South change so little following the Civil War, especially given the significant changes in political institutions? At first, this persistence of economic institutions appears at odds with the significant changes in the distribution of de jure power that took place after the Civil War, for example, with the enfranchisement of the freed slaves, and the repeal of the Missouri Compromise, which had previously cemented the political power of the South in the federal government.

We believe that the answer is related to the exercise of de facto political power by the Southern landed elites to compensate for the loss of their de jure political power. Consistent with our approach, considerable persistence was seen in the identity and power of the political elites. For example, Wiener (1978) studied the persistence of the planter elite in five counties of the black belt of western Alabama. Tracking families from the U.S. census and considering those with at least $10,000 of real estate, he found that "of the 236 members of the planter elite in 1850, 101 remained in the elite in 1870." Interestingly, this rate of persistence was very similar to that experienced in the antebellum period: "Of the 236 wealthiest planters families of 1850, only 110 remained in the elite a decade later." Nevertheless, "of the 25 planters with the largest landholdings in 1870, 18 (72 percent) had been in the elite families in 1860; 16 had been in the 1850 elite group" (Wiener 1978: 9).

After the end of the Civil War, more or less the same group of planter elites controlled the land and used various instruments to reexert their control over the labor force. Although the specific economic institution of slavery did not persist, the evidence shows a clear line of persistence in the economic system of the South based on plantation-type agriculture with cheap labor. This economic system was maintained through a variety of channels, including both control of local politics and exercise of potentially violent de facto power. As a consequence, in the words of W. E. B. Du Bois (1903: 88), the South became "simply an armed camp for intimidating black folk."

The planter elite successfully staffed or co-opted the members of the Freedmen's Bureau, whose remit was to supervise the freed slaves. In 1865 the state legislature of Alabama passed the Black Code, an important landmark toward the repression of black labor. Wiener (1978: 58) describes this as follows: "The Black Code of Alabama included two key laws intended to assure the planters a reliable supply of labor—a vagrancy law, and a law against the 'enticement' of laborers." These laws were designed to impede labor mobility and reduce competition in the labor market.

In addition to molding the legal system in their favor, "Planters used Klan terror to keep blacks from leaving the plantation regions, to get them to work, and keep them at work, in the cotton field" (Wiener 1978: 62). In his seminal study of the politics of the South after World War II, Key (1949: 9) sums up the pattern of persistence of the institutions of the South both before and after the Civil War as the "extraordinary achievement of a relatively small minority—the whites of the areas of heavy Negro population."

A key to the persistence of the antebellum system after the Civil War was the continued control over land. For example, in the debate over the redistribution of 40 acres of land to the freedmen (vetoed by President Andrew Johnson in 1865), Congressman George Washington Julian argued (quoted in Wiener 1978: 6): "Of what avail would be an act of congress totally abolishing slavery . . . if the old agricultural basis of aristocratic power shall remain?"

A third strategy, again consistent with the emphasis on the de facto political power of the elite in our theoretical analysis, was control of the local political system. Following the Civil War, the period called Reconstruction lasted until 1877. In this period Republican politicians contested power in the South and, with the help of the Union Army, engineered some social changes. Nevertheless, this induced a systematic backlash in the guise of support for the Democratic Party and the so-called Redeemers. In 1877, in the context of a log-roll between President Rutherford Hayes and Southern national politicians, Union soldiers were withdrawn from the South and the region left to its own devices. The period after 1877 then marked the real recrudescence of the antebellum elite. The "redemption" of the South involved the systematic disenfranchisement of the black (and poor white) population through the use of poll taxes and literacy tests (Key 1949, Kousser 1974) and the creation of the one-party Democratic regime.

Key (1949: 309–10), in his analysis of the primary elections of the Democratic Party, noted the hegemony of Southern society's "upper brackets" and the political marginalization of its "lower brackets." He discusses in detail the control of North Carolina's economic oligarchy over politics, noting that, "The effectiveness of the oligarchy's control has been achieved through the elevation to office of persons fundamentally in harmony with its viewpoint" (Key 1949: 211).

This picture is also confirmed by Wright's analysis (1986: 78), who writes: "Even in the 1930s, southern representatives in Washington did not use their powerful positions to push for new federal projects, hospitals, public works and so on. They didn't, that is, as long as the foundations of the low-wage regional economy persisted."

In addition to disenfranchisement, a whole gamut of segregationist legislation—the so-called Jim Crow laws—was enacted (see Woodward 1955 for the classic analysis). These laws turned the postbellum South into an effective "apartheid" society where blacks and whites lived different lives. As in South Africa, these laws were aimed at controlling the black population and its labor supply.

Consequently, the South entered the twentieth century as a primarily rural society: "It remained an agrarian society with a backward technology that still employed hand labor and mule power virtually unassisted by mechanical implements" (Ransom and Sutch 2001: 175–76). In 1900 the South's urbanization rate was 13.5 percent, as compared to 60 percent in the Northeast (Cobb 1984: 25).

Ransom and Sutch's (2001: 186) assessment of the implications of this economic and political system in the South for economic progress is representative of the consensus view: "Southerners erected an economic system that failed to reward individual initiative on the part of blacks and was therefore ill-suited to their economic advancement. As a result, the inequities originally inherited from slavery persisted. But there was a by-product of this effort at racial repression, the system tended to cripple all economic growth." The South remained relatively poor because

> When whites used threats of violence to keep blacks from gaining an education, practicing a trade, or purchasing land, they systematically prevented blacks from following the three routes most commonly travelled by other Americans in their

quest for self-advancement. With over half the population held in ignorance and forced to work as agricultural laborers, it is no wonder that the South was poor, underdeveloped, and without signs of economic progress. (Ransom and Sutch 2001: 177)

All in all, the Southern equilibrium, based on the exercise of de facto power by the landed elite, plantation agriculture, and low-wage, uneducated labor, persisted well into the twentieth century, and started to crumble only after World War II. Interestingly, it was only after the demise of this Southern equilibrium that the South started its process of rapid convergence to the North.

Case Study: The Reinvention of the Cambodian People's Party

In 1978 senior Khmer Rouge cadres, including Heng Samrin, Chea Sim, and Hun Sen, escaped to Vietnam after falling out with Pol Pot. In 1979 they were placed in power in Phnom Penh by the Vietnamese Army and formed the Communist Party of Kampuchea. In the 1980s they tried to implement socialism, but after the Berlin Wall came down, Hun Sen and his colleagues renamed their party the Cambodian People's Party (CPP), became democrats, and negotiated an opening of the political system (Hughes 2003). Although this involved the return of King Norodom Sihanouk from exile and necessitated that Hun Sen share power, his party, the CPP, managed to reinvent itself as a democratic political machine. For instance, in 2002 elections were introduced for commune chiefs, who had previously been appointed. The CPP won 1,591 of 1,621 positions. Primarily via its control of the bureaucracy and military, the CPP wins every election, and those who oppose it too strenuously, such as Sam Rainsy, are exiled or arrested. Here, despite the change in de jure institutions, the huge de facto power of the CPP means that it can dominate democratic politics through superior organization and resources, heavily aided by threats and intimidation.

General Lessons

Just as reforming economic institutions without changing the political equilibrium may not improve the institutional equilibrium, so changing de jure power, while leaving the sources of de facto power intact, may have little impact on economic performance. In the U.S. South, the same economic system based on the repression of cheap labor was reinstituted after Reconstruction. Even though the enfranchisement of the freed slaves meant that there had been a change in de jure power, and after the Civil War blacks exercised this power and voted in large numbers, Southern elites were able to use their de facto power to reassert control over labor and eventually by the 1890s disenfranchise the blacks. The persistence of de facto power stemmed from the fact that white elites had kept hold of the land after the Civil War and had avoided being killed during the Civil War and still had a huge comparative advantage over blacks in the ability to engage in collective action. Control was exercised via coercion, lynching, the Ku Klux Klan, and other extra-legal methods and eventually institutionalized via control of state legislatures.

In Cambodia, the transition away from socialism after 1989 and the opening of the political system and creation of de jure democracy after 1993 have not been sufficient to change the political equilibrium. The Cambodian People's Party, led by former Khmer Rouge cadres such as Hun Sen and Chea Sim, have been able to use their control of the bureaucracy and the army to win elections and have emasculated, co-opted, and sometimes banned the opposition. Although large changes have taken place in specific economic institutions, particularly with the move away from socialism to capitalism, as well as alterations in de jure political institutions, the society continues to be run to the benefit of a small elite who are free to enrich themselves at the expense of the wider society.

The general lesson seems to be that change in institutions, which affects the distribution of de jure political power, needs to be complemented by changes in the sources of de facto political power of the elite and reductions in the benefits that political incumbents have in intensifying their use of de facto political power (for example, use of paramilitaries, bribery, and corruption).

The Iron Law of Oligarchy

The conclusion one might make from the last section is that to change the political equilibrium there needs to be changes in both de jure and de facto power. For instance, if an elite is structuring institutions to its benefit with adverse aggregate effects, then to engineer a transition to a better equilibrium both their de jure and de facto power must be simultaneously reformed. To take a contemporary example, this would imply that to reform Iraq, it would not be sufficient to simply remove Saddam Hussein and introduce democracy, because the Ba'ath Party would still have considerable de facto power and would be able to capture the new political institutions. To really achieve reform it would be necessary to undermine the de facto power of the Ba'ath Party, something the U.S. government clearly succeeded in doing.

Unfortunately, things are not quite so simple as this, because even if de jure and de facto power changes, those who acquire the power in the new political equilibrium may not have the correct incentives either. More important, their incentives to use their power and the institutions they find it optimal to create may be fundamentally shaped by the status quo they replace—they may be path dependent. If an elite with power is initially structuring economic institutions to extract rents from society, then the fact that it is doing this may induce a new elite to do likewise. The replacement of one elite by another may therefore do little to improve economic performance. This pitfall is reminiscent of the classic idea in sociology of an *iron law of oligarchy* going back to the work of Mosca (1939), Michels (1962), and Pareto (1968). This hypothesis states that it is never possible to have real change in society, because when new groups mobilize or are created in the process of socioeconomic change, they simply replace preexisting elites and groups and behave in qualitatively similar ways (see Acemoglu and Robinson 2007). Many circumstances may exist in which "iron law" types of behavior may occur, and quite possibly many mechanisms may generate behavior like this. We focus on two that appear to be first order. The first is motivated by the experience of Bolivia following the Revolution of 1952. The second is motivated by the experience of Africa, where many countries have experienced a series of one bad leader after another.

The Bolivian Revolution and the Iron Law

Bolivia features centrally in accounts of comparative development in the Americas. It lay at the heart of the Inca Empire with a high density of indigenous peoples, and during the colonial period economic institutions designed to extract rents—the *encomienda, repartamiento,* and the *Potosí mita* (forced labor draft for the silver mines)—were all central. Although the *mita* was abolished at independence, a highly inegalitarian and authoritarian society persisted. In 1950, for example, 6 percent of landowners owned 92 percent of all lands, and the smallest 60 percent of landowners owned 0.2 percent. The tin mines, which formed the basis of the export economy, were owned by three families. A mere 31 percent of the adult population was literate, and only 4 percent of the labor force was employed in industry. Indians still were subject to unpaid *pongueaje* (personal services) for the landowners whose lands they worked.

The remains of this system were swept away by the Bolivian Revolution of 1952, which was masterminded by the Movimiento Nacionalista Revolucionario (MNR), a political party that had formed in urban areas in the 1940s to contest the power of the traditional elite. Following the revolution, the MNR formed a government that implemented land reform, expropriated large estates, and redistributed them to the labor force and Indian communities. It also introduced universal suffrage by abolishing the literacy requirement on voting and nationalized the mines of the tin barons.

These appear to be huge, radical institutional changes. In particular there was a shift in the distribution of both de jure and de facto power. Surely Bolivia was launched on a new path of institutional and economic development. At the least one would have anticipated a sustained fall in inequality. Unfortunately none of these good outcomes occurred. Following the revolution, the 1950s saw a failed attempt by the MNR to create a one party state, and in the process it rebuilt the military that had been disarmed in 1952. The party was also able to use clientelism to gain the support of the indigenous majority. Indeed, striking comparisons can be identified between the traditional clientelism that had existed before 1952 and that which emerged during the regime of the MNR afterwards. In a seminal study, Heath (1972) showed that although the identity of the patrons was different and the instruments of clientelism had changed following the institutional changes brought by 1952, very strong similarities were present in the basic structure of the political equilibrium. Kelley and Klein (1981) estimated that 15 years after the revolution, inequality had returned to 1952 levels.

How can we understand an outcome such as this? We believe that mechanisms exist that can generate persistence in the political equilibrium even when de jure and de facto power changes and that can produce an iron law of oligarchy. The idea is quite simple. Initially, in Bolivia, institutions were structured to the benefit of traditional elites. A new elite emerged, spearheaded by the MNR. The MNR needed to win support of the *campesinos* and other urban groups. To do this, MNR had to develop a political strategy, but the form that strategy took was highly influenced by the strategies being used by the traditional elite. The traditional elite were clientelistic, so it was optimal to use clientelism to compete with them. Similarly, the traditional elite ran a political system with few checks and balances. Would the MNR find it optimal to create a political system with checks and balances? Not necessarily. After all, although this might have appealed to citizens and garnered more support, it would also have been disadvantageous to them once they were in power. Hence there is a well-defined trade-off. Indeed, the MNR was able to attain power and create highly imperfect political institutions that it was then able to undermine.

General Lessons

One might conclude from our discussion of the U.S. South that the real problem was the persistence of the elite and their resources. If only the North had implemented land reform and given the freed slaves their 40 acres and a mule, everything would have been different. The example of the Bolivian Revolution shows that the situation is more complex than this. In Bolivia the previous elite were expropriated and their power taken away, yet the new elite that emerged (the MNR) used strategies that were very similar to those of the old elite and that had the same impact on economic institutions. Thus a huge path dependence can exist in political equilibria, even when de jure and de facto power changes hands from one group to another. This implies that, for reformers, a policy of changing political institutions and trying simultaneously to undermine the de facto power of incumbents may not work. To reform Iraq it is not sufficient to introduce democracy and undermine the Ba'ath Party. Instead, reformers must change the incentives for the new elites and decouple their choices from those of the previous elites.

Fighting Fire with Fire

A related phenomena to what happened in Bolivia, but that seems to involve different mechanisms, arises mostly in sub-Saharan Africa. Many African countries have experienced changes in the identity of elites and groups in power, but the new leaders seem to be as bad as the old. Most strikingly this happened with the transition from colonial authority. After suffering under King Leopold and then the Belgian colonial state, the Congolese were faced with Patrice Lumumba, Joseph Mobutu, and Laurent Kabila. Is this just a coincidence? Similar transitions occurred in many African countries. After the cocoa farmers in Ghana had protested against the policies of the British authorities, they were exploited even more vigorously by the government of Kwame Nkrumah. Other salient examples in British colonies are Siaka Stevens in Sierra Leone and perhaps the transition from Ian Smith to Robert Mugabe in Zimbabwe. Elsewhere on the continent the transition in Ethiopia from Haile Selassia to Mengistu Haile Mariam in the 1970s is yet another example (see Meredith 2005 on the extraordinary extent to which Mengistu ended up behaving like Haile Selassie). Transitions from one bad leader to another occurred not just at the time of decolonization, but also subsequently. In Zambia, for instance, the long struggle to remove Kenneth Kaunda and his United National Independence Party from power was headed by Frederick Chiluba and the Movement for Multiparty Democracy (MMD). Chiluba was elected president in 1991 after 27 years of United National Independence Party rule. Although Chiluba introduced economic reforms, he also engaged in massive corruption.

The succession of bad leaders seems to be another example of the iron law of oligarchy. On the surface change appears to take place, and often IFIs and foreign governments rush in to give aid and support to the new regime, only to become disillusioned with the lack of real change. Very good reasons for this phenomenon may exist, however (Acemoglu and Robinson 2007). Consider a situation in which a society has a very predatory ruler or ruling clique that is willing to use repression and violence and bend all the rules to stay in power. How can citizens remove such a ruler? To get rid of the regime, it may be necessary to "fight fire with fire" and support a challenger who can be as unscrupulous as the incumbent regime. Think perhaps of the difference between supporting Mahatma Gandhi or Nelson Mandela. Gandhi was obviously a highly principled leader who, had he attained office, would have had the public interest at heart. It turned out that this was also true of Nelson Mandela, but this must have been much less clear in the period before he attained office. In the 1960s Mandela was prepared to be tough, and he played an important role in the formation of Umkhonto we Sizwe, the armed wing of the African National Congress. Who would citizens back, Gandhi or Mandela? A Mandela is attractive because he has a much bigger chance of removing the apartheid state from power, yet when he wins will he be as bad? Gandhi was clearly better than British colonialism, yet he had a much smaller chance of winning. So there is a well-defined trade-off here. In African countries, where there are few checks and balances, it may be relatively attractive for citizens to fight fire with fire. Yet doing this runs the risk of replacing one bad leader with another and not experiencing any improvement in the economic environment.

General Lessons

When citizens decide to fight fire with fire, what can reformers do? The mechanism at work here is different from the one we hypothesized for

Bolivia, where the initial strategy of the incumbent elite influenced the strategy of a new elite. Here, however, it is the citizens who make the most important decisions, and this generates different implications. Again, direct reform of economic institutions is unlikely to be very useful, and this mechanism applies in environments in which political institutions probably place few constraints on the behavior of politicians. Nevertheless, this may be a case in which external intervention to remove bad rulers would imply that citizens no longer need to support unscrupulous opponents to generate change. Potential lessons could therefore be drawn from the recent experience of Sierra Leone, where the strong intervention of British soldiers in 2000 seems to have played an important role is destroying the power of various rebel movements and precipitating the movement of the country back to democracy and some stability. Now it may no longer be necessary for the citizens of Sierra Leone to fight fire with fire, as perhaps they did in 1967 when they put Siaka Stevens in power. The case of Sierra Leone, however, suggests how incomplete our understanding of dysfunctional political equilibria is. In the presidential election in September 2007, the people voted back into power the All People's Congress Party, the political machine built by Stevens that he and the ruling clique used as a basis to rule and loot the country for two decades before the onset of the civil war.

Successful Reform

In the last section we used our framework to explain why reform is so difficult and why patterns of relative economic performance are so persistent over time. Nevertheless, countries do reform their institutions and move onto different development paths. Obvious examples that come to mind from the post–World War II development experience include Taiwan, China, in the late 1950s; Botswana, the Republic of Korea, and Singapore in the 1960s; and Chile, China, and Mauritius in the 1970s. Important historical episodes of reform have occurred as well. As we noted earlier, Britain underwent an important process of institutional change in the seventeenth century, and again in the nineteenth century when it expanded democratic rights and began to invest more systematically in education. Obviously some of these instances of institutional transition took place under democracy, as in Botswana and Mauritius, and some took place under authoritarian regimes. Some countries, such as Spain, experienced institutional reforms under authoritarianism in the 1960s and democracy in the 1980s.

Earlier in the chapter we described what drove this process of change in Britain. In particular we argued that changes in economic opportunities altered both interests and the balance of de facto power in society, which in turn destabilized the initial absolutist equilibrium. This led to a process of cumulative change in political and economic institutions. This did not end with the Glorious Revolution but extended to the nineteenth-century

Reform Acts and many other subsequent changes in economic institutions. All of these other examples of successful reform can be described within our framework. Let us consider just one example, Botswana.

As is well known, Botswana, a small, partially tropical, landlocked country in sub-Saharan Africa, has had the fastest average rate of economic growth in the world in the last 35 years. What explains Botswana's success? At a proximate level Botswana has been aided by large quantities of diamonds, yet in general natural resources are not associated with successful economic outcomes in Africa. It has also had very good macroeconomic and microeconomic policies and ranks at the same level as Western European countries in terms of indexes of governance and corruption (Parsons and Robinson 2006). The argument of Acemoglu, Johnson, and Robinson (2003) and Parsons and Robinson (2006) is that Botswana's success is precisely because of its economic and political institutions. Botswana benefited immensely from having indigenous political institutions that put constraints on Tswana chiefs and political elites, and in the nineteenth century the Tswana tribes engaged in a quite successful process of defensive modernization that strengthened these institutions. Significantly, these institutions were not undone by the impact of colonialism, which was very marginal in the country. Thus at independence Bostwana emerged with political institutions that placed checks and balances on political elites. This was important for the security of property rights and governance, and it is an almost unique phenomenon in Africa. In consequence economic institutions were good. Economic institutions were also good because the Tswana chiefs and elite were heavily invested in the main economic sector, ranching, at independence. Hence, as in Britain after the Glorious Revolution, political elites had a vested interest in economic institutions that were socially desirable. In addition, other historical factors were certainly important, such as the fact that the modern nation of Botswana had a certain coherence that other African natures lacked, though much of the apparent homogeneity of Botswana is actually an outcome of the process of state formation, rather than a prerequisite for it (see Leith 2005).

Botswana did well because its political equilibrium facilitated good economic institutions in a way similar to the situation in late-seventeenth-century Britain. Indeed, we can even understand this in the same way in terms of the interaction of de jure political constraints and economic interests. The agenda ahead is to understand better how such an equilibrium can be created elsewhere in Africa.

Conclusions

We believe that several key conclusions can be drawn from this analysis. The main determinants of cross-country differences in income per capita are differences in economic institutions. Although institutions often persist for long periods of time and have unintended consequences, differences in institutions across countries primarily reflect the outcome of different collective choices. Different collective choices reflect differences in political institutions and different distributions of political power. As a result, understanding underdevelopment implies understanding why different countries get stuck in political equilibria that result in bad economic institutions. Solving the problem of development entails understanding what instruments can be used to push a society from a bad to a good political equilibrium.

Unfortunately, this is far beyond what we understand at the moment, and, as yet, we do not have a deep enough comprehension of the forces that lead to good or bad political equilibria. One can note robust patterns in the cross-national data and say a few obvious things. For instance, in the case of Africa, promoting democracy and accountability and checks and balances will almost certainly lead to better economic policies and institutions. Although it is true that developmental authoritarian regimes have held power in East Asia, one has never taken hold in sub-Saharan Africa, so creating one seems a good option from the point of view of neither political freedom nor economic growth. Nevertheless, clear pitfalls lie before those who promote both good economic and political institutions, and we cannot say that improvements in accountability, for instance, will push African countries onto much better growth paths. In this chapter we have focused on these pitfalls and showed that they demonstrate how cautious one must be in promoting reforms. For instance, one cannot necessarily change the political equilibrium by introducing democracy. These pitfalls also illustrate why, for example, so many people in Latin America have been disappointed by the results of the apparent application of the Washington consensus. It is not that these reforms would not be good, other things being equal; it is just that other things are not equal. Reform in one area leads other areas to become unreformed. Our analysis poses challenging problems for those who would wish to solve the problem of development and poverty. Nevertheless, experience strongly suggests that it is difficult to solve these problems, and we believe that the main reasons for this are the forces that we have outlined in this chapter. Better development policy will come only when we recognize this and understand these forces better.

Nevertheless, countries do reform their institutions and move from situations of stagnation to rapid growth. We have argued that this is because of changes in the political equilibrium. It can hardly be denied, for example, that the rapid take-off of growth in China after 1978 was a result of policy and institutional reforms. These were a direct result of the defeat of the "Gang of Four" and a dramatic shift in those who controlled the Communist Party. Growth did not occur because the culture of the Chinese changed, or because some geographical constraint was lifted. Growth also did not occur because previously the Chinese were mistaken about the correct form of policy. They did not suddenly discover what to do. Rather, growth occurred because the political equilibrium changed in a way that gave more power to those who wanted to push through reforms. Said in this way our analysis is an optimistic one. The institutional approach opens the promise that if we can understand the determinants of political equilibria, then we can design interventions that will make poor societies prosperous.

References

Acemoglu, Daron. 2008. "The Form of Property Rights: Oligarchic versus Democratic Societies." *Journal of the European Economic Association* 6: 1–44.

Acemoglu, Daron, Simon Johnson, and James A. Robinson. 2001. "The Colonial Origins of Comparative Development: An Empirical Investigation." *American Economic Review* 91 (Dec.): 1369–1401.

———. 2002. "Reversal of Fortune: Geography and Institutions in the Making of the Modern World Income Distribution." *Quarterly Journal of Economics* 118: 1231–94.

———. 2003. "An African Success: Botswana." In Dani Rodrik, ed., *In Search of Prosperity: Analytic Narratives on Economic Growth*. Princeton, NJ: Princeton University Press.

———. 2005a. "The Rise of Europe: Atlantic Trade, Institutional Change and Economic Growth." *American Economic Review* 95: 546–79.

———. 2005b. "Institutions as the Fundamental Cause of Long-Run Growth." In Philippe Aghion and Steve Durlauf, eds., *Handbook of Economic Growth*. Amsterdam: North-Holland.

Acemoglu, Daron, Simon Johnson, James A. Robinson, and Yunyong Thaicharoen. 2003. "Institutional Causes, Macroeconomic Symptoms." *Journal of Monetary Economics* 50: 49–123.

Acemoglu, Daron, and James A. Robinson. 2000. "Why Did the West Extend the Franchise? Democracy, Inequality and Growth in Historical Perspective." *Quarterly Journal of Economics* 115: 1167–99.

———. 2006a. *Economic Origins of Dictatorship and Democracy*. New York: Cambridge University Press.

———. 2006b. "Economic Backwardness in Political Perspective." *American Political Science Review* 100: 115–31.

———. 2006c. "De Facto Political Power and Institutional Persistence." *American Economic Review* 96: 325–30.

———. 2007. "A Model of the Iron Law of Oligarchy." Work in progress.

———. 2008. "Persistence of Power, Elites and Institutions." *American Economic Review* 75: 282–99.

Bateman, Fred, and Thomas Weiss. 1981. *A Deplorable Scarcity: The Failure of Industrialization in the Slave Economy*. Chapel Hill: University of North Carolina Press.

Bates, Robert H. 1981. *Markets and States in Tropical Africa*. Berkeley: University of California Press.

Coate, Stephen T., and Stephen E. Morris. 1995. "On the Design of Transfers to Special Interests." *Journal of Political Economy* 103: 1210–35.

———. 2005. "Policy Conditionality." In Gustav Ranis and James R. Vreeland, eds., *Globalization and the Nation State: The Impact of the IMF and World Bank*. New York: Routledge.

Cobb, James C. 1984. *Industrialization and Southern Society, 1877–1984*. Lexington: University Press of Kentucky.

Curtin, Philip D. 1964. *The Image of Africa*. Madison: University of Wisconsin Press.

Djankov, Simeon, Rafael LaPorta, Florencio Lopez-de-Silanes, and Andrei Shleifer. 2002. "The Regulation of Entry." *Quarterly Journal of Economics* 117: 1–37.

Du Bois, W. E. B. 1903. *The Souls of Black Folk*. New York: A. C. McClurg & Company.

Gibson, Edward L. 1997. "The Populist Road to Market Reform: Policy and Electoral Coalitions in Mexico and Argentina." *World Politics* 49: 339–70.

Heath, Dwight. 1972. "New Patrons for Old: Changing Patron-Client Relationships in the Bolivian Yungas." In Arnold Strickton and Sidney Greenfield, eds., *Structure and Process in Latin America*. Albuquerque: University of New Mexico Press.

Herbst, Jeffrey I. 1990. "The Structural Adjustment of Politics in Africa." *World Development* 18: 949–58.

Hughes, Caroline. 2003. *The Political Economy of Cambodia's Transition, 1991–2001*. New York: Routledge.

Kelley, Jonathan, and Herbert S. Klein. 1981. *Revolution and the Rebirth of Inequality: A Theory Applied to the National Revolution in Bolivia*. Berkeley: University of California Press.

Key, V. O., Jr. 1949. *Southern Politics: In State and Nation*. New York: Vintage Books.

Knack, Steven, and Philip Keefer. 1995. "Institutions and Economic Performance: Cross-Country Tests Using Alternative Measures." *Economics and Politics* 7: 207–27.

Kousser, J. Morgan. 1974. *The Shaping of Southern Politics: Suffrage Restriction and the Establishment of the One-Party South, 1880–1910*. New Haven, CT: Yale University Press.

Leith, J. Clark. 2005. *Why Botswana Prospered*. Montreal: McGill-Queen's University Press.

Levitsky, Steven. 2003. *Transforming Labor-Based Parties in Latin America: Argentine Peronism in Comparative Perspective*. New York: Cambridge University Press.

Lindert, Peter H. 2004. *Growing Public: Social Spending and Economic Growth since the 18th Century*. New York: Cambridge University Press.

Margo, Robert A. 1990. *Race and Schooling in the South, 1880–1950: An Economic History*. Chicago: University of Chicago Press.

Mauro, Paulo. 1995. "Corruption and Growth" *Quarterly Journal of Economics* 110: 681–712.

Meredith, Martin. 2005. *The Fate of Africa: From the Hopes of Freedom to the Heart of Despair: A History of Fifty Years of Independence*. New York: Public Affairs.

Michels, Robert. 1962. *Political Parties*. New York: Free Press.

Mosca, Gaetano. 1939. *The Ruling Class*. New York: McGraw-Hill.

North, Douglass C. 1981. *Structure and Change in Economic History*. New York: W. W. Norton.

———. 1990. *Institutions, Institutional Change, and Economic Performance*. New York: Cambridge University Press.

Pareto, Vilfredo. 1968. *The Rise and Fall of the Elites*. New York: Arno Press.

Parsons, Q. Neil, and James A. Robinson. 2006. "State Formation and Governance in Botswana." *Journal of African Economies* 15: 100–140.

Ransom, Roger L., and Richard Sutch. 2001. *One Kind of Freedom: The Economic Consequences of Emancipation*. 2nd ed. New York: Cambridge University Press.

Reno, William. 1998. *Warlord Politics and African States*. Boulder, CO: Lynne Rienner.

Roberts, Kenneth M. 1995. "Neoliberalism and the Transformation of Populism in Latin America." *World Politics* 48: 82–116.

Roberts, Kenneth M., and Moisés Arce. 1998. "Neoliberalism and Lower Class Voting Behavior in Peru." *Comparative Political Studies* 31: 217–46.

Rodrik, Dani. 2006 "Goodbye Washington Consensus, Hello Washington Confusion? A Review of the World Bank's Economic Growth in the 1990s: Learning from a Decade of Reform." *Journal of Economic Literature* 44 (4): 973–87.

Schulman, Bruce J. 1994. *From Cotton Belt to Sunbelt: Federal Policy, Economic Development and the Transformation of the South, 1938–1980*. Durham, NC: Duke University Press.

Stigler, George. 1971. "The Economic Theory of Regulation." *Bell Journal of Economics and Management Science* 2: 3–21.

———. 1982. "Economist and Public Policy." *Regulation* 6: 13–17.

Tawney, R. H. 1941. "The Rise of the Gentry, 1558–1640." *Economic History Review* 11: 1–38.

van de Walle, Nicolas. 1993. "The Politics of Nonreform in the Cameroon." In Thomas M. Callaghy and John Ravenhill, eds., *Hemmed In: Responses to Africa's Economic Decline*. New York: Columbia University Press.

———. 2000. *The Politics of Permanent Crisis: Managing African Economies, 1979–1999*. New York: Cambridge University Press.

Weyland, Kurt G. 1998. "Swallowing the Bitter Pill: Sources of Popular Support for Neoliberal Reform." *Comparative Political Studies* 31: 539–68.

———. 2002. *The Politics of Market Reform in Fragile Democracies: Argentina, Brazil, Peru, and Venezuela.* Princeton, NJ: Princeton University Press.

Wiener, Jonathan M. 1978. *Social Origins of the New South: Alabama, 1860–1885.* Baton Rouge: Louisiana State University Press.

Woodward, C. Vann. 1951. *Origins of the New South, 1877–1913.* Baton Rouge: Louisiana State University Press.

———. 1955. *The Strange Career of Jim Crow.* New York: Oxford University Press.

Wright, Gavin. 1986. *Old South, New South.* New York: Basic Books.

CHAPTER 6

Leadership, Policy Making, and Economic Growth in African Countries: The Case of Nigeria

Milton A. Iyoha

Nigeria's economic performance since Independence in 1960 has been decidedly unimpressive. It is estimated that Nigeria received over $228 billion from oil exports between 1981 and 1999 (Udeh 2000), and yet the number of Nigerians living in abject poverty—subsisting on less than $1 a day—more than doubled between 1970 and 2000, and the proportion of the population living in poverty rose from 36 percent to 70 percent over the same period. At official exchange rates, Nigeria's per capita income of $260 in 2000 was precisely one-third of its level in 1980 (World Bank 2005). Meanwhile, during this period Nigeria's external debt rose almost continuously, as did the share of its gross domestic product (GDP) owed annually in debt service.

Nigeria's story is one of missed opportunities and, more specifically, of misspent natural resource rents. Basically, Nigeria failed to surmount the two fundamental challenges generally faced by natural resource dependent economies:

The author gratefully acknowledges the invaluable assistance of Susan Iyoha in researching and editing this chapter. He also thanks the Commission on Growth and Development for financial assistance and useful comments on previous drafts of the chapter.

- Addressing the culture of corruption and rent seeking created by the availability of "easy" oil rents, which reduces the incentives to create wealth by productive work and
- Managing the economy in a way to build and enhance competitiveness of the non-oil sector in the face of large inflows of oil revenues.

Thus, corruption is an important part of the story, as is a pervasive lack of transparency and accountability in governance under military dictatorships. Above all, serious mistakes have been made in macroeconomic management, notably including a Dutch disease–generating syndrome in which policy makers erroneously treated favorable but transitory oil shocks as permanent.

The Political Economy of Economic Growth in Nigeria

Nigeria's poor economic performance during the 1960–2000 period is attributable to several political economy factors, including especially the following:

- The dominance of military despotism in governance[1] during most of the period (see table 6.1)
- Acute regional rivalry and ethno-religious fragmentation, and
- Leadership (both military and civilian) motivated by extreme regional bias resulting in what Fosu has dubbed an "adverse redistribution" syndrome (Fosu 2008).

---

1 A careful examination of the economic outcomes shows that Nigeria does not fit well into the "Structural Model" of "The Logic of Authoritarian Bargains" proposed by Desai, Olofsgard, and Yousef (2007). In Nigeria's case, little or no economic gain was present to compensate for the political rights relinquished to the military dictators.

Table 6.1. Executive Transitions

Year	Leader	Mode of Assumption of Office
1960	Sir Abubakar Tafawa Balewa	Elected
1963	Nnamdi Azikiwe	Establishment of Republic with Azikiwe as president
1966	Johnson T. U. Aguiyi-Ironsi	January coup
1966	Yakubu Gowon	July coup
1975	Murtala Mohammed	Coup
1976	Olusegun Obasanjo	Coup
1979	Shehu Usman Shagari	Elected
1983	Muhammadu Buhari	Coup
1985	Ibrahim Babangida	Coup
1993	Ernest Shonekan	Selected head of interim national government in August 1993
1993	Sani Abacha	Palace coup in November after a federal high court declared the interim national government unconstitutional
1998	Abdulsalam Abubakar	Selected mainly because of unexpected demise of Sani Abacha
1999	Olusegun Obasanjo	Elected
2003	Olusegun Obasanjo	Elected
2007	Umaru Musa Yar'Adua	Elected

Source: Compiled by the author, 2008.

These three issues are interrelated and intertwined. This chapter suggests that Nigeria's failure to effectively harness and utilize its resource rents resulted mainly from distributional struggles between ethno-regional interests, and that imprudent macroeconomic policies in particular were motivated by the single-minded attempt by Northern political leaders to transfer resources from the Southern to the Northern part of the country (see table 6.2).

Note that in the 1960s the economy relied heavily on export-driven primitive agriculture, small- to medium-scale manufacturing, and petty

Table 6.2. Regional Bias in Oil Revenue Allocation

Leader	Notable Actions on Oil Revenue Sharing
Alhaji Tafawa Balewa (1957–66)	Supported the construction of the first Port Harcourt refinery by Shell B.P. in 1965. Established several industries in the Northern part of Nigeria (Funtua Seed Cotton Mill, Arewa Textile Mill, and others).
General J. T. Aguyi-Ironsi (1966)	No notable action.
General Yakubu Gowon (1966–75)	Yakubu Gowon Dam in Kano. Established the Volkswagen and Peugeot plants in Lagos and Kaduna. Responsible for the construction of dual road network across the country. Built the national stadium and the national arts theater in Lagos. Carved out 12 states from the original four regions in 1967. Established the Nigerian Agricultural Bank with headquarters in the North. Seized the offshore oil and made it federal property without regard to state of location.
General Ramat Murtala Muhammed (1975–76)	Created additional seven states out of the existing 12 to make 19 in 1976. Set up the machinery for the movement of the federal capital territory from Lagos to Abuja. Completed the fertilizer plant in Kaduna.
General Olusegun Obasanjo (1975–79)	Initiated the construction of the Ajaokuta Steel Company, Delta Steel Company, Aladja, and established the Oshogbo Steel Rolling Mill, Nigerian Machine Tools Limited, Oshogbo, and the Katsina and Jos Steel Rolling Mills. Ensured the takeoff of the Warri refinery in 1978. Reduced the oil royalties and rents due to the state of origin from 50 to 30 percent.
Alhaji Shehu Shagari (1979–83)	Established the Aluminum Smelter Company of Nigeria at Ikot Abasi in 1983 to make up for several industries located in the North by his administration, including the Kaduna refinery, which started operation in 1980. Completed an additional steel plant and three rolling mills at Ajaokuta. Reduced the share of oil royalties and rents to state of origin from 30 to 2 percent.
General Muhammadu Buhari (1984–85)	Probed and detained several corrupt military governors and ministers. Reduced the share of oil royalties and rents to state of origin from 2 to 1.5 percent.
General Ibrahim Badamosi Babangida (1985–93)	Increased the share of oil royalties and rents to state of origin from 1.5 to 3 percent. Established the Oil Mineral Producing Area Development Commission in 1992. Established the Federal Environmental Protection Agency in 1985, with headquarters at Abuja. Created two additional states (Akwa Ibom and Katsina) and several local government councils. Built Toja Bridge in Kebbi, established Jibia Water Treatment Plant and the Challawa Cenga Dam in Kano. Moved the seat of the federal government to Abuja on December 12, 1991. Annulled June 12 election results. Commissioned Ajaokuta Steel Company. Introduced the SAP in 1986. Created 11 more states with a bias toward the North.
Chief Ernest Shonekan (August 1993–November 1993)	No notable action.

Table 6.2. Continued

Nigerian Leaders	Notable Actions on Oil Revenue Sharing
General Sani Abacha (1993–98)	Created six new states and 181 new local government councils with a heavy bias toward the North on December 5, 1996. Looted the Nigerian Treasury; initiated the vision 2010 economic blueprint for Nigeria; promulgated Decree No. 18 in 1994 to support the trial of the executives of failed banks.
General Abdulsalam Abubakar (1998–99)	Granted autonomy to the Central Bank of Nigeria in the formulation and implementation of monetary policies. Established the Independent Electoral Commission and facilitated the handover of power to a civilian administration in 1999.
Chief Olusegun Obasanjo (1999–2007)	Established the Niger Delta Development Commission and increased the 3 percent for oil-producing states from the federation account to 13 percent to enhance development and solve ecological problems. Introduced the Universal Basic Education Program to enhance the literacy level of Nigerians. Introduced the Independent Corrupt Practices Commission to check fraudulent financial activities of Nigerians. Resuscitated the National Fertilizer Company in Kaduna and (Onne) Port Harcourt.

Source: Iyoha and Oriakhi 2008.

trading. However, with crude oil becoming the dominant product among Nigeria's exports, political elites and their administrations failed to harness the receipts from oil for a proper diversification of the export base of the economy. Instead they engaged in capital flight (see table 6.3) and massive importation of consumer goods, to the detriment of the balance-of-payments position.

Ethnic affiliations and nepotism acted over time to constrain the growth process: between 1960 and 2000, the majority of leaders directed their attention to the diversion of state resources—public investments, infrastructure improvements, public sector employment—to the regions that constituted their political base. This phenomenon is central to the political instability that has been a permanent feature in Nigeria since the 1960s, with dire consequences, including the discouragement of foreign investment and the encouragement of capital flight and brain drain.

Table 6.3. Capital Flight, 1972–89

Year	Capital Flight (in millions of dollars)	Year	Capital Flight (in millions of dollars)
1972	106.4	1981	2,132.3
1973	636.1	1982	−3,805.8
1974	325.0	1983	2,016.1
1975	119.8	1984	−169.8
1976	124.8	1985	3,569.4
1977	2,490.0	1986	5,502.9
1978	508.4	1987	5,814.6
1979	−86.3	1988	1,043.8
1980	2,713.3	1989	−2,997.0
Total 1972–89	**32,801.3**		

Source: Ajayi 2000: 232.

The continued importance of oil rents in Nigeria's economy mirrors their importance as a flash point for political conflict. Nigeria is a striking example of what Sachs and Warner (2001) have labeled the "natural resource curse": the systematic tendency for narrowly specialized primary commodity exporters to grow more slowly than countries with more diversified exports. Where did Nigeria's natural resource rents end up, if not as productive domestic investments capable of supporting economic growth? One answer is in capital flight: virtually all the former military rulers amassed huge fortunes in foreign bank accounts. It can indeed be argued that the political environment of military rule rewarded rent-seeking activities, bribery, and corruption.

Another answer is that domestic investment, particularly by the public sector, was often highly inefficient. Ethnic rivalries encouraged Northern political elites to ignore the Southern part of the country, where oil resources originate, in favor of developing the North. In pursuance of this goal, many costly mistakes were made regarding the location of investment projects. The leaders appeared to be unduly interested in redistribution of resources, which, of course, could be favorable to growth—especially in cases in which it reduces polarization. However, its effect might be perverse if it increased polarization, especially in cases in which government officials used redistribution as a mechanism to reward their cronies or regional constituencies that were often ethnically defined. This latter form, adverse redistribution, could be vertical as well.

This is what happened in Nigeria between 1960 and 2000 when the incumbent governments engaged in adverse redistribution as a mechanism of shoring up their respective power bases, usually based on ethnicity. It may therefore be postulated that Nigeria perfectly illustrates the challenges of natural resource management under conditions of ex ante ethno-regional polarization. As emphasized by Iyoha and Oriakhi (2008), Nigeria rushed to independence as an uneasy federation of a militarily powerful but economically weak interior (the North) and two smaller coastal regions, each home to a dominant ethnic group.[2] Oil hardened regional political identities, replacing the North's development agenda with one of continued political domination and placing issues of revenue allocation at the center of political competition—to the detriment of economic growth. This point has also been forcefully made by Suberu (2001). Relying on the communiqué of a major national conference on Nigerian federalism, Suberu (2001: 9) concluded that Nigeria's federal system was perched precariously on a

---

2 Nigeria is composed of more than 250 ethnic groups. The following are the most populous and politically influential: Hausa and Fulani, 29 percent; Yoruba, 21 percent; Igbo (Ibo), 18 percent; Ijaw, 10 percent; Kanuri, 4 percent; Ibibio, 3.5 percent; and Tiv, 2.5 percent. There are three dominant ethno-linguistic groups: Hausa/Fulani, Yoruba, and Igbo, which account for 68 percent of the total population. In terms of geographical location, the Hausa/Fulani live in the North, and the Yorubas and Igbos live in the South (with the Yorubas occupying the Southwest and the Igbos the Southeast coastal areas). In terms of religious breakdown, Muslims account for 50 percent of the population, Christians for 40 percent, and indigenous practitioners for 10 percent. The Hausa/Fulani are mainly Muslims, whereas the Yorubas and Igbos are mainly Christians.

"weak productive base" because of the preoccupation of local, religious, and ethno-regional interests with redistributing a shrinking national cake rather than producing a bigger one. According to Suberu, ethno-regional conflict continues to express itself in a wide variety of ways, including ongoing debates over the rules for intergovernmental sharing of revenues, calls for further subdivision (or amalgamation) of the 36-state structure, frequent repudiation of population census figures that appear to favor a particular section of the country, and debates over the "federal character principle," which constitutionally mandates the equitable representation of states in federal public services and institutions.

A common feature of these struggles is the tension that they bring out between politically motivated redistribution and economic efficiency. Several reasons have been adduced, for example, for requiring roughly proportional representation of states in some important political positions and in recruitment into the senior echelons of the federal Civil Service: a leading one is the relative educational backwardness of the Northern part of the Nigerian Federation. However, although this imbalance provided an equity rationale for educational investment in the North, the argument for proportional recruitment seems clearly weaker given its potentially discouraging effect both on bureaucratic efficiency and on educational investment within Nigeria as a whole. As this example suggests, distributional conflict has acted over time to reduce the drive for growth and development of the Nigerian economy, both directly, via the misallocation of existing resources (and their wastage via court cases, work stoppages, and ethnic clashes), and indirectly, via the undermining of incentives for productive new investment.

Economic Outcomes

Nigeria's long-run growth performance has been extremely poor. For the 1960–2000 period, real income per capita grew at only 0.43 percent per year at constant domestic prices (figure 6.1). The importance of economic growth for poverty reduction has been established by numerous empirical studies and has recently been underscored by the phenomenal progress of China and other countries in East Asia and the Pacific region. In Nigeria, the consequence of long-run stagnation in average income was a sharp cumulative increase in poverty, both in terms of absolute numbers and as a share of the overall population.

As indicated in figure 6.1 and table 6.4, Nigeria's long-run stagnation has occurred in a context of acute short- to medium-run volatility. Nigeria was a poor country at independence in 1960, with a per capita income in constant 2000 U.S. dollars of less than $250 at official exchange rates (about $1,000 in PPP-adjusted terms). Real per capita income rose impressively between 1960 and the mid-1970s, with the exception of a brief but sharp interruption immediately before and during the civil war of 1967–70. In the mid-1970s, income fluctuated with little overall trend, but then it plummeted in 1981 with the onset of an acute economic crisis.

Figure 6.1. Real GDP per Capita, 1960–2000

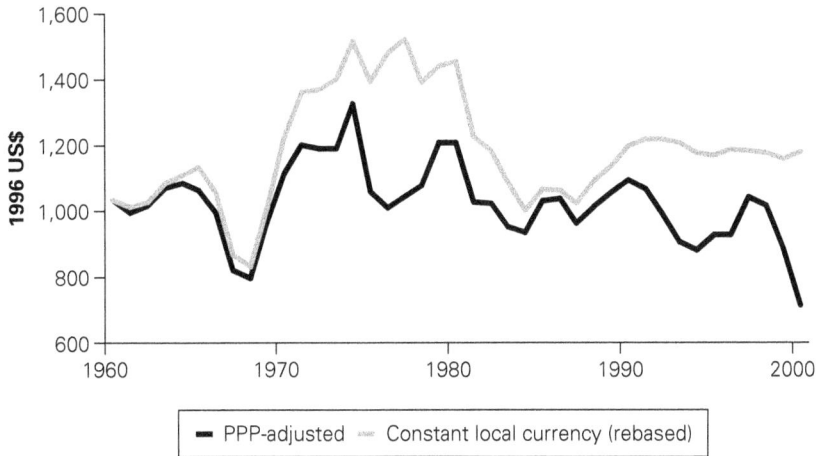

Source: World Bank 2006c.

Table 6.4. Per Capita Real Income and Its Growth Rate (U.S. dollars)

Pre-Liberalization Era			Economic Liberalization Era			Democratic Era		
Year	Level	Growth Rate	Year	Level	Growth Rate	Year	Level	Growth Rate
1965	318.60	—	1987	287.70	−3.59	2001	338.0	1.9
1966	297.00	−6.78	1988	307.20	6.78	2002	359.0	1.8
1967	243.60	−17.98	1989	320.02	4.17	2003	438.0	6.8
1968	234.20	−3.86	1990	336.50	5.15	2004	528.0	3.8
1969	283.05	20.86	1991	342.64	1.82	2005	653.0	3.4
1970	344.30	21.64	1992	342.60	−0.01	2006	808.0	3.3
1971	382.60	11.12	1993	340.10	−0.73			
1972	384.70	0.55	1994	330.60	−2.79			
1973	394.20	2.47	1995	328.90	−0.51			
1974	425.95	8.05	1996	333.40	1.37			
1975	392.20	−7.92	1997	333.20	−0.06			
1976	415.45	5.93	1998	330.60	−0.78			
1977	427.67	2.94	1999	325.90	−1.42			
1978	391.10	−8.55	2000	331.60	1.75			
1979	404.99	3.55						
1980	409.18	1.03						
1981	344.51	−15.80						
1982	332.96	−3.35						
1983	305.50	−8.25						
1984	281.83	−7.75						
1985	299.90	6.41						
1986	298.40	−0.50						

Source: World Bank 2005.

Between 1981 and 1984, real output fell at an average annual rate of nearly 6 percent. The Structural Adjustment Program (SAP) adopted in 1986 brought about temporary relief, with real growth averaging over 5 percent per year between 1988 and 1990. The 1990s, however, witnessed nearly complete stagnation, with average income growing at a rate of less than half a percentage point per year.

Note that although the growth rate of real income per capita averaged 0.43 percent between 1960 and 2000, it averaged a robust 3.4 percent between 2001 and 2006, and the average growth rate of real per capita income was an outstanding 4.2 percent between 2003 and 2006. The first decade of the twenty-first century therefore showed an unprecedented growth spurt in Nigeria. Accordingly, these years will be studied carefully in this chapter to determine the roles played by leadership, policy making, the quality of economic policies, and institutions.

The next section will examine Nigeria's economic growth performance between 1960 and 2000, with special emphasis on the reasons for the dismal record. The following section will investigate the reasons for the rapid growth during the 2001–06 period. Particular attention will be given to the economic reform program of the Obasanjo administration, and specific policies that were implemented will be discussed. Also, the key role of leadership will be highlighted. Next, the analysis will be devoted to a further study of the roles played by leadership, policy making, the quality of policies, learning, and institutions in the growth outcomes of the entire period. The last section provides a summary and concluding remarks.

Nigeria's Economic Growth Performance, 1960–2000

This section begins by examining the impact of investment on income growth during the 1960–2000 period.

Aggregate Investment

Figure 6.2 shows the ratio of investment to GDP in Nigeria for the years under study. A comparison of figures 6.1 and 6.2 shows a distinct co-movement of real GDP per capita with the aggregate investment share. Both variables fall sharply during the civil war and again, after a protracted boom, during the economic crisis of the early 1980s. Consistent with the dominant share of the public sector in total investment, revenues from oil exports seem to have served as an extremely powerful driver of the overall investment rate. Because investment has a domestically produced component, changes in the investment share affect growth both from the demand side and from the supply side. Short-run aggregate demand effects of oil-financed investment are readily apparent in figure 6.1. Sustained impacts on productive capacity, in contrast, are less evident, consistent with severe inefficiencies in the allocation of domestic investment, documented below.

Figure 6.2. Investment as a Share of GDP

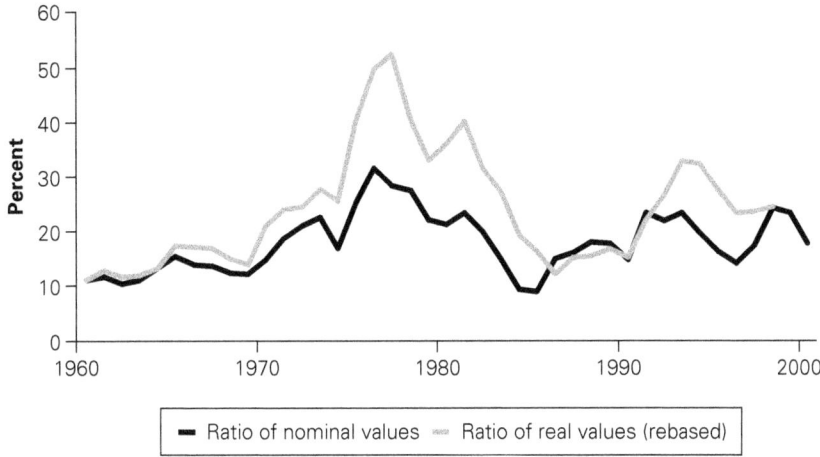

Source: World Bank 2006c.

To fully explain the economic events of the 1960–2000 period, it was found desirable to split the period into two subperiods, with the line of demarcation given by the initiation of major economic reforms under the aegis of the 1986 SAP. These periods will be referred to as the pre-liberalization era (1960–86) and the economic liberalization era (1987–2000).

The central objective of Nigeria's SAP was to restructure and diversify the productive base of the economy to reduce dependence on the oil sector and on imports. The main SAP measures included deregulation of the exchange rate, trade liberalization, deregulation of the financial sector, rationalization and privatization of public sector enterprises, and adoption of appropriate domestic pricing policies (by eliminating subsidies), especially for petroleum products (Federal Government of Nigeria 1986).

Originally planned to last for only two years (July 1986 to June 1988), the SAP period was extended several times to allow for the phased introduction of the requisite policy reforms and provide a period within which results could come to fruition. In policy analysis, therefore, the SAP epoch is now generally taken to cover the period from 1987 to 1992. Unfortunately, the SAP did not deliver all the benefits that its protagonists promised. Deregulation and liberalization improved conditions for agriculture and led to positive developments in the financial sector and to an economic growth spurt during the first few years of SAP. As of the early 1990s, however, little evidence was at hand that reforms had transformed the overall climate for growth. Indeed, overall economic growth differed only marginally between the two periods, amounting to 0.18 percent during the period of economic controls and 0.80 percent during the liberalization era. Additionally a drastic fall in public sector employment took place, which served to lower the welfare of the citizenry. However, it should be noted that, as indicated in figure 6.1 and table 6.4, the intertemporal pattern of growth differs markedly—with the first period characterized by a massive boom and bust cycle and the second by protracted stagnation following an initial burst of growth. However, although 1986–87 marks the outset of a cumulatively substantial reorientation of economic policy in Nigeria, the legacies of the earlier period, combined with the continued realities of political conflict, prevented any fundamental transformation of the growth environment through the end of the century.

As already mentioned, the continued importance of oil rents in Nigeria's economy mirrors their importance as a flash point for political, ethnic, and regional conflict. Nigeria is indeed a remarkable example of what Sachs and Warner (2001) have labeled the "natural resource curse," that is, the systematic tendency for countries highly dependent on the exportation of a single primary commodity to grow more slowly than countries with more diversified exports. Given Nigeria's peculiar circumstances, it turned out that a significant proportion of Nigeria's natural resource rents ended up in capital flight[3] because virtually all the former military rulers amassed huge fortunes in foreign bank accounts. Also, it turned out that domestic investment, particularly by the public sector, was often highly inefficient. Ethnic rivalries encouraged Northern political elites to ignore the Southern part of the country, where oil resources originate, in favor of developing their constituencies in the Northern part of the country, albeit inefficiently. Thus, in pursuance of this ethnic and sectional goal, many costly mistakes were made regarding the location of investment projects, for example, the Ajaokuta Steel Mill and the Kaduna refinery.

Periodization

For each of the two major subperiods—the pre-liberalization era of 1960–86 and the liberalization era of 1987–2000—this section undertakes a detailed study of the determinants of growth performance, focusing in turn on economic policies and outcomes at the macroeconomic and sectoral levels, the changing institutional organization of key markets, the response of microeconomic agents to the policy environment, and the political economy of policy and governance.

Nigeria's Growth Performance: 1960–86

The pre–economic liberalization period was characterized by what Collier and O'Connell (2006) call "soft controls," reflecting direct government intervention in prices and often quantities in key markets throughout the economy. National planning was in the ascendancy, with rapid economic development to be brought about through a series of fixed-term National Development Plans. During the pre–civil war period, growth in per capita income was moderate, driven by agricultural exports (mainly cocoa, groundnuts, palm oil, and rubber) and the massive drawdown of foreign

---

3 Data given by Ajayi (2000) show that between 1972 and 1989 capital flight from Nigeria amounted to $32.8 billion. For yearly amounts, see table 6.3.

exchange reserves and Marketing Board surpluses accumulated during the Korean War agricultural export boom of the 1950s. Growth accelerated sharply after the civil war, driven mainly by petroleum exports, but then these, as we have seen, collapsed under the weight of falling oil prices during the first half of the 1980s.

Oil already accounted for 57.5 percent of total exports in 1970, but by 1977 it accounted for 93.3 percent (Iyoha 1995). During the boom, balance of payments surpluses and buoyant government revenues led to a major expansion in government expenditures, including capital expenditures. Commendably, much of the federal government's recurrent spending during the 1970s went into educational expansion. The Western and Eastern regions had already introduced Universal Primary Education to the Southern parts of the country, but during this period the Northern region introduced free primary and secondary education and even adopted a program of awarding overseas scholarships to its indigenes. The percentage of the federal government budget devoted to education was between 5 percent and 10 percent in the 1970s as compared to less than 1 percent committed by the colonial government (Central Bank of Nigeria 2002). The number of federally owned universities expanded from one to six during the period.

Investment, and particularly public investment, rose very sharply during this period: in 1976 the aggregate investment–income ratio was an impressive 31.5 percent whereas the public investment–income ratio amounted to 24.4 percent. The absence of sustained growth in the Nigerian economy despite these high investment rates is partly traceable to the inefficiency of the public sector's investment response. As Bevan, Collier, and Gunning (1992: 2) observe, the public investment response was intertemporally inefficient both in terms of its ultimate magnitude and in terms of the domestic investments undertaken. The ideal response to an export price boom is to invest the proceeds in income-earning assets abroad and to repatriate them only as the economy develops domestic investment projects with a social rate of return at least as high as that of the nation's overseas portfolio. Nigerian policy makers succeeded initially in accumulating international reserves, but public investment programs were then pushed rapidly and with little concern for efficiency. Policy makers fell prey to a vision of import-substituting industrialization that was already discredited at the time, allocating vast sums to public-sector megaprojects (including two steel mills built at a cost of some $11 billion) that were never able to compete in world markets.

Although this period was dominated (from the civil war forward) by military rule, the brief periods of civilian rule in between—1979 and 1983— did not bring greater coherence to economic policy in Nigeria. Instead, although military administrators had depended heavily on the civil service to initiate and implement economic policies, the civilian administration of President Shehu Shagari saw a drastic reduction in the powers of the civil service and an increase in rent-seeking activity. Maximization of political support through patronage became the order of the day. Patronage was made easier by increasing the number of states and by failing to enforce legal rules against corruption. Kickbacks appear to have increased the costs of investment projects dramatically: the contract for the construction of a dam, for example, which had been concluded by the military government for $120 million, was renegotiated by the civilian government for $600 million (Bevan, Collier, and Gunning 1992: 8).

Over the full period of the oil boom, the excessive and highly inefficient public investment response is consistent with successive governments having viewed the boom as effectively permanent. Bevan, Collier, and Gunning (1992) observe that it was not until after the fall of oil revenues in 1980–81 that the Nigerian government recognized the transitory nature of the shock. During the period of military government, however, the public investment strategy reflected in addition the capital-accumulation dogma of the civil service, whereas during the civilian period public investment became a focal point for patronage and corruption. Thus, throughout the period, the oil-financed investment boom contributed little to the underlying growth process of the economy.

Nigeria's Growth Performance: 1987–2000

The SAP and post-SAP periods were marked by deregulation and economic liberalization. However, the success of market liberalization was constrained throughout by haphazard implementation, frequent policy reversals, weak institutions, and the regional redistribution syndrome. Thus, in spite of a determined effort to deregulate and liberalize both the real and financial sectors of the economy, the average rate of economic growth barely exceeded that of the pre-liberalization period.

The performance of the manufacturing sector was extremely poor during this subperiod. Although weak growth in domestic aggregate demand may have played some role, the more fundamental problem appears to be a consistent failure to meet price and quality competition from imports at the more modest levels of protection afforded by post-liberalization policies. The high price of domestic manufactures reflects, among other influences, inordinately high energy costs, inefficient and old equipment, and inadequate infrastructure. Other constraints that have been identified as militating against output growth are the incidents of civil and religious disturbances in some parts of the country, as well as the general insecurity of lives and property arising from banditry and armed robbery (Central Bank of Nigeria 2002). The issue of poor infrastructure, however, bears particular emphasis. The supply of electricity is erratic and unreliable, with frequent power outages, load shedding, and power rationing. The erratic nature of the power supply has forced high-income households and businesses to purchase generators at prohibitive initial and operating costs. The failure of infrastructural services extends to the areas of water supply and telecommunications. All these issues have implications for the cost of producing manufactured goods and by extension the competitiveness of domestic industry.

Leadership, Policy Making, and Economic Growth: The Case of Nigeria

The SAP introduced in 1986 constituted the institutional framework for the design and application of trade and commercial policies for a substantial part of the 1987–2000 period. The government abolished Commodity Boards and deregulated the pricing and marketing of agricultural commodities. The import and export licensing system was also abolished, and the number of import-prohibited items reduced. In 1988 the desire to provide a more stable and predictable tariff regime prompted the introduction of tariff reform. Hence, a tariff structure expected to last seven years was initiated. A variety of incentives were introduced to promote non-oil exports and foreign direct investment, including duty and tax concessions.

Toward the end of the 1980s, the continuation of economic distress led to the introduction of a new set of reform-oriented measures, some of which were a direct reversal of measures introduced under the SAP. Selected crops and their derivatives were placed under an export prohibition list, to lower food prices and stimulate the output of agro-allied industries. The 1988 tariff reform was reversed before its seven-year expiration period, through amendments implemented in 1989, 1990, and 1991. In 1994 the Abacha government pegged the exchange rate at N22 to the U.S. dollar, a direct reversal of the move to a market-determined exchange rate. These policy reversals (possibly triggered by political pressure from vested interests that had lost windfalls they formerly gained from rent seeking under the regime of controls) acted over time to undermine the supply response to economic reforms.

From the early 1980s to the inception of the SAP in 1986, it became obvious that the agricultural sector could not keep up with domestic demands for food and raw materials. In addition to creating of the Directorate for Foods, Roads and Rural Infrastructure in 1986, the government developed an agricultural policy as part of a sectoral Perspective Plan up to the year 2005. The Perspective Plan stressed the introduction of financial policy measures to improve credit allocation to the agricultural sector, and in pursuance of this objective, new financial institutions were established, including community banks and the Peoples Bank of Nigeria. The removal of price distortions under the SAP, however, probably bore the greatest responsibility for the revival of agricultural production after 1986. Aggregate output of the agricultural sector grew by 7.5 percent per year between 1986 and 1996, a rate significantly higher than during the pre-SAP period.

In the attempt to correct "government failures" in the agricultural sector, SAP policies and measures apparently paid less attention to the possibility of market failures. Thus although SAP reforms greatly reduced the output price distortions facing Nigeria's farmers, they also removed government input subsidies to the sector—subsidies that may have been justifiable as a means of encouraging the adoption and diffusion of yield-enhancing technologies (for example, seed varieties intensive in fertilizer).

The SAP introduced broad-based regulatory and institutional reforms in the financial sector with a view to deregulating the system and creating a level playing field for the growth and development of financial institutions, markets, and instruments. In 1992 bank-by-bank credit ceilings were lifted and replaced by Open Market Operations as the primary method of monetary management. Interest rates, which had previously been administratively fixed, were left to market forces through the removal of all controls on bank deposit and lending rates. Although controls were reintroduced in 1991 and between 1994 and 1996, interest rates on deposit and lending were decontrolled again in October 1996. In 1997 the Central Bank of Nigeria (CBN) was vested with the control and supervision of all commercial, merchant, and community banks; the Peoples Bank of Nigeria; finance companies; discount houses; primary mortgage institutions; bureaux de changes; and all development banks. In 1988 the Nigerian Deposit Insurance Corporation was established to complement the regulatory and supervisory role of the CBN. It was set up to provide deposit insurance and related services for banks, to promote confidence in the banking industry. The Securities and Exchange Commission (SEC), which had been established in 1979, was strengthened by the SEC Decree of 1988 to perform its role of effective promotion of an orderly and active capital market.

Other major changes in the Nigerian financial system during the 1987–2000 period include the promulgation of the Failed Banks (Recovery of Debt) and Financial Malpractices in Banks Decree No. 18 of 1994, aimed at prosecuting those who contributed to the failure of banks and to recover the debt owed to the failed banks. In 1994 the CBN inaugurated the Financial Services Regulatory Coordinating Committee to coordinate and standardize the regulatory policies of all financial institutions in the system and evolve cooperation among regulatory agencies. In 1995 three decrees to further regulate the financial system were promulgated: Money Laundering Decree No. 3, Nigerian Investment Promotion Commission Decree No. 16, and Foreign Exchange (Monitoring and Miscellaneous Provisions) Decree No. 17, which established an autonomous foreign exchange market.

Financial sector reforms during this period led to the expansion of the number of banks and financial institutions. They also significantly reduced government domination of the capital market and enhanced its capitalization. The value of new issues of securities rose steadily, from N399.9 million in 1988 to N10,814.0 million in 1997. This gives an average annual rate of growth of 36.6 percent in nominal terms. However, given that the average annual rate of inflation was 36.9 percent during the subperiod, hardly any growth was seen in the value of new issues in real terms. Also, the number of listed securities increased from 180 in 1985 to 264 in 1997. In spite of the increase in the number of banks in the economy, however, the ratio of savings to GDP declined steadily over much of the liberalization period, from 16.0 percent in 1988 to 7.8 percent in 1997. At least through the early 1990s (figure 6.2), investment remained below its levels in the early 1970s. The basic structure of the financial system changed very little, as commercial banks continued to dominate institutionalized savings, providing about 80 percent of total savings. Despite some progress, the overall performance of the Nigerian financial system was not impressive, especially with the many cases of bank distress reported between 1989 and 1996. The number of banks classified as distressed increased from 8 to 52, and the licenses of five banks were revoked. The CBN also took over the management of 17 distressed banks in 1995 and one in 1996.

In recognition of the lack of access to credit by many citizens who sought to be self-employed, the federal government introduced a policy to liberalize access to credit. To this end, the Peoples Bank of Nigeria was established in October 1989, and the community banks were established in 1990. Other programs introduced to boost employment include the National Directorate of Employment and Mass Agricultural Projects in seven states of the federation in 1993. The Family Economic Advancement Program was introduced in 1997 to empower locally based producers of goods and services and potential entrepreneurs in the cottage industries through the provision of loans and training, and the acquisition of skills.

With the adoption of SAP, the foreign exchange market was completely liberalized, and the exchange rate largely left to market forces. To enhance the smooth operation of the foreign exchange market, bureau de change offices were introduced in 1989 to handle small-scale foreign exchange transactions based on funds from unofficial sources. Possibly succumbing to pressure from vested interests whose opportunities for rent seeking had been blocked by the reforms, the Abacha government reversed exchange-rate reforms and pegged the naira for a wide range of transactions starting in 1994. In 1995 the government formalized its reversal by adopting a policy of "guided deregulation." Given ongoing Nigerian inflation, foreign exchange available at the pegged rate was increasingly overvalued, and the black market premium skyrocketed. The exchange rate remained effectively pegged until 1998, although restrictions on external payments began to be lifted even in advance of the devaluation of 1999.

The Babangida administration introduced the SAP in 1986 and was responsible for its initial implementation. The efforts of this administration were hampered by continuous declines in oil revenues and increases in external debt, as well as by its commitment to an unending program of political transition. The quality and consistency of economic policy management declined sharply. The government yielded to domestic political pressures and, despite repeated official pronouncements that it would continue with reforms, could not sustain the original objectives of the SAP. Ad hoc policies were implemented instead, to meet short-term expediencies. The most serious issue was irresponsible fiscal behavior, primarily in the form of excessive spending—mainly to shore up dwindling political support and pacify the government's constituency. The early 1990s were thus characterized by rising fiscal deficits, increasing poverty, and mounting discontent, a situation that resulted in several anti-SAP protests, riots, and strikes. The SAP led to a major decline in expenditure on the social sector and created a new class of the poor. It forced down capacity utilization in industry, from an average annual rate of 53.1 percent between 1981 and 1985 to 39.8 percent between 1986 and 1993. It may also have contributed to the widespread distress in the banking system, which destroyed the confidence of the public in the financial system and caused hardships to bank customers (Iyoha 1996).

Economic Performance in the Third Republic, 1999–2006

For the first two years after the return to democratic rule in 1999, the Nigerian economy continued to report poor overall economic performance, contrary to the hopes and expectations of Nigerians, donor partners, and the entire international community. It was widely expected that with the dawn of democratic revival in Nigeria, economic growth would resume and accelerate, leading to a significant reduction in poverty. Unfortunately, this did not immediately happen, and economic growth continued to be lackluster and unprepossessing. Indeed, the poor growth performance of the economy during the first two years of President Obasanjo's first term made it clear that fundamental economic reforms were warranted. Additionally, in the new millennium, it became necessary to make a concerted attempt to actualize the U.N.'s Millennium Development Goals. Thus, starting in 2001, the government began to introduce economic reforms. In 2003, having consolidated his political position and keen to deliver the "dividends of democracy," the president decided to formalize, systematize, and intensify the reform program. His government therefore began to implement a comprehensive reform program known as the National Economic Empowerment and Development Strategy (NEEDS).

Nigeria's Growth Performance, 2001–06

According to the document issued by the Nigerian government, NEEDS is a nationally coordinated framework of action in collaboration with the state and local governments and other stakeholders to reduce poverty. Indeed, NEEDS is Nigeria's homegrown equivalent of a World Bank poverty reduction strategy. In effect, the State Economic Empowerment and Development Strategy of each state of the federation is to be coordinated with NEEDS as a weapon to reduce poverty and underdevelopment in the country. In addition to the state and local governments, the implementation of NEEDS will be predicated on a close collaboration and coordination between the federal government and donor agencies, the private sector, civil society, and nongovernmental organizations. As articulated by the Nigerian authorities, poverty reduction is the core objective of NEEDS. Accordingly, NEEDS includes interventions and policies aimed at poverty reduction, and the policies are intended to benefit virtually all segments of the Nigerian society.

NEEDS also encompasses important structural reforms designed to enhance the transparency and accountability of public-sector policies and institutions. In the process, it is expected that many deep-rooted macroeconomic and structural challenges will be addressed to restore macroeconomic stability and promote rapid and sustainable economic growth. The NEEDS document declares that the strategy is to be implemented by creating a conducive environment for business and foreign investment so as to ensure a partnership between the public and private sectors for growth. In particular, government's attention is to be focused on the provision of basic services and the empowerment of Nigerians to take advantage of new livelihood opportunities while encouraging the private sector to become the engine of growth in the economy. Empowerment of people will especially focus on the areas of health, education, the environment, integrated rural development, housing, employment, gender mainstreaming, and youth development.

NEEDS has also become an umbrella organization for the various poverty eradication programs established by the Obasanjo administration since its inception in 1999. Chief among these programs is the National Poverty Eradication Program (NAPEP), which was established in 1999. The objectives of NAPEP include the following:

- Poverty eradication
- Economic empowerment of the citizenry, especially women
- Provision of skill acquisition for youths and reduction of unemployment among youths
- Provision of universal basic education to all Nigerians
- Revitalization of agriculture as a means of raising the incomes of rural dwellers and
- Provision of motorable roads in rural areas to enhance evacuation of produce to markets.

To summarize, the comprehensive reform programs have been implemented in four main areas: Macroeconomic Reform, Structural Reform, Governance and Institutional Reform, and Public Sector Reform. Under the Macroeconomic Reform Program, government adopted a prudent oil price–based fiscal rule, introduced a Medium-Term Expenditure Framework and a Medium-Term Sector Strategy, improved implementation of monetary policy by the Central Bank, undertook a bank consolidation exercise to strengthen the financial sector, adopted trade liberalization policies, and undertook the privatization of some government enterprises. Under the Structural Reform Program, there has been a bank consolidation exercise to strengthen the financial sector, implement trade liberalization reform, encourage deregulation of the economy, and promote privatization of some government enterprises. Under Institutional and Governance Reforms, the government introduced the Due Process mechanism in public procurement, adopted the Extractive Industries Transparency Initiative, and established the Economic and Financial Crimes Commission and Independent Corrupt Practices Commission to address corruption in public offices. Under the Public Sector Reforms, there has been a restructuring of some government agencies and an increased focus on improving service delivery, an anticorruption drive, and civil service reform. For a more detailed discussion of the economic and structural reforms adopted, see Okonjo-Iweala and Osafo-Kwaako (2007).

It should be pointed out that improvement in oil revenue management and monetary policy implementation was complemented by better debt management strategies. In particular, the erstwhile stubborn problem of external debt overhang was successfully resolved. During the 2003–06 period, Nigeria's external debt stock was drastically reduced.

Arising largely from a successful debt relief agreement with the Paris Club of creditors, Nigeria's external debt stock fell dramatically from $35.9 billion in 2004 to approximately $5.5 billion in 2005, after award of a comprehensive debt relief package on its $30.4 billion Paris Club debt. As explained by Okonjo-Iweala and Osafo-Kwaako (2007: 11), the unprecedented debt relief package involved payment of outstanding arrears of $6.4 billion, a debt write-off of $16 billion, and a debt buyback of the remaining $8 billion (at a 25 percent discount) for $6 billion.

The improvement in macroeconomic policy making in the post-2003 period has started to yield identifiable dividends. Real GDP growth has improved, averaging 7.1 percent per year since 2003. Similarly, inflation has improved, falling from over 20 percent in 2003 to below 10 percent in 2006. Foreign exchange reserves have skyrocketed from about $7 billion in 2002 to approximately $45 billion in 2006, and total external debt fell from $35 billion in 2003 to under $5 billion in 2006 (table 6.5). Since 2003 the non-oil sector, which provides livelihoods for the majority of Nigerians, has grown at 5.9 percent annually, accelerating to 7.4 percent in 2004 and to 8.2 percent in 2005. In 2006 the growth rate of the non-oil sector reached 8.9 percent. Growth of the non-oil sector has been largely driven by growth in agriculture and the global commodity boom. Foreign direct

Table 6.5. Economic Performance Indicators, 2001–06

Indicator	For the Year Ending December 31					
	2001	2002	2003	2004	2005	2006
Real GDP	4.7	4.6	9.9	6.6	6.2	5.6
Oil sector	5.2	(5.7)	23.9	3.3	0.5	4.7
Non-oil sector	4.5	8.3	5.2	7.8	8.2	8.9
Oil production	2.2	2.1	2.3	2.5	2.5	2.5
Gross national savings (% of GDP)	5.3	3.5	7.2	18.4	19.4	20.6
Inflation rate (%, Dec.-over-Dec.)	16.5	12.2	23.8	10.0	11.6	8.5
GDP per capita ($)	530.7	539.1	620.7	673.0	847.1	1,114.0
Population (million)	118.8	122.4	126.2	129.9	133.5	140.0
Population growth rate (%)	2.8	2.8	2.8	2.8	2.8	2.3
Life expectancy at birth (years)	54.0	54.0	54.0	54.0	54.0	55.0
Adult literacy rate (%)	57.0	57.0	57.0	62.0	62.0	67.0

Source: Central Bank of Nigeria 2007.

Table 6.6. Nigeria—Foreign Investment Inflows, 2001–06

Year	Foreign Direct Investment $ (billions)	Portfolio Investment $ (billions)
2001	1.18	0.827
2002	1.87	0.134
2003	2.00	0.147
2004	1.87	0.350
2005	2.30	2.860
2006	4.40	—

Sources: Economic Associates 2007; World Bank 2006a.
Note: — = not available.

investment (FDI) inflows into the country have ballooned, exceeding $5.16 billion in 2005 (table 6.6). Foreign investment has occurred not only in oil and gas but also in the telecommunications, transportation, and banking sectors. It can be convincingly argued that the relaxation of the external debt constraint brought about by the Paris Club debt relief package has contributed to the observed increase in FDI inflows and portfolio flows.

Leadership, Policy Making, and Economic Growth, 1960–2006

It is now increasingly accepted in the development literature that leadership, policy making, the quality of economic policies, and good institutions play important roles in bringing about rapid growth in developing countries. This section shall analyze the differential effects of leadership, institutions, and policy making on economic growth during the dismal 1960–2000 period and during the successful 2001–06 period. It will show that good policy making and high-quality economic policies during the 2001–06 period largely account for the rapid growth during the period. In turn, good leadership largely accounts for the effective and consistently good economic policies during the period.

Leadership and Macroeconomic Policy Making, 1960–2000

Thirty of the first 40 years after independence in Nigeria were spent under the heavy handed rule of military dictators and despots. Much of the failure of policy and the lack of development have been attributed to the abnormal situation in which a country was denied democracy and the rule of law, but rather was forcibly subjected to military misrule. Unfortunately, the quality of leadership was low because the military establishment was led by poorly educated and often ill-trained soldiers. During much of this period, there was the problem of ethno-religious violence and a vicious struggle for resource control. Although oil resources were located in the South, the leaders (military and civilian) were usually from the North. These Northern leaders were bent on transferring the oil resources to develop the North.

This regional redistribution syndrome resulted in an unending tribal and religious strife during most of the period. The development conundrum was exacerbated by the fact that many of the military rulers were corrupt. Thus, the nation's oil resources were stolen when they were not misspent on "white elephant" projects in the Northern parts of the country.

The quality of economic policy making was also poor. Given the prevailing orthodoxy that industrialization was a prerequisite for rapid economic growth, the aim of government was to promote industry and manufacturing through import substitution, using development planning. Between 1962 and 1985 the country used the approach of fixed medium-term plans. Four Development Plans were adopted and implemented:

First National Development Plan, 1962–68
Second National Development Plan, 1970–74
Third National Development Plan, 1975–80
Fourth National Development Plan, 1981–85

During the era of development programming, macroeconomic management policies were used as the key tools for achieving plan objectives. However, in the end, the policy of import-substituting industrialization failed. The discovery of oil and its predominant position after 1974 soon led to the relative neglect of agriculture, but the oil boom lasted only until 1982.

With the end of the oil boom in 1982, Nigeria found itself in a quagmire of economic problems. The internal problems included recession, inflation, high unemployment, and rising fiscal deficits, while the external problems consisted of chronic current account and balance-of-payments deficits, an escalating external debt stock, and a crushing debt-service burden. Ample evidence of sectoral disequilibrium was also present, as demonstrated by the destruction of the agricultural sector, the stunted development of the industrial sector, a lop-sided dependence on the oil sector, and the repression of the financial sector. Between 1982 and 1986, the government made a valiant attempt to combat the economic crisis by adopting various austerity measures, as reflected particularly in the Economic Stabilization Act of 1982 and the National Economic Emergency Act of 1985. However, because of the fundamental nature of the economic and financial disequilibriums, the government found that mere austerity without structural adjustment constituted an inadequate response to the economic crisis. Matters came to a head in early 1986 when the world oil market collapsed and the price of oil fell by over 50 percent. With Nigeria's earnings from petroleum exports tumbling from approximately $25 billion in 1980 to $6.4 billion in 1986, trade arrears piling up, and international credit lines drying up, the nation was on the verge of economic collapse.

Accordingly, in July 1986 the government adopted the SAP to bring about a fundamental restructuring of the economy to ensure its long-term survival. Unfortunately, the SAP policy of economic liberalization and deregulation did not succeed, mainly as a result of poor implementation and policy inconsistency. In the manufacturing sector, there was a weak supply response by private-sector firms to the incentives offered by SAP policies. This limited response has been ascribed to several factors including, especially, the infrastructure deficit. Poor infrastructure availability, particularly in the power and transportation sectors, has militated strongly against private-sector production. Table 6.7 gives comparative infrastructure data for Nigeria, South Africa, and other sub-Saharan countries. An examination of the data shows that a wide gap exists between the availability of electricity in Nigeria (82 kilowatts per capita) and in South Africa (3,793 kilowatts per capita) (Okonjo-Iweala and Osafo-Kwaako 2007). The problem of poor and directionless leadership also continued. Thus, in the end, economic growth performance during the liberalization period was only marginally different from what was recorded during the preceding period of economic controls. Table 6.8 shows data for sectoral shares in output since 1960, and table 6.9 for sectoral annual growth rates in output from 1960 to 2006. Table 6.10 provides data on the exchange rate, and table 6.11 gives data on the terms of trade.

Table 6.7. Selected Data on Infrastructure

Infrastructure	Nigeria	South Africa	SSA	LIC	HIC
Electric power consumption—kW per capita (2001)	82	3,793	456	317	8,421
Road-to-population ratio—1,000 km per million people (1995–2001)	1.1	8.5	2.6	—	—
Paved primary roads—percent of roads (1995–2001)	30.9	20.3	13.5	1,692.9	—
Telephone—mainlines per 1,000 people (2002)	6	107	15	28	585
Access to sanitation—percent of population (2000)	54	87	54	43	—
Access to safe water—percent of population (2000)	62	86	58	76	—

Source: World Bank, World Development Indicators, various years.
Note: HIC = high-income countries, LIC = low-income countries, SSA = sub-Saharan Africa.

Table 6.8. Sectoral Shares in Output, 1960–2006 (percent)

Year	Agriculture	Industry	Manufacturing	Services
1960	63.85	7.68	3.81	28.47
1961	61.83	8.29	4.10	29.88
1962	61.92	8.76	4.41	29.32
1963	61.20	9.03	4.66	29.73
1964	57.88	9.67	4.69	32.45
1965	54.90	12.47	5.43	32.64
1966	54.94	12.32	5.38	32.74
1967	55.40	11.78	5.50	32.81
1968	51.65	10.79	5.65	37.56
1969	49.49	15.56	6.35	34.95
Average 1960–69	57.31	10.64	5.00	32.06

Table 6.8. Continued

Year	Agriculture	Industry	Manufacturing	Services
1970	41.28	13.76	3.67	44.95
1971	40.04	17.34	3.38	42.61
1972	38.27	19.94	3.90	41.79
1973	35.14	25.09	4.04	39.78
1974	31.83	35.24	3.33	32.93
1975	31.73	28.50	5.03	39.77
1976	29.12	32.27	5.06	38.60
1977	29.57	31.42	4.57	39.01
1978	30.48	33.33	6.53	36.18
1979	28.65	37.82	8.79	33.52
Average 1970–79	33.61	27.47	4.83	38.91

Year	Agriculture	Industry	Manufacturing	Services
1980	20.63	45.57	8.38	33.80
1981	26.91	37.58	9.18	35.51
1982	30.84	33.33	9.55	35.82
1983	33.22	29.73	9.90	37.05
1984	37.77	27.78	7.82	34.45
1985	37.31	29.18	8.74	33.51
1986	38.66	26.00	8.73	35.34
1987	36.68	33.31	6.76	30.01
1988	40.60	30.83	7.52	28.57
1989	31.34	43.19	5.29	25.47
Average 1980–89	33.40	33.65	8.19	32.95

Year	Agriculture	Industry	Manufacturing	Services
1990	32.71	41.37	5.54	25.92
1991	30.43	45.57	5.90	24.00
1992	23.80	58.26	4.32	17.94
1993	24.16	58.65	4.00	17.18
1994	28.57	50.24	4.94	21.19
1995	31.61	46.68	5.36	21.71
1996	30.70	49.17	4.84	20.12
1997	33.63	44.79	5.08	21.57
1998	38.98	33.43	5.24	27.58
1999	36.56	35.24	4.89	28.20
Average 1990–99	31.11	46.34	5.01	22.54

Table 6.8. Continued

Year	Agriculture	Industry	Manufacturing	Services
2000	28.81	43.55	4.01	27.63
2001	30.60	47.78	3.89	21.62
2002	31.18	43.80	4.58	25.02
2003	26.41	49.37	3.99	24.21
2004	16.61	56.93	3.68	26.45
2005	16.9	56.2	3.79	26.9
2006	17.5	54.0	3.79	28.4
Average 2000–06	24.0	50.2	4.12	25.75

Sources: World Bank 1999, 2006c; *Economist* Conferences 2007.
Note: Shares may not add up to 100 percent because of rounding.

Table 6.9. Sectoral Annual Growth Rates, 1960–2006 (percent)

Year	Agriculture	Industry	Manufacturing	Services
1960	—	—	—	—
1961	−3.0	29.6	18.8	−1.9
1962	3.6	18.3	12.4	0.9
1963	8.3	14.5	29.1	8.6
1964	−0.4	18.8	−4.2	5.8
1965	0.6	49.6	−28.3	−4.7
1966	−7.0	9.1	70.6	−4.6
1967	−15.5	−20.0	−14.3	−12.1
1968	−1.5	−19.9	5.5	9.2
1969	15.0	79.3	31.5	7.9
1970	17.5	54.4	27.9	20.8
1971	5.2	32.9	−3.1	8.5
1972	−7.3	19.3	23.9	3.3
1973	8.9	−1.2	11.3	13.5
1974	10.4	17.2	−3.3	8.2
1975	−10.4	−13.7	23.6	20.6
1976	−1.6	23.5	23.4	5.4
1977	6.8	5.0	−49.6	7.0
1978	−8.6	−3.7	13.7	−5.7
1979	−3.0	18.9	46.9	2.4
1980	4.9	−2.2	28.1	5.1
1981	−16.5	−10.1	15.1	−5.7
1982	2.5	−4.2	12.9	2.5
1983	−0.3	−14.7	−29.4	2.8
1984	−4.8	−0.5	−11.2	−11.1
1985	16.8	5.3	19.9	6.2

Table 6.9. Continued

Year	Agriculture	Industry	Manufacturing	Services
1986	9.2	−5.7	−3.9	7.3
1987	−3.2	−2.9	5.1	6.1
1988	9.8	9.9	12.8	10.0
1989	4.9	9.0	1.6	8.6
1990	4.2	6.3	7.6	15.0
1991	3.5	8.6	9.3	2.1
1992	2.1	0.3	−4.8	6.9
1993	1.4	−0.8	1.2	5.4
1994	2.4	−2.8	1.6	0.5
1995	3.7	1.2	4.6	2.3
1996	4.1	6.0	2.4	3.0
1997	4.2	1.5	0.9	4.9
1998	4.0	−1.7	−5.4	1.8
1999	5.2	−2.5	2.1	0.7
2000	2.9	6.1	3.5	4.0
2001	3.8	2.6	5.2	3.3
2002	4.2	−8.0	13.7	6.6
2003	6.5	22.4	6.2	6.9
2004	6.5	4.6	3.7	6.9
2005	8.2	4.8	3.9	6.5
2006	8.0	0.1	−1.4	10.5

Sources: World Bank 1999, 2006c; *Economist* Conferences 2007.

Table 6.10. Exchange Rate, 1965–2006

Year	Exchange Rate	Year	Exchange Rate	Year	Exchange Rate
1965	0.7142	1979	0.6040	1993	22.0654
1966	0.7142	1980	0.5468	1994	21.9960
1967	0.7142	1981	0.6177	1995	21.8953
1968	0.7142	1982	0.6735	1996	21.8844
1969	0.7142	1983	0.7244	1997	21.8861
1970	0.7142	1984	0.7665	1998	21.8861
1971	0.7142	1985	0.8938	1999	92.3381
1972	0.6579	1986	1.7545	2000	101.6973
1973	0.6579	1987	4.0160	2001	111.2312
1974	0.6302	1988	4.5370	2002	120.5782
1975	0.6155	1989	7.3647	2003	129.2224
1976	0.6266	1990	8.0383	2004	132.888
1977	0.6447	1991	9.9094	2005	131.300
1978	0.6353	1992	17.2984	2006	127.400

Sources: World Bank 1999, 2006c; *Economist* Conferences 2007.

Table 6.11. Terms of Trade, 1980–2005

Year	Terms of Trade	Year	Terms of Trade
1980	181.25	1993	59.41
1981	192.00	1994	56.12
1982	163.63	1995	55.56
1983	155.17	1996	86.90
1984	154.54	1997	65.09
1985	143.48	1998	43.88
1986	70.27	1999	59.60
1987	72.60	2000	100.00
1988	60.94	2001	88.90
1989	75.71	2002	89.92
1990	88.51	2003	101.94
1991	74.39	2004	122.35
1992	65.04	2005	125.00

Sources: World Bank 2006a, c.

Leadership, Policy Making, and Institutions: 2001–06

Apart from the sustained commodity export boom (as exemplified by skyrocketing oil prices) in the new millennium, the main explanation for the exemplary economic growth performance in Nigeria was leadership. Going hand-in-hand with improved leadership was the adoption and implementation of good economic policies (as exemplified by NEEDS). Some analysts question whether the Nigerian economic reforms are truly "home grown" as claimed by their architects. The issue is moot because although parts of the reform program are "orthodox"—conforming to Williamson's (2003) "Washington Consensus"—the program was nevertheless adopted without prodding from the International Monetary Fund or World Bank and was not supported by a loan from either of the two Washington institutions. Although NEEDS has both state-level and local government–level components, it has yet to be as fully embraced by the subnational units as it has been embraced at the national level. It seems clear that economic reform is more likely to promote sustainable growth over time if it is also enthusiastically implemented at the subnational level. Thus, a priority of any future government should be the extension of these economic reforms to the subnational units.

Good governance and institution building have also been part of the Nigerian success story. The Obasanjo government introduced a "fiscal rule" to delink public expenditures from oil revenue earnings, thus effectively insulating the domestic economy from internationally transmitted business cycles. An attempt is being made to institutionalize this by passing a Fiscal Responsibility Act. Other useful reforms in this area were the establishment of a due process mechanism for public procurement and the adoption of the Extractive Industries Transparency Initiative as a means of promoting transparency in the oil and gas sector. Two anticorruption agencies, the Independent Corrupt Practices and Other Related Offences Commission and the Economic and Financial Crimes Commission, were also established to promote accountability and good governance. It may well be true that without good governance other reforms have limited impact, because good governance includes issues such as the absence of rent-seeking behavior, transparency, accountability, proper enforcement of property rights, and the rule of law. Good governance thus plays a critical role in attracting investment to a country, improving productivity and competitiveness, promoting political stability, and in the end contributing to rapid economic growth.

Summary and Concluding Remarks

This study of Nigeria's growth experience will conclude by referring briefly to a resource-rich African country at the other end of the growth tables. Botswana reported an average real GDP growth rate of 11 percent between 1982 and 1989 and 7.5 percent between 1990 and 2000. Nigeria grew at 3.7 percent between 1960 and 2000. Thus, Nigeria's average real GDP growth rate was one-third that of Botswana's in the 1980s and one-half that of Botswana's in the 1990s. However, Nigeria's average growth rate of 7 percent between 2003 and 2006 is close to what was reported by Botswana during the 1990–2000 decade. This buttresses the belief of many that given Nigeria's abundant human and natural resources, its average growth rate could approximate that reported by Botswana if good macroeconomic policies are consistently implemented. Table 6.12 shows that Nigeria's average per capita real income growth compares favorably with the world average during the 2001–06 period but was well below the world average during the 1960–2000 period. Table 6.13 provides data indicating that the primary sector contributed 50.6 percent to GDP growth during the 2001–05 period but is expected to contribute 64.9 percent to GDP growth during the 2006–10 period. In contrast, the secondary sector, which contributed 16 percent to GDP growth during the 2001–05 period, will contribute only 6.5 percent to GDP growth during the 2006–10 period.

Table 6.12. Comparative Real per Capita GDP Growth Rates

Region	1980–2000	2001–05
World	2.2	3.1
Developing countries	2.4	5.1
Emerging market economies	2.6	5.0
Industrial countries	2.1	1.4
Nigeria	0.4[a]	4.2[b]

Sources: IMF World Economic Outlook Database (September 2006) and author's calculations.
a. 1960–2000.
b. + 2003–2006.

Table 6.13. Growth Outlook, Sectoral Contribution to GDP Growth (percent)

Economic Sector	2001–05	2006–10
Primary	50.6	64.9
Crops	35.5	39.8
Oil and gas	11.1	21.7
Livestock	2.4	2.1
Fishing	1.6	1.3
Secondary	16.0	6.5
Electricity	8.5	3.2
Manufacturing	5.2	2.9
Construction	2.3	0.4
Tertiary	33.7	22.4
Wholesale and retail trade	16.3	10.5
Financial institutions	7.6	4.0
Telecommunications	4.4	4.5
Road transport	3.9	2.1
Real estate	1.5	1.3

Sources: 2001–05, Bureau for National Statistics; 2006–10 forecasts, Economic Associates 2007.

Finally, it must be noted that the manufacturing sector is still very weak. Although it contributed 5.2 percent to GDP growth in the 2001–05 period, it is expected to contribute only 2.9 percent to GDP growth during the 2006–10 period. Clearly, then, policy makers still have much work to do to significantly increase the contribution of manufacturing to GDP and GDP growth in Nigeria.

Why, then, did Nigeria fail to develop between 1960 and 2000 in spite of the enormous amount of petrodollars that it received starting in the early 1970s? The simple answer is that Nigeria's petrodollars were misused, misspent, and mislaid. As proximate causes for these outcomes, this chapter has stressed in particular poor leadership and governance combined with ineffective macroeconomic policies during the 1960–2000 period. Also important was the acute regional ethno-religious rivalry in the polity. The issue of poor leadership and governance should not be underestimated, because during most of the first 40 years after independence, Nigeria was governed by leaders excessively motivated by narrow ethnic and sectional loyalties and who lacked the intellect required to develop viable strategies for sustained growth and development in a pluralistic and multiethnic country such as Nigeria. In short, the country did not have a pro-development leadership in its first 40 years of existence. As has been argued, the situation has changed for the better since 2000. If this goes on, Nigeria has a chance finally to take its place among the rapidly growing countries of the world.

It is now accepted in the development orthodoxy that policies can matter profoundly for development outcomes. This chapter has argued that by and large, between 1960 and 2000, Nigeria's policy choices were poor, and the reforms that sought to correct them starting in the mid-1980s were plagued by inconsistencies, reversals, and a general lack of policy coherence. In contrast, the reforms adopted in 2003 were consistent, and an attempt has been made to implement them in a coherent manner. The main difference has been a focused and committed leadership

During the last few decades of the twentieth century, uncertainty in the Nigerian economy was brought about as much by social and political instability as by macroeconomic policy errors. A case in point was the early 1990s, when the nullification of presidential election results by General Babangida brought about an acute political crisis and proved a harbinger of major policy reversals. Deeper institutional problems of governance still remain, including a lack of grassroots participation in politics, malfunctioning formal political institutions, and inadequacy of democratic structures. Resolution of these stubborn social and political problems will go a long way in reducing perceived uncertainty and increasing confidence in the stability of the Nigerian economy. In turn, this will clear the way for a return of flight capital and an increase in both domestic and foreign investment, as well as the sustenance of rapid economic growth in the years ahead.

References

Ajayi, S. I. 2000. "Capital Flight and External Debt in Nigeria." In *External Debt and Capital Flight in Sub-Saharan Africa,* ed. S. I. Ajayi and M. S. Khan. Washington, DC: International Monetary Fund.

Bevan, D., P. Collier, and J. W. Gunning. 1992. "Nigeria: 1970–1990." International Center for Economic Growth, Budapest, Hungary.

Central Bank of Nigeria. 2002. *Annual Report and Statement of Accounts.* Abuja: Central Bank of Nigeria.

Collier, P., and S. A. O'Connell. 2006. "Opportunities and Choices." AERC Explaining African Economic Growth Project, June.

Desai, R. M., A. Olofsgard, and T. M. Yousef. 2007. "The Logic of Authoritarian Bargains: A Test of a Structural Model." Working Paper No. 3. Brookings Global Economy and Development. Washington, DC: Brookings Institution.

Economic Associates. 2007. *Economic Outlook in 2007.* Lagos: Economic Associates.

Economist Conferences. 2007. *Third Business Roundtable with the Government of Nigeria.* Abuja.

Federal Government of Nigeria. 1986. *Structural Adjustment Programme for Nigeria, July 1986–June 1988.* Lagos: Government of Nigeria.

Fosu, A. K. 2008. "Anti-Growth Syndromes in Africa: A Synthesis of the Case Studies." In *the Political Economy of Economic Growth in Africa, 1960–2000,* vol. 1, ed. Benno J. Ndulu and others. Cambridge: Cambridge University Press.

Iyoha, M. A. 1995. "Economic Liberalization and the External Sector." In *Macroeconomic Policy Issues in an Open Developing Economy,* ed. A. Iwayemi. Ibadan: NCEMA.

———. 1996. "Macroeconomic Policy Management of Nigeria's External Sector in the Post-SAP Period." *Nigerian Journal of Economic and Social Studies* 38 (1): 1–18.

Iyoha, M. A., and D. E. Oriakhi. 2008. "Explaining African Economic Growth Performance: the Case of Nigeria." In *The Political Economy of Economic Growth in Africa, 1960–2000.* Vol. 2, *Country Case Studies,* ed. Benno J. Ndulu and others. Cambridge: Cambridge University Press.

Okonjo-Iweala, N., and P. Osafo-Kwaako. 2007. "Nigeria's Economic Reforms: Progress and Challenges." Working Paper No. 6. Brookings Global Economy and Development. Washington, DC: Brookings Institution.

Sachs, J., and A. Warner. 2001. "Natural Resources and Economic Development: the Curse of Natural Resources." *European Economic Review* 45: 827–38.

Suberu, R. T. 2001. *Federalism and Ethnic Conflict in Nigeria.* Washington, DC: United States Institute of Peace Press.

Udeh, J. 2000. "Petroleum Revenue Management: The Nigerian Perspective." Paper presented at World Bank/IFC Petroleum Revenue Management Workshop, Washington, DC, October 23–24.

Williamson, J. 2003. "From Reform Agenda to Damaged Brand Name." *Finance and Development* 40 (3): 10–13.

World Bank. 1999. *World Development Indicators.* Washington, DC: World Bank.

———. 2005. *World Bank Africa Database CD-ROM 2004.* Washington, DC: World Bank.

———. 2006a. *The Little Data Book on Africa.* Washington, DC: World Bank.

———. 2006b. *Nigeria: Competitiveness and Growth.* Report No. 36483-NG. Washington, DC: World Bank.

———. 2006c. *World Development Indicators.* Washington, DC: World Bank.

CHAPTER 7

Political Leadership and Economic Reform: The Brazilian Experience in the Context of Latin America

Fernando Henrique Cardoso and Eduardo Graeff

Brazil grew 2.4 percent per year on average in the last 25 years—somewhat less than Latin America, a good deal less than the world, far less than the emerging countries of Asia in the same period, and indeed far less than Brazil itself in previous decades. If anything stands out favorably in recent Brazilian experience, it is not growth but stabilization and the successful opening of the economy. To this should be added a political achievement: democracy. Democracy was the grand cause of the people and groups who have governed the country since the departure of the military in 1985. Democracy, it should be stressed, rather than economic stability and growth. These are not mutually exclusive goals, of course, although authoritarian regimes sometimes display faster gross domestic product (GDP) growth rates. For Brazil, as for other Latin American countries, there would be no trade-off among these goals—all three presented themselves as inseparable challenges at the start of the 1990s.

To assume that a political leader in today's world can freely determine the pace and direction of a country's economy as he or she wishes is as questionable as believing that an inspired military leader alone could ensure victory on the battlefield. In *War and Peace* Tolstoy mocks the princes and generals who behave as if their attitudes, words, and resolutions dictate the course of history. His most acid irony is directed at the military theorists who claim to extract scientific laws from the infinite multiplicity of events. The paradox, as he sees it, is this: "The higher soldiers or statesmen are in the pyramid of authority, the farther they must be from its base, which consists of those ordinary men and women whose lives are the actual stuff of history."[1] Spy satellites, smart bombs, guided missiles, and other technological wonders may have dispelled the "fog of war" (albeit only to some extent). Advances in information technology and financial engineering, in contrast, have shown an immense capacity to increase the unpredictability of markets at certain times. Anyone who has been in charge of the foreign-exchange trading desk at the central bank of a peripheral country during a global crisis knows how hard it can be to keep calm and hold a steady course in this kind of fog on a stormy sea.

Without venturing into a philosophical discussion of the limits to free will imposed by the course of nature and history, one must acknowledge the virtual impossibility of distinguishing between what was due to the initiatives of local governments and what was imposed from outside in the economic changes experienced by Brazil and its neighbors in the region. The second oil shock (1979) and the U.S. interest-rate shock (1982) plunged almost the whole of Latin America into a decade of stagnation and inflation, while the industrialized world was recycling its economy. The search for solutions to the crisis inevitably responded to the new forms of operation adopted by investors, multinational corporations, governments of central countries, and multilateral economic agencies.

This does not mean, as some market economics theorists seem to suppose, that there are complete recipes for development that will open the doors of globalization to all countries if they are prepared to "do their homework." Nor that Latin Americans are condemned forever to underdevelopment or merely reflex development, as used to be supposed by vulgar dependency theorists and as some people still believe. Countries experience specific historical courses, which are not limited to mechanically reproducing the global structural "model."

A historical and structural analysis of this complex reality would start with the rules according to which the global economy operates—the general, abstract determinations, in Marxist jargon—and reconstitute how they were experienced, adapted, or transformed in each relatively homogeneous group of peripheral countries. This would be the way to expose the dynamic relations between local and international social forces, as well as to see how adaptations and innovations in the linkages between

---

1 The quotation and the points about Tolstoy are from Berlin (1979: 22–80).

each country or group of countries and the global economy produce different results, albeit subject to the same general conditioning factors. The framework for change is established by globalization and the information economy, but each country fits into it or defends itself from it in different ways. The responses can be creative; some may be more advantageous than others, and each will depend both on circumstances such as the country's location, population, and natural resource endowment and on political decisions. National societies have different degrees of economic and cultural development, which facilitate better or worse alternatives for adapting to new circumstances.[2]

The purpose of this chapter is more modest. It is limited to setting out our particular view of recent efforts to consolidate democracy in Brazil while controlling inflation and resuming economic growth. At the same time the chapter presents, as objectively as possible, some thoughts on the limits but also the relevance of action by political leaders to set a course and circumvent obstacles to that process. On occasion the chapter refers to the experiences of other Latin American countries, especially Argentina, Chile, and Mexico, not to offer a full-fledged comparative analysis, but merely to note contrasts and similarities that may shed light on the peculiarities of the Brazilian case and suggest themes for a more wide-ranging exchange of views.[3]

From Inflationary Crisis to the Consolidation of Stability: Democracy in the Expectations Race

In October 2006, Luiz Inácio Lula da Silva was reelected president of Brazil, winning 60 percent of the valid votes cast in the runoff ballot, after leading the first round with 49 percent, 10 points ahead of the runner-up. Reelection was the crowning achievement for a politician with extraordinary talent as a mass communicator at the service of a democratic symbol—a migrant from the Northeast who became a union leader, the founder of a political party, and president of the Republic. To voters in the least developed regions, who ensured his victory, it also embodied their recognition of the poverty alleviation policies introduced by the previous administration, which Lula extended and converted into a material anchor for his symbolic relationship with the poor. At the same time it represented a renewal of the somewhat reticent support shown for his economic policies during his first term, when expectations of faster growth were frustrated but inflation was kept low and Brazil's integration with the global flow of trade and finance was deepened. The challenge Lula faces in his second term is to convert the contradictory messages from the ballot box into government actions that reaffirm belief

---

2   This was the approach used to analyze "dependency situations" in Latin America by Enzo Faletto and Fernando Henrique Cardoso in the 1960s. See Faletto and Cardoso (1979).

3   This account of the Brazilian experience of stabilization and economic reform is based extensively on Cardoso (2006).

not merely in symbols but in democratic institutions and their ability to foster new social and economic advances without relinquishing stability.

There are uncertainties on the horizon, as usual: doubts about the long-term sustainability of the economic policies in place, with high interest rates and taxes and with a strong real, especially if the long cycle of global economic expansion should end. Difficulties in continuing to finance the rising cost of social programs and the government machine by increasing the tax burden, cutting investment, and incurring more debt. Conflict between the president's appeals to private investors and the statist tendencies preferred by so many in the ruling coalition. Concern with the disrepute into which politicians have fallen after a series of corruption scandals involving senior government officials, their party, and allies in Congress.

None of this seems to disturb the perception of most Brazilians that "the country is doing all right," in the words of one of Lula's campaign jingles—far from brilliantly, not as well as other developing countries, but "all right." Translation: there is political and economic stability and some income distribution to the poorest of the poor, but with losses for the middle class. The assessments of analysts and local and foreign investors are also positive for the most part. Banks and major corporations closed 2006 with modest investments but strong earnings. At the start of 2007 projected inflation was around 4 percent per year; the international reserves were close to $100 billion, for imports of $91 million and external debt of $192 billion; and country-risk premiums fell below 200 basis points, the lowest level since calculations began.

Brazil's situation was very far from being as comfortable at the start of the 1990s. Economic stagnation prevailed, a foreign debt moratorium had been declared, hyperinflation was at the gates, and the hopes and expectations awakened by democratization were giving way to widespread despondency. A consensus had formed among political scientists, economists, and observers that a combination of anachronistic ideas, defective institutions, and lack of leadership was preventing Brazil from making the changes needed to control inflation and resume economic growth. While sectors of academia, the state techno-bureaucracy, the business community, and the media were discussing reforms, the national-statism that had inspired several provisions in the "economic order" chapter of the 1988 constitution continued to exert a decisive influence on the opinions of most politicians. In the everyday scrimmage of political activity, old clientelist and populist practices sprang back like weeds in the shade of democracy. Major decisions concerning the design of the nation's institutions weakened the parties and undermined support for the legislative proposals sent to Congress by the president, threatening to reproduce the pattern of executive-legislative conflict that had led to the 1964 coup. The prospect was not of a complete breakdown but of slow deterioration in democracy for lack of governability.[4]

---

4 A representative sample of this view can be found in papers delivered by Brazilian and American experts at a conference organized by the University of Miami and Fundação Getúlio Vargas in late 1991. See Marks (1993).

The political literature uses the term *doble minoria* to describe the recurrent situation in Latin America in which a president is brought to power by a minority of the electorate and faces difficulties in governing for lack of a majority in Congress (Lins and Valenzuela 1994). In Brazil the two-round system for presidential elections introduced by the 1988 constitution solved the first problem, but fragmentation of the party system worsened the second. The Partido do Movimento Democrático Brasileiro (PMDB) had been the sole party of opposition to the authoritarian regime and won a large majority in the 1986 Constituent Assembly, but then split over key issues in the constitutional debate and whether to support President José Sarney or remain in opposition. Collor de Mello won the 1989 presidential election even though he formally belonged to a practically nonexistent party, evidencing the premature decay of the parties that had led the transition to democracy. In the 1990 elections the PMDB's share of the lower house fell to a fifth, representing a slim relative majority among the 19 parties with seats in the Chamber of Deputies.

Lacking a majority in Congress was not a problem for Collor in his first year as president because he was at the height of his popularity and a congressional election was looming. In his second year he realized that he would have to negotiate with the main parties that had won seats in the new Congress, but by then it was too late. With his popularity rapidly eroded by the failure of his anti-inflation policy and a massive corruption scandal, the lack of a consistent majority in Congress prevented him from implementing the reforms he had promised and in December 1992 forced him out of office.

Rising inflation and falling governability seemed to have caught Brazil in a trap that was draining its energy. This inspired pessimistic prognostications about democracy's ability to win or at least tie the race with the expectations of social and economic progress that democracy itself had aroused.

The Real Plan

Peaceful mass demonstrations against Collor and compliance with due process of law during his impeachment rekindled confidence in democracy. Vice President Itamar Franco, an experienced politician, took over as president and appointed a cabinet based on a broad coalition of parties that ensured him a stable majority in Congress.

The economic climate continued to deteriorate, however. The wage-price spiral accelerated, fueled by indexation, and deprived business and government of any stable value reference on which to base medium- and long-term decisions. Investors remained retrenched, although corporate rates of return and liquidity were generally positive. Inflation had reached 30 percent *per month* when President Itamar Franco appointed his fourth finance minister, in May 1993.

As if this were not enough, political turbulence was back with a vengeance as Congress plunged into rancorous investigation of a corruption scandal involving kickbacks in the distribution of budget resources that was to lead to the expulsion of several congressmen, including the majority leader.

Under these circumstances it is understandable that our promise of frontally combating the inflation scourge was received with skepticism, albeit tempered with good will, by the media, business, most congressmen, and the general public. With a president who had not been elected to that office (in Brazil, unlike the United States, the vice president is simply the running mate of the presidential candidate, and most voters do not even know who he is) and with Congress semiparalyzed, few believed the political conditions existed to wage this battle against inflation. Time was running out, moreover: general elections were scheduled for October 1994, and a constitutional amendment had brought forward the presidential election to coincide with them. In little over a year, congressmen would leave for their constituencies to campaign, and it would be impossible to pass complex legislation requiring the physical presence of a majority on the floor of the house.

What Congress, the president, and the people actually preferred was a price freeze in the style of the 1986 Cruzado Plan, which had been followed by short-lived euphoria but was still recalled with gratitude. Analysts accustomed to project the future as a rerun of the past predicted that the fiscal austerity measures included in the FHC Plan, as it was initially called, would end up like similar proposals in the Sarney and Collor administrations, gathering dust on some shelf in Congress or the Office of the President.

The success of the Real Plan, as it later became known, and the cycle of change unleashed by the plan refuted or at least relativized the diagnoses that stressed political obstacles to stabilization of the economy and the implementation of reforms in Brazil.

Even in the short time frame allowed by the electoral calendar, it proved possible to assemble at the Finance Ministry an experienced and creative technical team to furnish indispensable support for a minister who was not an economist, formulate an innovative stabilization strategy combining orthodox and heterodox measures, and win the political support to implement it. In this case the minister's experience as a member of Congress was valuable.

Fiscal policy had undermined the credibility of previous stabilization programs under Presidents Sarney and Collor. The first stage of the Real Plan comprised a series of measures designed to cover this flank: cuts in public spending, de-earmarking of some revenues that the constitution had automatically allocated to specific expenditures, a new tax to be collected by banks on all financial transactions including the cashing of checks, and debt renegotiations with the states, several of which had been in or close to default for some years. Although they were insufficient to assure long-term fiscal equilibrium, these measures were submitted to the president, to Congress, and to the nation as a first step in tackling the structural causes of inflation. In bringing forward the proposals, the government made clear that it had no intention of repeating the discredited "shock therapy" tactics applied under previous anti-inflation programs with a heterodox core, and it showed the determination to dissolve the marriage between inflation and the public purse that had become a hallmark of the Brazilian fiscal regime.[5] In passing the measures, Congress indicated that it would be possible to build a consensus around a broader reform program, giving economic agents a positive signal about the stabilization policy's chances of success. This momentum and the resulting credibility were boosted in October 1993 when Brazil ended its debt moratorium in direct negotiations with creditor banks and only informal support from the International Monetary Fund.

We believed that orthodox fiscal measures were a necessary but not sufficient condition to tackle inflation at the very high levels that it had reached. At some point it would be necessary to dismantle the wage and price indexation mechanisms that had become generalized in the 1980s and were feeding back into inflation via inertia, making past inflation rates the floor for future inflation. The innovative, and to a certain extent audacious, aspect of this operation was the radicalization of indexation as an antidote to indexation itself, in a move that recalled homeopathy's first law, *similia similibus curantor*. A daily indexation mechanism was introduced in February 1994 (the "real value unit" or URV) as a reference for spontaneous resets to contracts and prices before the new currency began circulating on July 1. This avoided litigation among private agents, or between them and the state, to "decouple" contractual rights and obligations before and after the onset of the stabilization program. Litigation arising from previous programs has resulted in a towering stack of liabilities for the National Treasury. In the case of the Real Plan, only one provision has ever been invalidated by the courts, with comparatively minor consequences. Legal armor plating was a key factor in the Real Plan's credibility.

From 47 percent per month on the eve of the currency change, inflation fell to less than 3 percent per month after 30 days and has remained at a single-digit-per-year level ever since.

The first batch of opinion polls on the presidential election, released in May 1994, had shown Lula clearly in the lead with 40 percent. In October we won the election outright in the first round with over half of all valid votes cast. This result was due mainly to the optimism aroused by the Real Plan, which also cemented the coalition of parties that backed our campaign, comprising our own party, the Partido da Social Democracia Brasileira (PSDB), and two center-right parties, the Partido da Frente Liberal (PFL) and Partido Trabalhista Brasileiro (PTB), broadened in the center by the inclusion of the PMDB after the election. Although our program was by no means limited to this issue, consolidating stabilization (or "holding on tight to the real" as the popular saying put it) became the basic commitment as a function of which our government sought support from Congress and society and would be assessed at the end of the day.

---

5 The implicit rationale for this marriage was that nominal revenue growth coupled with corrosion of expected expenditure in real terms guaranteed a balanced budget a posteriori, or something along these lines, allowing the government and Congress to avoid the discomfort of negotiating priorities and spending cuts a priori.

Stabilization and Structural Reform

Controlling inflation was to be not the end but the beginning of an ambitious agenda for change, as we had insisted all along. We had a clear vision of the course to steer. The overall vision as well as several specific measures on this agenda had been outlined in the original planning documents for the Real Plan.[6] The path was made by walking, however, and many unexpected boulders and bends lay ahead.

The initial impact of price stabilization on wages and incomes in general at the base of society anticipated the bonus and deferred the onus of the reforms needed to consolidate stability. A neoclassical economist would have advised us to do the opposite, anticipating the onus while fueling expectations of the bonus. Recalling Machiavelli's teachings about the risks that lie in wait for a reforming ruler, we saw this inversion of conventional economic logic as a political opportunity to sustain the support of the unorganized majority who stood ultimately to gain from the reforms and neutralize resistance from well-organized affluent minorities. We were by no means unaware of the risk of "reform fatigue." However, we were confident that relief at the sharp reduction in inflation would help Brazilian society finally see its age-old ills for what they were and fuel demands for more progress in combating them. We would have to walk a razor's edge between these two collective sentiments: the blossoming of aspirations in response to the changes we had begun, and frustration with the pace and cost of completing the changes.

Our starting point was the conviction that the combination of superinflation, fiscal disequilibrium, foreign debt, and economic stagnation, which had dragged on since the 1980s, signaled the end of a development cycle in Brazil without the foundations having been laid for another cycle. The crisis had well-known proximate causes, from external oil and interest-rate shocks to mistakes and omissions by successive governments. Its underlying cause, however, was the bankruptcy of the centralist interventionist state founded by the dictatorship of Getúlio Vargas (1937–45) and reinforced by the military regime (1964–85). Having enabled Brazil to enjoy 50 years of strong growth, albeit with income concentration and social marginalization, this state model had exhausted its ability to drive industrialization via state-owned enterprises, protectionist barriers, and subsidies to private enterprise.

In our view there could be no lasting economic stability, let alone a sustained resumption of growth, if Brazil remained outside the expanding international flow of trade, investment, and technology. Despite the crisis, many Brazilian companies had managed to modernize their production and management methods, albeit less so their plants and equipment. In contrast with the public sector, private enterprise was not excessively indebted. Although business organizations had been taken by surprise by

---

6   See the Explanatory Memoranda to the July 1993 Immediate Action Plan and the July 1994 measure that introduced the real. Both can be accessed on the Finance Ministry's Web site: http://www.fazenda.gov.br/portugues/real/realhist.asp.

the abrupt trade liberalization promoted by the Collor administration, generally speaking they displayed the capacity to face greater exposure to international competition.

To make its economy more competitive overall, however, Brazil needed a different state model. Neither the grand protagonist of development, as in the past, nor the neoliberal minimalist state, but the "necessary state," as we preferred to call it: with more brains and muscle than bureaucratic mass to respond in a timely manner to the opportunities and turbulence of globalized capitalism. More focused on coordinating and regulating private enterprise than on intervening directly in the economy. Just as important, capable of fulfilling the promises of democracy in the social sphere without making the very beneficiaries of those promises—workers, pensioners, the poorest in general—pay for them via inflation "tax."

The 1988 constitution was not only vast, rambling, and excessively detailed; it was also highly contradictory, and still is to a large extent. It embodied major advances for fundamental citizens' rights and safeguards, as well as generous provision for social rights, yet at the same time it reflected the entrenchment of vested interests linked to the structures of the Vargas state, as well as privileges typical of the deep-seated patrimonialism of Brazilian culture and political institutions.

The state-owned enterprises were accommodated by inclusion in the constitution of the monopoly that they already held in oil and gas as well as telecommunications. In mining and shipping there was no state monopoly, but the constitution established exclusivity for Brazilian-owned companies. In both cases the consequence was insufficient investment or none at all. The state-owned electric power utilities were also lagging behind with investments. The severe fiscal crisis meant that it was necessary to eliminate or ease the constraints written into the constitution and define rules whereby the effort to foster expansion in these sectors could be shared with private enterprise, including foreign capital. Otherwise the incipient resumption of growth would be aborted by infrastructure bottlenecks.

For public-sector workers and civil servants the constitution guaranteed a highly privileged pension scheme, both in terms of the age, length of service, and contribution requirements and in terms of the cash values involved. Private-sector employees covered by the official scheme had far fewer advantages but nevertheless saw their benefits guaranteed, extended, or both. Expenditure was rising faster than the capacity to generate revenue, and as a result both systems began to display growing deficits that would eventually place a huge burden on society as a whole, by forcing an increase in taxation, driving up inflation, or pressuring interest rates. Any increase in payroll taxes for the private sector as a palliative measure to contain deficit growth, on the other hand, would lead to a rise in informality, whereby a large proportion of the workforce would be left without any social security coverage at all. In sum, contrary to the promised universalization of rights, the constitution enshrined a social security and pension system that was highly stratified, lopsided, and unsustainable in the long term.

Public-sector workers also benefited from the extension to all civil servants, including the large number hired without competitive examinations, of job security for life and a ban on pay cuts, both of which are reserved for judges in most countries. This hindered any more ambitious effort to modernize the machinery of government, as well as making payroll expansion almost inevitable in all three tiers of government (federal, state, and municipal).

It was imperative to correct these distortions for reasons of both efficiency and equity. This is what we proposed in a series of bills to amend the constitution's provisions on state monopolies, the definition of a Brazilian-owned company, social security and pensions, and public service. The package was submitted to Congress shortly after the new government took office in January 1995. The committee stage and voting on the entire swathe of constitutional amendments lasted throughout the 1995–98 presidential term. Passage of enabling legislation took longer, with pension reform extending until the end of our second term in 2002.

Battle on Several Fronts

For the general public the debate about reform was basically indistinguishable from the marches and countermarches that revolved around the constitutional amendments. These were an important part but only a part of the state reforms carried out in this eight-year period. Consolidation of stability entailed efforts on several fronts.

Financial relations, and behind them the balance of power, in the sphere of the federation were arduously renegotiated until agreement was reached on a legal framework that would limit the future indebtedness of states (as well as some medium and large cities), encourage them to adjust their accounts, and guarantee payment of installments on debts assumed by the federal government. In this process several state banks used by the respective governments for uncontrolled debt issuance were closed or privatized.

Private-sector banks were affected to varying degrees by the loss of the inflation revenue that they were accustomed to pocketing on unremunerated deposits. A program was established to restructure and strengthen the banking sector; this led to changes of ownership for distressed institutions, limiting the losses to depositors, and above all averting systemic or cascading bank failure, whose effects would have been devastating. Federal financial institutions were also restructured and capitalized.

The Collor administration had removed most nontariff barriers and reduced import tariffs. Currency stability and appreciation against the dollar made trade liberalization effective. Contrary to widespread predictions, this did not lead to the destruction of Brazilian industry. Despite difficulties in certain areas, industry as a whole responded positively to liberalization. It took advantage of the favorable exchange rate to import high-tech plant and inputs, benefited from expansion of the domestic market, and basically maintained the same level of complexity and integration across branches.

The state had to make its own contribution toward the reforms needed for growth to resume under the new conditions arising from economic opening.

BNDES, the national development bank, increased disbursements fivefold in the period 1994–98, to a level above R$20 billion per year. The presence of such a large development bank is unique among the emerging countries and was of key importance to the restructuring of production capacity in Brazil's private sector.

Government agencies of no significance or simply nonexistent in a closed economy had to be strengthened or created in areas such as export promotion, antitrust, agricultural defense, intellectual property, and support for innovation. Structuring such agencies helped to pave the way for strong export growth in both commodities and manufactures beginning in 1999.

The entry of private enterprise into infrastructure sectors required a new legal framework for the granting of public service concessions and the creation of a hitherto unknown entity in the organization of the Brazilian state: regulatory bodies with the powers and political independence to protect the rights of consumers in their relations with service providers. Several such regulators were created following the passage of constitutional amendments on oil, electricity, and telecommunications.

The real was born close to parity with the dollar but not legally pegged to the dollar as the Argentine peso had been by the Cavallo Plan (1991). Rather than dollarization, we insisted on less attractive issues, such as combating the public deficit and balancing the budget. This had important implications for the consolidation of stability in Brazil. Successive attempts to realign the exchange rate in terms more favorable to Brazilian exports were aborted by external financial crises in the second half of the 1990s. Gradual devaluation of the real against the dollar until the end of 1998 lagged behind domestic inflation. Realignment eventually happened of necessity in January 1999, when the risk that our foreign-exchange reserves would be dangerously depleted by a fierce speculative attack forced the Central Bank to float the real. Widespread fears of a banking crisis and inflation acceleration proved unfounded. The structural changes already in place, albeit incomplete from our standpoint, proved sufficient to stabilize the economy without the "exchange-rate anchor."

The battle to bring states, municipalities, and the federal sphere itself into line behind the banner of fiscal sustainability intensified with the introduction of a floating exchange-rate regime and inflation targeting in 1999. To crown this normative effort, the Fiscal Responsibility Act passed in May 2000 applied strict rules to all three tiers of government regarding indebtedness and the creation of payroll and other permanent expenses.

Last but by no means least, instruments of state action had to be redesigned to fulfill promises of rights universalization in the social sphere. Also via constitutional amendment, new rules were established for participation by the federal, state, and municipal governments in the financing of primary education and health care, and a Fund to Combat Poverty was created. The criteria for investment of these funds represented a major advance toward equity in public spending, because they prioritized the poorest and most vulnerable strata of the population, who had traditionally benefited least from social programs. Comprehensive changes to the design and execution of essential programs in these areas enhanced spending efficiency, especially through decentralization via the transfer of federal funds and activities to states and municipalities, partnerships with civil society, and systematic assessment of outcomes.

Not all the reforms advanced as much as we would have liked. We lack the necessary distance to judge how far they succeeded, and we cannot guarantee that they have reached the point of no return. However, it seems undeniable that they have now helped sustain the stability of the Brazilian economy for more than 12 years. It may be too soon to say whether they have also laid the foundations for such a significant long-term change as the creation of a new development model, as we intended.[7]

The Drawbacks and Force of Democratic Reformism

Modern formulations of the notion of political leadership emphasize institutional position and "mission." Outside this context the discussion of a leader's motivations and personal attributes falls into the banality of psychological and even biological generalization (Petracca 2004). Our thoughts on the role of leadership in the reform process start from these two dimensions. In the case of the head of a democratic government, position is basically defined by power sharing and "mission" by the expectations of the led in their triple status as citizen-voters, voices of public opinion, and members of organized social sectors.

Plebiscitary or Consensual Democracy?

Let us begin with the relations with Congress and the parties, which are critical to any president's ability to lead in Brazil and other Latin American countries with presidential systems.

Our reform agenda was extensive and complex, and (it bears repeating) took up most of the order of business in Congress for several years. In all, 35 constitutional amendments were passed between 1995 and 2002—36 if the amendment is included that enabled the requisite fiscal adjustment to be made in preparation for the Real Plan in 1993.[8] Each could be passed only by three-fifths of both houses, with two readings in each house, the Chamber of Deputies and Senate. Because the rules of the lower house allowed (and, within certain limits, still allow) any party to demand that

---

7 Mauricio Font (2003) speaks of "structural realignment" in referring to the balance of change in Brazil in this period. For an analysis of the reforms by Brazilian scholars, some of whom participated actively in their implementation, see Giambiagi, Reis, and Urani (2004).

8 The text of the Brazilian constitution, including all passed amendments, can be found at the Office of the President's Web site: http://www.planalto.gov.br/ccivil_03/Constituicao/Constitui%E7ao.htm.

parts of a bill be voted separately, the three-fifths quorum had to be achieved for hundreds of votes. Over 500 supplementary laws, ordinary laws, and relevant provisional measures were passed in the same period.

It is most unlikely that a reform process would have entailed such a huge effort at building a consensus with the legislative branch in any other Latin American country. Did this represent a disadvantage? Considering the gap between our goals and what we actually succeeded in achieving, the answer is perhaps affirmative: the need to negotiate with Congress and the social sectors represented there every single step of the way did result to some extent in a slower pace and a narrower scope for the measures we proposed. However, democracy and economic efficiency are not mutually negotiable goals in our view, as noted at the start of this chapter. Nor has Brazil done worse than those of its neighbors that implemented reforms in the authoritarian way.

Chile under General Augusto Pinochet (1973–90) is always cited as an example of successful reforms imposed without consulting Congress, which had been closed, or society, or at least the working class, which was silenced by vicious repression. Dictatorship is said to have been a necessary evil that enabled the Chilean economy to steer the "right course to growth" from the liberal standpoint, including deregulation, privatization, trade liberalization, and fiscal equilibrium. This view underestimates the price paid by the Chilean people, not only in lost liberties and rights but also in terms of material hardship. An orthodox shock program to tackle inflation caused a recession of more than 11 percent in 1975. The financial crisis that forced devaluation of the peso (Pinochet's "Chicago boys" also used an exchange-rate anchor) triggered another recession in 1982. Unemployment soared to nearly 20 percent and fell below 10 percent only in the late 1980s.[9] The proportion of the population living below the poverty line reached 45 percent in 1985; today it has returned to the level prevailing at the end of the 1960s, around 17 percent (Racynski and Serrano 2005: 259–60).

Nor can it be said that Concertación por la Democracia was lucky enough to receive the house in order in 1990. Inflation was 17 percent in Pinochet's last year and did not fall to single-digit levels until 1995. Although the Concertación coalition retained the principles of deregulation, privatization, and economic openness, it introduced a more rigorous fiscal policy while also restoring workers' rights and investing strongly in social policies.[10] It did this by consensus building in Congress and with organized sectors of society despite the discretionary resources conferred on the executive by Chile's hyper-presidentialist constitution (Siavelis 2000). Chile's GDP grew 5.5 percent per year on average in the period 1990–2004, under Concertación-led governments, compared with only 3.1 percent in the period 1974–89 (Landerretche 2005).

9   Unless otherwise noted, all data on GDP, unemployment, and inflation in Latin American countries are from the World Bank, compiled for this paper by Juliana Wenceslau at the Brasília office of the International Bank for Reconstruction and Development.

10 For a detailed analysis of the economic and social orientations and achievements of Concertación-led governments compared with the legacy of the dictatorship, see Meller (2005).

If Chile stands out in Latin America as a successful case of integration into the global economy, it is thanks not to the legacy of the dictatorship but to what its democratic leaders have been able to achieve by leaving that legacy behind.

In Argentina the military junta that seized power in 1976 attempted liberal reforms similar to Chile's via the same authoritarian road, but the results were disastrous, and the Malvinas/Falklands war made a handover to civilian rule inevitable in 1983. President Raúl Alfonsín (1983–89) received an economy that had been in deep recession for two years with inflation running at over 300 percent.

In contrast with Chile's, Argentina's democratic leaders had a difficult time establishing a lasting consensus on the direction of the economy. Alfonsín's reform proposals foundered in the face of Peronist opposition and lack of support from his own Unión Cívica Radical (UCR). A price freeze attempted under the Austral Plan ended in more recession and inflation of more than 600 percent in 1985, opening the gates for the Peronists to return to government with President Carlos Menem (1989–99). In 1991, as hyperinflation threatened to break out, Menem managed to wrest support from the Peronist Partido Justicialista (PJ) and the opposition for the stabilization program mounted by Finance Minister Domingo Cavallo. In addition to fixing the peso by law at parity with the dollar, the plan included a fast-track privatization process. In 1992 the Olivos Pact between Peronists and Radicals laid the basis for convening a Constituent Assembly that introduced some of the reforms proposed previously by Alfonsín. But Menem's preferred instrument for implementing economic policy, including privatization, deregulation, and what little downsizing of government he undertook, was legislative delegation to the executive, which freed the president of the need to negotiate measures point by point with Congress.[11]

Without ceasing to be democratic, the road to reform in Menem's Argentina appears to have had a pronounced plebiscitary element, in which the inflationary crisis predisposed the parties and society to accept "heroic" measures and concentrated the initiative in the hands of the president. In contrast, the Chilean and Brazilian experiences fell distinctly into the camp of "consensual democracy," in which the executive must negotiate and trade concessions with the groups that have the power to veto its proposals.[12]

Argentina's shortcut to stabilization may look faster at first sight, but it did not go so far in terms of structural reform, and ultimately seems to have resulted in weaker rather than stronger institutions, as evidenced by the 2001–02 foreign-exchange and financial crisis. A preference for tortuous consensus building led Chile and Brazil to more solid results from the institutional standpoint. There is a significant difference between the two

---

11 On Argentina's experience with stabilization and reform, see Palermo (2004).

12 The distinction between majoritarian and consensual democracy is explored in Lijphart (1984: 177–207).

countries in this regard: whereas the agenda pursued by the Concertación can perhaps be said to have focused on rebuilding democratic social and political institutions on the scorched earth left behind by the dictatorship, the Brazilian reforms simultaneously addressed the need to build new institutions and to remove the detritus of the old Vargas state, possibly paying a higher political price for that.

The "Political Preconditions" Fallacy

The inflationary crisis also functioned as the "midwife of history" in Brazil. With almost daily price rises averaging more than 20 percent per month, practically no sector was immune from the burden of superinflation. Everyone was affected in some way: wage workers, pensioners, and retirees, by accelerating corrosion of the purchasing power of their fixed earnings; self-employed workers and small business owners without access to the banking system, by depreciation of their limited cash assets; the upper-middle class and business, by the immense difficulty of calculating, planning, and investing in a superinflationary environment, even with access to index-linked financial instruments. This boosted potential support for any plausible proposal to control inflation insofar as it diminished resistance to the necessary sacrifices.

Thus Brazil under the Real Plan and Argentina under the Cavallo Plan are examples of the tendency detected by Albert Hirschman in the early 1980s, when he investigated what he called the social and political matrix of inflation in Latin America: "Beyond a threshold of tolerance, inflation certainly is the kind of pressing policy problem that increases the willingness of governments to take action, in spite of opposition from powerful interests, if there is firm expectation that the action will help restrain the inflation" (Hirschman 1981: 206).

To this effect of inflation was added in our case the weakening of traditional political forces for strictly political reasons. We mentioned earlier the exceptional circumstances that justified skepticism about the chances of success of a frontal attack on inflation after the impeachment of Collor: lack of direct electoral backing for his legal alternate, the corruption scandal that had all but paralyzed Congress, and pressure from the electoral calendar. Paradoxically, these very circumstances were what made the Real Plan possible. What analysts diagnosed as a lack of political preconditions turned out to be a window of opportunity. In normal conditions the groups that benefited one way or another from inflation and state disorganization, including segments of Congress, the private sector, and the state bureaucracy itself, would have mobilized more effectively to defend their interests. Only the disarray in which traditional political forces found themselves can explain why they allowed themselves to be defeated—or persuaded—by a minister and his small group of aides and sympathizers in the government, with the president's support, it is true, but with very hesitant backing from other parties apart from our own, the PSDB.

The art of politics consists of creating the conditions to achieve an objective for which the conditions are not given in advance. This is why politics is an art and not a technique. Its principal weapon in a democracy is persuasion. Thanks to persuasion, to the winning over of public opinion, it eventually proved possible to build a minimum of consensus where it was presumably most difficult and certainly most necessary: inside the government, in Congress, and in the parties—that is, among the actors who make political decisions or prevent them from being made. In the midst of many doubts we had one certainty, grounded in the values of our democratic upbringing: that only a program capable of being explained and understood by ordinary people would be able to inflict a lasting defeat on inflation and set in motion the reorganization of the Brazilian state.

Credibility was a key prerequisite in a country that had suffered the consequences of the failure of successive stabilization programs in recent years. We benefited from the good will of the media, most business leaders, other organized sectors of society, and Congress itself. Despite skepticism about our chances of success they trusted the minister's seriousness of purpose and the competence of his team. Aware of the importance of maintaining and broadening this basis of trust, we decided that there would be no surprises and no promises that could not easily be met: each step in our stabilization strategy would be announced in advance and explained to the general public, always making clear that what was involved was not unilateral action by the government but a *process* whose outcome depended on the continuing convergence of the efforts of government, Congress, private economic agents, and society as a whole.

We often came close to losing the battle for trust. As the months went by, society became more and more anxious about the acceleration of inflation, pressure built up in the government itself for decisive action, and there was increasing resistance from parties and leaders who saw the possibility of a successful stabilization program as a defeat for their own political plans.

The removal of an entire currency from circulation and its replacement with a new one brought a fundamental reinforcement to this battle for trust and credibility: the *symbol* represented by the real, which synthesized the expectations of change diffused throughout society.

Even before the new currency began circulating, the parties' and politicians' radars had begun capturing the public's change of mood. The perception that this could drive a competitive presidential candidacy facilitated the task of winning support for our proposals in Congress.

This is how the breakthrough was achieved: launched under the sign of a "lack of political preconditions," the Real Plan was itself to become the precondition for a realignment of political forces in favor of the reforms.

Almost by saturation, the old order gave way to the new. Victory in the presidential election provided the opportunity and responsibility of anchoring this new situation in the bedrock of the nation's institutions, of moving forward with an extensive agenda of reforms necessary to "hold on tight to the real" and keep the hopes deposited in it alive.

Testing the Limits of Latin American Presidentialism

The success of the Real Plan owed much to this seizing of a window of opportunity. It took eight years of unremitting effort to consolidate stability. The continuity of the progress that was possible to achieve throughout this period depended on a political strategy with two pillars: (1) building a stable majority in Congress by sharing power in the executive with the parties in the ruling coalition and (2) leveraging the president's leadership to bring to bear both the government's forces and those of the coalition parties to push for reform, with the support of public opinion and the organized sectors of society.

A president can often use constitutional instruments to transform his will, if not into law, at least into decrees or provisional measures with the force of law,[13] and even the authority to ensure his orders are obeyed through recognition of the legitimacy of his decisions. However, to be politically effective by winning more support or smoothing the way to implementing his proposals, he does not fully exercise this virtual power but instead goes about creating situations in which, although his will is not entirely patent, the policies and decisions he aims to pursue stand a greater chance of success.

It so happens that the executive, represented by the president and his cabinet, is only a part of the system of power (not to mention the domination structurally exercised by classes and segments of classes, organized in the nonformal command structure, and that bring pressure to bear on a day-to-day basis and have at their disposal power resources entrenched in a thousand ways in social practices). Congress, the parties, and the courts, to cite only the formal components of the command structure, condition the political game.

The crises that led to the resignation of President Jânio Quadros and the ouster of President João Goulart in the 1960s, as well as to the impeachment of Collor, left a clear lesson: the main question for the president is not *if* but *how* he should share power. The worst mistake he can make is to imagine he has a mandate to govern alone. To do what he has promised those who voted for him, he needs Congress. And to ensure himself of a majority in Congress, he needs to build alliances, because the heterogeneity of the federation and the peculiarities of the Brazilian system of proportional representation produce party-political fragmentation in which no single party wields a majority.

With these lessons of history in mind, we set out to weld an alliance between our own party, the PSDB, and the PFL and PTB in the presidential election, and later to include the PMDB and Partido Progressita Brasileiro (PPB) in the ruling coalition. A balance among the larger parties, preventing our own party from controlling Congress even when it won a majority in

---

13 The Brazilian constitution authorizes the president in cases of urgency to issue provisional measures with the force of law, which lose validity unless they are ratified by Congress in 90 days.

the lower house after the 1998 elections, proved fundamental to ensuring political stability.

A respectable current of political scientists considers Latin American presidentialism a lost cause. Party fragmentation, on the one hand, and the independence and rigidity of the mandates of the president and Congress, on the other, are believed to lead to recurrent political impasses.[14] The PSDB, inspired by this sort of diagnosis, declared itself parliamentarist in its 1988 founding manifesto. Parliamentarism sustained a crushing defeat in a plebiscite held in 1993. In an irony of history, we lost the plebiscite and a year later won the presidential election, thus having to assume the task of ensuring not just the survival but the good health of the system we had considered doomed.

More recent studies underscore the idea that in Latin America, instead of presidentialism it is more appropriate to speak of presidentialisms in the plural. The risk of an impasse is ever present. The means and modes of avoiding it vary according to the specificities of executive-legislative relations, party organization, and the contents of the decisions on the agenda. Only by taking these variables into account, in addition to generalizations about systems of government, would it be possible to explain the positive, albeit problematical, results achieved by democracy in some countries of the region.[15]

A peculiarity of Brazil in this regard is the coexistence between the relative weakness of the parties and the strength of Congress as an arena for negotiating and decision making. We are an extreme case of multiparty politics, with some 20 parties represented in the Chamber of Deputies, five or six of them relevant, and none with more than 20 percent of the seats. Argentina, Chile, and Mexico, in contrast, are cases of moderately concentrated pluriparty systems.

The Argentine and Chilean dictatorships closed Congress and banned parties but were unable to destroy them in practice, at least not the largest parties. The UCR (Radicals) and PJ (Peronists), which had polarized Argentine politics since 1945, like Chile's Partido Demócrata Cristiano (PDC; Christian Democrats) and Partido Socialista (PS; Socialists), which date back to the 1920s and 1930s, survived and again assumed a leadership role after redemocratization. Their strength is due to long-standing loyalty on the part of voters and card-carrying members, as well as the discipline of backbenchers. This discipline derives from the electoral system—closed-list proportional representation in Argentina, two-member ("binominal") districts in Chile—and is reinforced by tradition. The usual penalty for congressmen who vote systematically against the party line is removal from the list at the next election or expulsion before it. Given the weight of tradition and the relative concentration of votes for the larger parties, the chances of reelection for those who leave or are expelled are slim.

---

14 Lins and Valenzuela (1994) is representative of this type of approach.

15 For analyses that emphasize possibilities for executive-legislative cooperation, despite the conflict, see Morgenstern and Nacif (2002).

We Brazilians often imagine that fewer and more united parties would facilitate negotiations between the president and Congress and ensure a faster, more consistent decision-making process. Our neighbors' experience suggests that may not always be the case. United and pugnacious parties may be a synonym for governability under parliamentarism. Under presidentialism they sometimes serve to organize gridlock. Polarization between the PJ and UCR in Argentina, and exacerbated rivalry between right-wing, centrist, and left-wing blocs in Chile, set the stage for the collapse of democracy in both countries.

Polarization persisted in postauthoritarian Argentina, and although it did not reach a breaking point, it severely hampered both UCR-led administrations. The intransigence of the Peronist opposition and galloping inflation led President Alfonsín to resign months before the official end of his term. President Fernando de la Rúa, who succeeded Menem, failed to complete a year in office. His government was stymied by its inability to halt or manage the crisis of confidence in the peso's parity with the dollar. In response to popular rejection of all politicians (*¡Que se vayan todos!*), the UCR broke up and shrank, while the PJ, despite electoral damage, strengthened its relative predominance, sustained by the Peronist party-union machine and its symbolic identification with the *descamisados* (Torre 2004). Argentina thus appears to be shifting away from a virtual two-party system to a pluriparty system with a dominant party, in which executive-legislative relations will tend to oscillate between cooperation and confrontation depending on whether the president is a Peronist.

Argentina's military junta departed the scene without leaving anyone to claim a political legacy. Pinochet's legacy, in contrast, was recognized until the end of his life by the right-wing UDI and RN, which have consistent social and electoral grassroots. This led to an alliance of the center and left represented by the PDC and PS. The unstable triangle of the past was thus replaced by a sort of virtuous circle in which the Concertación's political consistency and economic success reinforce each other, ensuring control of both the executive and Congress.

Mexico's transition to pluralist democracy is a case apart in this mosaic: it was somewhat of a Latin American perestroika, in which a semi-authoritarian regime opened up from the inside out and from the top down in a process led by those who were both head of government and head of the almost single party. This concentration of power enabled Presidents Miguel de la Madrid (1982–88) and Carlos Salinas de Gortari (1988–94) to overcome the Partido Revolucionario Institucional's (PRI) deep-seated national statism and implement the economic reforms that paved the way for Mexico to join the North American Free Trade Agreement in January 1994. Successive electoral reforms since 1978 enabled the opposition to strengthen its representation in the lower house from 17 percent of seats to 48 percent in 1988 and 52 percent in 1997, leaving President Ernesto Zedillo (1994–2000) with a minority in Congress in the second half of his term. The 2000 presidential election brought the democratic routine of party alternation and made Mexico a member of the club of presidents in *doble minoria*. Partido Acción Nacional (PAN) candidate Vicente Fox was elected president (2000–06) with 48 percent of the votes and failed to win congressional approval for his main fiscal, energy, and labor reforms.

The PRI's hegemony for more than 70 years forged a peculiar mechanism whereby the party controlled its representatives: prohibition of reelection to Congress. Without the possibility of a second consecutive term, congressmen depended on the party for access to other elective offices or political appointments. Far from questioning this legacy, the PAN and Partido de la Revolución Democrática (PRD), which grew in the electoral soil lost by the PRI, used it to increase the power of their national leaderships. One wonders whether this party setup will lead to negotiating and coalition practices similar to those in Chile today or to a three-sided tug of war more like that of Chile before Pinochet.

Unique to Brazil: Strong Congress, Weak Parties

The iron law of what in Brazil has been called "coalition presidentialism" says that to maintain a stable majority in Congress the president must share power in the executive sphere by appointing representatives of allied parties to seats in the cabinet and other positions.[16]

If power sharing safeguards the president, other political actors, and the nation from the unforeseeable consequences of an impasse between president and Congress, it does not in itself guarantee the support of a majority in Congress for the legislative measures proposed by the executive. This has to be won vote by vote, bill by bill, in a Sysiphean labor for the president and his inner circle—within which the function of "political coordinator," normally performed by a minister with an office in the presidential palace, stands out as a high-turnover job.

The key problem here is that except for the so-called left-wing parties, from the variants of communist origin to the Partido dos Trabalhadores (PT), Brazilian parties have little control over how their elected members vote in Congress.

Although some people insist on seeing our parties through European eyes, Brazilian society is entirely different. It has less hierarchy, more mobility, and far fewer stable reference points. Ideologies are too weak to define behavior. Under the dictatorship there was a straightforward alternative: some supported the regime, others fought for democracy. In a free country other choices are available. At the same time, however, there is less difference between the ideologies professed by the parties. Their platforms are very similar, and unfortunately so are their practices.

Unlike the Argentine and Chilean dictatorships, the Brazilian military kept Congress open and shut down existing parties on two occasions: in 1965, when it imposed a two-party system, and in 1979, when it abolished it. This effectively truncated evolution of the party system. The Brazilian

---

16 The Brazilian institutional system up to 1964 was first characterized as "coalition presidentialism" by Abranches (1988).

dictatorship itself did not leave behind an electorally competitive right-wing party or bloc, as did the Chilean, and this in turn deprived the democratic forces of a common adversary that could prevent them from dispersing. Several leaders and some of the old parties reappeared, but the political system was reorganized on a different basis: first, for a short time, it revolved around the PMDB; more recently, it has revolved around the polarization between the PT and PSDB.

Moreover, Brazil has an electoral system that tends to push party indiscipline to extremes. The existence of a large number of parties is a typical effect of proportional representation, particularly in a large heterogeneous federation like Brazil. The weakness of the link between elected representatives and their parties is characteristic of the open-list proportional representation system adopted in Brazil, where a candidate's position on a party list depends on the number of votes he or she receives individually.

Adopted in the 1940s when Brazilian society was still predominantly rural with strongly oligarchic features, this system has long shown signs of fatigue. In a democratic mass society with whole states for electoral districts, in which hundreds of candidates contest seats in the lower house, individually competing for tens of thousands of votes, the open-list system has become a game of roulette in which the "banker"—economic power and influential corporations embedded in the state apparatus, in the private sector, or worse still in the interface between the two—always wins in the end. The rate of reelection to the Chamber of Deputies remains low at 50 percent or less, but the high turnover does not mean renewal in any measurable sense, let alone improvements in quality. Election campaigns are growing more and more expensive. Congress members' chances of reelection depend less and less on whether they perform their duties well as a lawmaker and scrutinizer of the government's actions, and more and more on how well they cater to local or sectoral clienteles. This makes the typical congressman a representative in search of people to represent, that is, of new clienteles for whom they strive to cater via amendments to the budget, government favors, or legal advantages. Thus Brazil has a representative system in which "representation," if any, is postelectoral.

In practice this form of relationship between congressmen, parties, and the electorate, as well as the executive, makes it difficult to characterize our system of government with precision. How can one properly speak of "coalition presidentialism" when the fragmentation of interests and power foci overflows party channels? The notion is useful but needs to be contextualized. It would be greatly preferable to be able to organize stable party alliances and coalitions. The "imperial" aspect of Brazilian presidentialism derives less from the will of the president than from the effective conditions under which politics functions. Given the relative weakness of the parties and the strength of Congress, regardless of what the president wants, if he lacks strength, then clientelism and patronage (or *fisiologismo,* to use the popular term for the system whereby congressmen lobby for material and political public resources) predominate over the government's capacity to define and implement a change agenda for the nation.

Executive-legislative relations become much more volatile in the context of this type of representation. This is why attempts at building an "institutional" relationship between president and parties produce precarious results. For the same reason political negotiations, however legitimate, are seen by the public as "horse trading" and "logrolling": they are conducted almost individually or, in the case of "parliamentary fronts," by caucuses comprising members of an array of different parties, ranging for example from the PT to the PPB, who join forces to pursue a specific goal, such as farm debt relief, opposition to the easing of restrictions on abortion, or advocacy of parliamentarism.

Nevertheless, with all its delays, peculiarities, and convolutions, Congress represents the interests and visions existing in society. It is up to the government (and especially the president) to understand the rules of the democratic game. The president must be balanced enough to realize that the obstructions, amendments, and feints of the legislature often create the opportunity for understandings that produce better results. Not always, of course, and in such cases it is the president's responsibility to put his foot down, insofar as the rules of the game allow. If even so the results are not forthcoming, then he must go back to public opinion and persistently defend his views. This is why in a democracy the battles are incessant and the improvements incremental.

Tension is inevitable between the president's roles as representative of the majority of the nation and organizer of a parliamentary majority. Without alliances the president cannot govern. Neither, however, can he govern, in the sense of carrying out his agenda, if he "surrenders" to Congress.

Alliances to what end? Just to stay in power or to achieve broader goals? This question must be faced right at the start of his term, when the parties (the president's, those of his allies, or, when even so a majority cannot be assured, those of his former adversaries) sit down with a voracious appetite to discuss what shares they will each have in the spoils of power. This is the time to appoint a cabinet and leaders in Congress (to control and manage the lower and upper houses as well as lead the coalition caucus). The broader goals set limits on the concessions the president may make to allies and his own party. If he is not capable of identifying and safeguarding those parts of the executive that are essential to the accomplishment of his projects, he may end up appointing the wrong people to key positions. In our case the economic area, including ministries and federal financial institutions, and the most important portfolios in the social area, starting with health and education, were not included in any power-sharing deals. Privatization of many large state-owned enterprises (SOEs) took out of the equation dozens of top executive positions that had traditionally been part of these negotiations. The introduction of formal procedures to choose regional and middle managers in social security, land reform, and environmental protection, among others, had the same effect. Otherwise, even in positions open to nomination by allied parties, it proved possible to match political criteria, technical competence, and alignment with the government's goals.

Members of the opposition and other critics of the government accused us of subjecting Congress to a "steamroller," lubricated by handouts of jobs and budget allocations. In actual fact the scope for political appointments was made narrower for the reasons given above, as was the scope for so-called parochial amendments after the scandal involving members of the budget committee in 1993. If the clientelistic use of jobs and funds were the key to ensuring a pro-government majority in Congress, it would be impossible to explain how we enjoyed broader support for a longer time to pass a much larger and more complex reform agenda and with far fewer resources with which to bargain than previous governments.

In our view the key to the majority was none of the above, but the project itself: the "mission" legitimated by the ballot box and public opinion, and in whose name the government made alliances and sought backing in Congress. Common sense suggests that the more the government asks of Congress in terms of lawmaking, the higher the price it must be prepared to pay in "retail" negotiations with the parliamentarians who support it. Our experience suggests the contrary: the consistency of the government's legislative agenda, with its overarching commitment to "holding on tight to the real," did not hinder but rather facilitated the task (in itself always arduous) of keeping the extent to which specific demands from parties and allies were met within reasonable limits.

Support from the street is no substitute for support from the parties. Without stable party alliances it would have been hard for the government to overcome the 1999 foreign-exchange crisis, when the commitment to saving the real seemed momentarily endangered and the president's ratings took a plunge. A combination of tactical flexibility to negotiate and renegotiate a parliamentary majority, and strategic obstinacy to pursue the key points of the reform agenda, made it possible to traverse the inevitable ups and downs in presidential popularity while maintaining both the majority and the direction of the government (Graeff 2000).

Turning the Page on National-Statism

The "mission" that legitimates the president's actions is almost always couched by the people in generic terms, although not necessarily vague ones: controlling inflation, eradicating poverty, creating more jobs, combating crime. The leader must translate these diffuse expectations into a *project*, a sequence of actions that consistently lead toward the desired common good. This depends on the scope of his *vision*—his understanding of the country's past and outlook on its future—and his ability to assemble a team to formulate and implement concrete measures in accordance with this vision.

Our efforts to translate the mission of controlling inflation into a more ambitious reform project would have to surmount one major obstacle: the national-statist vision with which Brazilian culture and political institutions are imbued, as well as a constellation of interests linked to that vision.

Mentioned above was the relative backwardness of this discussion among Brazilian politicians. They were not alone in this respect. In Brazil, as elsewhere, a significant number of intellectuals remained attached to a basically statist vision—self-labeled left-wing, socialist, nationalist, or progressive—even after the collapse of the Soviet Union and the acceleration of capitalist globalization had resoundingly discredited statism. Surprising alliances were seen between these fellow travelers. In discussions on fiscal adjustment, the traditional budgetary populism of those who advocate "spending now and the money will turn up later" often resorted to the pseudo-Keynesian arguments of economists venerated by the left.

The influence sustained by national-statism in Brazil is proportional to the advances that it claimed in the last century. Brazil's economy grew more than any other country's between 1930 and 1980. Industrialization by import substitution bequeathed an industrial base unrivaled in Latin America, vast, diversified, and, as became clear after economic opening, reasonably competitive. Expansion of the protected domestic market sustained levels of employment at a time of explosive demographic and urban growth. The Vargas state extended to the masses who had only recently flooded into the towns a precarious web of social protection but one that was unprecedented and far better than the insecurity to which they were exposed in the countryside.

Economic decline in the 1980s sapped the strength of the military regime, but confidence in the old form of the state and its economic model remained unscathed. Most delegates to the Constituent Assembly (1987–88) assumed that democracy would be enough to put the national locomotive back on the rails of development, merely adding safeguards for individual and social rights to the pillars of the autarkic statist economy. (The same credo, by the way, was expressed by Alfonsín in his vibrant inauguration address as president of Argentina in 1983: "Con la democracia se come, se educa y se cura." In a loose translation: "Democracy will grant us food, education, and health care.")

Besides attachment to the past, alongside special interests best accommodated under the mantle of state protection, what fueled the resistance to change was a lack of clear alternatives—an ideological fog that now shrouded, now merged with the institutional obstacles to decision making. The alternatives were not self-evident in fact. Unlike Mexico, Brazil did not have the largest capitalist economy in the world on its doorstep offering purportedly unlimited possibilities for trade and industrial integration and an exit for surplus labor. Over 10 times the size of Chile, it could not afford to confine itself to modernizing and diversifying exports of primary goods to secure jobs and incomes for its population. Exports of manufactures, in which the military regime invested with some success, took time to be recognized not as a mutually exclusive alternative but as a complement to expansion of the domestic market.

In any event, a critique of the national-statist vision matured in the five years between promulgation of the constitution and the Real Plan, driven by shock waves from the fall of the Berlin Wall and the realization that advancing information technology and the formation of regional economic blocs had opened a new stage of global capitalism. Initially waged outside the political system, the debate among specialists (mainly economists) in a few universities, centers of excellence belonging to the federal administration, and research institutions linked to trade associations gradually distilled a new vision of Brazil and its place in the world, alongside proposals for a development strategy to match the new reality. Collor embraced some of these proposals in the name of a vague "modernity." His meteoric passage shook the political world and created more room for discussion of the reforms in the media. By taking presidential intervention in politics and the economy to the ultimate level, he may actually have helped to convince public opinion of the need for a leader who, without retreating into a vision of the past, would be capable of restoring confidence in a less traumatic reform agenda.

When the gathering inflation crisis after Collor's impeachment crossed the threshold of society's tolerance and lowered resistance to change in Congress, a sufficiently mature agenda was ready to be offered to the nation.

Our thoughts on this subject had advanced during the Constituent Assembly. The manifesto of the PSDB, founded in July 1988 by a group of dissidents who had split from the PMDB, incorporated many of the new ideas we would try to put into practice after the Real Plan was launched: less protectionism and more technological development, less corporatism and more permeability of the state to grassroots demands and participation. We criticized both the dyed-in-the-wool advocates of state monopoly and those who saw any state intervention as a threat to the market economy. Nationalization versus privatization, we warned, was a false problem when it was reduced to a matter of principle without taking into account the limits and possibilities of state and private action in each sector.

It was too late to try to dissuade the Constituent Assembly from bowing to the pressure of corporatist and national-statist opinions. Later, however, when the Real Plan opened a window of opportunity, the conversation with reformist sectors of society gave us both the intellectual critical mass and the support of public opinion to move forward.

The presence of a hybrid of intellectual and politician at the head of the Finance Ministry, and later as president, helped build and sustain a bridge between the government, the parties, and Congress, on the one hand, and reformist groups in the universities, the technobureaucracy, and the business community, on the other.

Once an alternative direction had been defined and the ideological fog had been dispersed, resistance to change came to the fore, led by a battle-hardened minority parliamentary opposition with the PT at its core and an important segment of the labor movement, whose main constituency was among public-sector workers in the state apparatus and SOEs.

The debate about the reforms never reached the point of causing a split in society. When it became apparent that this could happen, the government preferred to limit its goals rather than fueling polarizations that might undermine democracy itself. On several occasions, however, just before difficult votes in Congress, the president appealed publicly to the sectors favorable to the government's proposals—not to force Congress's hand but to counterbalance adverse pressures and legitimate the aye votes that the majority were disposed to cast, albeit without much enthusiasm, as in the case of pension reform.

The interplay of presidential leadership, Congress, and organized sectors of society would have left out the vast majority of the population and would therefore have produced limited results if it had not been for the intervention of another fundamental political factor in today's world: public opinion mediated and engendered by the mass media.

Brazil is a country with proportionally fewer readers than in most other countries but with vast numbers of people who watch television and listen to the radio—practically the entire population. The supply of information from both sources, radio and television, is reasonably pluralistic and independent. The political strength of the masses informed by the electronic media made itself felt for the first time in the 1984 campaign for direct presidential elections (*diretas-já*), which heralded the end of the military regime. All important political developments since 1984 have evidenced the same phenomenon, from the indirect election of Tancredo Neves to the presidency to the impeachment of Collor, from the Cruzado Plan to the Real Plan, and including all the elections in between.

The presence of this diffuse actor profoundly changes the ways in which power is democratically wielded. It is not enough to be voted into office, even with tens of millions of votes, or to be vested with legal authority. Legitimation of decisions requires an unremitting effort to explain the reasons for them and convince public opinion. We made intensive use of the media to explain every step of the Real Plan and the reforms and to sustain the support of public opinion.

Objective missteps—the abrupt floating of the exchange rate in January 1999, above all, whose inflationary impact was absorbed but which impaired society's confidence in the government—and subjective difficulties to sustain our political agenda in the public debate cost us the 2002 presidential election. Alternation in power, not desired by the outgoing group, obviously, but planned and conducted with serenity by the incumbent and by the president-elect, proved an acid test not only for the consolidation of democracy but also for the reform agenda itself.

Lula surprised foreign investors, the nation, and most of his own party by exchanging the rhetoric of radical opposition to the "neoliberal model" for an explicit commitment, maintained until today, to the premises of stability and economic openness. He also maintained the fundamental premise of political stability by opting—also against the PT's hegemonistic impulses—for a broad coalition including parties in the center and on the right to ensure a majority in Congress.

This is not the place to emphasize the differences that persist between the poles symbolized by the PT and PSDB. The fact is that the political process has somehow reduced the intensity of those differences. No longer does anyone advocate demolishing one form of state and laying the foundations of another. In practice this issue has been decided, although it still echoes in the public debate. The dispute between "monetarists" and "developmentalists," which was a heated one inside our administration and has recently come to the fore, does not call into question concepts such as privatization, trade liberalization, or fiscal responsibility. The political cost of specific changes in these areas will tend to diminish in coming years. At least in theory this makes room on the agenda for other topics on which little progress has been made, such as the tax system, judicial, and electoral reforms.

Opportunity, Passion, and Perspective

In complex societies change sometimes comes about through a "short circuit." A gesture, a strike, an emotional shock, or a galvanizing proposal can trigger a chain reaction that leads to far deeper transformations than imagined or desired at the outset. This also depends, of course, on the history of the demands, class conflicts, and ideological strife and frustrations, for example, that existed beforehand.

This is what happened with the Real Plan. Tired of inflation and its negative effects, Brazilian society saw the Real Plan as a solution and backed it against the opinions of many people and many vested interests—and at certain times, against a majority of *bien-pensants* and leaders who claimed to "own" the masses.

"Responsible pragmatism," however, does not explain the change. Without leaders who can present a perspective accepted as valid by the majority, significant transformations do not happen in a democratic society. That acceptance is not blindly given. There has to be a democratic pedagogy, persuasion, an effort to "win together"; otherwise the traditional order prevails over the forces of modernization and change.

The inflationary crisis opened the ears of society, including both influential organized sectors and the unorganized mass of voters, to proposals for change that in other circumstances would have been ignored or rejected. That a leadership was there with the ability to take advantage of this window of opportunity was ultimately a fortunate accident. Pressing ahead with the changes required much obstinacy and some art.

Implementing policy is a collective process. The word *process* is one that must be stressed. The press, public opinion, Congress, and members of the government itself often expect and even beg for an act, for a heroic gesture, that can rapidly resolve the problems faced by the citizenry or cater to the interests of a group. The latter may perhaps be won over through a heroic gesture, but not the interests of an entire nation. That depends on continuous action to change practices, mind-sets, and structures.

It is no accident that reform is so difficult or that anyone who genuinely desires change sometimes feels lonely. Structures resist change. Vested interests oppose them. Having a dream is part and parcel of the art of politics, in the ancient form of crystallized ideology or, in modern times, inspired to a greater extent by visions than by certainties. In any event, it is always necessary to have goals and to strive to achieve them, even if they are limited to holding on to power for its own sake. There is as well a permanent interplay between national and international structures (parties, churches, labor unions, companies, multilateral organizations, civil and military bureaucracies, and the media), on the one hand, and movements, proposals, and leaders, on the other, alongside a continuous search for ways of persuading more people and building up more strength to achieve one's goals.

If you overlook one side, whether it be the established order, albeit antiquated or apparently fragile, or the forces that can lead to change, with their proposals and working toward the new, albeit based on the old, you make no progress. How many times in our eagerness to pursue change are we obliged to make concessions to the other side? When the journey begins there are no certainties about who will win the wager. Political will and firmness in pursuing the goal do not ensure victory. The outcome will always depend on the actions of many and the repercussions of the actions and desires of those in command.

How can a head of government, for example, promise to create this or that number of jobs if neither he nor his government controls the variables of economic life? Changes in technology, capital flows, corporate strategies, and a huge number of factors directly influence the level of employment, often dramatically reducing the number of jobs in this or that sector. The leader can, and evidently should, be committed to implementing ideas, adopting programs, and taking measures designed to improve the economic situation and increase employment, but he will be wrong to promise hard numbers.

Pragmatism with clearly defined goals involves a calculation and a wager. The calculation relates to the support required to implement the government's overall policy, even when it is detrimental to specific targets. The wager has to do with the leader's belief that he is capable of inducing (or, if necessary, forcing) his allies, including the last-minute ones, to accept the goals he has set.

The risk of losing control of the process or of the government betraying its commitments is permanent. It is a dangerous adventure, because even with the best of intentions a mistaken wager can be made. Success depends on objective conditions as well as dispositions that are neither defined nor limited by the broader circle of power alone. People will be indifferent to the will and motivation of the principals, and in certain circumstances even to their successes, if the latter are not sufficiently broad and consistent to convince the majority.

In any event, politics is not just a continuation of war by other means, nor is it the substitution of force by submission. It is not a method for counting and separating the good from the bad. It is the art of persuading the "bad" to become "good," or at least to act as if they were, even if they do so for fear of the consequences. It is the art of transforming enemies into adversaries, and adversaries possibly into allies. When co-optation occurs instead of persuasion (by different means), politics is replaced by bartering between petty interests. The drama is that the borderline between greatness and perdition is very thin indeed.

To practice this difficult art it is not indispensable to have an academic background or even to spend many hours reading. Several noteworthy leaders have had or done neither. Yet a certain comprehension of history is a great help. At a time when everything is "of the world," everything is global, it is necessary to have a reasonable vision of the totality and to be capable of understanding the social conditions of one's day and age, to be able to exercise effective leadership, not to make tabula rasa of what others have done but to give a better direction to what has come from the past and lay the foundations for what one wants for the future.

It also helps to have a "persuadable" temperament, to borrow a term from Jane Austen. Democracy today is a process in which the citizenry wants to participate not just by voting or even approving (in a referendum, for example), but also by deliberating. Albert Hirschman, contradicting the tradition that values vigorous and rigid political opinions, has stressed the importance of opinions being formed not before but during the process of discussion and deliberation. Open minds, spirits psychologically more inclined to convergence and compromise, who favor dialogue, among both leaders and led, would therefore be better suited to playing the democratic game on a long-term basis (Hirschman 1995).

This shake-up in today's world has made Cicero highly relevant again, in his praise of rhetoric as a foundation for the education of the Prince. For him the noblest way of life is devotion to virtuous public service. Friendship among men, good will, enables good government to be grounded in the free cooperation of citizens. For these values to sustain the republic, there must be laws, and people must be persuaded of their validity, which in turn requires that the statesman be capable of using reason and emotion. The interplay of these two qualities develops through what was called "rhetoric," the basis for persuasion. Obedience is obtained not through fear and coercion, but through reason and love built on a kind of Socratic dialogue and embodying the apex of leadership.[17]

The word is the "message" in our time, and the means for its diffusion is no longer the pulpit or tribune but the electronic media. The impact of radio, and later television, could already be seen in the "mass politics" that characterized fascist and authoritarian mobilizations in general and that served as cement for Third World populism. Now it is democratic politics itself that appeals to these media and the Internet. Everything happens in real time regardless of physical distance, but with a difference: the Internet

---

17 To understand the topicality of Cicero, see chapter 6 of the excellent book by Wegemer (1996).

is essentially interactive, and little by little radio, TV, and even newspapers and magazines are creating democratic spaces for "the other side," for people's reactions.

Everything is made easier when there are symbols that help people visualize change. Politics deals with symbolic content, and leaders seek to exercise the modern form of what Gramsci called cultural hegemony, albeit with a different connotation. This requires an "actor's" qualities, although these cannot be dissociated from the individual's prior experience.

In the interplay between symbolism and practical achievements, leaders must be capable, through intuition or knowledge, of elaborating and transmitting a "vision" of the problems they face, a vision of society and the nation. In the case of politicians with a national following, given the framework of globalization, they must have some feeling of world affairs. Statesmanship is projecting the nation's future, seeing it in the world context, and being capable of leading it in that direction.

In a world of intercommunicating messages and increasing participation, democratic leaders, albeit conscious of class conflicts and differences, must propose values that can be shared by a majority of society. Otherwise they lose strength. Because their relationship with those they lead is not static, leaders will attempt to persuade them all the time, running the risk of losing some of the time but winning at other times. On those occasions when they win, they must strive to attract more and more people, groups, movements, and institutions to their side. When they lose, they must try to find out why, to identify the mistakes they made, and based on their convictions humbly to rebuild the widening circle of persuasion that can lead to victory.

At bottom, the capacity to symbolize and transmit messages is identical to the virtue of discerning and proposing to society a way forward that is acceptable to the led, albeit temporarily. In an interactive society this "project" cannot be conceived as an act of reason or will, but as a collective construction in which certain people—the leaders—express more completely and symbolize for a specific moment the movement of society, which is necessarily conditioned by values, by cultural models, with which and on which they act. Leaders either point the way and blaze a trail or lose power.

In any event, the personal attribute that is critical to the exercise of leadership, in the new politics as in the old, is still courage, because there comes a time when it is unavoidable to make decisions that upset a lot of people. It will even be necessary to make decisions almost alone, however "persuadable" one may be. A leader is someone who, once persuaded that an important decision is the right one to make, accepts only one attitude of him- or herself: making the decision. However hard it may be, the leader takes a road and resolves to move forward on it, even if it means being against everyone else, and persists until success is won, because what can be seen farther ahead shows that this and not something else is what needs to be done.

Max Weber despised politicians who shrug off the consequences of their actions, blaming the pettiness of others or the world, cozily reliant on their own clear conscience and clean hands. Weber reserved his respect for the mature person (young or old) who in particular circumstances decides, "I must do this and nothing else," and takes responsibility for doing so. "That is something genuinely human and moving," he says. "In so far as this is true, an ethic of ultimate ends and an ethic of responsibility are not absolute contrasts but rather supplements, which only in unison constitute a genuine man—a man who can have the 'calling for politics'" (Weber 1958: 127).

The possibility proposed by Weber of reconciling pragmatism with ethical values and limits that transcend immediate circumstances is encouraging for a political leader in government who wonders, as we so often wondered, whether he will be capable of implementing the necessary changes with the necessary speed by the meandering highways and byways of democracy.

Let us stay with Weber for our conclusion:

> Politics is a strong and slow boring of hard boards. It takes both passion and perspective. Certainly all historical experience confirms the truth—that man would not have attained the possible unless time and again he had reached out for the impossible. But to do that a man must be a leader, and not only a leader but a hero as well, in a very sober sense of the word. And even those who are neither leaders nor heroes must arm themselves with that steadfastness of heart which can brave even the crumbling of all hopes.

The experience of Brazil, like that of other important countries in Latin America, gives us reasons to keep alive our hopes of democratic reformism and renewing its political agenda.

References

Abranches, Sérgio. 1988. "Presidencialismo de Coalizão: O Dilema Institucional Brasileiro." *Dados* 31 (1): 5–33.

Berlin, Isaiah. 1979. "The Hedgehog and the Fox." In *Russian Thinkers*. London: Penguin Books.

Cardoso, Fernando Henrique. 2006. *A Arte da Política: a história que vivi*. Rio de Janeiro: Civilização Brasileira.

Faletto, Enzo, and Fernando Henrique Cardoso. 1979. *Dependency and Development in Latin America*. Translated by Marjory Mattingly Urquidi. Berkeley: University of California Press.

Font, Mauricio. 2003. *Transforming Brazil. A Reform Era in Perspective*. Lanham, MD: Rowman and Littlefield.

Giambiagi, Fabio, José Guilherme Reis, and André Urani, eds. 2004. *Reformas no Brasil: balanço e agenda*. Rio de Janeiro: Nova Fronteira.

Graeff, Eduardo. 2000. "The Flight of the Beetle: Party Politics and the Decision-Making Process in the Cardoso Government." Paper presented to the V Congress of the Brazilian Studies Association, Recife, Brazil, June. Translated by Ted Goertzel. http://www.crab.rutgers.edu/~goertzel/flightofbeetle.htm.

Hirschman, Albert. 1981. "The Social and Political Matrix of Inflation: Elaborations on the Latin American Experience." In *Essays in Trespassing: Economics to Politics and Beyond.* Cambridge: Cambridge University Press.

———. 1995. "Opinionated Opinions and Democracy." In *A Propensity to Self-Subversion.* Cambridge, MA: Harvard University Press.

Landerretche M., Oscar. 2005. "Construyendo solvencia fiscal: el éxito macroeconómico de la Concertación." In *La Paradoja Aparente. Equidad y eficiencia: resolviendo el dilema,* ed. Patrício Meller. Santiago de Chile: Aguilar Chilena.

Lijphart, Arend. 1984. *Democracies: Patterns of Majoritarian and Consensus Government in Twenty-One Countries.* New Haven, CT: Yale University Press.

Lins, Juan, and Arturo Valenzuela, eds. 1994. *The Failure of Presidential Democracy: The Case of Latin America.* Volume 2. Baltimore, MD: Johns Hopkins University Press.

Marks, Siegfried, ed. 1993. *Political Constraints on Brazil's Economic Development: Rio de Janeiro Conference, Edited Proceedings and Papers.* Miami, FL: North-South Center Press.

Meller, Patrício, ed. 2005. *La Paradoja Aparente. Equidad y eficiencia: resolviendo el dilema.* Santiago de Chile: Aguilar Chilena.

Morgenstern, Scott, and Benito Nacif, eds. 2002. *Legislative Politics in Latin America.* Cambridge: Cambridge University Press.

Palermo, Vicente. 2004. "Melhorar para piorar? A dinâmica política das reformas estruturais e as raízes do colapso da convertibilidade." In *Brasil e Argentina hoje: política e economia,* ed. Brasílio Sallum Jr. Bauru, Brazil: EDUSC.

Petracca, Orazio M. 2004. "Liderança." In *Dicionário de Política,* ed. Norberto Bobbio and others. São Paulo: Editora UnB e Imprensa Oficial do Estado de São Paulo.

Racynski, Dagmar, and Claudia Serrano. 2005. "Las políticas y estrategias de desarrollo social. Aportes de los años 90 y desafios futuros." In *La Paradoja Aparente. Equidad y eficiencia: resolviendo el dilema,* ed. Patrício Meller. Santiago de Chile: Aguilar Chilena.

Siavelis, Peter M. 2000. *The President and Congress in Postauthoritarian Chile: Institutional Constraints to Democratic Consolidation.* University Park: Pennsylvania State University Press.

Torre, Juan Carlos. 2004. "A crise da representação partidária na Argentina." In *Brasil e Argentina hoje: política e economia,* ed. Brasílio Sallum Jr. Bauru, Brazil: EDUSC.

Weber, Max. 1958. "Politics as a Vocation." In *From Max Weber: Essays in Sociology,* trans. and ed. H. Gerth and C. Wright Mills. Oxford: Oxford University Press.

Wegemer, Gerard B. 1996. *Thomas More on Statesmanship.* Washington, DC: Catholic University of America Press.

CHAPTER 8

Economic Reforms, Growth, and Governance: The Political Economy Aspects of Bangladesh's Development Surprise

Wahiduddin Mahmud, Sadiq Ahmed, and Sandeep Mahajan

Bangladesh emerged from its war of independence desperately poor, overpopulated, and reeling from overwhelming war damage to its institutional and physical capital. It was not until 1978–79 that per capita income had recovered to its pre-independence level. The economy was ravaged by acute food shortages and famines during the early years. According to some authors, Bangladesh was designated as a "test case" for development, and Henry Kissinger called it "an international basket case" (Faaland and Parkinson 1976).

More than 30 years later, doubts and doubters have been proven wrong. With sustained growth in food production and a good record of disaster management, famines have become a phenomenon of the past. Bangladesh's per capita gross domestic product (GDP) has more than doubled since 1975. Life expectancy has risen from 50 to 63 years; population growth rates of

The authors are grateful to Homi Kharas, T. N. Srinivasan, and Roberto Zagha for helpful comments and suggestions. They have also benefited from comments made by the workshop participants, including Steven Durlauf, Ravi Kanbur, Mustapha Nabli, Gobind Nankani, Klaus Schmidt-Hebbel, and Michael Spence. The views expressed in the chapter are those of the authors and should not be ascribed to the institutions of their affiliation.

3 percent a year have been halved, child mortality rates of 240 per 1,000 births have been cut by 70 percent, literacy has more than doubled, and the country has achieved gender parity in primary and secondary schools.

Most of these gains have taken place since the early 1990s, when the introduction of wide-ranging economic reforms coincided with transition to democracy. The growth of per capita GDP had been slow in the 1980s, at an annual average of 1.6 percent a year, but it accelerated to 3 percent in the 1990s, and to about 4 percent more recently (table 8.1). The acceleration resulted partly from a slowdown in population growth but also from a sustained increase in GDP growth, which averaged 3.7 percent annually during the 1980s, 4.8 percent during the 1990s, and 5.7 percent since then.

Progress in the human development indicators was even more impressive. Bangladesh ranked among the top performing countries in the 1990s in the extent of improvement in the UNDP Human Development Index, and it is among the few developing countries that are on target for achieving most of the Millennium Development Goals (World Bank 2003b, 2005a).[1] As a result, Bangladesh is now clearly an overperformer in most social development indicators in relation to its per capita GDP, whereas two decades or so ago it was a laggard among countries with similar per capita income levels.[2]

Bangladesh's achievements may appear as a "development surprise," given the country's desperate initial conditions and allegedly poor record in governance adversely affecting the investment climate and the quality of public service delivery (Ahluwalia and Mahmud 2004; Devarajan 2005; Mahmud 2008a). Bangladesh is rated extremely poorly according to most global indicators of political and economic governance.[3] Numerous questions have therefore been raised: How could the progress achieved thus far have been possible amid widespread governance failure and without concomitant institutional development? Is this progress sustainable, and what are the risks and challenges ahead? How did the prevailing political economy environment shape the policy-making process, including the design and implementation of policies and their outcomes? This chapter attempts to answer these questions.

Policy Shifts, Macroeconomic Trends, and Growth Performance

The development strategy and the associated economic environment in Bangladesh since the early 1970s have undergone successive shifts and refinements, often linked with change in the ruling political regime.

---

1   The absolute increase in the value of the Human Development Index for Bangladesh between 1990 and 2001 is surpassed notably only by China among countries for which such estimates are available; UNDP (2003: 241–44).

2   Regressions with cross-country data show that the current values of most social development indicators for Bangladesh are distinctly superior to the predicted values at the given level of per capita income; see Government of Bangladesh (2005: 9), table 1.

3   See, for example, World Bank (2007), vol. II: Main Report, ch. 7.

In the early years following the War of Liberation in 1971, economic management in Bangladesh was primarily aimed at reviving a war-ravaged economy in an overall framework of extensive state control and with an avowed ideology of socialism (Ahmed 2005; Mahmud 2008b). The state became the de facto owner of a large number of enterprises that had been abandoned by their Pakistani owners. With the change of government and emergence of General Ziaur Rahman as the military ruler, following the assassination of Sheikh Mujib in 1975, there was a policy shift toward privatization and the promotion of the private sector.[4] The denationalization of the earlier abandoned enterprises continued at varying speed into the 1980s, when a second wave of divestment was initiated under the military government of General Ershad.[5]

From the late 1970s to the beginning of the 1980s, there was a short-lived investment boom in both public and private sectors, with growth at nearly 15 percent annually in real terms (Mahmud 2001). This was made possible by relying on an increasing flow of foreign aid, adopting a privatization strategy based on lavish dispensation of cheap credit, and provision of other incentives such as highly protected markets for domestic industries. To a large extent, later problems regarding the so-called sick industries and the large-scale default of bank loans originated from this experiment with aid-dependent, state-sponsored private capitalism.[6] There was no mobilization of domestic savings, so that the investment boom ended abruptly when the external aid climate severely deteriorated in the early 1980s.

A major change of direction occurred in the early 1980s with the adoption of a market-oriented development strategy supported by a number of liberalizing policy reforms undertaken along the guidelines of the World Bank and the International Monetary Fund (IMF) and implemented under fairly rigid aid conditionality (Task Forces 1991). These reforms were initiated against the backdrop of serious macroeconomic imbalances, which had been caused in part by a decline in foreign aid and in part by a preceding episode of severe deterioration in the country's terms of trade. The policy reforms in the 1980s were mainly directed toward withdrawal of food and agricultural subsidies, privatization of state-owned enterprises, financial liberalization, and withdrawal of quantitative import restrictions. Nevertheless, many state controls remained along with heavy trade protection (Ahmed 2002).

The early 1990s saw the launching of a more comprehensive program of macroeconomic reforms, which coincided with a transition to parliamentary democracy from a semiautocratic rule. These reforms particularly were

---

4 General Ziaur Rahman later formed the Bangladesh Nationalist Party (BNP), which emerged as one of the two major political parties in Bangladesh, the other being Sheikh Mujib's Awami League.

5 Like General Ziaur Rahman, General Ershad also later gave a civilian face to his regime by forming a political party, although his regime remained characterized by its autocratic style and lack of legitimacy.

6 The subsequent decline of the development financing institutions was also closely linked to the shortcomings of that round of privatization in Bangladesh (Mahmud 2001).

aimed at moving toward an open economy and included such measures as making the currency convertible on the current account (leading to a floating exchange rate in 2003), reducing import duties generally to much lower levels, and removing virtually all controls on the movements of foreign private capital. There was also a tightening of fiscal and monetary discipline. The reforms also included further relaxation of restrictions on private investment, such as opening up telecommunications and power generation to private investment, financial liberalization with deregulation of interest rates, and fiscal reforms including the introduction of the value-added tax (VAT; Ahmed 2005; World Bank 2007).

Trends in Macroeconomic Indicators

The macroeconomic stabilization measures initiated in the 1980s were aimed at reducing the fiscal and external deficits to a sustainable level, partly in response to the reduced availability of aid. The trends in various macroeconomic indicators over the last two decades are shown in table 8.1. During the 1980s, although some success was achieved in reducing both the fiscal deficit and the external current account deficit, this was achieved at some cost. The macroeconomic balances were improved not so much by raising government revenue, domestic savings, or exports, but by squeezing public development spending, private investment, and imports (table 8.1). Thus, as in the case of most other early experiments in structural adjustment, the attempt to achieve macroeconomic stabilization in Bangladesh in the 1980s was made along the contractionary route.[7]

One reason that macroeconomic adjustment did not provide the required impetus to growth and resource mobilization was that the sectoral reforms needed to boost the supply response from the private sector were very limited. Numerous investment controls and trade protection prevented competition, and banking sector reforms did not happen.[8] Indeed, the lack of savings response and weak private investment may have been to a significant extent a reflection of the inefficient banking sector. Moreover, with deficits still deeply in the red and the inflation rate in double digits, the economy was not yet very stable.

The launching of wide-ranging policy reforms beginning in the 1990s was followed by some positive developments in economic performance.

---

7   One redeeming feature of the macroeconomic developments in the 1980s as shown in table 8.1 is the increase in public investment. This increase, however, barely compensated for the decline in private investment, resulting in a slight decline in the overall investment rate. However, the actual investment scenario of the decade was probably much worse. The figures in table 8.1 are based on the revised national income series, which was initially estimated from 1990–91 onward, but was subsequently extended backward to cover the period of the 1980s. In spite of the improved estimation methodology used in the revised series, the investment estimates suffer from many weaknesses, which are likely to have been made worse through backward extrapolation. In fact, the old series shows a substantial decline in the investment-GDP ratio during the 1980s, which is also borne out by a decline in the import of capital goods (see Task Forces 1991). It is also highly improbable that public investment was increasing at a time when public development expenditure was being curtailed, although the two are not exactly the same.

8   Banking reforms in Bangladesh started only after 2000. For a review of banking sector reforms and performance see Ahmed (2005).

Table 8.1. Macroeconomic Balances, 1980/81–2004/05; Five-Year Averages (percent of GDP)

	1980/81–1984/85	1985/86–1989/90	1990/91–1994/95	1995/96–1999/2000	2000/01–2004/05
External sector					
Exports of goods and services	5.0	5.6	8.7	12.7	15.4
Imports of goods and services	14.4	12.8	14.0	18.6	21.0
Trade deficit	9.4	7.2	5.6	5.9	5.7
Workers' remittances[a]	2.7	2.9	2.9	3.6	5.8
Current accounts deficit[b]	6.7	4.7	2.1	1.9	1.5
Investment and savings					
Gross investment	16.9	16.6	17.9	21.5	23.6
Public	4.8	6.1	6.7	6.8	6.4
Private	12.1	10.4	11.3	14.7	17.2
Gross domestic savings[c]	8.0	9.4	12.5	15.3	16.9
Gross national savings[d]	10.2	11.9	15.8	19.6	22.1
Government budget					
Total revenue	6.3	6.7	8.6	9.0	10.0
Tax revenue	5.2	5.4	6.9	7.2	8.4
Current expenditure	4.6	6.0	6.5	7.2	8.2
Development expenditure[e]	6.6	5.4	5.6	5.7	5.4
Total expenditure[f]	12.9	12.2	13.4	13.4	14.0
Budget deficit	6.6	5.6	4.8	4.4	4.0
Domestic borrowing[g]	1.0	0.5	0.8	1.9	2.2
Foreign financing[h]	5.6	5.0	4.0	2.5	1.8
Memorandum items Monetary policy					
Growth rate of real GDP (% p.a.)	3.7	3.7	4.4	5.2	5.4
Growth rate of population (% p.a.)	2.2	2.1	2.0	1.6	1.6
Inflation rate (CPI) (% p.a.)	13.0	8.0	5.6	5.6	4.3

Sources: Various publications of the Bangladesh Bureau of Statistics, Bangladesh Bank, IMF, and the World Bank.
Note: Figures are in percent of GDP at current market prices unless otherwise noted.
a. Remittances from Bangladeshi workers abroad.
b. Equals trade deficit minus net factor income from abroad; the latter includes private transfers (mainly remittances), interest payments on external public debt, and other investment incomes; it differs from the official estimates because of not including official transfers (foreign aid as grants); a negative value implies surplus.
c. Equals gross investment minus trade deficit; also equals gross national savings minus net factor income from abroad.
d. Equals gross investment minus current account deficit.
e. Expenditure under annual development plan.
f. Includes food account balance and certain capital expenditures and net lending not included in the development budget.
g. Includes net borrowing from the banking system and net sale proceeds of savings certificates.
h. Includes grants and concessional loans net of amortization.

A marked improvement was seen in the government's budgetary position, particularly in terms of increased revenue mobilization in the early 1990s (table 8.1). The growth of GDP has been accelerating in each successive period since the latter half of the 1980s. Although the net inflow of foreign capital has further declined to the current level of less than 2 percent of GDP, both investment and saving rates have steadily improved, thus paving the way for superior growth performance. Furthermore, the increase in the investment-to-GDP ratio has been almost entirely due to the dynamism in private investment, with the investment in the public sector remaining almost unchanged as a proportion of GDP. Meanwhile, because of robust and sustained growth in export earnings and the accompanying increase in imports, there has been a rapid increase in the trade openness of the economy (that is, the combined ratio of imports and exports to GDP).

All this was achieved along with remarkable success in keeping inflation under control. In the first half of the 1980s, the average annual rate of inflation as measured by the consumer price index was relatively high at 13 percent. It was only the contractionary effect of macroeconomic adjustment of that period that brought inflation down to around 8 percent in the second half of the decade. The 1990s saw a further decline in the inflation rate, down to 5.6 percent and even lower since then, and this time the reduction in inflation was accompanied by the relative buoyancy of the economy compared with the preceding decade. The period since the early 1990s thus has seen positive developments on several fronts: transition to parliamentary democracy, strengthening of economic growth performance, and consolidation of economic stabilization in the face of declining foreign capital inflows. It appears that the combination of macroeconomic adjustment to stabilize the economy along with a range of structural reforms in trade, finance, and domestic deregulation spurred private investment and generated a strong supply response. This said, some periodic lapses in the macroeconomic discipline particularly related to the timing of approaching national elections produced the symptoms of the so-called political business cycle.[9]

Sources of Growth Stimulus

All broad sectors of the economy—agriculture, industry, and services—have contributed to the growth acceleration since the early 1990s. The average annual growth of agricultural GDP accelerated from 2.5 percent in the 1980s to 3.2 percent in the 1990s, industrial GDP from 5.8 to 7.0 percent, and the service sector GDP from 3.7 to 4.5 percent.[10] In spite of fluctuations in crop production, the volatility in long-term GDP growth in Bangladesh is found to be remarkably low among developing countries (World Bank 2003a: 7–8).

Within manufacturing, growth has come largely from the ready-made garment industry; during the 1990s, medium- and large-scale manufacturing as a whole grew at about 7 percent annually, but at only

---

9 In 1995–96 and 2000–01, both preelection years, the government's domestic borrowing and the rate of credit expansion in the private sector were unusually high, and trade deficits increased substantially and foreign exchange reserves fell; see Mahmud (2004).

10 The estimates are derived from the official national income statistics. The industrial sector includes construction, mining, and utilities, besides manufacturing.

Table 8.2. Bangladesh: Growth of Exports since 1990
(annual export earnings in $ millions)

Export Item	1990/91	2004/05
Ready-made garments and knitwear	890	6,418
Frozen foods (mainly frozen shrimp)	142	421
Raw jute and jute goods	395	404
Leather and leather goods	137	221
All other exports	154	1,190
Total exports	1,718	8,654
Of which, manufactured exports	1,411	8,006

Sources: Official export data of the Export Promotion Bureau as reported in Bangladesh Bank's Annual Report, various years, and World Bank 2005b.

about 4 percent excluding the garment industry.[11] This implies that growth in the organized manufacturing sector has been mainly export led, but it also means that the manufacturing and export base of the economy has become more concentrated rather than more diverse (table 8.2). The growth of export items lumped under "other exports" is an encouraging sign that continued improvement in export incentives might foster the needed export diversification. However, the values of these exports are still too low to allow a definite conclusion about whether diversification is already under way.

Bangladesh has achieved robust and sustained growth of export earnings, averaging about 15 percent a year in nominal U.S. dollar terms in the 1990s, and 11 percent since 2000 despite a 7.5 percent decline in 2001–02 because of a global recession—the first such decline since 1985–86. In fact, Bangladesh seems to have successfully withstood the initial impact of the competition in the global markets for garment export following expiration of the Multifibre Agreement and the Agreement on Textiles and Clothing. Another positive factor has been continued growth of the inflow of migrant workers' remittances—from about 2.5 percent of GDP in the beginning of the 1990s to almost 8 percent in 2005–06, amounting to about $4.8 billion annually.

Exports are, however, only a part of the growth dynamics in Bangladesh. Although the structure of the economy is changing, the organized sectors of the economy still remain relatively small with no more than 12 percent of GDP currently originating from large- and medium-scale manufacturing. Agriculture still contributes about 20 percent of GDP, and a much larger share of GDP originates from the so-called informal sectors outside agriculture: small-scale processing and manufacturing and various informal services.[12] The growth rates of these informal activities accelerated in the 1990s, contributing substantially to the acceleration of overall GDP growth

11 These are estimated annual compound growth rates between the years 1991–92 and 1999–2000 and are based on the official national income statistics as reported in the annual *Statistical Yearbook of Bangladesh* of the Bangladesh Bureau of Statistics.

12 According to the official 1999–2000 Labor Force Survey, these informal activities employ about three-fourths of the country's nonagricultural labor force.

(Osmani et al. 2003). Many of these activities—being extremely labor intensive and requiring very little capital investment—are largely demand driven, responding to at least three major sources of increased income: crop production, ready-made garment exports, and workers' remittances, in that order of importance.[13]

Although these informal activities have expanded largely as the result of demand linkages with the leading productive sectors of the economy, they have had their internal growth dynamics as well. Evidence suggests that their growth acceleration in the 1990s was accompanied by a tilt toward relatively scaled-up activities that use labor more productively and can cater to more income-elastic demand (Mahmud 2006). Import liberalization is likely to have played a role here by allowing better access to imported inputs and technology. For example, in the postliberalization period, small-scale manufacturing activities (excluding handlooms and cottage industries) fared better than large-scale manufacturing, growing at an average rate of more than 9 percent annually in the 1990s.[14] Small industries seem to have benefited from the liberalization of imports of capital machinery and raw materials, whereas their products—being mostly remote substitutes for imported items—had an advantage over those of their large-scale counterparts, which faced stiffer competition from imports.[15]

Policy-Making Process: Economic Rationale and Political Incentives

It was out of pragmatism that the shift in policy away from socialism to private-sector development was initiated within a few years after independence. The state policy of socialism, which was included in the declaration of independence, was hardly taken seriously and was formally deleted from the country's constitution during the Ershad regime. The operation of the nationalized industries, previously abandoned by their Pakistani owners, was driven by the objective of enriching a few politically favored private individuals. As mentioned earlier, the initial process of private-sector development as pursued during the regime of General Ziaur Rahman turned out to be an early version of what is now called "crony capitalism." The market-oriented liberalizing policy reforms were initiated around the mid-1980s with the support of the IMF and the World Bank and have been followed through since then in various phases. Although aid conditionality did have an important leveraging role, the sequencing, design, and implementation of these reforms had much to do with the political incentives in relation to the economic rationale of such policies.

---

13 For an estimation of the relative importance of these growth stimuli, see Osmani et al. (2003).

14 Estimated annual compound growth rate between 1991–92 and 1999–2000.

15 Small industries are likely to have grown also at the cost of cottage industries, whose value added grew at only 2.8 percent annually during the same period.

Reducing Agricultural and Food Subsidies

As part of the reforms discussed above, the early emphasis on privatization of marketing of agricultural inputs and withdrawal of agricultural subsidies made sense on grounds of pragmatism. By the late 1970s, about one-third of the entire development budget was being consumed by agricultural input subsidies. To promote modern rice technology, government policies had emphasized the public distribution of fertilizers and renting of publicly owned irrigation equipment at a heavy subsidy. These policies did have a major role in the initial adoption of the modern high-yielding variety rice technology, but the budgetary costs became unsustainable. The rationale of providing input subsidies was also weakened once farmers became familiar with the use of modern inputs.

Debates on agricultural subsidies still reappear from time to time. The case for agricultural subsidies is made partly from a general populist stance, but partly also on grounds of helping poor farmers (who may lack access to credit to use inputs at optimal levels) and facilitating agricultural rehabilitation after natural disasters such as floods. It is true that the withdrawal of high input subsidies made rice production less profitable, because the subsidy withdrawal was not compensated by the avowed policy of supporting rice harvest prices through public procurement of rice—a policy that was hardly effective. Nevertheless, the promise of price supports, along with the absence of strong agricultural lobbies, helped the implementation of the policy of subsidy withdrawal. According to the findings of "participatory" research conducted later to assess the impact of structural adjustment reforms, the farmers did not think the reintroduction of large subsidies on agricultural inputs to be a realistic proposition, but they did expect the government to have a role in supporting agricultural growth.[16] The same study also found that the farmers did not also expect their agricultural loans to be written off, although successive governments did include this issue in their election manifestos. In this manner, electoral competition rather than genuine popular expectations seems to give rise to economic populism.[17]

Government control of tube-well irrigation was abolished by selling government-owned irrigation equipment and allowing free import of such equipment. The policy was criticized by some observers on the grounds that it favored the big farmers who emerged as the major suppliers of water to smaller farmers at a high price, particularly because such irrigation is like a natural monopoly in the so-called command area of a tube well (Khan and Hossain 1989: 164). This argument, however, did not gain much ground because subsequent evidence showed that the policy led to a spurt in private

---

16 This so-called Structural Adjustment Participatory Research was sponsored by the World Bank in collaboration with a coalition of international NGOs and national governments; see Mahmud (2002b), ch. 1.

17 Populist policies should be, however, distinguished from the genuine need to incorporate the "voice" and participation of the people in the economic decision-making process; see Mahmud (2002b), ch. 1.

investment in tube-well irrigation contributing to growth in food grain production (Ahmed 2001: ch. 5).

At about the same time as agricultural subsidies were being reduced, public food distribution in the form of food rations in urban and rural areas was also gradually phased out. The budgetary burden was again a consideration, but there was also a widely held view, supported by study findings, that the poorest families did not have access to the food rations. Even then, the abolition of the food rationing system was not an easy decision, given that the politically vocal urban middle class was its main beneficiary. In many other countries, attempts to abolish such food rations met with violent political protests. The success of the reform program regarding the public food distribution system in Bangladesh is partly explained by its gradualism and its clever design. In the years of high food grain prices, the ration prices were raised without creating much resentment (because of still higher market prices), but the ration prices were not reduced in years of low market prices (which again was acceptable, because only an increase in ration prices was a sensitive issue). The gap between the market and ration prices was thus gradually reduced, so that ultimately there was little incentive for the beneficiaries to access such rations (Rahman and Mahmud 1988). On the other hand, there was a strong case on equity grounds in support of the policy to continue, and even strengthen, the food distribution programs targeted to the poor, such as those relating to food-for-work and feeding vulnerable women and children.

External Sector Reforms

The reforms toward trade liberalization in Bangladesh followed a logical sequence: the relaxation and withdrawal of import quota restrictions along with the unification of the exchange rate and devaluation of the domestic currency during the late 1980s, followed by large reductions in import tariffs in the first half of the 1990s. Since then further import liberalization has been rather slow. Taking into account all import duties having a protective effect, the unweighted average import duty rate declined from 74 percent in 1991–92 to 32 percent in 1996–97 and 24.3 percent in 2006–07 (table 8.3). The slower decline since the mid-1990s is partly because cuts in customs duties were offset by other protective duties and para-tariffs (Mahmud 2004; World Bank 2005b). As a result, Bangladesh still has a relatively closed economy.

The devaluations of the exchange rate of the taka—in both nominal and real terms—during the late 1980s, along with relatively sluggish growth in import demand during that time, resulted in a gradual erosion of the premium on import licenses. There were thus no strong lobbies of import-license holders opposing the reforms. The removal of import restrictions and a flexible management of the exchange rate eventually led to making the taka convertible on the current account and, more recently, in a system of managed free float. This helped to provide incentives for export as well as for attracting migrant workers' remittances from abroad.

Table 8.3. Average Rates of Customs Duties and All Protective Import Duties[a]
(percent)

	1991–92	1995–96	2003–04	2006–07[b]
Average customs duty, unweighted	70.6	28.7	18.8	14.9
Total protection rate, unweighted[c]	73.6	32.0	29.1	24.3
Average collection rate[d]	28.7	23.7	18.0	n.a.
	(37.4)	(31.8)	(25.5)	

Source: Estimated from World Bank 2005b: 16, table 3.1.
a. The average rates reported here are based on eight-digit 6877 tariff lines; they do not include tariff exemptions or concessions, nor do they reflect "preferential" tariffs.
b. According to the budget for the fiscal year 2004–05.
c. "Total protection" incorporates, in addition to customs duty, protection provided by the infrastructure development surcharge, license fee, regulatory duty, as well as protection resulting from asymmetric implementation of the Supplementary Duty and VAT. Asymmetric implementation results when the so-called protection-neutral taxes are levied only on imports but not on domestic production and/or when higher rates are applied on imports than on domestically produced substitutes.
d. The collection rate reflects tax exemptions as well as tax evasion and includes duties on all lines of import items, but not the advance income tax on imports. Figures within parentheses relate to imports, excluding duty-free export-related ones.

An important concern regarding trade liberalization is the possible adverse effect of tariff reductions on government revenue. Thus far, the revenue effects of reductions in the rates of customs duties have been more than offset by the growth of imports (Mahmud 2004). More than half of total tax revenue still comes from import duties, even though the introduction of the VAT has reduced the dependence on such duties. In fact, revenue concerns rather than protectionist appeals seem to have a stronger deterrent to faster import liberalization. This is evident from the pattern of reductions in import duties: the government sought to protect revenue by reducing tariff on minor items rather than on those with a large recorded import value.[18]

One reason that tariff reforms have not been strongly resisted by domestic industrial lobbies is the end-use-based discrimination in protective duty rates. Capital goods and primary commodities are subject to much lower rates of tariffs compared with intermediate goods, whereas the highest rates apply to finished consumer goods. This has helped to retain relatively high rates of protection for the latter goods even within the much lower average import tariffs; at the same time, the anti-export bias of the tax system has been reduced to some extent because of lower taxes on imported inputs. Such a system of tariff escalation has suited the interest of the protectionist lobbies, because the domestic import-substituting industries mainly produce finished consumer goods.[19] Even within such a policy of tariff escalation, however, revenue concerns dominated over protectionist ones, so that

18 As a result, for the period of rapid tariff reductions in the early 1990s, the import-weighted estimates of average import duty rates (with respect to both total import duties and protective duties) showed a much smaller decline than the unweighted estimates; see Mahmud (2001: 55).

19 The system of incentives thus created has worked against a "deepening" of the domestic manufacturing structure, making it even more import dependent. In particular, there is evidence that the reforms of the duty structure have thwarted the growth of a nascent domestic engineering and capital goods industry; see Mahmud (2004).

duties on major imported intermediate goods remained higher than those on relatively minor ones (as reflected in the higher estimated import-value-weighted average duty rate compared with the unweighted rate in respect of this category of imports).

The prospect for export growth and diversification may provide further leverage for import liberalization. Most industrialists in Bangladesh now have a stake in the export-oriented garment industry. The other fast-growing industries such as pharmaceuticals and ceramics have gone into the export market after graduating from being entirely import-substituting industries. This may weaken the resistance to further reducing the anti-export bias in the duty structure that now exists.

The extent and speed of further import liberalization remain a contentious issue in the country's economic reform agenda. In the absence of any preannounced target and timetable, tariff reform in Bangladesh would seem to be a "learning-by-doing" process (even if not consciously recognized to be so). The credibility of such an approach depends on the government's willingness and capability to conduct trade policy reforms in an analytical way. The impact of protection afforded through tariff escalation and the selective interventions for export promotion are bound to be somewhat discriminatory in nature, although the room for such discrimination may be gradually reduced with further liberalization. The government conducts its trade and tax policies in close consultation with the business communities and is sensitive to their demands. In the absence of enough in-house analytical capability of its own, however, the removal of some "anomalies" in the tax structure in response to businessmen's demands often leads to other anomalies.

Fiscal Policy and Public Expenditure

As noted earlier, the transition to democracy resulted in improved fiscal management and macroeconomic discipline. More revenue mobilization was seen as well as a greater restraint on the growth of current expenditures. Budgetary deficits were prudently managed in the face of declining foreign aid so as not to crowd out private sector's borrowing. Overall monetary policy was conducted in a way to keep inflation low—and this was not just because of the IMF's stipulations, but perhaps more because of the government's political sensitivity to inflation.

The increase in the tax-GDP ratio in the early 1990s was largely due to the introduction of the VAT and turned out to be of a one-time nature. The revenue-GDP ratio is very low in Bangladesh even by the standards of developing countries, and the reason lies mostly in large-scale tax evasion. Enforcing better tax compliance has a political cost for the government in terms of alienating the better-off people and the business community, whereas the revenue foregone due to tax evasion curtails government's ability for development spending, which is the flexible part of budgetary expenditures. In this trade-off, the government seems to have chosen the option of a relatively low tax effort.

Table 8.4. Government Expenditure on Health and Education
(as shares of the budget and as percent of GDP)

	1980/81–1984/85	1985/86–1989/90	1990/91–1994/95	1995/96–1999/2000
Percentage of total budget expenditure				
Education	8.16	11.24	13.62	15.51
Health and population planning	5.40	5.88	6.77	7.13
Percentage of GDP at market prices				
Education	1.00	1.33	1.81	2.11
Health and population planning	0.66	0.70	0.90	0.97

Source: Based on the official "revised budget" figures as reported in Bangladesh Economic Survey, Ministry of Finance, various issues.

The patterns of public development spending have undergone significant changes, reflecting the changing developmental role of the government under the economic reforms (Mahmud 2002a; Ahmed 2005). The government has gradually withdrawn from the directly productive sectors, while concentrating more on providing public goods in the form of education and health, physical infrastructure, and rural development. As can be seen from table 8.4, the proportional budgetary allocations to education and health have continuously increased throughout the reform period beginning in the early 1980s.

The analysis of benefit incidence shows that the distribution of benefits from public spending on both health and education among households is weakly pro-poor: that is, the distribution is more equal than the overall income distribution in the economy, although it favors the relatively rich. Only expenditure on mother and child health and on primary education is strongly pro-poor, so that the poor get more absolute benefit than the rich (World Bank 2003a). Much inefficiency and wastage is also found in the delivery of public services in these social sectors (Mahmud 2002a). Clearly, ensuring adequate access of the poor to education and health services of sufficient quantity and quality requires much more than allocating more budgetary resources to these sectors. Moreover, the structural shift in the budget toward larger social spending has come about from a redefining of the role of the government and is, therefore, a one-time occurrence. In the future, higher allocations to social sectors will require more difficult reforms—for example, preventing tax evasion or downsizing the government. Nevertheless, it must be acknowledged that the public expenditure policy of Bangladesh deserves credit for raising the share of these sectors in the total budget, as well as for implementing at least a weakly pro-poor stance in the distribution of benefits.

Governance, Political Incentives, and Policy Making

It is generally agreed that economic reforms in Bangladesh have not been matched by progress in building the institutions of political and economic governance (Mahmud 2001; Ahmed 2006). The degree of resistance to reforms of different kinds depends on the nature of prevailing political cultures. Bangladesh has successfully implemented many reforms that are usually considered unpopular and sure to lose votes, such as the withdrawal of agricultural and food subsidies affecting large sections of the population. Considerable progress has also been made in implementing reforms that are liable to antagonize organized militant groups that can create short-term disruption through agitation, such as trade unions resisting the privatization of state-owned enterprises. In some areas of reforms, however, the government did hesitate in taking tough actions because of the fear of a backlash from the voters or organized labor (for example, adjustment of energy prices, or privatization of ports and public utilities).

By and large, Bangladesh did not see any significant reversal of reforms, even as governments changed, because both of the large parties—the Awami League and the Bangladesh Nationalist Party (BNP)—were broadly committed to carrying out the same economic reform agenda. However, the relative emphasis on specific policies and interventions did differ significantly. Thus, the Awami League, whose voter base tends to be more populated by rural residents and low-income groups, maintains a more populist and left-wing stance in its policy interventions, reflected in greater support for rural spending and agricultural subsidies and less enthusiasm about privatization and trade liberalization. The BNP, on the other hand, is relatively more dominated by urban and business interests and therefore has been generally more enthusiastic about pro-market reforms.

The most politically challenging reforms thus far have been the ones aimed at dealing with a whole range of governance-related problems: willful default of bank loans, large-scale tax evasion, electricity pilferage, corruption in public procurement, deteriorating quality of public administration, poor law and order, an inadequate justice system, and erosion of integrity of most other state institutions. These problems are largely related to the country's core governance systems as shaped by the nature of its politics. Although the concentration of political power in the two major parties has helped to form governments with large stable majorities, this has also resulted in a system in which winners in elections take all and the losers have difficulty in reconciling themselves to their loss. The result is a dysfunctional parliament and highly confrontational politics. Little democratic practice is seen within the major parties, which are run by authoritarian control from the top; this is a reflection of the personalized and patron-client relationships pervading the Bangladeshi society at large.

The structure of governance as described here provides an ideal breeding ground for corruption through the exercise of large discretionary powers with little accountability. Spoils and privileges are parceled out to different clientele groups as an essential tool of political management. On top of this, a large part of the bureaucracy is seen to be corrupt and incompetent, which further feeds this vicious cycle of poor governance. Economic liberalization has no doubt contributed to reducing the scope of rent seeking, such as from the import-licensing system, but this has been increasingly replaced by other means of patronage politics.[20] The overall evidence suggests that if there is a demand in the political system for illegal incomes and rent seeking, economic reforms alone will not be the remedy (Mahmud 2001).

In spite of the adverse governance environment, ample evidence suggests that the government has been committed to playing a major developmental role. This is reflected, for example, in the government's budgetary allocations, which have been broadly in concordance with its development goals. The compulsions of meeting public expectations and gaining political legitimacy in an environment of widespread political awareness of the people seem to have played a role.[21] In fact, certain yardsticks for judging the merits of the budget proposals are now generally accepted in Bangladesh. One such yardstick, for example, is whether there is enough fiscal prudence to contain inflation and ensure economic stabilization. Raising higher revenue and containing the growth of administrative expenditures, so as to generate more domestic resources for development spending, are regarded as a broad goal of budgetary measures. Within development spending, the higher the benefit seen to be going to the poor, the better. There seems to be a necessity for the finance minister to show (even with some jugglery of data, if needed) that the allocations to education are larger than the defense budget.

Even if the delivery of public services suffers from a serious governance problem, the government has shown genuine commitments to improve social development indicators, such as child mortality, primary school enrollment, and the adoption of modern birth control. Support from external donors has definitely helped to achieve these goals, but it cannot be said that the increased budgetary allocations and other public measures for achieving these goals have been dictated largely by aid conditionality.[22] The government also appears to have been genuinely committed to poverty reduction, as indicated by increased spending and expansion of various programs to achieve this goal. The government not only has had a record of good disaster management at times of severe floods, for example, but it has

---

20 For example, while new laws have been introduced to make the public procurement system more transparent and accountable, the system has hardly worked. Moreover, financial extortion (including illegal collections of tolls and protection money) under political patronage has been an increasing phenomenon contributing to the cost of doing business.

21 Thus, any deviant political motives have to remain as a hidden agenda, only to be pursued at the time of implementation of the budget; see Mahmud (2002a).

22 For example, the multidonor-supported Health and Population Sector Project (1998–2003) stipulated that a minimum of 60 percent of the entire sector's public expenditures must go to essential health care including reproductive health. However, it turned out that the government's previous patterns of health expenditures had already met this criterion. Similarly, the allocations to primary education within total public education expenditures have been high, more than 40 percent, without any conditionality imposed by donors. For a discussion on these issues, see Mahmud (2002a); Mahmud and Mahmud (2000).

also shown sensitivity to reported incidences of seasonal poverty in certain poverty pockets.[23]

Other explanations may reveal why some reforms were possible and others not. Broadly speaking, in selecting reforms successive governments have pursued the path of least confrontation and adopted reforms that were more in the nature of easy wins accomplished by "a stroke of the pen." Thus, many of the reforms in the area of macroeconomic management could be implemented without much political resistance. For example, the country's bad experience with runaway inflation during 1972–75 created the political support for tightening macroeconomic management. Similarly, the disastrous experience with nationalization and controls in this period was easy to dismantle because most people (except possibly trade unions) saw the merits of doing away with a controlled economy and moving toward a private-sector-led development strategy. Also, the support for social spending was seen as a political win-win because the members of parliament could take credit for the expansion of health and education programs in their constituencies. This was good for their voter base, and such spending also provided business opportunities for their clients.

The parliamentarians' political agenda of the creation of dedicated voter bases through control over the delivery of public services has obvious downsides. Members of parliament, instead of being concerned with lawmaking and national policies, become lobbyists for procuring projects for their respective constituencies—by no means a healthy process of selection of development projects. Much of the waste in public resource management at the local level, such as the alleged leakage of resources in the rural works program, is the result of the system described here. It also partly explains many weaknesses in the implementation of local development projects, which nonetheless have benefited the local communities.[24] The confluence of public good and political incentives is thus at best partial.

The policy reforms in the banking sector provide an example of how the opposing compulsions of patronage politics and sound economic order have shaped the evolution of such reforms. The banking sector has long been suffering from the widespread culture of willful default in loan repayment. The reasons for loan default on such a large scale have been many, such as politically influenced loans given by state-owned banks, "insider" loans given by private banks to their sponsor-directors, and the weakness of legal provisions for loan recovery. The adverse economic effects of such fiduciary indiscipline gradually took unsustainable

---

23 This is evident from the recent initiatives taken by the government to mitigate seasonal poverty, locally called *monga*, in some vulnerable areas in the northwestern part of the country.

24 For example, as noted earlier, disproportionately more funds are allocated for constructing new local roads rather than for the maintenance of the existing ones; the former is perceived as public service rendered by the local member of parliament, the latter as only the routine work of the concerned government agencies.

proportions and created widespread public resentment. Public opinion against loan defaulters was reflected in the introduction of a law in 1996 debarring such defaulters from participating in national elections. Bold banking reforms were subsequently adopted to prevent banks from giving more loans to defaulters, to remove unscrupulous sponsor-directors from the boards of the private banks, and to make the state-owned banks more disciplined and autonomous for their eventual privatization.[25]

One important development in Bangladeshi politics is that business interests have gradually gained influence over politics. The country's first parliament had few members whose principal occupation was business (politicians traditionally coming from the profession of law); the last parliament (2001–06) was, however, dominated by businessmen. This transformation in politics has had an important impact on the policy-making process. A parliament dominated by businessmen would try to enact or prevent laws to protect their sources of income, legal or illegal. It was only because of the pressure of public opinion that the legislature had to ultimately pass laws against the defaulters on bank loans. Many examples show how businessmen-turned-politicians exercised political influence to earn illegal incomes, but later moved into legitimate businesses. One potential advantage of the rise of this new breed of lawmakers is the effective pressure that they can create for promoting their legitimate interests, such as provision of better infrastructure, including power supply and port facilities. This advantage will materialize, however, only if the conflict of interest between lawmaking and pursuit of personal business can be managed through appropriate legal safeguards.

It would appear that public economic functions are influenced by both adverse and beneficial political incentives. Given the weaknesses of the democratic institutions, hardly any effective oversight mechanism exists to ensure the accountability of the government's fiscal operations and other economic functions. However, the national elections since 1991, held under a unique system of a nonparty caretaker government, have been seen as fair and credible. People seemed to have demonstrated a willingness to move against regimes once they crossed some vaguely defined threshold with respect to poor governance and corruption, as evidenced by the fall of the successive governments led by the Awami League and the BNP. This has created an incentive structure in which public representatives try to respond to the genuine popular sentiments to win reelection while still engaging in rent-seeking activities. Also at work, apparently, are noninstitutional mechanisms for ensuring public accountability, such as through civic activism, a lively media, and widespread political awareness among the people at large. This probably explains why, in spite of many perverse political incentives embedded in the system, governments have played overall an effective developmental role.

---

25 For a detailed account of these reforms, see Mahmud (2005).

Explaining the "Development Surprise"

Bangladesh's impressive record of economic growth and social development has been achieved despite apparently poor governance and is thus an outlier in cross-country comparisons relating governance to economic growth.[26] Recent studies show increasingly compelling evidence that good governance matters to growth, although many controversies surround these studies regarding the definition of "good governance," the biases in perception of governance, the direction of causality, and the problem of isolating the effects of country-specific institutional and other factors in explaining cross-national variations. Although it is quite evident that Bangladesh's economic performance has been negatively affected by some of the adverse governance factors, the more interesting question relates to why the country's economy has performed in the way that it has despite wide-ranging governance failures.

Deconstructing Growth

To understand Bangladesh's development conundrum, one needs to deconstruct the economic growth process and focus on the main drivers behind accelerated growth. As discussed earlier in this chapter, the acceleration of growth of Bangladesh's economy since the early 1990s has been underpinned by strong export growth, led almost entirely by the growth in ready-made garment export. The garment industry has flourished in Bangladesh because of the confluence of a number of favorable factors: the early relocation of garment producers and marketing intermediaries from East Asian countries (especially the Republic of Korea) to Bangladesh to evade import quotas in the U.S. and European markets; easy transfer and spread of garment-industry-specific managerial and production skills; preferential access of Bangladesh's garment exports in the major markets of the West; a flexible exchange rate policy and other policies adopted by the government in supporting the industry, especially by creating a set of enclave-type arrangements (for example, bonded warehouses and back-to-back letters of credit to facilitate duty-free import of fabrics); and the abundance of low-cost female labor.[27] Once the growth of the industry gathered momentum and became the main exchange earner, it gained in efficiency and could exercise more clout in shaping government policies in its favor.

The uniqueness of the garment industry in Bangladesh is demonstrated by the fact that other potential exports have not fared well even when generous government support has been provided to them. Besides various export-promoting schemes such as the duty drawback system for imported

---

26 World Bank (2007), vol. II: Main Report, ch. 7 and fig. 7.

27 Easterly (2001, ch. 8) elaborately describes how, by some historical accident, the Korean firm Daewoo and an influential Bangladeshi bureaucrat-turned-industrialist, Noorul Quader, got together to start the process of transfer of knowledge and skills for setting up an export-oriented garment industry.

inputs, cash incentives of up to 30 percent of the export value have been provided to certain export items without producing notable results. It is true that even the garment exporters complain about having to pay bribes to facilitate export formalities at the port, besides having to deal with other constraints such as inadequate infrastructure. However, the industry's early foothold has helped it to withstand these constraints.

Strong export growth has contributed to GDP growth both directly and indirectly by providing growth stimulus to other parts of the economy. An indirect route also exists through which export growth, coupled with import liberalization, has helped the growth in small-scale and informal sector activities. These latter activities produce mostly nontradables or poor substitutes for imports. A real devaluation of the taka can hurt these activities by increasing the prices of imported inputs and by turning the domestic terms of trade against their products compared with tradable products. Thanks to rapid growth of export and remittances, however, the real exchange rate of the taka remained more or less stable at a time when substantial import liberalization and a marked decline in external deficits were seen.[28]

In addition to garment export, growth impulses have come from workers' remittances and from growth in agriculture and small-scale industries and services, mostly belonging to the informal sector. The government has pursued policies since the early 1980s to encourage manpower export and attract remittances by negotiating with host countries, offering favorable exchange rates for workers' remittances during the previous exchange control regime, and facilitating remittances through banking channels by various means. Growth in agriculture has been helped by market-oriented reforms in agricultural input markets, as mentioned earlier. Moreover, because both agriculture and informal sector activities mostly remain outside the purview of the government's regulatory functions, these are likely to be less adversely affected by poor governance compared with the activities in the modern organized sectors of the economy.[29]

The growth of the urban centers, foremost among them Dhaka, has greatly contributed to economic growth by creating the complementarities that accompany urban growth. Dhaka, with 12 million inhabitants, has seen an eightfold increase in its population since 1970 and is reckoned to be among the two fastest-growing megacities in the world.[30] Not least because of the rapid growth of the export-oriented garment industry and the flow of remittances and the related housing construction boom, urbanization has been accompanied by job creation strong enough to accommodate

---

28 During the same period, the currencies of many developing countries, including India and Pakistan, underwent massive real devaluation; see Mahmud (2004, 2007).

29 There is, however, evidence that with a deterioration of law and order, small-scale and informal sector activities can be more vulnerable to illegal extortion and toll collection than larger-scale enterprise in terms of the proportionate increase in the cost of doing business; see Mahmud (2006: 42).

30 Lagos in Nigeria is the other.

over 10 million new entrants to the workforce between 1996 and 2003.[31] Study findings show that rural-to-urban migration, instead of being mainly driven by the so-called push factors, has been generally a means of upward economic mobility for the migrants (Khundker et al. 1994). Nevertheless, the problem of poor governance manifests here in the form of unplanned urbanization creating enormous problems for the future.

In the rural areas, the nonfarm sector has become more diversified, productive, and dynamic, especially with the growth of the rural towns. The clusters of habitation around these rural towns have helped to promote those nonfarm activities that can cater to urban-like and income-elastic consumer demand, and these are the kinds of activities that are found to have shown more dynamism within the rural nonfarm sector in terms of improved technology and higher labor productivity (Mahmud 2006). Very rapid expansion of microcredit since the early 1990s is also likely to have played an important part in this process.

Growth Inclusiveness and Poverty Reduction

With the acceleration in the growth of per capita income, Bangladesh has made considerable progress in poverty reduction. During the 1990s the national incidence of poverty declined from nearly 60 percent to about 50 percent, and a much more rapid reduction in poverty seems to have taken place in the following five-year period with the national poverty rate reduced to about 40 percent.[32]

More progress against poverty would have been made in the 1990s had income distribution not worsened in both rural and urban areas. In the recent periods, growth acceleration in many developing countries, including in South Asia, has been accompanied by increased income inequality (Devarajan and Nabi 2006; Mahmud and Chowdhury 2008). The growth-inequality links in the case of Bangladesh seem to be, however, of a different nature. The pattern of growth in Bangladesh would appear to be fairly pro-poor—with the main stimulus to economic growth coming from labor-intensive garment exports, micro- and small-scale enterprises in manufacturing and services, and remittances from migrant workers. All these sectors typically provide scope for upward economic mobility for the poor. Even then, inequality tended to increase because the more dynamic parts of the economy happened to be the ones with relatively unequal income—such as the urban/organized sector compared with the rural/informal sector or the dynamic part of the rural nonfarm sector compared with agriculture—and also because growth, although employment intensive, was not strong enough to pull wages in the vast agricultural and informal intensive markets (Osmani et al. 2003; Mahmud 2006).

---

31 World Bank (2007), vol. II: Main Report, ch. 5. See also Acharya (2006), who explains the contrasts between Dhaka's commercial and construction boom and the lack of it in Kolkata and Mumbai.

32 The official poverty estimates are made with reference to an "upper" and a "lower" poverty line. The national poverty incidence, according to the lower poverty line, is estimated to have declined from 43 percent in 1991–92 to 34 percent in 2000 and 26 percent in 2005.

Table 8.5. Trends in Poverty and Income Distribution in Rural and Urban Areas,
1991/92 to 2005

| Year | Population under Poverty Line (%) | | | Gini Coefficient of Consumption Expenditure | | Urban-Rural Ratio of per Capita Expenditure |
	Rural	Urban	National	Rural	Urban	
1991/92	61.2	44.9	58.8	0.24	0.31	1.65
2000	53.0	36.6	49.8	0.27	0.37	1.87
2005	44.5	28.8	40.6	0.28	0.35	1.67

Source: Reports of the various rounds of the Household Expenditure Survey published by the Bangladesh Bureau of Statistics 2003, 2006.
Notes: The poverty estimates are those of the Bangladesh Bureau of Statistics relating to the "upper poverty line" and derived from a cost-of-basic-needs methodology. The Gini coefficients are estimated by adjusting per capita income for spatial price variations, but urban-rural ratios relate to nominal per capita consumption expenditure.

However, the estimates for the most recent period from 2000 to 2005 suggest that the process of increasing income inequality has slowed down or even reversed. As a result, the impact of income growth on poverty reduction has been much more pronounced during this period than in the 1990s (table 8.5). Real wages in agriculture and construction—the sectors dominated by informal intensive markets—have shown strong upward trends since the late 1990s, after having been stagnant for a long time.[33] It would thus appear that Bangladesh is perhaps past the turning point of the "Kuznets curve" in the income-inequality link.[34]

Recent analyses of poverty dynamics in Bangladesh suggest that, compared with many other developing countries, upward economic mobility in Bangladesh is less constrained by class, ethnicity, or other socioeconomic barriers. Access to markets with extensive rural transport networks, increasing participation of women in work outside home, and a very rapid spread of microcredit have all contributed toward expanding the economic opportunities for the poor. Thus, everyone, even the poorest people, sees a chance of escaping poverty.[35] Such inclusiveness may contribute to social cohesion, and it raises awareness about economic opportunities, which may explain why even poor families are increasingly sending their children to school. It may also, however, raise people's expectations and lower their tolerance for governance failure.

Social Development: The Most Striking Development Surprise

Bangladesh's most striking development surprise is its rapid and spectacular improvements in human development indicators, particularly since the early 1990s (table 8.6). From being a laggard, Bangladesh now outperforms most Indian states and South Asia as a whole in such indicators as female school

---

33 World Bank (2007: 43), vol. II: Main Report, fig. 3.7.

34 Although the general validity of the Kuznets process has not been borne out by recent cross-country experience (see, for example, Anand and Kanbur 1993), this does not imply that it cannot be valid for specific country situations.

35 This is not to underestimate the problem of persistent or chronic poverty in Bangladesh. For empirical evidence, based on longitudinal studies, about the economic mobility of the poor, see Sen (2003) and Rahman and Hossain (1995), ch. 7.

Table 8.6. Improvements in Some Human Development Indicators since 1990, Bangladesh and South Asia

Indicators		1990	2002–04
Gross primary enrollment rate (%)	Bangladesh	80	109
	South Asia	95	103
Ratio of girls to boys in primary and secondary education (%)	Bangladesh	77	107
	South Asia	71	89
Under-five mortality rate (per 1,000 live births)	Bangladesh	144	69
	South Asia	130	86
Population with access to improved sanitation (%)	Bangladesh	23	48
	South Asia	20	37

Sources: Estimates of access to sanitation are from UNDP's *Human Development Report 2005;* all other estimates are compiled from the World Bank's World Development Indicators as reported in World Bank 2006a, 2006b.

enrollment, child mortality, and contraceptive adoption rates. The achievements of Sri Lanka and the Indian state of Kerala in this respect are well known, but the factors behind Bangladesh's success need a closer look.

How could these achievements be made in spite of still widespread poverty, relatively low although increasing public social spending, and the poor governance of service delivery systems in Bangladesh? The improvements in the human development indicators reflect a process of social transformation that is of a much broader scale and dates back to earlier decades (Mahmud 2008a). Much of this progress has resulted from adoption of low-cost solutions such as the use of oral rehydration saline for diarrhea treatment, leading to a decrease in child mortality. More progress has come from increased awareness created by effective social mobilization campaigns, such as for child immunization, contraception, or female child enrollment in school. The scaling up of programs through the spread of new ideas is helped in Bangladesh by a strong presence of nongovernmental organizations (NGOs) and by the density of settlements and their lack of remoteness.[36] Public support in the form of many innovative interventions has also helped.

Thus far, Bangladesh has not followed the typical pathways to human development, such as the income-growth-mediated path of Korea or the public-spending-driven path of Sri Lanka.[37] This is evidenced by the fact that, although Bangladesh compares favorably with some of the socially progressive states of India, it lags far behind those states in both per capita income and per capita public social spending in absolute terms (Mahmud 2008a). This also implies that further progress will require following either or both of the above pathways, as the gains from low-cost easy solutions are reaped and the amount of public spending, quality of services, and synergies with income-poverty all become important. Nevertheless, Bangladesh's experience shows that it is possible to make rapid initial progress in social

36 It is noteworthy that, according to the World Bank's *World Development Indicators 2005,* the percentage of children with diarrhea who were treated with oral saline was estimated at 61 percent in Bangladesh compared to 27 percent in India.

37 Sen, for example, distinguishes between "income-mediated" and "support-led" human development; see Sen (1999), ch. 2.

development by creating public awareness and using low-cost affordable solutions, and that social attitudes and behavioral norms can change over a much shorter period than usually assumed in the literature of institutional economics (see, for example, North 1997).

Unbundling Governance

The governance-growth nexus needs to be understood in the individual country contexts, in which institutions, historical and cultural settings, and the stage of development will matter. Most international comparisons show relatively poor perceptions of governance in Bangladesh. For example, in the most recent governance data set released by the World Bank Institute for 2005, Bangladesh's ranking among 210 countries varies from bottom 7th to 32nd percentile in the six indicators: 6.6 for political stability, 14.9 for regulatory quality, 19.8 for rule of law, 7.9 for control of corruption, 21.1 for government effectiveness, and 31.4 for voice and accountability. Bangladesh's position is significantly worse than its South Asian neighbors in most indicators; only with respect to voice and accountability is it ahead of Nepal and Pakistan. The information from the surveys on Investment Climate and Doing Business carried out by the World Bank Group is also not encouraging for Bangladesh in most respects.[38] Even more discouraging is Bangladesh's very poor ranking in the economic competitiveness index prepared by the World Economic Forum.[39]

In some respects of governance, however, Bangladesh does well. For example, Bangladesh ranks among the top 50 percent of countries in terms of the ease of doing business according to the World Bank's Doing Business survey of 2006. It ranks above many developing countries in terms of investor protection.[40] The perception indexes may also neglect many ground-level realities. Although Bangladesh scores very poorly in terms of enforcements of contracts, casual observation suggests that local business people do not regard this as any great hindrance in an environment where such enforcement can be biased to favor them and where informal methods based on business mores and customs and reputation play an important role. The corporate tax regime is relatively liberal in Bangladesh, and profits are fairly high in formal sector enterprises.[41]

As discussed earlier, Bangladesh has enjoyed governance successes in some key areas. The state has created space for the emergence of a vibrant domestic private sector through various policy reforms aimed at maintaining macroeconomic stability, keeping fiscal deficits low so as not to crowd out bank lending to the private sector, providing access to imported inputs through import liberalization, increasing competition by reducing entry

---

38 World Bank (2007), vol. II: Main Report, ch. 7.

39 Bangladesh ranks 98th out of 102 countries in business competitiveness according to the World Economic Forum's Global Competitiveness Index.

40 In terms of the investor protection index, Bangladesh scores 6.7 compared to the OECD average of 6.0 and the South Asian average of 5.0.

41 The World Bank's Doing Business survey does not take account of business profitability.

barriers, and improving the central bank's oversight functions in respect of commercial banking. The successive democratically elected governments have been able to make fairly prudent public expenditure choices. The government's disaster management capacity has also improved significantly over the years. The state has created space and forged partnerships with NGOs and the private sector to help deliver social services, and a certain degree of continuity in policy has been maintained in spite of changes in government. Overall, the state has played a significant developmental role.

Concluding Remarks: Future Challenges

Bangladesh has been successful thus far in converting the gains of economic stabilization and reforms into sustained and accelerated growth. To consolidate this process and to meet the risks of slippage, it has to address emerging challenges on many fronts. Institutional weaknesses may have already reached the tipping point beyond which they become binding growth constraints. Although the governance environment has been barely adequate so far to cope with an economy breaking out of stagnation and extreme poverty, it is increasingly proving a barrier to putting the economy firmly on a path of modernization, global integration, and poverty reduction. Fortunately, Bangladesh's problem is not to jumpstart growth, but to maintain, and to the extent possible, accelerate it.

The governance agenda is large and cuts across a wide range of institutions and threatens powerful vested interests. Developing a strategic, sequenced approach that relies on success in a few key areas to generate momentum and demand for reform in other areas will be crucial. Compared with the first-generation reforms, a need exists for deeper and more complex policy innovations to deal with the emerging binding constraints to growth, such as the inefficient and overburdened seaport, inadequate electricity and infrastructure, urban congestion and mismanagement, acute skill shortages, and limited successes in attracting foreign investments.

Future growth will have to come increasingly more from the urban organized sectors of the economy, which will need a better-functioning regulatory framework and improved infrastructure. Strengthening agricultural growth will also require modernization of the marketing infrastructure. The growth in crop agriculture over the past decades has come almost entirely from increased rice and wheat production. Beyond the attainment of self-sufficiency in rice, potential exists to accelerate agricultural growth through crop diversification (Mahmud, Rahman, and Zohir 2000). High-value crops such as fruits and vegetables could be profitably produced both for domestic consumption and for export, but a shift from rice to such crops will require technological dissemination, better integration with processing and marketing, and provision of other support services. For these products to enter the export market would require even more sophisticated marketing infrastructure.

Strong export growth is key to achieving any impressive growth performance of the Bangladesh economy. Bangladesh has made the transition from being primarily a jute-exporting country to a garment-exporting one. The transition has been dictated by the country's resource endowment, characterized by extreme land scarcity and a very high population density, which makes economic growth dependent on the export of labor-intensive manufactures. It is not, however, easy for a least-developed country like Bangladesh to specialize in manufactured exports. Having low wage costs can hardly compensate for its relative disadvantage in marketing skills and infrastructure (including transport, ports, product standards, and certification facilities). Thus, Bangladesh's export base remains low because the impressive success in garment export has yet to be replicated in other industries. Indeed, Bangladesh's experience with the garment industry has demonstrated the limitation of relying on enclave-type arrangements to facilitate export growth in a specific activity, while postponing institutional reforms for improving the investment climate generally (see Mahmud 2007).

Bangladesh's labor force has been increasing at a rapid rate because of the age composition of the population, resulting from a demographic transition, as well as because of a rapid increase in the female labor force participation rate. This is a potential strength of the economy, but enough jobs need to be created to reap the economic gains from it. A slackening of the labor market will keep wages from rising and may lead to political discontent. The garment industry is already facing labor agitation demanding higher wages. Bangladesh also needs more skilled and well-trained workers to boost productivity, and with it, global competitiveness. Improved governance of the education system will be needed to raise the quality of education and consolidate the earlier gains from the increase in primary school enrollment.

Bangladesh needs foreign direct investment (FDI) for facilitating technology transfer and for meeting its resource gap. Local entrepreneurs may have grown used to dealing with many aspects of the governance problems, but this is not true for prospective foreign investors. Besides the export-oriented garment industry, FDI mainly has come in sectors such as electricity generation and exploration and production of natural gas, which involves purchase or sale contracts with the government at "administered" prices. Because of the perceived high country risk for investment in Bangladesh, the prospective foreign investors include a high premium in their profitability calculations, so that the negotiated terms are less favorable to Bangladesh than they otherwise could be.

Without some political incentives, attempts at institutional reforms are unlikely to have much success. As mentioned earlier, the reforms in the banking sector could make progress in spite of strong vested interests because the government has realized the key importance of such reforms in maintaining a sound economic order. In some other key sectors, however, such incentives have not worked. In power generation, potential private investors have been put off by the interference of vested interests in the tendering and negotiation process. The result is an acute power shortage that has not only proved to be a brake on economic growth but also a source of great embarrassment for the erstwhile BNP government. Successive governments have also neglected to improve the management of the Chittagong port, which suffers from corruption in the customs procedures, deficient logistical capacity, and the interference of highly politicized labor unions. As a result, the country's only major seaport ranks among the world's least efficient container ports.

Bangladesh's economic growth prospects will ultimately depend on the viability of its core systems of political governance. Will political governance improve through increased civic activism and a lower tolerance shown by the public for weak governance? Or will the internal dynamics of the system lead to a "path-dependent" institutional deterioration as postulated by Douglass North (e.g., North 1997)? Bangladesh's recent political developments show both tendencies. On the one hand, there is no evidence of as much elite capture of the system as one would expect from the country's image of being one of the most corrupt and ill-governed countries. On the other hand, patronage politics and a winner-take-all system as exists in Bangladesh seems to have resulted in more and more rent seeking as an essential means of political management, thus raising the stakes in winning elections and rendering the system increasingly unsustainable. The shape of Bangladesh's political and economic future will largely depend on which of these opposing forces will prevail.

References

Acharya, Shankar. 2006. "A Tale of Three Cities." Unpublished paper. Indian Council for Research on International Economic Relations, New Delhi.

Ahluwalia, Isher J., and W. Mahmud. 2004. "Economic Transformation and Social Development in Bangladesh." *Economic and Political Weekly* 39 (36), September 4: 4009–11.

Ahmed, Raisuddin. 2001. *Retrospects and Prospects of the Rice Economy of Bangladesh*. Dhaka: University Press.

Ahmed, Sadiq. 2002. "The Political Economy of Poverty Reduction in South Asia: Role of Good Governance." South Asia Discussion Paper Series No. 183. World Bank, Washington, DC.

———. 2005. "Development Performance and Policy Reforms since Independence." In Sadiq Ahmed, *Transforming Bangladesh into a Middle Income Economy*. Delhi: Macmillan India for the World Bank.

———. 2006. "The Political Economy of Development Experience in Bangladesh." In Sadiq Ahmed and W. Mahmud, eds., *Growth and Poverty: The Development Experience in Bangladesh*. Dhaka: University Press for the World Bank.

Anand, S., and R. Kanbur. 1993. "The Kuznets Process and the Inequality-Development Relationship." *Journal of Development Economics* 40: 25–52.

Bangladesh Bureau of Statistics. 2003. *Report of the Household Income and Expenditure Survey 2000*. Dhaka: Ministry of Planning, government of Bangladesh.

————. 2006. *Preliminary Report of Household Income and Expenditure Survey 2005*. Dhaka: Ministry of Planning, government of Bangladesh.

Devarajan, Shantayanan. 2005. "South Asian Surprises." *Economic and Political Weekly* 40 (37), September 10: 4013–15.

Devarajan, S., and I. Nabi. 2006. "Economic Growth in South Asia: Promising, Unequalising, Sustainable?" *Economic and Political Weekly* 41, August 19: 3573–78.

Easterly, W. 2001. *The Elusive Quest for Growth: Economists' Adventures and Misadventures in the Tropics*. Cambridge, MA: MIT Press.

Faaland, J., and J. Parkinson. 1976. *Bangladesh: The Test Case of Development*. London: C. Hurst.

Government of Bangladesh. 2005. *Unlocking the Potential: National Strategy for Accelerated Poverty Reduction*. Dhaka: Planning Commission, General Economics Division.

Khan, A. R., and Mahabub Hossain. 1989. *The Strategy of Development in Bangladesh*. Basingstoke, UK: Macmillan in association with OECD Development Centre.

Khundker, N., W. Mahmud, B. Sen, and M. U. Ahmed. 1994. "Urban Poverty in Bangladesh: Trends, Determinants and Policy Issues." *Asian Development Review* 12 (1): 1–31.

Mahmud, W. 2001. "Bangladesh: Structural Adjustment and Beyond." In W. Mahmud, ed., *Adjustment and Beyond: The Reform Experience in South Asia*. Basingstoke, U.K: Palgrave-Macmillan in association with International Economic Association.

————. 2002a. "National Budgets, Social Spending and Public Choice: The Case of Bangladesh. IDS Working Paper 162. Institute of Development Studies, University of Sussex, Brighton, U.K.

————. 2002b. *Popular Economics: Unpopular Essays*. Dhaka: University Press.

————. 2004. "Macroeconomic Management: From Stabilization to Growth?" *Economic and Political Weekly* 39 (36), September 4: 4023–32.

————. 2005. "Ethics in Banking." Fifth Nurul Matin Memorial Lecture, Dhaka, Bangladesh Institute of Bank Management.

————. 2006. "Employment, Incomes and Poverty: Prospects of Pro-Poor Growth in Bangladesh." In Sadiq Ahmed and W. Mahmud, eds., *Growth and Poverty: The Development Experience in Bangladesh*. Dhaka: University Press for the World Bank.

————. 2007. "Bangladesh: Development Outcomes in the Context of Globalization." In Ernesto Zedillo, ed., *The Future of Globalization: Explorations in Light of Recent Turbulence*. London: Routledge.

————. 2008a. "Pathways of Social Development in Bangladesh: Surprises and Challenges." *Indian Journal of Human Development* 2 (1): 79–92.

————. 2008b. Chapter on Bangladesh. In Anis Chowdhury and W. Mahmud, eds., *Handbook on the South Asian Economies*. Cheltenham, U.K.: Edward Elgar.

Mahmud, W., and Anis Chowdhury. 2008. "Introduction: South Asian Economic Development: Impressive Achievements but Continuing Challenges." In Anis Chowdhury and W. Mahmud, eds., *Handbook on the South Asian Economies.* Cheltenham, U.K.: Edward Elgar Publishing.

Mahmud, W., and Simeen Mahmud. 2000. Chapter on Bangladesh. In S. Forman and R. Ghosh, eds., *Promoting Reproductive Health: Investing in Health for Development.* Boulder, CO: Lynne Reimer.

Mahmud, W., S. H. Rahman, and S. Zohir. 2000. "Agricultural Diversification: A Strategic Factor for Growth." In R. Ahmed, S. Haggblade, and T. Chowdhury, eds., *Out of the Shadow of Famine: Evolving Food Markets and Food Policy in Bangladesh.* Baltimore, MD: Johns Hopkins University Press.

North, Douglass C. 1997. "The Contribution of the New Institutional Economics to an Understanding of the Transitional Problem." Annual Lecture 1, United Nations World Institute for Development Economics Research (UN-WIDER), Helsinki.

Osmani, S. R., W. Mahmud, B. Sen, H. Dagdeviren, and A. Seth. 2003. *The Macroeconomics of Poverty Reduction: The Case of Bangladesh.* Dhaka and Kathmandu: UNDP Asia-Pacific Regional Program of Macroeconomics of Poverty Reduction.

Rahman, Akhlaqur, and W. Mahmud. 1988. Chapter on Bangladesh. In *Evaluating Rice Market Intervention Policies.* Manila: Asian Development Bank.

Rahman, Hossain Zillur, and Mahabub Hossain. 1995. *Rethinking Rural Poverty: Bangladesh as a Case Study.* Dhaka: University Press.

Sen, Amartya. 1999. *Development as Freedom.* Oxford: Oxford University Press.

Sen, Binayak. 2003. "Drivers of Escape and Descent: Changing Household Fortunes in Rural Bangladesh." *World Development* 31 (3): 513–34.

Task Forces. 1991. "Macroeconomic Policies." In *Report of the Task Forces on the Bangladesh Development Strategies for the 1990s.* Dhaka: University Press.

United Nations Development Program (UNDP). 2003. *Human Development Report 2003.* New York: Oxford University Press for the United Nations Development Program.

———. 2005. *Human Development Report 2005.* New York: Oxford University Press for the United Nations Development Program.

World Bank. 2003a. *Bangladesh Public Expenditure Review.* Washington, DC: World Bank; and Manila: Asian Development Bank.

———. 2003b. "Bangladesh Development Policy Review." Report No. 26154-BD. World Bank, Washington, DC.

———. 2005a. *Attaining the Millennium Goals in Bangladesh.* Washington, DC: World Bank (South Asia Region)

———. 2005b. "Bangladesh: Growth and Export Competitiveness." Report No. 31394-BD. World Bank, Washington, DC.

———. 2006a. *World Development Report 2006: Equity and Development.* Washington, DC: World Bank; and New York: Oxford University Press.

———. 2006b. *2004 World Development Indicators.* Washington, DC: World Bank.

———. 2007. "Bangladesh: Strategy for Sustained Growth." Bangladesh Development Series Paper No. 18. World Bank Office, Dhaka.

Index

electoral systems
in Argentina, 212
in Brazil, 199
in Chile, 212
disenfranchisement in, 152
political frameworks and, 10–11
proportional representation, 215
electricity supply. *See* power supply
infrastructure
El Salvador, persistence of institutional
framework in, 146
Eng, Alvin, 99
England. *See* United Kingdom (UK)
entrepreneurship entry barriers, 137
Equatorial Guinea, growth and
development success in, 102*t*, 103
Ethiopia, persistence of institutions in, 157
ethnicity. *See* race and ethnicity
EU-Africa Economic Partnership
Agreements, 65–66
Europe and European Union
See also specific countries
democratization in, 149
development assistance to Africa, 23
property rights, 142–44
Rwanda and, 91–92
Everything But Arms program, 56
e-waste disposal, 63–64
exchange rate
in Bangladesh, 236
in Brazil, 205
in Latin America, 147
in Nigeria, 173, 179, 182, 185, 188*t*
exports
from Bangladesh, 233–34, 245, 251
from Singapore, 112–14, 113*f*
transportation costs and, 81
Extractive Industries Transparency
Initiative, 181, 189–90
extractive institutions, 138, 155–56
Ezemenari, Kene, 84–85

F

Failed Banks (Recovery of Debt) and
Financial Malpractices in Banks
Decree No. 18 (Nigeria), 178
failed states, 71–72

Family Economic Advancement Program
(Nigeria), 179
Fanon, Frantz, 28
Farouk (King of Egypt), 45
Ferry, Jules, 27
financial sector
in Bangladesh, 242
liberalization of, 173
in Nigeria, 178
Financial Services Regulatory Coordinating
Committee (Nigeria), 178
fiscal policy. *See* monetary policy
Fiscal Responsibility Act (Brazil), 205
food security
in Bangladesh, 236, 240
poverty reduction and, 22
foreign direct investment (FDI)
in Africa, 52, 55–56
in Bangladesh, 251
in Brazil, 198
economic model choice and, 16
effectiveness of, 66–68
military coups and, 46
in Nigeria, 182–83, 183*t*
in Singapore, 113, 115
foreign exchange. *See* exchange rate
Foreign Exchange (Monitoring and
Miscellaneous Provisions) Decree
No. 17 (Nigeria), 178
Fosu, A. K., 166
Fox, Vicente, 214
France
colonialism in Africa and, 27, 37
Guinea independence and, 32
Franco, Itamar, 199
Freedmen's Bureau (U.S.), 151
freedom of the press, 77
Frontline States, 53
Fujimori, Alberto, 147
Fund to Combat Poverty (Brazil), 205

G

G-8
on development assistance to Africa, 23
Investment Climate Facility and,
61, 61*b*
Gaddafi, Muammar, 45

income inequality
  in Africa, 57
  in Bangladesh, 246, 247*t*
  ethnic fractionalization and, 122–23
  growth and development success and, 5, 12
  international comparisons, 100–102, 101–2*f*
Independent Corrupt Practices Commission (Nigeria), 181, 190
Independent Monitoring Group, 68
indexation, 201
India
  democratic reforms, 5
  economic growth model choice, 7
  growth and development success, 4, 106
Indonesia, growth and development success in, 3*t*, 12, 106
industrial development
  in Bangladesh, 245
  economic crises and, 50
  import-substitution model, 111–12, 111*f*, 175, 184
  in Nigeria, 184, 185–88*t*, 185*t*
  in Singapore, 114–17, 114*f*, 116*f*
  in Tanzania, 20
inflation
  in Africa, 52
  in Bangladesh, 232, 242
  in Brazil, 199, 201, 221
  in Chile, 207
  in Nigeria, 179, 182
  in Singapore, 115
informal sector
  in Bangladesh, 233–34, 245
  in Tanzania, 56–60, 58–59*f*
information and communication technology (ICT), 64–65, 196, 219
  See also technology
infrastructure
  in Africa, 60
  in Bangladesh, 247, 251–52
  in Brazil, 203
  economic growth and, 22, 83
  import costs and, 81
  in Nigeria, 168, 176–77, 185, 185*t*
  private investment in, 205, 230
  in U.S., 149

Institute for Liberty and Democracy (ILD), 58
Institutional and Governance Reform Program (Nigeria), 181
institutional framework, 135–64
  in Africa, 22, 74, 147–48
  in Brazil, 202–4
  defined, 136–37
  impact of, 2, 137–40
  incentives and, 146–48
  iron law of oligarchy, 154–58
  modeling differences, 140–42, 142*f*
  in Nigeria, 181–82, 189–90, 191*t*
  persistence in, 146–48
  policy implementation and, 109–10
  power and, 146–54
  recommendations, 158–59
  reform challenges, 144–46
  in Rwanda, 81, 87–88
  in Singapore, 119–23, 120*t*, 124*t*, 158
intellectual corruption, 69
International Criminal Tribunal for Rwanda (ICTR), 89
international financial institutions (IFI), 147–48, 157
Internationalist Magazine, Nyerere interview in, 42
International Monetary Fund, 20, 201, 229, 234
Internet and participatory governance, 223–24
intra-Africa trade, 64, 66
investment
  See also foreign direct investment (FDI)
  in Bangladesh, 232
  in Brazil, 198
  corruption impact on, 176
  in education, 150, 175
  in market and economic infrastructure, 22
  in Nigeria, 172–74, 173*f*, 183*t*
  in Rwanda, 92–93
  in science and technology, 94, 95*t*
Investment Climate Facility (ICF), 60–62, 61*b*
Investment Climate survey (World Bank), 249
Iraq, persistence of institutions in, 154, 156
iron law of oligarchy, 154–58
Iyoha, Milton A., 165, 169

literacy
  in Bangladesh, 228
  in Rwanda, 82
  tests for voting, 152
local government
  in Brazil, 205
  in Nigeria, 189
  participation in, 54
Local Industry Upgrading Program
        (Singapore), 116
Lockwood, Matthew, 42, 72
Lucas, R. E., Jr., 99
Lula da Silva, Luiz Inácio, 197–98, 201, 220
Lumumba, Patrice
  assassination of, 35–36
  military coups and, 46
  persistence of institutions and, 157
  Soviet Union and, 32

M

Macroeconomic Reform Program (Nigeria),
        181
Madrid, Miguel de la, 213
Mahajan, Sandeep, 227
Mahmud, Wahiduddin, 227
Makerere College, 29*b*
Malawi, one-party political system in, 40
Malaysia, growth and development success
        in, 3*t,* 102*t*
Mali
  one-party political system, 40
  recommendations, 71
Mandela, Nelson, 38, 53, 157
manufacturing
  in Bangladesh, 232–33, 234
  infrastructure and, 176
  in Nigeria, 166, 185–88*t*, 191
  in Singapore, 114, 115–16
  in U.S., 149
Mao Tse-tung, 6, 11
Mariam, Mengistu Haile, 157
market reforms
  in Africa, 56–60
  in China, 11–12
  infrastructure investments, 22
  in Nigeria, 176
  in Rwanda, 92–93

Marxism, 43
Mauritius, institutional reforms in, 158
Mauro, Paulo, 137
MDGs. *See* Millennium Development Goals
media
  accountability and, 76–77
  in Bangladesh, 243
  in Brazil, 220
  participatory governance and, 223–24
  policy implementation and, 125
  in post-Cold War Africa, 52
Medisave insurance program
        (Singapore), 115
Menem, Carlos, 148, 208, 213
Meredith, Martin, 39, 40
Mexico
  persistence of institutional framework, 146
  presidential political system, 213–14
  state-owned enterprise, 14
Michels, Robert, 154
microfinance, 59, 246, 247
migration, rural-urban, 57, 246
military rule
  in Africa, 44–46
  in Argentina, 208
  in Bangladesh, 229
  in Brazil, 202, 214–15, 218
  in Nigeria, 45, 166, 166*t*, 175, 176, 183
Millennium Development Goals (MDGs),
        53, 180, 228
Ministry of Finance and Economic Planning
        (MINECOFIN), 92
Mkapa, Benjamin William, 19
MMD (Movement for Multiparty
        Democracy, Zambia), 157
MNCs (multinational corporations), 113,
        115–16
MNR (Movimiento Nacionalista
        Revolucionario, Bolivia), 155, 156
Mobutu, Joseph, 45, 157
monetary policy
  in Bangladesh, 230, 238–39, 239*t*
  in Brazil, 200–201
  in Nigeria, 178
  in Rwanda, 93–94, 93*t*
Money Laundering Decree No. 3
        (Nigeria), 178

Morris, Stephen E., 148
mortality rates, 139, 228
Mosca, Gaetano, 154
Movement for Multiparty Democracy
(MMD, Zambia), 157
Movimiento Nacionalista Revolucionario
(MNR, Bolivia), 155, 156
Mozambique
decolonization and, 47
recommendations, 71
Mugabe, Robert, 157
Multifibre Agreement and the Agreement on
Textiles and Clothing, 233
multilateral development partners, 23, 54
See also official development assistance
multimember districts, 9, 10
multinational corporations (MNCs), 113,
115–16
multiparty political systems, 9–10, 72–73, 213
Mungoshi, Charles, 28

N

NAFTA (North American Free Trade
Agreement), 213
Namibia
education, 30
land reforms, 50
NAPEP (National Poverty Eradication
Program, Nigeria), 181
Nasser, Gamel Abdel, 45
National Bank of Rwanda (NBR), 92, 93
National Commission for Reconciliation
(Rwanda), 88
National Commission to Fight against HIV/
AIDS (Rwanda), 88
National Development Plans (Nigeria), 174,
184
National Directorate of Employment and
Mass Agricultural Projects
(Nigeria), 179
National Economic Emergency Act
(Nigeria), 184
National Economic Empowerment and
Development Strategy (NEEDS,
Nigeria), 180–81, 189
National Poverty Eradication Program
(NAPEP, Nigeria), 181

national-statism, 198, 217–21
National Wages Council (NWC,
Singapore), 114, 116
nation building, 38–42
natural endowments
economic dependence on, 165–66
political-economy framework and, 107
in Singapore, 119–23, 119t, 124t
natural resource curse, 169, 174
NBR (National Bank of Rwanda), 92, 93
NEEDS (National Economic Empowerment
and Development Strategy, Nigeria),
180–81, 189
neoliberalism, 147, 203, 220
nepotism, 168
New Partnership for Africa's Development
(NEPAD), 20, 54, 61b, 94
New Zealand, colonial institutions in, 138
Ngoma, Naison, 46
NGOs (nongovernmental organizations),
248, 250
Niger, growth and development in, 103t, 119
Nigeria, 165–93
business entry barriers, 137
economic outcomes, 170–72
executive transitions, 166, 166t
growth performance (1960–2000), 171f,
171t, 172–80
growth performance (1999–2006),
180–83, 182t
institutional framework, 189–90, 191t
international comparisons, 190, 190t
investment, 172–74, 173f, 183t
leadership role in growth and
development, 183–90, 185–89t
military coups and, 45
nation building in, 39
political framework, 166–70, 167–68t
Nigerian Deposit Insurance
Corporation, 178
Nigerian Investment Promotion
Commission Decree No. 16, 178
Niou, E., 10
Nkrumah, Kwame
on land ownership and usage, 50
on liberation struggles, 46
military coups and, 45

public investment
   in Bangladesh, 238–39, 239*t*
   economic growth and, 85
   in Nigeria, 168, 169, 175
   oil revenues and, 172–73
public opinion, 220, 243
public-private partnerships, 64, 250
public sector
   in Brazil, 203–4
   downsizing of, 148
   in Nigeria, 168, 173
Public Sector Reform Program
      (Nigeria), 181
public service concessions, 205
purchasing power parity (PPP). *See* real per
      capita GDP

Q
Quadros, Jânio, 211

R
race and ethnicity
   in Africa, 74–75
   fractionalization, 122–23
   in Nigeria, 166, 168–70, 174, 183, 191
Rahman, Ziaur, 229, 234
Ransom, Roger L., 152
Reader, John, 35, 45
real per capita GDP
   global trends, 100–102, 100*f*
   in Nigeria, 170–72, 171*f*, 171*t*,
      190–91, 190*t*
Real Plan (Brazil), 199–201, 209–11, 220
Reconstruction (U.S.), 151–52
Redeemers (U.S.), 152
redistribution of wealth, 13, 147
reform fatigue, 202
regional bias in Nigeria, 166, 167–68*t*
regional integration, 54, 94, 95*t*
regional redistribution syndrome, 184
religion, 74–75, 166
Reno, William, 147
Republican Party (U.S.), 152
Republic of Korea
   democratic reforms, 11
   growth and development success in, 3*t*,
      7–8, 12, 13–14, 102*t*

institutional framework, 140, 158
   political framework, 9, 10, 16
resources
   economic dependence on, 165–66
   growth and, 119–23, 119*t*
   market economies and, 11
   natural resource curse, 169, 174
   political framework and, 107–9
responsible pragmatism, 221
Roberts, Kenneth M., 147
Robinson, Edward, 99
Robinson, James A., 120, 135, 138, 139,
      140, 142, 159
Robinson, James H., 32
Rodney, Walter, 28
Roh Tae Woo, 14
Rome Declaration on Aid Harmonization, 67
Romer, P., 99
RPF (Rwanda Patriotic Front), 86
Rúa, Fernando de la, 213
rule of law
   growth and development impact of, 2
   informal sector and, 56–60
   in political framework, 16
   Singapore's institutional framework
      and, 111
rural areas
   in Bangladesh, 246
   decentralization policy and, 91
   electoral systems and, 10
   migration from, 57, 246
   poverty reduction and, 22
   Rwanda monetary policy and, 93–94, 93*t*
   in Tanzania, 19–20
Rural Investment Facilities, 93–94, 93*t*
Rusuhuzwa Kigabo, Thomas, 81, 84
Rwanda, 81–97
   decentralization policy, 89–91
   economic growth, 83–84, 84*t*, 86–87
   economic reforms, 92–95
   genocide impact on, 82, 83
   institutional framework, 87–88
   judicial reforms, 89
   leadership role, 86–92
   liberation conflicts, 47
   monetary policy, 93–94, 93*t*
   participatory governance, 91–92

Sri Lanka, growth and development success in, 106
State Economic Empowerment and Development Strategy (Nigeria), 180
state-owned enterprises
in Bangladesh, 229
in Brazil, 203, 204
economic growth and, 14
privatization of, 173, 216, 229
in Rwanda, 83, 92–93
in Tanzania, 20
Stevens, Siaka, 157, 158
Stigler, George, 148
strategic planning, 71, 199–201
Strategic Planning and Poverty Monitoring Department (Rwanda), 92
Structural Adjustment Program (SAP, Nigeria), 49, 172, 184–85
Structural Reform Program (Nigeria), 181
Suberu, R. T., 169–70
subsidies
agricultural, 14, 177, 229, 235–36, 240
food, 235–36, 240
Sutch, Richard, 152
Switzerland and tax havens, 70*b*

T

Taiwan, China
democratic reforms, 11
growth and development success, 3*t*, 7, 13, 102*t*
institutional reforms, 158
party system in, 9, 10, 16
Tanganyika. *See* Tanzania
Tan Yin Ying, 99
Tanzania
aid effectiveness in, 68
decolonization impact on, 47–48
democratic political system, 72
growth and development prerequisites, 19–20
informal sector, 57–60, 58–59*f*
land ownership and usage, 50–51
media in, 76–77
nation building in, 39–40
political framework, 23, 40–42, 41*b*

recommendations, 71
socialism and, 43–44, 48–49
tariffs
in Africa, 65, 66
in Bangladesh, 237, 237*t*
in Brazil, 204
in Latin America, 146
in Nigeria, 177
in Singapore, 112
taxes
in Bangladesh, 238
corporate, 112–13, 249
corruption and, 70, 70*b*
economic growth and, 85
poll, 152
in Rwanda, 83, 93
Tax Justice Network, 70, 70*b*
technology
Africa and, 62–65
economic model choice and, 7
globalization and, 62–63
infrastructure, 176
private investment in, 230
Rwanda and, 94, 95*t*
Temple, J., 100
Thiongo, Ngugi wa, 28
Time magazine
on Nyerere's pro-Western attitude, 43
on Tanzania economy, 37
Tolstoy, Leo, 196
total factor productivity, 99
Touré, Sékou, 32, 47, 53
trade
in Africa, 65–66
conflict and, 87
intra-Africa, 64
liberalization of, 83, 94, 146, 173, 176, 203, 204
in Nigeria, 185, 189*t*
tradenetINTL service, 64
transparency
in Africa, 75–76
in oil and gas sector, 189–90
in political framework, 16
Transparency International (TI), 69–70, 69*b*
transportation infrastructure
in Bangladesh, 247